# RESISTING HISTORY

JEWS, CHRISTIANS, AND MUSLIMS

FROM THE ANCIENT TO THE MODERN WORLD

SERIES EDITORS

*R. Stephen Humphreys, William Chester Jordan, and Peter Schäfer*

*Imperialism and Jewish Society, 200 B.C.E. to 640 C.E.*
by Seth Schwartz

*A Shared World: Christians and Muslims in the Early
Modern Mediterranean*
by Molly Greene

*Beautiful Death: Jewish Poetry and Martyrdom in
Medieval France*
by Susan L. Einbinder

*Power in the Portrayal: Representations of Jews and
Muslims in Eleventh- and Twelfth-Century Islamic Spain*
by Roass Brann

*Mirror of His Beauty: Feminine Images of God from
the Bible to the Early Kabbalah*
by Peter Schäfer

*In the Shadow of the Virgin: Inquisitors, Friars,
and* Conversos *in Guadalupe, Spain*
by Gretchen D. Starr-LeBeau

*The Curse of Ham: Race and Slavery in Early Judaism,
Christianity, and Islam*
by David M. Goldenberg

*Resisting History: Historicism and Its Discontents in
German-Jewish Thought*
by David N. Myers

# RESISTING HISTORY

## HISTORICISM AND ITS DISCONTENTS IN GERMAN-JEWISH THOUGHT

*DAVID N. MYERS*

PRINCETON UNIVERSITY PRESS

PRINCETON AND OXFORD

Published by Princeton University Press, 41 William Street, Princeton, New Jersey 08540
In the United Kingdom: Princeton University Press, 3 Market Place,
Woodstock, Oxfordshire OX20 1SY

Library of Congress Cataloging-in-Publication Data

Myers, David N.
Resisting history : historicism and its discontents in German-Jewish
thought / David N. Myers.
p. cm. — (Jews, Christians, and Muslims from the ancient to the modern world)
Includes bibliographical references and index.
ISBN: 0-691-11593-1
1. Jewish learning and scholarship—Germany—History—19th century. 2. Jewish
learning and scholarship—Germany—History—20th century. 3. Judaism—Historiography.
4. Historicism—History. 5. Cohen, Hermann, 1842–1918—Views on historicism.
6. Rosenzweig, Franz, 1886–1929—Views on historicism. 7. Strauss, Leo—Views on
historicism. 8. Breuer, Isaac, 1883–1946—Views on historicism. I. Title. II. Series.

BM195.M94 2003
181'.06—dc21        2003049790
British Library Cataloging-in-Publication Data is available

This book has been composed in Sabon
Printed on acid-free paper. ∞
www.pupress.princeton.edu
Printed in the United States of America

10 9 8 7 6 5 4 3 2 1

*For Nomi*

שנינו ביחד וכל אחד לחוד

*Yehuda Amichai (1924–2000)*

# CONTENTS

# ACKNOWLEDGMENTS

A pair of grants in 1995 provided the initial impetus to embark on this project. A Leo Baeck Institute/DAAD Fellowship in German-Jewish History allowed me to delve into the life and thought of Franz Rosenzweig, a key figure in this book, by combing the archival holdings at the Leo Baeck Institute in New York. Shortly thereafter I had the good fortune of spending a semester as a fellow of the Center for Advanced Judaic Studies in Philadelphia. The Center's wonderful library, superb staff, convivial intellectual surroundings, and indefatigable director, David Ruderman, assisted me in laying out the first blueprint of this book.

I would also like to thank the staff and faculty colleagues at the Institute for Advanced Study at the Hebrew University in Jerusalem, where I served as a visiting scholar in the fall semester of 1997. This half-year in Israel gave me an opportunity to present my still rudimentary ideas on the problem of history in German-Jewish thought to learned audiences in Jerusalem and Beersheva. Three years later I was able to offer a more refined version of my thinking when a trusted colleague, Shmuel Feiner, invited me to deliver the Braun Lecture on the History of the Jews in Prussia at Bar-Ilan University in May 2000.

The bulk of this book was written in the following year in Los Angeles, when I had a sabbatical from the UCLA Department of History. I would like to extend sincere thanks to Dean Scott Waugh (Social Sciences), Dean Pauline Yu (Humanities), and Professor Brenda Stevenson (then chair of the History Department) for their generous support. Likewise, I thank the UCLA Academic Senate for its ongoing commitment to faculty research on campus, including my own.

A number of colleagues were generous enough to read parts of this book at different stages of writing. They include Arnold Band, John Efron, David Ellenson, Shaul Friedländer, Maurice Kriegel, and Adam Rubin. I would especially like to thank a number of outstanding young scholars, all trailblazers in the study of German-Jewish thought, who offered illuminating comments upon various chapters: Leora Batnitzky, Peter Gordon, Samuel Moyn, and Eugene Sheppard. Excellent research assistance came from Jeff Blutinger, Dante Camargo, Stephanie Chasin, Tal Gozani, Didier Reiss, and the irrepressible Barry Trachtenberg. For stimulating conversation that contributed to (and, at times, thankfully distracted me from) this book, I owe a debt of gratitude to Jackie Ellenson and Chaim Seidler-Feller.

In the final stage of preparing the book for publication, Michael Brenner, Moshe Idel, and Richard Wolin read the entire manuscript and offered many valuable suggestions. I have tried to incorporate most of them, but fear that I have not done full justice to the richness of their insights. Thanks are also due Peter Schäfer, who graciously agreed to consider this book for a series he coedits at Princeton University Press and then shared a most illuminating chapter of his own work that overlaps substantially with mine. The Press has been a delight to work with, especially Marsha Kunin, who copyedited the book and, above all, Brigitta van Rheinberg, who has been a most supportive and sage editor.

Finally, I want to express my gratitude to two women who have left an indelible imprint on me. My grandmother, Libbye Myers z"l, passed away in 2002, less than three months shy of her 106th birthday. In the course of her long and extraordinary life, she imparted to me an abiding respect for tradition (and its dynamism), perseverance, and the benefits of unconditional love.

Last but not least, Nomi Maya Stolzenberg has been my partner for half of my life. We have grown up together and, in the process, created our own familial web in which Avital, Noa, and Sara are enmeshed. For reasons not entirely clear, Nomi continues to tolerate me. For reasons that are much clearer, she continues to inspire me. Nomi is the true spiritual custodian of this book, having presided over its conception and maturation with her customary love, generosity, and keen mind.

# A NOTE ON THE COVER

The cover of this book features a painting entitled *The Jew Etc.* by R. B. Kitaj (in black-and-white on page xiv), an artist whom I have always admired. It was one of the typically unexpected pleasures of living in Los Angeles that I came to meet Kitaj a short while after he moved back to the United States from London. Since that time, he has become a wonderful friend and conversation partner. When I asked him if I could use one of his paintings for the cover of this book, Kitaj instantly agreed, believing that reproduction was not only a sincere form of flattery, but also a continuation of the ceaseless interpretive practices of the Jews. Ever faithful to that tradition, Kitaj explains in an accompanying text to *The Jew Etc.* that the figure is possessed of "an aesthetic of entrapment and escape, an endless, tainted Galut-Passage." I can think of no more fitting visual and textual entry into this book. Like those who most interest Kitaj, its main characters are Jews of *Mitteleuropa*, caught between East and West, Exile and Redemption, and, as I explore in detail, historicism and anti-historicism. Indeed, they dwell in the space between "entrapment and escape," much like the resigned and searching Joe Singer in *The Jew Etc.* I thank Kitaj for his generosity in sharing with me his most fitting deeds and words.

# RESISTING HISTORY

FIGURE 1 "The Jew Etc." © R. B. Kitaj. Courtesy of Marlborough Gallery, New York.

# INTRODUCTION

I

Acentury and a half ago, Søren Kierkegaard issued a powerful indictment against one of the main pillars of modern intellectual life.
Caught in the throes of spiritual turmoil, the Danish philosopher
took aim at the kind of historical thinking that reduced human experience
to a long series of disconnected moments. This modern mode of thinking
reached its most offensive, Kierkegaard lamented, when applied to the
personality of Jesus. He had thorough contempt for the efforts of European historians of his day to attempt a reconstruction of the life of the
"historical Jesus," whom they portrayed as a decidedly human figure born
and raised in first-century Palestine. Against the historians, Kierkegaard
insisted that:

> one can "know" nothing at all about "Christ"; He is the paradox, the object
> of faith, existing only for faith. But all historical communication is communica-
> tion of "knowledge," hence from history one can learn nothing about
> Christ. . . . History makes out Christ to be another than He truly is, and so one
> learns to know a lot about—Christ? No, not about Christ, for about Him noth-
> ing can be known, He can only be believed.[1]

Kierkegaard feared that the most sacred and transcendent of realms
had been infected by a destructive contagion: historicism and the practice
of modern critical history. The historian's careful measurement of change
over time—for instance, in depicting the history of Christianity after
Jesus—obscured for him far more than it illuminated. Indeed, Kierkegaard felt compelled to emphasize again and again that, in matters per-
taining to the divinity of Christ, "the 1,800 years (or if there were 18,000
of them) have nothing whatever to do with the case."[2]

Powerful and poignant as it was, Kierkegaard's plaint was hardly the
first and surely not the last of its kind. Criticism of modern historical
thinking has been almost as common as the thinking itself. Frequently,
it has been trained on "the quest of the Historical Jesus," as in Albert
Schweitzer's well-known book of that (English) title from 1906.
Schweitzer was far more immersed in and sympathetic to historical scholarship on Jesus than Kierkegaard. But at the end of the day, the renowned
missionary-physician arrived at a conclusion not altogether dissimilar:
namely, "it is not Jesus as historically known, but Jesus as spiritually
arisen within men, who is significant for our time and can help it."[3]

But what exactly was so distasteful or unsettling about modern historical thinking? What prompted scholars of different disciplines and denom-

inations to attack it with such fervor? In the first instance, it was history's ubiquity. Friedrich Nietzsche bemoaned this fact in his 1874 essay "On the Use and Abuse of History" when he wrote of the dangerous "surfeit of history."[4] A half century later, Ernst Troeltsch, the German Protestant theologian, called attention to "the historicization of all our knowledge and perception."[5] Both Nietzsche and Troeltsch realized that one could hardly think of an event from the past without relying on the causal logic of modern historicism. This logic dictated that each event be understood as an individual unit, assessed on its own terms and according to its own unique development. Caught in the fast-moving current of history, events floated like petrified wood, drifting in no particular pattern or direction. Each discrete event had its own distinct properties; the aggregate of such events yielded no coherent design.

This state of fragmentation pointed up another major concern issuing from historicism: the problem of relativism.[6] According to their critics, historians went about evaluating each event on its own terms, but never set in place any overarching standard, or Archimedean point, of measurement. In the first place, they were captives of their own context, and thus incapable of achieving anything but a relativist or relational perspective on the past.[7] Constrained by such a perspective, they produced an endless string of historical pearls, each carefully polished and catalogued, but at the same time constant reminders of a certain fall from a state of wholeness. In this fallen state, it was no longer possible to assert spiritual or moral truths with certainty. For example, while one might be able to adduce historical evidence to prove the existence of an individual named Jesus, one could never marshal comparable evidence to prove the existence of the mythic Christ of faith.

In the language of historicism's critics, this condition marked a descent from supernaturalism into "naturalism." Following centuries of tumultuous theological struggle, modern historians now asserted their right to displace God as the primary causal force in history.[8] Borrowing liberally from natural scientific models, they anchored historical causation in a wide array of natural or human forces. The result, according to Ernst Troeltsch, was a steadfast alliance "between naturalism and historicism . . . the two great scholarly creations of the modern world."[9]

Troeltsch was keenly aware of the dangers of this double-barreled assault on transcendent values. He was present and vocal at a particularly acute moment of anti-historicist distress after the First World War.[10] He knew well that the devastation of the war must be assessed not only in the massive loss of life, but also in the staggering blow to epistemological confidence. And so it was in this period that Troeltsch surveyed the universe around him and declared a "crisis of historicism." This call in 1922 resonated throughout intellectual circles in Weimar Germany, from the reactionary right to the radical left. As we shall see in due course, the "crisis of historicism" came to be seen as a major symptom of the broader malaise of modernity that so characterized the Weimar sensibility and stimulated its frenetic political and cultural activity. A decade after Troeltsch, another Protestant theologian and historian, Karl Heussi, was still attempting to get a firm grasp on this social and intellectual crisis. Heussi's 1932 book, *Die Krisis des Historismus* offered a detailed analysis of objections raised to historicism, while also containing a glimmer of hope that historicism and systematic theology need not stand in diametric opposition.[11]

Clearly, the Weimar milieu, with its mix of social instability and intellectual audacity, was fertile ground for the kind of debate that ensued over the "crisis of historicism." And yet, if anything, the long and dark decades after the Weimar republic have presented even more formidable challenges to historicism.[12] The Holocaust triggered its own epistemological upheaval, leading many to question the value or even possibility of historical representation (preeminently of the Holocaust itself).[13] Meanwhile, the prominence of post-structuralist literary theories over the past several decades has done little to affirm, and much to call into question, the value of the historian's contextualizing methods. When faced with these methods, post-structuralist critics have often seemed "uncertain and confused, overcome by what appears to them an infinite array of possible contextual relations, each equally fulfilling the claim to stand as 'the context.' "[14] In this regard, post-structuralism has had the effect—consistent with its own skepticism of foundationalist claims—of highlighting the very relativism to which anti-historicists have taken frequent and vociferous exception.

## II

So the old problems of historical relativism and fragmentation have not disappeared. They are with us today. At the same time, we find ourselves more deeply saturated in an historicist mindset than ever. I am reminded of this paradox by a controversy that recently broke out in the Jewish community of Los Angeles.

During the Passover holiday of April 2001, Rabbi David Wolpe of Sinai Temple in Los Angeles ignited a firestorm by delivering a sermon that called into question the historical authenticity of the biblical account of the Exodus story. The rabbi pointed out that there was no persuasive historical or archaeological evidence to validate the tale of Israelites escaping the clutches of Pharaoh's army across the Red Sea. By extension, it was not clear that the Israelites had ever been in Egypt as slaves.

Wolpe's sermon stunned his audience, some of whom deemed his words sacrilege and others of whom regarded them as intellectually courageous. Soon enough, news of the address spilled out beyond the synagogue's walls, due in no small measure to front-page exposure in the *Los Angeles Times* under the headline "Doubting the Story of Exodus."[15] At both local and national levels, the sermon provoked fiercely divergent reactions. One supporter, writing in a local Jewish paper, insisted that "defending a rabbi in the 21st century for saying the Exodus story isn't factual is like defending him for saying the earth isn't flat." Modern notions of Judaism had moved far away from "a literal understanding of the Torah."[16] Meanwhile, a detractor in the same paper declared simply that "if the Exodus did not occur, there is no Judaism." According to this writer, "logic and common sense" dictate that the Exodus story is more than a fairy tale. Otherwise, why would Jews have continued to repeat it in ritual fashion for three thousand years?[17]

For many observers from the scholarly world, the wide rift opened by this Passover sermon—if not its content—came as a considerable surprise. For years, historical and archaeological research has challenged the veracity of the Exodus story. One journalist surveying the state of the field in 1993 concluded that "there isn't a shred of hard evidence—not a single potsherd unearthed or one Hebrew letter scratched into a stone—to prove that the Israelites were ever slaves in Egypt, or that they ever wandered in the desert."[18] To be sure, not all scholars would accept this sweeping assertion or the claim that the absence of hard and fast evidence attesting to their presence means that there were no Israelites in Egypt. But ongoing research by archaeologists, including a number of prominent Israelis, has added more fuel to the fire. Their work calls into question not only the presence of Israelites in Egypt, but also the claim that the post-Exodus Israelites went on to conquer Canaan.[19]

In drawing upon this search, David Wolpe was not seeking to unhinge the faith commitments of Jews. Rather, he hoped to confront head-on the brittleness of literalist readings of the Bible, and in doing so, to "maintain the Jewish tradition of sustaining faith by seeking truth."[20] Whether he succeeded in this task is a matter of opinion. Differences on the question of how to read the Bible have left deep denominational tracks in European and now American Judaism. Rabbi Wolpe's own Conservative affiliation, anchored in a healthy respect for modern scholarship, led him to a stance that was fundamentally unacceptable to the vast majority of Orthodox Jews. At the same time, his words revealed that the gap between academy and community was quite substantial: what many scholars had taken for granted for years was nothing short of scandalous to many in his lay audience.

Most germane for our purposes is the yawning chasm that this episode revealed between history and faith. Kierkegaard made clear in the mid–nineteenth century that this chasm is a central feature of intellectual life in the West. The Wolpe controversy demonstrated that the conflict between history and faith is not a *Christian* problem alone, but an ongoing one in the lives of twenty-first century Jews. After all, Rabbi Wolpe declared to his audience that spiritual truths—the exalted ideals of freedom and justice contained in the Exodus story—were independent of historical facts.[21] Ironically, he chose to make the point in decidedly historicist fashion—by summoning up modern scholarly evidence to challenge the historicity of Exodus itself.

And thus we come up again against a curious paradox hinted at above: ambivalence over the utility of history coincides with an unavoidably historicist way of thinking. We yearn to discover a source of meaning for past events that transcends the single historical fact, but are confined by the limitations of our historicist mode of thinking—just as the Kabbalists were constrained in their efforts to decipher the Divine Word by their unavoidable reliance on human language. The roots of this dilemma surfaced well before the Golden Age of Historicism in the nineteenth century; they reach back at least to the seventeenth century when the tools of critical historical scholarship were first applied by figures such as Spinoza and Richard Simon to Holy Scripture, the bedrock of religious faith and authority. The underlying methodological imperative even then was to contextualize—which often meant to dissolve the veneer of transcendence in which sacred texts were wrapped.

Over the course of more than three centuries, the *tools* of critical history have become ubiquitous. So too has the broader *worldview* out of which these tools have been forged. This worldview proclaims that human history belongs to a long, undulating, but ultimately chartable current—not to a vast Divine terrain whose grand design eludes full human comprehension. Charting this natural current—noting carefully its width, length, and depth, as well as its frequent bends and curves—has become a main historicist occupation.

In this sense, as a mode of cognition, historicism has been a remarkable success story. It has come to dominate our way of thinking about the past, conditioning us to place the single event in context and then link it to a chain of other contextually bound events. Its ubiquity has also bestowed a dignified status onto a field of inquiry once deemed a second-tier discipline—indeed, once scorned as a "waste of time" by the greatest of medieval Jewish thinkers, Maimonides.


III


The paradoxical coexistence of historicism and anti-historicism is a recurrent theme throughout this book. Anti-historicism has been a constant foil, casting its long shadow over historicism precisely as the latter climbed to a position of intellectual dominance in the modern West. In this regard, historicism, despite its very considerable success, has never fully vanquished its intellectual opposite. On the contrary, critics can and do still argue that historicism has pushed us to the brink of total relativism—that it has created a world marked by the "end of meaning."[22]

But can this be so? Does historicism, with its obsessive demand to situate every historical datum in a discrete local context, preclude the prospect of enduring meaning?[23] My personal inclination, which admittedly overlaps with the need for professional self-justification, is to suggest that the study of history *can* serve a useful and, at times, vital function in illuminating the path from past to present. But I have not stopped wondering about historicism or its discontents since my first encounter with Yosef Hayim Yerushalmi's *Zakhor*—that sober and soaring meditation on Jewish history and historians. Soon after reading this book, I decided to undertake graduate studies under Professor Yerushalmi's supervision. My doctoral research there focused on a group of European-born scholars who moved to Palestine in the 1920s with the hope of erecting a new edifice of Jewish historical research. This cohort of scholars—the founders of the Institute of Jewish Studies at the Hebrew University—seemed to be an ideal case for exploring the space between the poles of history and memory that Yerushalmi traced in *Zakhor*. On the one hand, their years of training in European universities endowed them with a deep appreciation for the historicist craft and creed, as well as for the ethos of scientific labor (*Wissenschaft*) that undergirded both. On the other hand, the Jerusalem scholars often sought to use their historical labor to nurture a new Jewish—or more properly, Zionist—collective memory rooted in the soil of the ancestral Jewish homeland.[24]

While studying these scholars, I often wondered why virtually none succumbed to a crisis of historicist faith. After all, the European intellectual world in which they were trained was consumed with anxieties about history—and in the very decades in which they were university students. Were there no Jewish historians chastened by Nietzsche's admonitions in "On the Use and Abuse of History"? Were there no Jewish intellectuals who recoiled from "German fact-grabbing," as early twentieth-century French sociologists had?[25] Were there no Jewish parallels to the German intellectuals studied by Charles Bambach in his fine book *Heidegger, Dilthey and the Crisis of Historicism* (1995)? With few exceptions (notably Gershom Scholem's cri de coeur in "From within Reflections on Jewish Studies" from 1944), the transplanted Jerusalem scholars held firm to their historicist faith.[26] My sense is that they did so because historical scholarship had become a way of life, as it had for dedicated researchers of other ethnic or religious groups. But it also struck me that the historical discipline and its methodological protocol provided the Jerusalem scholars—quite like their Zionism—with an anchor of stability, a standard of fixity, as they made the tumultuous physical and cultural journey from Europe to Palestine.

Having completed a study of this group of scholars in 1995, I began to concentrate on a question that took form in the late stages of the first project: where were the Jewish critics of historicism? Here too Yosef Yerushalmi proved to be a prescient guide, outlining a lineage of Jewish anti-historicists (e.g., S. R. Hirsch, S. D. Luzzatto, and Franz Rosenzweig) in some brief, but illuminating pages of *Zakhor*.[27] Surprisingly, few subsequent scholars seized upon Yerushalmi's opening. To be sure, there is no dearth of research on the history of Jewish historiography, much of it written in the wake of *Zakhor*.[28] There are also interesting new studies of Jewish conceptions of time.[29] And there is a burgeoning scholarly literature on the early twentieth-century German-Jewish intellectuals who appear frequently in these pages.[30] But Jewish anti-historicism, in its German or any other guise, has not received the kind of sustained attention that it deserves.[31]

This book is a first attempt at exploring the phenomenon. Contrary to the initial plan, it does not seek to cover the entirety of anti-historicist expression in modern Jewish thought up to the present. Its mission is more limited: to record the diverse but concerted expressions of anti-historicism by Jewish thinkers during a fateful period of German history extending from the last quarter of the nineteenth century through the first third of the twentieth. This more limited scale reflects a desire to yield a manageable and coherent text. But it also stems from the recognition that anti-historicism—despite its own aspirations—does not operate in an historical vacuum. It too must be situated within a complex and dynamic historical milieu.

The historical milieu of late nineteenth- and early twentieth-century Germany is a compelling arena in which to study anti-historicist expression by Jew and non-Jew alike. From the time of Bismarckian unification (1871), one notices a combustible mix of liberal and illiberal forces, of growing military boldness and crushing military defeat, of radical innovation and reactionary conservatism, of messianic optimism and deep *Kulturpessimismus*. In this environment, historical scholarship assumed a position of intellectual centrality, often being called into service to validate the antiquity, virtue, or prowess of the state. Indeed, history had become, in Ernst Troeltsch's famous phrase, "the leaven, transforming everything and ultimately exploding the very form of earlier theological methods." Its influence was so great, Troeltsch insisted, that "we are no longer able to think without this method or contrary to it."[32]

And yet, if historicism had grown from a fragile sapling at the end of the eighteenth century into a sturdy tree by the end of the nineteenth, its very maturation had sown seeds of discontent. In addition to Nietzsche's critique of the eviscerating effects of historicism on life, a wide range of European thinkers began to challenge the hegemony of historicism in the turn-of-the-century period. But nowhere, as Søren Kierkegaard had intuited decades earlier in Denmark, were the stakes of historicism's success as high as in the field of theology. After all, one of the aims of this field was to preserve a realm of inspired faith and sacred scripture removed from historical contingency. Historicism, by contrast, was a relentless encroacher, constantly challenging or subverting the assertion of timeless sanctity.

What complicates the picture of the apparent antagonism between history and theology—much like the relationship between historicism and anti-historicism—was the fact that the two were locked in a tight, if uncomfortable, embrace. Given historicism's role as a potent leaven, theologians could scarcely avoid absorbing and making use of historical method to clarify their own religious traditions. In doing so, they themselves attested to the fact that history had ceased to be "a handmaiden of theology" and had become "the dominant form of humanistic scholarship" in Europe.[33] But with so much to lose, theologians were perforce obliged to attack the frailty and hubris of historical method with particular urgency. One result, as Thomas A. Howard argues in *Religion and the Rise of Historicism*, is that the modern "crisis of historicism stemmed from and found its center of gravity in explicitly theological problems."[34]

Consistent with that theme, this book will highlight the tension between history and theology in Jewish thought in late Wilhelmine and Weimar Germany. We will note the overlap and occasional contact between the four main Jewish protagonists studied here and a tradition of renowned *philosophical* critics of historicism (e.g., Nietzsche, Dilthey, Windelband, Rickert, Heideigger). We will also note—and in fact, pay more attention to—a related, though lesser-known tradition, that of *theological* anti-historicism. This current of dissent, whose origins extend back to (and even beyond) the first wave of opposition to David Friedrich Strauss's *Life of Jesus* (1835), assumed particular prominence in the late nineteenth and early twentieth centuries. Immersed in a world of explosive mobility and growing instability, theologians like Martin Kähler, Franz Overbeck, Friedrich Gogarten, and Karl Barth sought to gain a measure of religious certainty by abandoning the relativist practices of the historian. These theological anti-historicists lamented what Franz Rosenzweig called "the curse of historicity" that cast a pall over modern Western culture.[35] In diverse ways, each sought to lift this curse through a mix of recourse to traditional religious authority and more modern intellectual strategies.

Of course, we should not assume that the tension between critical history and traditional religious culture is the exclusive preserve of Europe (or America). It is also present in the cultures of Africa and Asia, and has shown interesting signs of life in the Islamic world of late.[36] It is perhaps a measure of the highly charged nature of this tension for Muslims that recent challenges to the received tradition have come more notably from novelists—for example, Tariq Ali, Kanan Makiya, and Salman Rushdie—than from historians.[37] Notwithstanding their vocation, these writers make clear that the history-faith tension cuts across religious and cultural dividing lines.

Seen from this perspective, our decision to focus on late nineteenth- and early twentieth-century Germany may seem a bit parochial. And yet, as we have already suggested, the German context offers a number of unique virtues: first, it was rife with sharp and recurrent debates over historicism; second, proponents of both sides of the divide were unusually articulate in advancing their views; and third, these debates formed part of a larger discursive world to which Christians and Jews both belonged.

In fact, one of the reasons Germany is such an intriguing venue to study is because of the complicated texture of Jewish-Christian interaction. For centuries, and most noticeably from the time of the late eighteenth-century *Aufklärung* (Enlightenment), Jews and Christians in Germany engaged one another economically and—in intense, thought not always hospitable ways—socially and culturally as well. While there may not have been a full dialogue between equals, as Scholem famously claimed, there was most certainly not silence either. The study of Jewish anti-historicism points to a level of communication between respectful dialogue and icy silence.

To give a sense of that ambivalent cultural register, we can foreshadow here some of the questions that will concern us throughout. If Jewish assimilation in the nineteenth century entailed absorbing the regnant historicist ethos of the day, did movement away from that integrationist goal in the twentieth century—"dissimilation"—require its rejection? Did Jewish anti-historicism coincide with renunciation of the ideal of *Bildung*—the program of intellectual, moral, and cultural betterment—that many German Jews held sacred? Did it mandate at the same time a renewed commitment to Judaism, understood not in the historicist categories of the nineteenth century, but in self-consciously ahistoricist terms? And so was there not a curious dynamic at work—namely, Jews participating in an impassioned debate over historicism in the broader German milieu even as they sought to disengage from that milieu?

These questions point in divergent directions. On one hand, they assume a centrifugal thrust that pushed Jewish intellectuals, particularly in the Weimar period, away from the German (and German-Jewish) cultural mainstream. On the other, we know full well that there was a high degree of cultural interaction—to the point of inextricability—between German Jews and their non-Jewish hosts. Rather than regard the two positions as irreconcilable, this book argues that they can and must be understood in tandem, for they reflect the multiplicity, or bi-directionality, of the cultural vectors shaping Jewish life in modern Germany.

In making this point, we tend to avoid use of the term "influence" to describe the continuing process of borrowing, lending, and negotiation between German Jews and non-Jews. Influence often implies the triumph of a dominant cultural group over a more passive recipient. Our own understanding of cultural interaction is far more reciprocal than the model of influence allows, even in a case in which the differential in political power is considerable. One need not deny this differential to appreciate the creative capacity of minority groups like the Jews not only to *adopt*, but to *adapt* cultural norms from the host society to their own needs. In this regard, adaptation is not the terminus of cultural activity. Rather, it is a midpoint in a process of give and take that continually redefines the malleable boundaries of Jewish history.

This view of the elasticity of cultural borders is elaborated in the final chapter of the book. While convention might dictate that it be addressed in the opening chapter, I have followed the wise adage that methodological ruminations are perhaps best left for last—after the evidentiary and conceptual foundation has been laid. Consequently, the book commences in chapter 1 with a discussion of the term historicism and then traces the rise and partial fall of an historicist sensibility in German and German-Jewish culture. Each of the following four chapters focuses on a distinctive Jewish intellectual for whom historicism came to pose a formidable problem to his vision of Judaism. Chapter 2 analyzes the eminent German-Jewish philosopher Hermann Cohen (1842–1918), who is not usually thought of as a frontline anti-historicist. However, beginning with one of his earliest neo-Kantian writings from 1871, Cohen evinced concern for the atomizing impact of historicism that was reiterated on a number of crucial occasions later in life. The following chapter discusses Cohen's student and friend Franz Rosenzweig (1886–1929), who abandoned a career as an historian to become one of the most innovative Jewish thinkers of his time, as well as one of the most trenchant Jewish critics of historicism. Chapter 4 explores the fascinating early career of Leo Strauss (1893–1973), whose conservative critique of Enlightenment politics and epistemology led him to search out a pre-modern intellectual tradition that eluded the clutches of history. The penultimate chapter treats of Isaac Breuer (1883–1946), the idiosyncratic Orthodox thinker who, over the course of a prolific writing career culminating with his 1934 novel *Der Neue Kusari*, developed the notion that the Jewish people inhabited the realm of *Metageschichte* (Metahistory).

The temporal boundaries marked by Cohen's early essay of 1871 and Breuer's last novel of 1934 delineate a period of heightened agitation over the nature and aims of historicism in German culture. The Jewish figures studied here were eager consumers and producers of that culture, as well as interesting critics of one of its dominant features. They offered diverse strains of criticism of historicism, each of which issued from a peculiar biographical and intellectual point of view. At the same time, these critics shared in the particular malaise over historical thinking, as well as the more general sense of crisis, that affected much of European intellectual culture.

One of the most interesting commonalities that linked these thinkers, and that reveals the importance of contextualizing them within a discrete cultural setting, was their ambivalence toward Zionism. At a time of highly charged polemics among Weimar Jewish intellectuals about the virtues of Zionism vis-à-vis assimilation, the four thinkers all struggled to forge a path that resisted these two perceived extremes. In doing so, they compel us to widen the spectrum of German-Jewish—and more broadly, Diaspora Jewish—identities to allow for an expanded and conflicted middle ground. On a more personal level, they stand as interesting foils to the Jerusalem scholars who were the central figures in my previous book.

The choice of the four principals here was not meant to be exhaustive, but rather illustrative. A good number of other Jewish intellectuals in the German sphere might have been as worthy, most notably Leo Baeck, Walter Benjamin, Martin Buber, and Gershom Scholem (all of whom appear in cameo roles). Moreover, there are Jewish thinkers from other cultural spheres who might have fit the bill such as Nachman Krochmal, Ahad Ha-am, Micha Yosef Berdyczyewski, and Henri Bergson. Later thinkers like Hannah Arendt, Abraham Joshua Heschel, Baruch Kurzweil, and Yeshayahu Leibowitz might have found a place had the chronological range been expanded. What made the four chosen here so interesting to bring together into conversation was not their univocality, but rather the diverse inflections—political, theological, generational—of their shared anti-historicist language.

Finally, I would be less than ingenuous—and a fool to boot—if I suggested that my interest in these figures and their anti-historicist critique was a matter of dispassionate scholarly concern. "Un historien est toujours obligé de s'investir," Jean Delumeau has written of his dual commitments as professional historian and Christian.[38] Likewise, my own investment in the phenomenon of Jewish anti-historicism is unmistakably that of a professional historian and of a Jew—and, I must add, of a Jew for whom matters of belief and practice have become more vexing, consuming, and central with the passage of time. The result of this inquiry is far from a definitive resolution of the tension between history and faith; nor has it allowed me to overcome the periodic desire to leap beyond the historicist mode of cognition that defines my personal and professional being. But it has sensitized me to the inevitability, even desirability, of living with tension. I take some comfort in the fact that Jewish history offers an extended, exhilarating, and at times sad lesson in living in two worlds at once, within two spheres of time, with two visions of history—indeed, with the two dates that appear at the end of these lines as the competing and complementary tempos of the rhythm of life.[39]

*September 6, 2002*
*Erev Rosh Ha-Shanah 5762*

## Chapter One

## JEWISH HISTORICISM AND ITS DISCONTENTS:
## AN INTRODUCTION

> At bottom, man will never partake of eternity; his eternality is merely
> an *incessant temporality*. His temporality never ends; it is, therefore,
> an essential part of his permanency and inseparable from it.
> —Moses Mendelssohn, *Jerusalem*

Throughout much of their lengthy history, Jews have inhabited two temporal realms: one anchored by belief in Divine supervision and regulated by their own ritual calendar; the second marked by their immersion in a social, economic, and political world that revolves around a Gentile calendar. The contrast between these two calendars—often designated sacred and profane—has been a source of perennial tension for Jews. And yet, surprisingly for such a literate culture, it has not generated a large corpus of writing. Or to qualify the point: the contrast did prompt philosophically inclined rabbis in the Middle Ages to take note, on occasion, of competing Jewish and Gentile notions of time.[1] But chronicles of the Jewish past rarely gave voice to this tension, much less wove the narrative strands of Jewish and Gentile history into a single thread.

Of course, pre-modern Jews did not produce a large library of historical works in the first place.[2] Perhaps the most important piece of medieval Jewish historiography, the pseudepigraphic *Sefer Yosifon* (attributed to the first-century Josephus, but written in southern Italy in the tenth century), was somewhat exceptional within this small corpus. It presented a detailed narrative of the political and military events surrounding the Jewish rebellion against Roman rule in first-century Palestine. By contrast, works like the contemporaneous *Sefer Ha-Kabbalah* or the Hebrew Crusade Chronicles subordinated the description of specific historical events to the elaboration of a grand spiritual drama in which the Jewish people played a unique role. This kind of historical writing—the antithesis of *l'histoire evenementielle*—was hardly confined to the Jews; it bore a strong resemblance to the ecclesiastical history favored by Christians from Eusebius through the Middle Ages.[3]

We notice another similarity between Jewish and Christian historical writing that extends from the medieval into the early modern period: their shared proclivity for the genre of chronology. In the Jewish case, the *shalshelet ha-kabbalah* (chain of tradition) literature sought to give a precise genealogy of the transmission of the Oral Law from Revelation to the present. Not only was this genre the most common and "legitimate" form of Jewish historical writing in the Middle Ages;[4] it also was well represented in the spate of new Jewish historical works that appeared during the sixteenth century.[5] Even those who did not write a purely linear record of transmission—for example, the great Italian savant, Azariah De' Rossi (1511–1577)—were intent on establishing a fixed chronological order for important patches of the Jewish past.[6] Meanwhile, Christian scholars were working in parallel on resolving their own questions of calendar and chronology. As Anthony Grafton notes, they had long regarded chronology "as a fascinating and important subject—indeed as part of the core of civilization."[7]

Yet even as early modern scholars continued the genres and inclinations of their predecessors, they evinced signs of a novel attitude to the past. The older ecclesiastical model of historical writing, focused on the inspiring acts of God, church (or synagogue), and holy men, now competed with the Renaissance ideal of erudition that began to value events or texts from the past on their own terms. In his recent *Barbarism and Religion*, J.G.A. Pocock follows Arnaldo Momigliano in suggesting that early modern European historiography was forged at the site of contest between ecclesiastical and civil notions of law and history. The new civil history, according to Pocock, rested on the emerging prominence of the sovereign state whose defining norms (*moeurs*) it aimed to describe.[8] The Jewish case posed something of an anomaly: the absence of a sovereign state, and accompanying *moeurs*, would seem to be a significant deterrent to historiographical creativity, a point that Robert Bonfil has made in dismissing the claim of a sixteenth-century revolution in Jewish historical writing.

Nonetheless, Bonfil does notice in figures like De' Rossi, Eliyahu Capsali, and David Gans an attempt to push beyond traditional ecclesiastical history toward "a genuinely historical mode of writing by contemporary standards"—that is, toward an appreciation of history on its own terms.[9] Of particular interest in this regard is the last of the major sixteenth-century works of Jewish historiography: David Gans's *Tsemah David* from 1592.[10] What is particularly noteworthy in *Tsemah David* is its organization, which sought to accommodate both Jewish and Gentile—and thus in some fashion, sacred and profane—chronologies. Whereas Jews up to this point had attended to their own chronology, and Christians to theirs, Gans endeavored to combine the two, or at least to stand them in contiguous relation to one another: the first part of *Tsemah David* was a chronicle of Jewish history from creation to Gans's own day; the second traced the history of the Gentile world to the present.

*Tsemah David* did not rest on bold new research. As Mordechai Breuer has shown, it borrowed liberally from Hebrew, Latin, and German sources.[11] Nevertheless, the book is an intriguing symbol of transition from old to new in Jewish historical thinking. On one hand, it adopted a traditional Jewish framing of Gentile history—according to the archetypal pattern of the Four Kingdoms (Babylonia, Persia, Greece, and Rome) outlined in the Book of Daniel (8:22). Consistent with this framing, Gans announced in the introduction to part I that he treated Jewish history apart from Gentile history precisely in order "to separate the holy from the profane."[12]

On the other hand, Gans's clear recognition of the two spheres of history—despite their segregation—is a novelty over and against the usual neglect or denigration of the Gentile realm in medieval Jewish chronicling. Furthermore, Gans's declared principle of separating sacred and profane is belied by the periodic intrusion of sources, events, and actors from one sphere into another—that is, by a kind of historiographical border-crossing. And finally, Gans adds a new entry to the catalog of rationales for writing Jewish history. While admitting that his book might provide succor to Jews by demonstrating their survival (as against the ephemerality of the Gentiles), he also allowed that it could provide reading entertainment to Jews, particularly after an exhausting day of work.[13] This criterion of entertainment, especially when applied to a genre whose reading was proscribed by the contemporaneous legal code *Shulhan 'Arukh*, merits our attention.[14] It reveals a new openness to the developing culture of leisure in Europe.[15] But more importantly, it reveals cracks in the edifice of Jewish historical exceptionalism. The history of the Gentiles could no longer be ignored altogether; nor could the entirety of human history be ascribed to the machinations of the Divine Hand. Gans told the story of kings, wars, and earthquakes without recourse to the role of God.

The juxtaposition of Jewish and Gentile chronologies in *Tsemah David* was still a distance from—but nonetheless, an important step toward—the fusion of historical horizons that more modern Jewish historians have often regarded as an ideal. Gans had not yet seen fit to insert Jewish history into the diverse social contexts in which Jews dwelt. But he was keenly aware that there was utility—the Hebrew term *to'elet* abounds in the introduction to part II—in studying the history of the Gentile nations. In fact, he enumerated ten virtues accruing to this study, including impressing one's Gentile neighbors with knowledge and good sense.[16] This list of virtues suggests that Gans was angling to justify history as a literary genre distinct from traditional religious sources, and thus worthy in its own right. In this respect, he might be said to exhibit a *historical sense* that was an essential precondition of a later, more developed *historicism*.[17]

It has often been assumed, following Salo Baron, that sixteenth-century Jewish historians like Gans "found no successors" until the first generation of *Wissenschaft des Judentums*—that a vast gulf separated the historical sense of the sixteenth century from the historicism of the nineteenth.[18] Arguing against this view, Amos Funkenstein maintained that "[s]omewhere between the sixteenth and eighteenth century, a revolution occurred that was no less radical than the concurrent scientific revolution." This revolution, according to Funkenstein, introduced a new sense of *context* into historical thinking of that period.[19] But Funkenstein did not elaborate on the claim of revolution in the sixteenth-century Jewish historians. In fact, it may well be that "revolution" is too dramatic a term to define their approach, that their contextualist sensitivities were not as refined as he implies. Nonetheless, Funkenstein's intuitions about Jewish and Christian thinkers of the early modern era point to a richer canvas of historical thought than that painted by Baron.

For example, Funkenstein observes that beginning with Giambattista Vico (1668–1744) in the seventeenth century, mention of "the 'finger of God' disappeared from the course of human events," to be replaced by the more veiled image of the "invisible hand."[20] Some traces of that causal shift were present in the sixteenth-century Jewish historians.[21] But they become much more prominent in the work of Baruch Spinoza (1632–1677), the great philosopher, Biblical critic, and excommunicated Jew from Amsterdam. In his *Theologico-Political Treatise* (1670), Spinoza assaulted the foundations of traditional Judaism, first by casting Sinaitic Revelation as little more than a set of time-bound laws whose validity has lapsed, and then by challenging the claim of Mosaic authorship of the Pentateuch.[22] In the process, Spinoza fundamentally reconceptualized the biblical narrative, "transforming it from a sacred history (*historia sacra*) to a secular history (*historia profana*)."[23]

This transformation was a significant departure from David Gans's earlier *juxtaposition* of sacred and profane histories in *Tsemah David*. Spinoza neither believed in nor felt compelled to uphold two parallel universes. His entire philosophical being was devoted to the idea of a single universe in which God and nature were one. Within that world, everything—every text and event—could be explained in mundane natural or historical terms. Even the Bible, the most sacred of sources, could and must be subjected to critical philological and historical scrutiny. While no longer radical in our day, it was this belief that distinguished Spinoza from Gans, De' Rossi, and other sixteenth-century Jewish authors. And it was this belief that counted as one of the "horrible heresies" of which the young Spinoza was accused in 1656 by the Amsterdam Jewish community in its writ of excommunication against him.[24]

Although Spinoza began to engage in the kind of source criticism that would later undergird historicist approaches, he did so both in adversity and isolation. A more pervasive and textured "historical-mindedness," as Lord Acton termed it, emerged a century later, in the age of the great Jewish Enlightenment thinker, Moses Mendelssohn (1729–1786).[25] This is not to say that historicism reached full maturity with Mendelssohn. After all, the philosophical proclivities of the renowned *juif de Berlin* and other Enlightenment-era thinkers were more suited to creating holistic systems of thought than to contextualizing individual historical events. Moreover, Mendelssohn differed sharply from the earlier David Gans over the entertainment value of history. In a letter to his friend, the mathematician and fledgling historian, Thomas Abbt, Mendelssohn complained in 1765: "Whatever goes by the name of history: natural history, geological history, political history, history of scholarship, is beyond me; I yawn every time I have to read something historical, unless the style cheers me up."[26]

And yet, Mendelssohn's boredom with historical writing was not consistent. Several years before complaining to Thomas Abbt, he recalled reading David Hume's *History of England* (1762) with great enthusiasm.[27] Even more significantly, Mendelssohn operated in an environment in which recourse to history was increasingly common. Indeed, the eighteenth century, the age of Enlightenment, was hardly, as Ernst Cassirer pointed out seventy years ago, the " 'unhistorical' century."[28] To take one notable example, the Protestant theologian H. S. Reimarus (1694–1768) set out to challenge important features of the New Testament account of Jesus. Most provocatively, he was among the first to describe Jesus as a flesh and blood human who was the product of a concrete historical context. Mendelssohn's own historical-mindedness was less dramatic. But it was still present, for example, in his ruminations on Revelation—an event that played a key role in his (and Spinoza's) understanding of Judaism. According to Mendelssohn, the weight of thousands of eyewitnesses at Sinai rendered the occurrence of the event incontrovertible—to the point that he felt confident in asserting that Revelation is "a matter of *history* on which I can rely with certainty."[29]

While historical narrative was not always captivating to Mendelssohn, history as an ontological category was increasingly relevant as a source of authority to confirm events of great religious import. Mendelssohn's stance, which David Sorkin has described as "historical without being historicist," reflected both resistance and surrender to the growing historical-mindedness of the era.[30] In recognition of this Janus-faced view, Hans Liebeschütz has asserted that "the debate between Judaism and histori-

cism that formed such an important theme in Enlightenment-era thought
. . . began with Mendelssohn."[31] That is to say, Mendelssohn, as a product
of his time, absorbed some of the causal logic of historicism. But he did
not share Spinoza's willingness to submit Judaism to the razor-sharp tools
of the critical historian. In fact, Mendelssohn exemplified the ambivalence
toward history that characterized and unsettled many subsequent Jewish
thinkers—and that stands at the center of inquiry in this book.

Meanwhile, Mendelssohn's philosophical colleagues in the late eighteenth century labored to gain a hold on the growing prominence of history. Immanuel Kant (1724–1804) called for a "philosophical historiography of philosophy, written from a 'transcendental,' not an empirical point
of view."[32] For Kant, history was still subordinate to the systematizing
ambitions of philosophy. Sounding a different tone, Kant's one-time student, J. G. Herder (1744–1803), wrote of the need to develop a regimen
for the meticulous examination of unique historical events. This regimen,
Herder added, would "guard us from attributing the facts that appear in
history to the particular hidden purposes of a scheme of invisible powers."[33] Herder was clearly marking distance from the once-regnant medieval scheme of divine causality, as well as from the succeeding early modern image of an all-powerful "invisible hand." Concomitantly, he was
eschewing the demand for a coherent and transcendent metaphysics to
which many philosophers of the day still held. Rather, Herder was articulating a belief in the centrality of the historical *individuum*, a belief that
anchored the worldview that would come to be known as historicism.[34]

## HISTORICISM: A BRIEF HISTORY OF THE CONCEPT

In his classic *Die Entstehung des Historismus* (1936), the German historian and political theorist Friedrich Meinecke (1862–1954) focused on
the late eighteenth-century German milieu in which figures like Herder
struggled to assert "a new kind of historical thought." This new thought
held that history "as a whole is a countless number of individual foci,
each charged with energy, and each carrying a particular destiny." The
commitment to study each of these foci spelled for Meinecke a dramatic
breakthrough. As he wrote in the oft-quoted opening to his book, "the
rise of historism was one of the greatest intellectual revolutions that has
ever occurred in Western thought."[35]

Although the revolution began, according to Meinecke, in the late eighteenth century, he dated the introduction of the term "Historismus" to
the late nineteenth century. Scholars have since determined that this
term—from which the English variants "historism" and the more common "historicism" derive—was used by contemporaries of Herder such

as the poet-philosopher Novalis and the literary critic Friedrich Schlegel in the last years of the eighteenth century.[36] Schlegel's use of the term hints at a mode of thought at odds with philosophical practice of the day, which stripped away "all personal indicators" from the object of inquiry.[37] The desire to restore the individual and personal to humanistic study became a key feature of the concept as it was employed—periodically—throughout the first half of the nineteenth century (e.g., Ludwig Feuerbach, C. J. Braniss, and Carl Prantl).

It was not until the last decades of that century that the term entered common intellectual parlance. Curiously, it did not make its biggest mark among members of the historians' guild. That may well be because "Historismus" often carried a pejorative connotation. For instance, in 1884 the Austrian economist Carl Menger famously inveighed against the "errors of historicism" in the work of his colleague, Gustav Schmoller. Menger took Schmoller's reliance on an historical rather than purely theoretical approach to economics as evidence of the hegemony of historicism.[38] His fear was compounded by that of contemporaneous philosophers and theologians, who increasingly saw the individualizing thrust of historicism as the source of a dangerous cultural and moral relativism.[39] The rising chorus of criticism, often emanating from outside of the historical discipline, prompted Ernst Troeltsch several decades later to declare a "crisis of historicism." In response to this crisis, he and Friedrich Meinecke felt compelled to defend historicism by re-articulating its core premises.

In particular, they sought to defend historicism's liberation from the clutches of an unchanging natural law. Herein lay the genius, for Meinecke, of the "substitution of a process of *individualising* observation for a *generalising* view of human forces in history."[40] This new process rested on an important assumption: as distinct from static natural law principles, the individual historical organism continually evolved and developed. The task of the historian, informed by historicist norms, was to provide a thick contextual description of the evolving historical individuum.

To be sure, not all have agreed on the virtue or, for that matter, the very definition of *historicism*. On the contrary, the term has spawned a remarkable range of definitional progeny.[41] One observer, Calvin Rand, went so far as to opine in 1965 that the ongoing debates over historicism "have distorted whatever clear meaning the term might have developed." Undaunted, Rand went on to offer a helpful distinction. Historicism, he argued, can best be understood in two senses. The first refers to a methodological regime that studies "each person, event, nation, or era as a unique individual which develops over a period of time through its own internal means." The second refers to an overarching ideology or Weltanschauung that *values* the past on its own terms—and as an interconnected series of individual historical organisms.[42]

Rand's two connotations, if inverted, allow us to gain a firmer grasp on the formative period of Jewish historicism. The "historical sense" that we noticed in sixteenth-century Jewish chroniclers—for example, as found in the new attention to the history of the Gentile nations—helped lay the foundation for an historicist Weltanschauung that developed gradually from their time up to the nineteenth century. Eventually, this Weltanschauung came to dominate European intellectual culture, leading to what Troeltsch called in 1922 "the historicization of all our thinking and perception."[43] The effects of this sweeping tide on European Jewish life were palpable. Virtually no aspect of Jewish high culture—from literature to painting—went untouched. Moreover, large numbers of Jews, not merely isolated individuals à la Spinoza, now became familiar with the methodological arsenal of historicism. One group that stood at the cusp between old and new, between the early modern historical sense and modern historicism, was the Maskilim of Berlin, devoted disciples of Moses Mendelssohn and partners in the cause of a Jewish Enlightenment.

## HASKALAH AND HISTORICISM

As we have seen, Moses Mendelssohn was neither a formulator of historical theory nor a devoted practitioner of its method. But Mendelssohn's disciples, the Maskilim (Jewish Enlighteners) of Berlin, did embark on a program of educational reform that entailed a new appreciation for secular subjects including history. Emblematic of this impulse was the Hebrew-language journal, *Ha-Measef*, that first appeared in Germany from 1784. The journal's opening statement spoke of the importance of biographical surveys of illustrious rabbinic sages. These surveys, bearing a mix of celebratory prose and contextual backdrop, were to highlight the rabbis' "place and time of birth, the events of their lives, and the good that they have done for their fellow men."[44] As Shmuel Feiner has demonstrated, the journal in which these surveys appeared articulated an agenda for intellectual expansion in which history was to play "an important and essential" role.[45] The Maskilim's view of history was not yet imbued with the "scientific" spirit of nineteenth-century scholarship.[46] But they did move cautiously toward a contextualized understanding of the past.

Consequently, we can identify the Berlin Maskilim as the direct forebears of modern Jewish historical scholarship in Europe. The two main branches of that scholarly tradition in the nineteenth century were *Wissenschaft des Judentums* and *Hokhmat Yisrael*. Though the latter term is often used simply as the Hebrew equivalent for *Wissenschaft des Judentums*, it connotes for us a distinct variant of modern Jewish scholarship, written in Hebrew and maintaining a reverential and referential relationship to traditional Jewish sources.[47] The juxtaposition of the two variants is instructive in reminding us that Jewish scholars of the nineteenth century, like the Maskilim before them, did not simply or uniformly renounce the theological premises or ritual values of traditional Judaism. Rather, a number of different stances can be detected in the two nineteenth-century variants, as well as within each. Typical of the enterprise of *Hokhmat Yisrael* was Shlomo Yehuda Rapoport (1790–1867), the Prague-born scholar who published major studies of medieval rabbinic figures beginning in the 1830s. Rapoport advanced beyond the Maskilim in terms of source utilization, attention to context, and a well-developed technical apparatus. Moreover, Rapoport urged his readers to assume a critical stance by searching out thinkers or ideas from the past that did not conform to their own perspective. Still, for all his scholarly acumen, Rapoport's narrative casting of medieval rabbis such as Saadia Gaon, Hai Gaon, and Nathan of Rome bore traces of veneration that were noticeably absent in contemporaneous German-Jewish scholarship.

Indeed, the scholars of *Wissenschaft des Judentums* used their command of German and their newfound access to university training to distance themselves from the objects of their research. Significantly, they also distanced themselves from the language of classical Jewish scholarship: Hebrew.[48] With all its traditionalist resonances, Hebrew conveyed the cadences and sensibilities of a sacred tradition.[49] For this reason, the move to a non-Jewish language—German—was a major stimulus to the rise of the dominant tradition of critical Jewish scholarship in the nineteenth century: *Wissenschaft des Judentums*.[50] At the same time, it was a clear signal that the circle of scholars associated with it had begun to embrace the fundaments of the historicist creed. Still, the process by which history became the discipline of choice for nineteenth-century Jewish scholars was delayed somewhat for reasons that we will now explore.

## The Rise of *Wissenschaft* in Judaism

Leopold Zunz (1794–1886), one of the founding figures of *Wissenschaft des Judentums*, reflected a momentous and rapid shift in linguistic and cultural perspective. Raised in a traditional Jewish household, the young Zunz was sent, after the premature death of his father, to study at the Samsonsche Freischule in Wolfenbüttel. It was there, at the age of eleven, that Zunz first acquired facility in the German language.[51] It was there that he also developed his growing interest in the annals of the Jewish past, consuming classics of Jewish history in his spare time, including the *Sefer Yosifon*. Following the Freischule, Zunz spent a number of years at a non-Jewish gymnasium in Wolfenbüttel before moving to Berlin to commence study at the newly established university there. His chief mentors in Berlin were the classical philologists Friedrich August Wolf and August Boeckh, as well as the Bible scholar, W.M.L. de Wette.[52] Whereas the first two imparted to Zunz a clear sense of philological method, de Wette stood as a symbol of unsparing rigor and integrity. De Wette was renowned as a fiercely independent scholar who did not shy away from a critical historical approach to early Christianity, an impulse that earned him his dismissal from the University of Berlin in the age of reaction that followed Napoleon's defeat.[53]

Emboldened by the example of his teachers, Zunz began work in 1817 on a sweeping essay that laid out a comprehensive agenda for Jewish scholarly research.[54] Published in 1818 as "Etwas über die rabbinische Literatur," this essay became one of the cornerstones of modern Jewish historical scholarship. Similar to Wolf and Boeckh, Zunz heralded in this essay the unique clarificatory powers of *Wissenschaft* (scientific scholarship), especially in its philological guise.[55] And similar to de Wette, Zunz regarded critical scientific method as a means of ridding distortion and superstition from the past, particularly a past religious tradition.[56] Armed with this new method, Zunz called for the systematic study of "neo-Hebraic" literature (*neuhebräische Literatur*) in its widest possible sense—amounting to the entirety of Jewish literary creativity after the Bible. It is interesting to note that Zunz regarded Hebrew as an appropriate object, but not vehicle, of research. Signaling a clear break with the residual traditionalism of the Maskilim, Zunz insisted on an exacting inventory of Hebrew literature. The task was particularly urgent, Zunz asserted, because in his day "Hebrew books are more readily available than they will likely be in 1919."[57]

Without a trace of sentiment (or clairvoyance) for Hebrew's future, Zunz made clear that German was the language in which to conduct such a critical analysis. He was duly mindful of the fact that fellow Jews "are seizing upon German language and learning and are thus, perhaps unwittingly, carrying the neo-Hebraic literature to its grave." But this was an inevitable and not altogether infelicitous development, given that Jewish learning had declined precipitously over the centuries. Indeed, an important subtext of Zunz's essay was the desire to wrest the classical sources of Judaism away from the hands of traditionalist rabbis whose wisdom, he boldly claimed, "had, perhaps, been extinguished forever." To facilitate this task, Zunz called upon *Wissenschaft* to "step in demanding an account of what has already been sealed away."[58] The proposed sealing of the canon of "neo-Hebraic literature" was not an act of sanctity. On the contrary, it reflected Zunz's unsentimental approach to classical Judaism.

The scale of Zunz's program owed much to his Berlin teachers Wolf and Boeckh; in their studies of classical antiquity, they attempted to provide systematic classifications of distinct literary genres within the framework of "encyclopedias."[59] Like them, Zunz envisaged philology as the ideal method to comprehend his wide-ranging subject. It alone "is capable of removing the veil of the past." As part of his philological labor, Zunz declared the need to place the evolution of Hebrew and its classical sources in a broader non-Jewish context—for instance, by studying ancient Chaldean in order to "make any claims for a basic history of Hebrew language."[60]

If Zunz's first teachers, the Maskilim, cautiously inched toward a new appreciation of Jewish history, he willingly leaped into a new methodological world. It is curious to note that this new critical perspective did not initially go by the name "history."[61] In his 1818 essay, Zunz did indicate that an historical approach was one of the three pillars of a systematic analysis of "neo-Hebraic literature." But he tended to describe his work in terms other than history—e.g., philology, statistics, or most inclusively, *Wissenschaft*.[62] Likewise, the scholarly circle that Zunz and his colleagues formed in 1819 was the Verein für Cultur und Wissenschaft der Juden (Society for the Culture and Science of Jews). Although Zunz contemplated other names for the society, none of these options mentioned the word "history."[63] And the Verein's journal, inaugurated in 1822, was the *Zeitschrift für die Wissenschaft des Judentums*, the Journal for the Science of Judaism. In commenting on this nomenclature, Leon Wieseltier observed that "[m]odern Jewish historiography was thus born not as *Geschichte* but as *Wissenschaft*; under the aegis of philology, not history."[64]

One can easily explain Zunz's terminological choice as the result of the pervasive allure and magical resonance of *Wissenschaft* in German intellectual circles. Thomas Nipperdey has noted that *Wissenschaft* came to represent in this period not merely a method, but also a new, quasi-religious faith in scientific validation.[65] For Zunz and other young Jewish scholars, *Wissenschaft* forged a path toward the illumination of the Jewish past. But it also served as an anchor of stability in the midst of a turbulent social environment.

Following Napoleon's defeat, a rising tide of conservative German nationalism, including virulent forms of anti-Jewish expression, placed German Jews on the defensive. The very university halls in which Zunz and his comrades acquired the tools of critical scholarship echoed with hostile words. One of Zunz's erstwhile teachers in Berlin, Friedrich Rühs, was in the forefront of those calling for a reversal of Jewish integration into German society. Stung by Rühs's call, Zunz "seized the weapon of *Wissenschaft* and turned it on his academic adversary."[66] He saw critical scholarship as a means of rebuffing those who possessed a simpleminded and essentialist image of Judaism—by distinguishing between "what is old and useful, what is outmoded and detrimental, what is new and desirable."[67]

Zunz's devotion to *Wissenschaft*—as source of scientific *and* social validation—may explain why he and his colleagues did not brand their scholarly labors "history." But a related reason may be that the study of history was increasingly identified in this period with German nationalism. Whereas eighteenth-century historians in Germany tended to focus on "universal history," their nineteenth-century successors began to define history as the narrative account of a distinct political nation or state.[68] One notices this tread in Berlin, where scholars such as Leopold von Ranke and F. K. von Savigny represented a new "Historical School" whose focus of research was the development of the nation.[69] One also notices it in leading scholarly journals such as the *Historisch-Politische Zeitschrift*, which Ranke founded in 1832. Enthusiastically supported by the Prussian foreign minister, Count von Bernstorff, this journal was intended to reveal the historical roots and glory of the Prussian state, as it sought to ward off criticism from both right and left.[70]

Caught in the throes of a developing nationalist enthusiasm, Leopold Zunz and other German-Jewish scholars faced a challenge. If history was increasingly seen as the story of the nation, how were they to cast the story of the Jews? Only at great risk could they treat the object of their study as a living national organism parallel to the German nation. For to do so was to strengthen the hand of the anti-Jewish agitators of the illiberal, post-Napoleonic era who continually raised the specter of Jewish clannishness and disloyalty. It was also to undermine the still unfulfilled claims to citizenship that German Jews advanced. Indeed, members of the Verein had to confront not merely antagonistic individuals like Friedrich Rühs, but a Prussian state bureaucracy willing to roll back the incremental emancipatory gains of an earlier era.[71]

This may be why it was rare for Zunz in his early career to refer to his labors as "history."[72] But regardless of any fear he may have had of dire consequences, Zunz simply did not regard the Jewish collectivity as a vibrant *nation* in the political sense of the word.[73] To the extent that Jews had a history at all, it took the form of a depoliticized *Judaism*. Zunz's instincts in this latter regard were shared by his one-time schoolmate in Wolfenbüttel, Isaak Marcus Jost. Unlike Zunz, Jost did choose the form of a narrative history in his major scholarly enterprise, the nine-volume *Geschichte der Israeliten* (1820–1828). But Jost was unmistakably guided in this undertaking by the belief that "the Israelite (of today) is no longer a member of an Israelite nation, rather only of the Israelite faith."[74]

In short, the equation of nation and history did not fit the scholarly or political agenda of the founders of *Wissenschaft des Judentums*.[75] While this equation increasingly animated the efforts of their non-Jewish teachers and contemporaries, they clung to the broader standard of *Wissenschaft*, which included but was not subsumed under the methods of history. It was only a matter of time before history and historicism per se began to gain ground—both in name and deed—within German-Jewish culture. Indeed, in the generation after Zunz and Jost, the scientific study of Judaism increasingly became the study of Jewish history. Even more significantly, history became an indispensable arbiter of both the Jewish past and present.

## FROM *WISSENSCHAFT DES JUDENTUMS* TO JEWISH HISTORY

The years in which Zunz and his colleagues first became active inaugurated a decades-long period of reaction in German lands that left a deep imprint on their lives. In a gesture of major symbolic import, Eduard Gans, one of the most distinguished young scholars of the Verein and its one-time president, decided to convert to Christianity after being denied a university professorship because of his religion. Gans could not escape a confounding paradox that would endure throughout the nineteenth and twentieth centuries: although Jews had demonstrated considerable upward mobility in the economic and social realms, they still had to contend with the persistent claim that they were incapable of integration into German society. This claim was a cornerstone of late eighteenth-century opposition to Jewish emancipation, but was also frequently intoned in the first half of the nineteenth century. One of its most painful iterations was Friedrich Wilhelm IV's insistence in 1841 that the "individual assimilation [of Jews] into the civil life of the Christian population of the land" could never be achieved. The king of Prussia proposed instead that his country's 200,000 Jews be organized into distinct corporations, prompting torrents of protest that quickly led him to rescind his proposal.[76]

These expressions of protest also led to a renewed struggle for full Jewish emancipation. Throughout the 1830s and 1840s, figures such as Gabriel Riesser (1806–1863) tirelessly pushed this cause in various legislative forums in Germany. Riesser, a Jewish lawyer who had been denied the right to teach in a university, framed his argument in terms that indicated his own acculturation into German society. He declared that Jews "are committed to struggle and to strive (for emancipation) until the very last breath of our lives—this is what we believe makes us worthy to be *German* and to be called *German*."[77] This kind of argument, suggesting both a new status and boldness for Germany's Jews, found a receptive audience in the 1840s; the parliaments of various German states, including the Prussian *Landtag* in 1847, moved closer to full citizenship rights for Jews.

Cast between the poles of recurrent anti-Jewish hostility and new legal remedies, the second generation of German-Jewish scholars continued to cling to *Wissenschaft*. And yet, the goal toward which *Wissenschaft* was applied differed from the founding generation. In the earlier years, *Wissenschaft* had been used to highlight Judaism's suitability for modern society. Now it was used as a tool to accentuate differences within Judaism, specifically among the emerging denominations of German Jewry. Indeed, the 1840s witnessed an intensification of denominational debate within German Jewry, as liberal, "positive-historical," and Orthodox camps battled for the soul of the community. Historical methods were employed in this battle, and became an important marker of denominational affiliation: the more radically one applied them, the more committed one was to the reform of Judaism; conversely, the more guarded one was in using these methods, the closer one was to the traditional, or Orthodox, position.[78]

Closely related to this development was the ascendance of history as the discipline of choice for German-Jewish scholars of the mid–nineteenth century. In contrast to the *Zeitschrift für die Wissenschaft des Judentums*, the leading Jewish scholarly journal of this later generation was the *Monatsschrift für Geschichte und Wissenschaft des Judentums*—the Monthly Journal for the *History* and Science of Judaism. The inclusion of "history" in the title of this journal signaled a new turn in German-Jewish scholarship.[79] The journal's editor, Zacharias Frankel (1801–1875), acknowledged the novel focus in his opening statement from 1851. Frankel understood that history was somewhat alien to the Jews, in large measure because Judaism was deemed alien from history—in the regnant sense of history as the plane of political activity. But Frankel was not content to accept that common connotation. He sought to reclaim history for the Jews, in part by expanding its definition. History was not only the story of a powerful political nation or, in the case of the Jews, of a passive victim acted upon by the nations of the world. It was also the story of "vigorous spiritual capacity, of deep and profound inspiration, of the overcoming of external circumstances." And it was these features that forged a "distinctive history of Judaism."[80]

These features inspired Frankel's notion of a "positive-historical Judaism." Frankel used his scholarly expertise to study the evolving history of the Oral Law. Through this line of inquiry, he aimed not only to chart new intellectual terrain, but to forge a middle course between two denominational poles of German Jewry. His approach was more "positive" toward the Jewish oral tradition than that of Reformers. At the same time, it was a good deal more "historical" than that of most Orthodox.[81]

Frankel's younger colleague, Heinrich Graetz (1817–1891), shared the denominational sensibility of his elder. Moreover, he shared Frankel's strong historical orientation. Five years before Frankel inaugurated the

*Monatsschrift*, the twenty-nine-year-old Graetz published a sweeping essay in which he proclaimed the indispensability of history for the Jews. Writing in 1846, Graetz declared that "the totality of Judaism is discernible only in its history. Its complete nature, the sum of its powers, becomes clear only in the light of history."[82]

Over the rest of his career, Graetz acted upon this historicist proposition, producing an eleven-volume *History of the Jews* that made him the most renowned Jewish historian of his time. Graetz's volumes were history of a grand scale, marked by a narrative passion so fierce that he was later accused by the historian Heinrich von Treitschke of anti-German chauvinism. In this regard, Graetz wrote a "quintessentially national history"—not of the Germans but of the Jews. Indeed, his *History* was more consonant with the national framing of his non-Jewish contemporaries than with the denationalized perspective of his Jewish predecessors.[83]

A year after the first volume of his *History* was published in 1853, Graetz joined the faculty of the new rabbinical seminary founded by Zacharias Frankel in Breslau. It was in the modern rabbinical seminary that the subject of Jewish history was systematically introduced as a field of study for rabbis, signifying an important shift not only in curriculum but in the worldview of modern Jewry. Whereas students in traditional yeshivot had been taught rabbinical literature in a contextual vacuum, the introduction of regular historical study in the seminary exposed students to new methods and notions of causality.[84]

Breslau was not the first seminary in Europe to attempt curricular innovations in rabbinic education.[85] But it was at Breslau that the new curriculum for rabbis received wide implementation, in large measure because the seminary employed an elite cadre of university-trained scholar-teachers suffused with the ideals of modern critical scholarship. In this respect, the Breslau seminary followed the model of Protestant theological faculties at German universities, where scholarship assumed an increasingly historical bent from the 1830s. Figures such as F. C. Baur at Tübingen were less interested in rehearsing standard dogmatic positions than in uncovering new historical perspectives on the history of Christianity. A similar critical impulse animated Frankel and Graetz at Breslau, where they imparted an historically textured understanding of Judaism to students. Mindful of the change in educational norms from the old-style yeshivah, Frankel asserted that in the case of the modern rabbi, "to be intimately familiar with the Talmud is not enough; the Muses must also not be strange to him."[86]

The weekly Jewish history lectures that Graetz delivered at Breslau could be jarring to the uninitiated.[87] A young student by the name of Hermann Cohen recalled his bewilderment when Graetz unmasked in one of his classes a revered medieval scholar known to Cohen only by the traditional acronym—RaDaK—as Rabbi David Kimchi from Provence.[88] Assigning biographical and historical details to seemingly timeless rabbinic figures could be unsettling to some of the Breslau students. Yet it was part of the ongoing historicization that transformed not only rabbinical education, but German-Jewish intellectual life more generally in the nineteenth century.[89]

The rabbinical seminaries of Germany—in addition to Breslau, Liberal and Orthodox seminaries were created in Berlin in the 1870s—had a particularly important role to play in this process. In the first instance, they served as home to professional Jewish scholars who were trained in, and subsequently discharged from, German universities.[90] Throughout the nineteenth century, there were no regular university positions (at the rank of *Ordinarius*) in the fields of Jewish history, literature, or theology. Hence when Jewish scholars—and only a lucky handful among them—found employment as professors, it was in the rabbinical seminary. As a result, the seminary became a significant institution in the "subculture" of German Jewry, parallel to the university in the broader German sphere, though a good deal more limited in function.[91] It was in the seminary that Jewish scholars pursued their research and taught in their chosen fields of expertise. Thus, for an historian like Graetz, the Jewish history lectures he gave at Breslau provided an unparalleled opportunity to impart the methods and conceptual framework of Jewish history to future teachers and scholars.

At the same time, the seminary served another important function. It allowed, even encouraged, its faculty to play an active role in the denominational battles within German Jewry. Graetz, for example, was both the initiator and target of vehement criticism in these battles. Meanwhile, scholars such as Abraham Geiger on the left and D. Z. Hoffmann on the right—each of whom taught in a rabbinical seminary representing his denomination—did vigorous battle in the name of their respective positions. In the midst of this disputatious climate, historical scholarship became a major tool both of assault and differentiation. The degree of historical perspective with which one read the Bible or the Talmud reflected not only a methodological stance, but an entire way of thinking about and practicing Judaism.[92]

In little more than half a century, from the time of the Haskalah until the founding of the Breslau seminary, a stunning transvaluation had occurred: history had become *the* authority to which Judaism answered.[93] One could no longer think except historically. As one scholar noted of Heinrich Graetz, "any concept of Judaism outside the perspective of history was meaningless."[94] This cognitive universe was not Graetz's alone. Nor was it confined to the exclusive cadre of Judaica scholars in mid-century Germany. Rather, its reach extended into many spheres of German-Jewish cultural life, reaching a high point at the fin de siècle.

## The Historicization of German-Jewish Culture

In his recent attempt to understand the phenomenon of modernism, Carl Schorske observed the pervasive rise of historicism following the Enlightenment:

> Never in the history of European culture had Clio enjoyed such preeminence—not to say hegemony—as in the mid–nineteenth century. . . . History's mode of thought and its temporal perspective penetrated most fields of learning, while the models of the past inspired the nineteenth century's arts. . . . Historical painting and the historical novel acquired new salience in artistic practice, while the study and criticism of the arts were reconceived as the *history* of art, literature, etc.[95]

As an urban, bourgeois presence seeking to integrate into the social mainstream, German Jews readily fell under the sway of history. Many areas of Jewish culture other than scholarship bore the imprint of history. Architecture,[96] painting,[97] and literature[98] all redefined themselves—and in the process, redefined Jews—in response to the new historicist imperative. Moreover, a new crop of journals and periodicals, scholarly as well as popular, arose over the course of the century to satisfy the expanding historical appetite of German Jews. Pride of place among them belongs to the *Allgemeine Zeitung des Judentums*, founded in 1837 by Ludwig Philippson. Material of an historical nature occupied a surprisingly large number of the *Allgemeine Zeitung*'s pages. In addition to works of historical fiction (such as a novel on Marranos by Phlippson's brother Phöbus), articles dealing with the history of Jewish communities old and new, as well as reviews of important works of historical scholarship, abounded. The historical-mindedness of the journal inevitably influenced and responded to the tastes of its readership. For as an observer of the paper noted in 1887, "the history of the Allgemeine Zeitung is essentially the history of [German] Jews and Judaism in the last half-century."[99] And if history had become a major preoccupation of the *Allgemeine Zeitung*, so too had it for German Jewry.

The process of historicization would continue to find new outlets in German Jewry toward the end of the century. Jacques Ehrenfreund has argued recently that the true historicization of German Jewry commenced only after 1871. Presenting Graetz (and Jost before him) as exceptions, he suggests that it was the establishment of the Second Reich that led to the rise of a professional Jewish historiography, as well as to popular interest in the Jewish past. Organizations such as the Historische Commssion für die Geschichte der Juden in Deutschland (1885), the Gesellschaft zur Förderung der Wissenschaft des Judentums (1902), and the Gesamtarchiv der deutschen Juden (1905) all reflected this new interest, and were particularly intent in an age of renewed nationalist fervor to establish the antiquity and legitimacy of Jewish existence in German lands.[100]

We concur with Ehrenfreund that the late nineteenth century witnessed both a growing professionalization and popularization of historicism among German Jewry. Jacob Borut highlights this latter trend, demonstrating that lay circles for Jewish history and literature (e.g., the Vereine für jüdische Geschichte und Literatur) proliferated in turn-of-the-century Germany, counting more than 12,000 members in 131 societies in 1900.[101] These societies provided an outlet for a Jewish public—young and old, women and men—increasingly hungry for knowledge about a rapidly vanishing Jewish past.

Through such institutions, historicization seemed to enhance, not diminish, the communal commitments of German Jews. But the very pace of historicization in German-Jewish culture inspired a strong current of discontent. Among critics, historicization and historicism were synonymous with the most debilitating features of modern life: brazen impiety, alienated individualism, and an unrestrained subjectivity masquerading as truth. Indeed, critics saw historicism not as the remedy, but the cause, of modernity's ills. It is to this tradition of criticism that we now turn.

## The Problem of History in the Age of Historicism

The author of a study of Orthodox Jewish attitudes toward history recently averred: "The truth is that historical 'truth,' per se, as an independent value in and of itself, has not fared well in Jewish tradition."[102] Jacob J. Schacter had in mind the long-standing tradition of Orthodox indifference or antagonism to historical study. Perhaps its most noteworthy expression of late came from Rabbi Shimon Schwab, a leading rabbinic figure in the German Orthodox community of Washington Heights, New York. In an essay devoted to Jewish history, Rabbi Schwab declared: "Rather than write the history of our forebears, every generation has to put a veil over the human failings of its elders and glorify all the rest which is great and beautiful."[103]

Schwab is but a late link in a chain of religiously observant Jews concerned by the growing encroachment of historical methods onto the sacred terrain of religion. More than a century earlier, a forceful articulation of this position came from the man who founded the community of German Orthodox Jews to which Rabbi Schwab belonged: Samson Raphael Hirsch (1808–1888). Hirsch did not favor a retreat from active engagement with the surrounding world. On the contrary, his celebrated notion of *Torah im derekh erets* urged Jews to embrace the literary and cultural treasures of the host society. But he had his own clear limits.

More than any other German Jew of his day, Hirsch sought to counter the prevailing norm of justifying Judaism according to history. Judaism, he maintained, was a force that did not submit to the dictates of historical contingency. This position placed him at odds with much of contemporaneous Jewish culture, including elements of the Orthodox community, which was awash in historicism.[104] Historical scholarship was a constant presence in that culture, fueling the publication of hundreds of monographs and thousands of pages in German-Jewish periodicals. To stem this powerful tide, Hirsch founded his own journal, *Jeschurun*, in 1854. Writing in the first issue, Hirsch observed that if Jews accept the veracity of the biblical phrase "and God spoke to Moses":

> so we must hold to it, fulfill it, without shortcuts or finding fault, in all circumstances and at all times. The Divine Word must reign eternal over all human judgment and we and all our deeds must be shaped by it. Instead of complaining that it is no longer suitable to the times, we should recognize only one legitimate complaint: that the times are no longer suitable to the Divine Word.[105]

Hirsch's view of the eternity of the Divine Word directly challenged the contextual logic of historicism. At the same time, it provided an unchanging standard against which to measure what he called the "sickly subjectivism" of modern Jewish historiography.[106]

When thinking of the dangerous effects of historicism, Hirsch had no clearer villain in mind than Heinrich Graetz. Beginning in the second volume of *Jeschurun*, Hirsch commenced a ferocious attack on the first published volume of Graetz's *History of the Jews* (dealing with the Talmudic period). What adds genuine intrigue to the story is the fact that Graetz had gone to Oldenburg as a young man to study with Hirsch from 1837 to 1840. To be sure, he left this apprenticeship with a less flattering view of Hirsch than when he came. But Graetz still maintained a good deal of admiration for his teacher.[107] Indeed, he dedicated his dissertation to Hirsch in 1845, describing him as "the profound fighter for historical Judaism, the unforgettable teacher, the fatherly friend."[108]

Notwithstanding Graetz's gesture of fondness, Hirsch came to regard his erstwhile disciple as the embodiment of history's destructive tendencies. The fact that Graetz chose to begin his multi-volume history with the Talmudic period set Hirsch on notice. Graetz's own aim in starting with this era, rather than the biblical age, was "to portray the disembodied rabbis of the Mishnah and Talmud as vibrant men, each with his own style and philosophy and personal frailties, who collectively resisted the disintegrating forces of their age."[109] Hirsch branded this attempt pure hubris. In the first instance, he excoriated Graetz for reducing the rabbis' actions to a jumbled mass of base human motivations. According to Hirsch, "he [Graetz] interprets them subjectively, in terms of what he perceives to be the temperament, the psychological makeup, the hierarchic positions and the political aims of these teachers."[110] Even more unsettling to Hirsch was the implication that the Oral Law—for example, the Mishnah and Talmud—was of human, not divine, origin. Hirsch wrote:

> Instead of viewing the moral and spiritual heroes of Jewish history as products of the theoretical study and practical observance of the Law, he regards the Law as the product of individuals of greater or lesser creative or spiritual talents. As a result, we receive, in place *of a true history of the development of the Jews*, a fictional account of the development of Jewish law.[111]

It is interesting that Hirsch, the vocal critic of the excesses of modern historical scholarship, came to attack Graetz on some of the very grounds favored by the modern historian. To begin with, Graetz's psychologization of the rabbis failed as good history, because it relied on thoroughly subjective speculation. Continuing the barrage, Hirsch analyzed many cases in Graetz's text in which, he claimed, the historian had misread the Talmudic sources. Indeed, Graetz had a tendency to "distort facts" and "invent motives," which was "truly puzzling to any genuine, scholarly student of history." For it resulted, Hirsch concluded, in "a history of things that did not happen."[112]

The reward in reviewing Graetz's work so exhaustively was clear-cut: to "show novices in the field of historiography how not to treat documentary sources, how not to establish facts, and how not to interpret historical events and personalities." But we must wonder how sincere Hirsch's reliance on the language and standard of history was. Unlike Orthodox scholars such as Esriel Hildesheimer, David Zvi Hoffmann, and Jakob Barth, Hirsch raised the banner of proper historical method only for defensive purposes—in this case, to beat back Graetz's perceived assault on the Oral Law. Hirsch also differed from a seminal earlier scholar, Nachman Krochmal (1785–1840), the Galician Jew renowned for his posthumously published meditation on Jewish history, *Moreh nevukhe hazeman*. Both Hirsch and Krochmal asserted that the spirit of Judaism soared above the plane of mundane history. But Krochmal also recognized, as Jay Harris has noted, that Jew themselves "remain subject to the laws that pertain to all physical things; as such, as far as their material existence is concerned, they have a history as do all other peoples." Krochmal's mediation between "metahistorical and historiographical claims" was not tactical.[113] It was a sincere attempt to contend with competing historicist and anti-historicist impulses, with the material existence of Jews and the Divine supervision of Judaism, in his thought.

By contrast, S. R. Hirsch operated according to the principle: "Rather a Jew without *Wissenschaft* than *Wissenschaft* without Judaism."[114] At the end of the day, historical research—and the realm of mundane history—had value for him only insofar as they were subordinate to an irrefutable religious truth. Hirsch could brook only a tactical and fleeting compromise with historicism. This position set him apart from Reform, positive-historical, and even some traditional thinkers of his day. Likewise, it has made him a revered (if misunderstood) figure within the Orthodox Jewish world today.[115]

## FAITH VERSUS HISTORY: A JEWISH PROBLEM TOO

We began this chapter by tracing the gradual rise of an historicist worldview among European, particularly German, Jews in the modern age. This rise was inextricably linked to developments in the contiguous Christian world. The link is hardly coincidental, since the two groups struggled jointly to make sense of their respective religious identities in a radically new historicist world. Thus, in the period in which S. R. Hirsch took aim at the historiographical hubris of Heinrich Graetz, a raging storm was sweeping Christian Europe. Reduced to its simplest form, the storm pitted faith versus history, with theologians battling historians to preserve the supernatural character of Christianity, and above all the mythic Christ of faith. A chief catalyst in igniting this storm was the Protestant scholar David Friedrich Strauss, whose monumental 1835 book, *The Life of Jesus*, struck a blow at the authenticity of the Gospel accounts of the life of Jesus. Although preceded by historically minded scholars like H. S. Reimarus, Strauss nonetheless broke new ground—both in method and boldness—in claiming that Jesus could be understood in historical-contextual (as opposed to mythological) terms.[116]

"Scarcely ever has a book," declared Albert Schweitzer, "let loose such a storm of controversy." Schweitzer thought little of the quality of response, branding Strauss' first critics a "crop of toad-stools."[117] As a matter of fact, Strauss's book did not initially spawn a body of serious scholarship on the life of Jesus; rather, research tended to focus on later Christian figures and sources.[118] Only in the 1860s did a new wave of research surface, inspired by a substantially revised edition of Strauss's *Life of Jesus* (1864), as well as by Ernest Renan's massively popular *Vie de Jésus* (1863). It was in the midst of this subsequent—and ongoing—debate over the historical Jesus that the problem of history became "*the fateful question*" for modern Christianity.[119]

We have seen that for nineteenth-century German Jewry as well, history was a potent tonic. For most, it was an indispensable mode of apprehending the world; for others, it was a source of instability and fear. The battle raging in adjacent Christian quarters only deepened divisions within the German-Jewish world. For instance, the liberal scholar Abraham Geiger regarded D. F. Strauss's challenge to Christian theological convention as "epoch-making." In the spirit of the religious reform that he so passionately embraced, Geiger confessed that "my most fervent wish is that things everywhere will be shaken up now, but with dignified seriousness, and thus in all sciences the consciousness of the necessity of a reorganization emerges."[120] But others, including notable Jewish historians, were less enthralled. Heinrich Graetz wrote to his friend Moses Hess in 1865 that he planned to expand a chapter on Christianity in his *History* "in order to refute the stupidity of Strauss and Renan."[121] Graetz had in mind not only their insufficient attention to Jewish sources, but more significantly, their view of Christianity as a radical rupture from, and spiritual advance over, Second Temple Judaism.

In the midst of this tumult, an Orthodox thinker like S. R. Hirsch found himself on the defensive. He and his like-minded friends were surrounded by an array of prospective enemies, the most serious of whom were Jewish.[122] It was one thing for a Christian scholar to dissolve the supernatural aura of Jesus; it was quite another for a Jewish scholar like Graetz to question the divine origin of the Oral Law. For Hirsch, such an act marked the total corruption of the modern project of secularization of which historicism was a standard-bearer.

When thinking of Hirsch, we can hardly avoid raising doubts about a statement made by Salo Baron in 1935. The great Jewish historian wrote then that "the entire problem of *Glaube und Geschichte* (faith and history), so troublesome to many modern Protestant theologians, loses much of its acuteness in Judaism through the absence of conflict between the historical and the eternal Christ."[123] Samson Raphael Hirsch's assault on Heinrich Graetz's historicization of the Oral Law, however, suggests a Jewish analogy to the Christian problem of *Glaube und Geschichte*. And as we shall see in the next chapter, Herman Cohen's resistance to Ernst Troeltsch's historicization of the Hebrew prophets performs a similar task.

Cohen's objections remind us that it was not only Orthodox Jews who feared the excesses of history. Nor were theologians the only critics. Philosophers, economists, and cultural commentators began to take aim at one or another aspect of historicism with great vigor—not surprisingly, in a period in which historicism was at its apex of strength. Most of these critics shared the fear that the methods of critical history, once deemed liberating, had eviscerated their core values to the point of disappearance. As the turn of the century approached, this fear assumed urgency, spreading rapidly into many realms of intellectual life and giving rise to a new culture of crisis in which history stood at the center.[124]

## Chapter Two

## HERMANN COHEN AND THE PROBLEM
## OF HISTORY AT THE FIN DE SIÈCLE

> How can something of a historical nature be decisive for an eternal happiness?
> —S. Kierkegaard

The historian Walter Köhler commenced his biography of Ernst Troeltsch with a memorable episode from the early career of the renowned scholar. Following a "learned, somewhat scholastic lecture" by a leading German theologian, the thirty-one-year-old Troeltsch, who had received his doctorate only four years earlier, leaped to the podium to declare to his senior colleagues: "Gentlemen, everything is tottering."[1] Troeltsch's audacious pronouncement from 1896 bespoke a sense of profound generational alienation, as well as deep despair over the current state of intellectual affairs. His cri de coeur long preceded the sweeping indictments of Western culture and philosophy issued by diverse figures such as Spengler and Heidegger in the 1920s.[2] And it preceded his own assertion a quarter-century later that a "crisis of historicism" was afflicting German academic life.[3]

And yet, Troeltsch's warning was a clear sign of an emerging "crisis consciousness" in European intellectual life.[4] The imminent turn of the century heightened anxieties over the rapid and uncontrollable pace of change. In the midst of this "reorientation of European social thought," as H. S. Hughes described it, stood the problem of historicism.[5] Ernst Troeltsch's exclamation to his scholarly elders reflected his particular awareness of the widening gap between theology and history. Under the relentless scrutiny of critics like D. F. Strauss, Christian faith was no longer assumed to rest on "supernatural foundations."[6] Troeltsch's evolution from theologian to historian of religion paralleled—in fact, owed to—the very intellectual current that seemingly undermined traditional faith. He was a major figure in what was known as the *religionsgeschichtliche Schule* (the history of religion school), which from the last decades of the nineteenth century sought to replace received wisdoms regarding the absoluteness of faith with a comparative historical perspective on the study of religion.[7]

But it was precisely this approach that contributed to the fragility of European intellectual culture, a point that was apparent to theologians and philosophers alike. One need only consider Friedrich Nietzsche in "Vom Nutzen und Nachteil der Historie" of 1874. Shortly before the publication of this essay, Nietzsche (1844–1900) underwent, not unlike Ernst Troeltsch, a change of scholarly direction. His early studies in classical philology had led to signal academic achievements, including a professorial appointment to the University of Basel at the age of twenty-four. But Nietzsche came to regard the philological discipline as "the misbegotten son of the goddess philosophy, born an idiot or a cretin."[8] His growing alienation from the empiricist pretenses of philology and its sister-discipline, history, led to his searing critique of 1874. Fearful of the numbing effects of historicism, Nietzsche rhetorically asked: "What if, rather than remaining the life-promoting activity of a historical being, history is turned into the objective uncovering of mere facts by the disinterested scholar—facts to be left as they are found, to be contemplated without being assimilated into present being?" Nietzsche apprehended that his fears were being confirmed, that the prevailing culture of historicism ceased to "serve life." One realm in which the deficiencies of this culture manifested themselves, and a somewhat surprising one given Nietzsche's later reputation, was religion. He declared that a religion which is "to be transformed into historical knowledge, a religion which is to be thoroughly known in a scientific way, will at the end of this path also be annihilated."[9]

Nietzsche's concerns in "Vom Nutzen und Nachteil" recall, at least fleetingly, Ernst Troeltsch's in 1896. Both men, erstwhile students of the theologian and philologist Albrecht Ritschl, contemplated the complex and often destructive relationship between history and religion. Both sensed that the "historical-mindedness" of the modern age could be ameliorated but never fully overcome. We need not overstate the similarity, for Nietzsche's and Troeltsch's intellectual paths diverged sharply: whereas the former excoriated the current profession of history in rather pungent fashion, the latter devoted much of his life not only to the practice of history, but to a sustained attempt to lay a firm foundation for that discipline.

Nevertheless, the two scholars serve as landmarks in an important debate surrounding the utility and method of history that took place in the late nineteenth and early twentieth centuries. Indeed, this debate represents not only an important prelude to the post–World War I "crisis of historicism," but a significant intellectual moment in and out itself. It is perhaps more accurate to say that this debate was a series of debates, each of which concerned the widespread perception that history was both a dominant and problematic realm of intellectual activity. Particularly in the German cultural sphere, rancorous disputes about historical method broke out among theologians, philosophers, sociologists, and econo-mists—and even within the ranks of historians themselves. For example, Karl Lamprecht, disturbed by the hyper-specialization and atomization that he saw in his discipline, eschewed prevailing historiographical norms by attempting to establish general laws of historical development. Toward this end, he advocated an historical science that was unburdened by "planlessly individualistic research . . . for its own sake."[10]

Lamprecht's angle of attack, in fact, identified a major new fault line in German academic culture—that separating the description of a single phenomenon or event from the attempt to identify laws or norms of social behavior. Advocates of the former approach regarded history as the para-digmatic individualizing discipline. Advocates of the latter looked to the model of the natural sciences for help in discerning recurrent patterns or series.[11]

Into this contested methodological terrain stepped the philosopher Wil-helm Dilthey. Dilthey asserted in his *Einleitung in die Geisteswissen-schaften* from 1883 that "the point of departure for understanding the concept of systems of societal life consists of the richness of life of the *individual himself.*"[12] His aim in highlighting the centrality of the individ-ual was to provide clarity to the mission of the human sciences (*Geistes-wissenschaften*)—and thereby distinguish them from the natural sciences. A decade later, Wilhelm Windelband undertook a similar task, but with an important terminological twist. In his 1894 rectorial address at the University of Strasbourg, Windelband also sought to clarify the nature of humanistic methods, although he attempted to move beyond the prevail-ing bifurcation between human and natural sciences.[13] Thus, Windelband distinguished between "nomothetic" inquiries intent on establishing gen-eral laws and "idiographic" disciplines that seek to describe fully the sin-gular and individual.[14]

The fact that philosophers like Dilthey and Windelband rallied to the cause of history was, at first glance, surprising. After all, history and phi-losophy were hardly equivalent in goal or method. In fact, they had been disciplinary rivals at least since the late eighteenth-century Enlightenment. But an important inversion of power occurred throughout the nineteenth century: As history soared to new heights in the latter half, the study of philosophy fell into disrepair. The once regnant Hegelianism of the early nineteenth century could no longer withstand serious scrutiny. As one historian of philosophy noted, "the great [Hegelian] system no longer responds to the needs of a disillusioned epoch, which does not want to hear talk about great speculative constructions."[15]

The crisis in philosophy impelled its practitioners to shift their focus from large metaphysical concerns to more modest epistemological mat-ters. Cloaked in the language of *Wissenschaft*, a new generation of philosophers began to inquire into the capacity of the human sciences to frame and enrich human knowledge. This effort received considerable impetus in the 1860s, when the call of "back to Kant" resounded loudly in German philosophical circles.[16] Those who heeded it turned to Kant for assistance in laying a stable epistemological foundation for the *Geisteswissenschaften*.[17] In particular, they sought to revive a Kantian "transcendental philosophy" that, despite its name, eschewed metaphysics for a careful examination of the relations among experience, logic, and knowledge.[18]

This was also a moment in which the concerns of philosophy and history intersected, if only fleetingly. Adepts of the former lent theoretical rigor to the latter, examining the ways in which we come to think and know about history—and, in the process, confirming the ubiquity of historicism in the academic culture of the day. A prime example was the important group of neo-Kantian thinkers known as the South-West German, or Baden, School, which included Windelband and Heinrich Rickert. Similarly, Dilthey, with a distinct nod to Kant, declared that his life mission was to "examine the nature and condition of historical consciousness—a critique of historical reason."[19] He shared the basic Kantian proposition that consciousness frames human experience. But against Kant and his followers, Dilthey did not believe in the existence of *logical* a prioris that condition consciousness. Rather, history was the only "genuine a priori condition of life."[20] The philosopher's task was to analyze and illuminate that historical a priori, thereby conjoining the two fields of knowledge into one. Indeed, history and philosophy, as Dilthey understood it, both served the same master. "In my way of working," he averred, "these are two names for the same preoccupation with historical facts."[21]

## BADEN, MARBURG, AND THE QUESTION OF HISTORY FOR NEO-KANTIANISM

Dilthey's fusion of history and philosophy was not universally embraced by philosophers of his day. Many saw it as their task to disentangle the two, primarily in order to preserve a particular and autonomous function for philosophy. Among the latter was Hermann Cohen (1842–1918), one of the founding fathers of a second school of neo-Kantians located at the University of Marburg.[22] The Marburg neo-Kantians did not set the critique of historical reason at the center of their scholarly agenda. Their goal was not to undertake à la Windelband and Rickert a systematic inquiry into the nature of history as an idiographic discipline. Rather, they admired and drew upon mathematical and natural scientific models as a means of identifying the logical a prioris that frame human consciousness.

True to his Marburg roots, Hermann Cohen was not a leading participant in the brewing debate over history stirred by the Baden School.[23] Yet part of the drama of our story is that neither Cohen nor his Baden counterparts—nor any modern for that matter—could escape the irrepressible force of historicism.[24] Windelband, Dilthey, and Rickert made it their life mission to explore the potential and limits of historical methods. While he did not share this commitment, Hermann Cohen nonetheless developed a peculiar and multifaceted relationship to history that it is our task to explore.

To begin to understand this relationship, we must recognize that Cohen sought to marshal his considerable philosophical talents to illuminate the logic and autonomy of ethics. It is this concern for the realm of ethics that he transmitted to leading Marburg disciples such as Paul Natorp, Rudolf Stammler, and Ernst Cassirer. In his own thinking, ethics provided a key clue to grasping the "ultimate meaning of the universe." For indeed "God's essence is morality," as Cohen wrote in a famous essay on the "profound correspondence" between Kantianism and Judaism.[25] This moral essence could not be reduced to the contextual fragments of history; rather, it soared above them. Consequently, the philosopher's mission was altogether distinct from that of the historian, who had "neither the need nor the competence to define essence."[26]

This view of the philosopher's mission was based on Cohen's veneration for the person and milieu of Immanuel Kant. The period in which Kant lived represented for Cohen an age of philosophical and ethical holism. By contrast, the ascent of historicism in the nineteenth century led to the atomization of holistic spiritual and intellectual values. On this point, Hermann Cohen anticipated Friedrich Nietzsche's more famous admonition against historicization from 1874.[27] In an essay from 1871, Cohen asked: "So if an age allows itself to be dominated by the trend of history, it will find its full satisfaction in the fulfillment of this trend, and the longer this state of affairs lasts, the less will it be affected by the question: what will be, and even less by the more urgent question: what *must* be?"[28]

Like Nietzsche, Cohen was troubled that the present age was "dominated by the trend of history." But unlike Nietzsche, Cohen believed in the progressive movement of European society, propelled by human reason and the ongoing development of *Wissenschaft*. As part of this optimistic worldview, Cohen even held out hope for history.

Here it is imperative to recall the diverse and often confusing connotations of the word in German (and other languages). On one level, Cohen followed Kant in depicting History (*Geschichte*) as the broad and indispensable plane on which all human activity unfolded.[29] On another level, Cohen was wary of a history (*Historie*) that was the product of the dissecting methods of professional historians. Even at this point Cohen held out a measure of hope. The excesses of these methods could be tempered by demoting history from a position of dominance in the hierarchy of the *Geisteswissenschaften*. Hence, to the extent that it "aspire[d] to fashion a whole out of its member parts"—to the extent that it served the philosopher's quest for holism—then history could perform a valuable role.[30] Stated otherwise, if mobilized to the task of clarifying grand philosophical and ethical principles, then history was both capable and worthy of redemption. In this regard, Hermann Cohen can be seen as attempting to salvage some utility for history without succumbing to historicism.

Recent researchers have devoted little attention to this stance, notwithstanding the impressive renascence of scholarly interest in Cohen over the past decades.[31] The aim here is to overcome the neglect by presenting a sustained reading of Cohen's ambivalent posture toward history. In the process, we hope to understand more fully the problem that history posed for European and Jewish intellectual culture in the late nineteenth and early twentieth centuries. We will also notice that Cohen affords us a most interesting angle on the predicament of the German Jew for whom assimilation was deemed a noble *Jewish* path. Cohen's biography will assist us in unraveling the nuances of this view, although he himself might have recoiled a bit at the attempt to embed his ideas in a thick contextual description.[32]

This is because our own recourse to historicization leads us to focus on tension rather than unity. Indeed, the very contingency of ideas renders untenable the principle of seamless coherence that Hermann Cohen held precious.[33] As a result, we are drawn to the tensions underlying Cohen's quest to find essentialist values in a modern historicist age. He was hardly alone in this quest. As we saw in the last chapter, Samson Raphael Hirsch assailed the ascendant role of history in modern Jewish life. Cohen, for all his difference in Jewish outlook from Hirsch, also expressed concern over the deleterious effects of history. Moreover, he directed these concerns at the same target as Hirsch: the prominent nineteenth-century historian Heinrich Graetz. And yet, like Hirsch, Cohen could not avoid the presence of history in his own work—both as the ontological plane of *Geschichte* and as *Historie*. He favored at times a kind of abstract history of ideas in his encounter with the Kantian oeuvre—an approach that he passed on to his charges Natorp and Cassirer.[34]

Beset by ambivalence over history, Cohen was part of a cohort of Jewish and Christian thinkers in Germany who struggled to balance the competing demands of religious faith and critical humanistic inquiry at the turn of the century. Some among them like Ernst Troeltsch or Adolf Harnack were deeply committed to history as the primary lens through which to grasp the essence of religion. Nowhere was this more evident than in Harnack's famous lectures from 1899 to 1900 in Berlin, published as *Das Wesen des Christentums*, which set in motion a wide-ranging and repercussive theological debate.[35]

While Harnack spoke of the indispensability of history in understanding the evolution of Christianity, his opponents trembled at the specter of an unrestrained historicism. Christian theologians like Martin Kähler and Cohen's Marburg colleague Wilhelm Herrmann insisted that the application of historicist methods threatened the spiritual foundations of Christianity.[36] Jewish theologians like the young rabbi Leo Baeck (1873–1956) warned that Harnack's misuse of historical methods went to support the claim of Christianity's supersession of Judaism.[37] Hermann Cohen was sympathetic to these criticisms. After all, he had first expressed his own concerns some thirty years earlier. And he would continue to do so throughout his career, with particular vigor in the last years of his life. For this reason, we will argue that Cohen, without being fully cognizant, was among the inaugurators of a critical discourse on Jewish historicism that emerged from within the secular academy and has continued, with interruptions and eruptions, to the present.

## BETWEEN WITTENBERG AND DESSAU

It was a fellow Jewish townsman who noted that Hermann Cohen's birthplace, Coswig, was poised between Wittenberg, home of Martin Luther, and Dessau, birthplace of Moses Mendelssohn.[38] These two locales symbolized the poles between which Cohen's intellectual worldview was forged. It is hardly surprising that Moses Mendelssohn would have inspired Cohen. Not only was Mendelssohn a contemporary and philosophical colleague of Immanuel Kant. He exemplified the very Enlightenment-era accommodation between Judaism and modernity that Cohen so valued in his own synthesis of *Deutschtum* and *Judentum*.

Cohen's attraction to Luther would seem a bit more complicated, given the latter's periodic anti-Jewish outbursts.[39] And yet, Luther was one of the most storied heroes in Cohen's cultural pantheon. For Cohen, Luther was the prototypical German patriot, and a pioneering influence in the formation of German language and cultural identity. More significantly, Cohen identified in Luther a principle that resonated deeply with his own (and Mendelssohn's) philosophical tenets—namely, that religion should be dictated by individual conscience, not ecclesiastical authority.[40]

In his introduction to Cohen's Jewish writings, Franz Rosenzweig observed, with Cohen foremost in mind, that "all modern Jews, and German

Jews more than any others, are Protestants."[41] Later, Hans Liebeschütz called attention to Cohen's "radically liberal interpretation" of Luther which bespoke a deep and abiding sympathy with Protestantism.[42] Jacques Derrida rendered this point even more explicit in referring to Cohen as a "Judeo-Protestant."[43] The roots of this hybrid identity reach back to Cohen's formative experience in the town of Coswig. As one of a handful of Jews in the town, Cohen was raised in an environment dominated by the Protestant church. This powerful cultural presence informed Cohen's self-understanding as a Jew throughout his life. Indeed, it shaped Cohen's unwavering commitment to a Judaism of ethical perfection rather than ritual observance. On the basis of this "protestant" vision, Cohen constructed an intellectual and spiritual genealogy that commenced with the biblical prophetic tradition and included Plato, Maimonides, Luther, and Kant before culminating in the modern German Jew represented by Cohen himself. It was this genealogy that prompted Cohen to view Jewish and Protestant-German identities as harmonious, if not identical.

## From Cantor's Son to Neo-Kantian

Hermann Cohen was born on July 4, 1842, in Coswig, a small town in central Germany that belonged at the time to the principality of Anhalt-Bernburg. Nestled on the Elbe River, this town hosted a tiny Jewish community that numbered some eleven families at the beginning of the nineteenth century. In 1800, twenty-three years after gaining the right of settlement, the Jews of Coswig were permitted to construct a synagogue on Domstrasse that was renovated in 1843. This institution assumed a central role in Hermann Cohen's early life. Indeed, the family lived on the same street, since Cohen's father served as cantor at the synagogue, as well as teacher of the town's Jewish youth.

The Cohen household reflected the traditional piety of the parents, Gerson and Friederike (née Salomon). On the Sabbath, the family welcomed passing Jewish travelers into their home during which time the father would engage the visitors in Talmudic discussion.[44] Hermann Cohen's deep Jewish ethos—the sense of tribal affinity that would later manifest itself in his activist stance against anti-Semitism—was born in this intimate ambience. So too was his often-ignored, yet expansive Jewish knowledge, which enabled the mature Cohen to draw freely on ancient and medieval Jewish sources.

Cohen's father, described by a former student as a "pedagogical genius," oversaw his son's Jewish education. He began to teach Hebrew to Hermann from the age of three and a half, and continued to instruct him in Jewish subjects even after the young Cohen left for Dessau at age eleven to study at the gymnasium. Much later in life, when Gerson moved to Marburg, Hermann Cohen, then a renowned philosophy professor, would fill in for his ailing father in leading prayers at the local synagogue.[45] Even though Cohen fils did not lead a scrupulously observant life, his reverence for Jewish tradition and ritual, as embodied by his father, remained firm. Franz Rosenzweig affirmed this point in the closing sentence of his introduction to Cohen's Jewish writings when he recalled that Cohen's great Jewish book, the posthumous *Religion der Vernunft*, was dedicated neither to a philosophical school nor to an intellectual influence, but rather to the man who bestowed upon him a grounded sense of Jewish identity: his father.[46]

If Hermann Cohen's allegiance to the Jewish religion was forged in the intimate confines of Coswig, his equally steadfast faith in the virtue of the German nation was born there as well. By his own account, he grew up in an environment largely free of anti-Jewish expression. His father typified the sense of social optimism that this environment yielded and to which his son would later give clear expression. Although a traditional Hebrew instructor (*melamed*), Gerson Cohen was friendly with Protestant teachers who respected his learning and regarded him as a colleague. He also was a proud German patriot, who at the outbreak of the Franco-Prussian War prayed for his country along with fellow Coswig residents in the town's Protestant church.[47]

The example of the father's patriotism left an indelible imprint on Hermann Cohen. Throughout his life, from his response to Heinrich von Treitschke in 1880 to his polemic with Martin Buber over Zionism in 1916, Cohen remained convinced that Germany was the most enlightened nation known to history, a beacon of humanism to the rest of the world. While this view troubled many later critics, it emerged quite naturally out of Cohen's formative environment. In this regard, Cohen was a classic representative of the kind of German Jew, ever loyal to the cherished ideal of *Bildung*, to whom George Mosse has famously called attention.[48]

This ideal was fortified during Cohen's many years of studying and teaching in German academic institutions. At the Herzogliche Gymnasium in Dessau, where Cohen was the first Jewish student admitted, he was in a class with eleven others boys, of whom seven went on to study Protestant theology. After four years of study at the gymnasium, Cohen went to the new Jüdisch-Theologisches Seminar established in Breslau in 1854. This decision was a fitting Jewish parallel to the study of Protestant theology, and perhaps already reflected Cohen's vision of the proximate, parallel, and even confluent paths of Judaism and Protestantism.

At Breslau, the fifteen-year-old Cohen began to study with some of the most distinguished Jewish scholars in nineteenth-century Germany: Jakob

Bernays, Heinrich Graetz, and Zacharias Frankel. Each of these scholars exerted a deep, though not necessarily favorable, impression on Cohen. The classicist Bernays was a powerful intellectual personality, and yet, Cohen recalled fifty years later, "there was no living, creative, constructive thought at work in this powerful machine." Bernays's chief sin, in Cohen's eyes, was that he could not grasp the inner essence of philosophy: "he knew it, he understood it, *but only as a philologian and historian.*"[49]

Bernays's sober and dispassionate attitude stood in contrast to the personality of Heinrich Graetz, who taught Talmud and history at the Seminary. Graetz was then in the midst of writing the first volumes of what would become the most important historical survey of the Jews of the century, the eleven-volume *Geschichte der Juden.* Unlike Bernays, Graetz possessed an untamed "impulsivity" that informed "his interesting and lively presentation of the great men of our literature" and that, Cohen once recalled, "elevated us to our spiritual heights."[50] At the same time, it was Graetz who first exposed Cohen to critical historical analysis of inspired figures and texts from the past. Consequently, Graetz appears at crucial points in Cohen's intellectual life as the arch historian, emblematic of the perils of historical research for Jewish thought.

This image is striking in light of Cohen's youthful recollection. Indeed, he remembered that at Breslau "there was stirring in me in those young years a kind of historical consciousness, and it did not always harmonize with the profound and sharp personality" of his revered teacher, Zacharias Frankel. On its own terms, this admission is curious given Cohen's later hesitations about history. All the more curious is the suggestion that this "kind of historical consciousness" was foreign to Zacharias Frankel. After all, Frankel gained considerable notoriety as one of the first Jewish scholars to adopt a systematic and critical historical approach to the Oral Law.[51] Moreover, when Frankel came under attack from Orthodox thinkers who objected to the historical approach adopted in his book *Darkhe ha-Mishnah* (1859), Hermann Cohen leaped to his defense. In 1861 Cohen wrote glowingly of Frankel to Samson Raphael Hirsch, who was one of the Breslau scholar's chief critics. Admittedly, Cohen did not argue for Frankel on the grounds of the legitimacy of his method, but rather on the basis of his teacher's deep piety.[52] But he recalled how "contrary to the spirit of history" he found Hirsch's criticism of Frankel.[53]

The Frankel-Hirsch controversy coincided with Cohen's decision to leave the Breslau Seminary in 1861. No evidence exists to suggest a causal relationship. But it seems clear that Cohen decided at that point to leave the world of Jewish studies—and the historical study of Judaism—and commence a career in the secular academy. In that year, he began studies in philosophy and philology at the university in Breslau, while simultaneously completing requirements for the matriculation certificate (*Abitur*) from a local gymnasium. Cohen demonstrated promise at the university by winning a prize in 1863 for an essay contest in philosophy.[54] But like many bright university students in Germany, Cohen did not remain at the institution where he first commenced his formal education. Rather, he moved the next year to Berlin to study at the university there. Cohen continued his philosophical studies, but also came into close contact with the renowned Jewish scholar Heymann Steinthal (1823–1899). He heard Steinthal's lectures on Völkerpsychologie, a new field of inquiry that Steinthal and his brother-in-law, Moritz Lazarus (1824–1903), had a large hand in developing.

Völkerpsychologie was, to a certain extent, the late nineteenth-century heir of philology, whose combination of history, linguistics, and psychology led scholars earlier in the century to regard language as the gateway to a group's culture. The new discipline used a similar scholarly mix to comprehend the "particular psychological relationships, occurrences, and creations" that obtained among groups of people.[55] According to Lazarus and Steinthal, the search for the "objective Spirit" (*objektiver Geist*) of a particular "collectivity" (*Gesamtheit*) proceeds along two interrelated methodological paths: first, the scholar attempts to trace the broad historical outlines of the *Volksgeist* through a "collective-historical psychology"; second, the scholar uses a "psychic ethnology" to focus in concrete detail on the manifold features of the group spirit (including language, myth, religion, ethics, law, art, crafts, and institutions of public life).[56]

This historically grounded approach to psychology proved appealing to the young Cohen.[57] His first published article, devoted to Plato's theory of ideas, not only appeared in 1866 in Steinthal and Lazarus's *Zeitschrift für Völkerpsychologie und Sprachwissenschaft*. It reflected Heymann Steinthal's own preference for historical and philological analysis in tracing psychological and philosophical development.[58]

Even earlier, Cohen affirmed the importance of this distinctly historicist approach to psychology in an essay written for a contest in Berlin that he did not win. In the expanded Latin version of this essay, "Philosophorum de antinomia necessitatis et contingentiae doctrinae," Cohen concluded his discussion with a series of general theses, the first of which declared "Omnem philosophiae progressum in psychologia constitutum esse" (all progress in philosophy has been based on psychology).[59] This essay was sent to a committee of three scholars at the University of Halle, and on September 25, 1865, Cohen was examined and "promoted"; in the following month, he received his official doctoral diploma from Halle.[60]

While searching for a university appointment, the twenty-three year-old Cohen continued to live in Berlin, relying on the material support of his parents. From time to time, Cohen supplemented his income by tutoring young students. He also continued to publish scholarly articles that bore the traces of his debt to Völkerpsychologie. In a number of exceptional instances, these articles engaged Jewish themes.[61]

It is important to note that while in the throes of his infatuation with Völkerpsychologie, Cohen was aware of and in contact with leaders of the Kantian revival that was penetrating German universities in the 1860s. One of Cohen's acquaintances from his Berlin student days, Adolf Trendelenburg, achieved a good deal of fame as the polemical opponent of the Heidelberg philosopher Kuno Fischer in a fierce scholarly battle over how to interpret Kant. In 1871 Cohen joined the fray with a book on the Kantian idea of experience, as well as a long essay on the Trendelenburg-Fischer debate.[62] Published in the Steinthal/Lazarus *Zeitschrift für Völkerpsychologie*, the essay on Trendelenburg and Fischer marks an important moment in Cohen's development as a philosopher. Not only did it signal his growing enthusiasm for the "return to Kant" movement. It also gave voice to his emerging belief that history must now be subordinate to philosophy in the hierarchy of the *Geisteswissenschaften*.[63]

To the extent that Cohen was attempting a disciplinary reordering, his "break" with history was not a full rupture. In fact, when he moved to Marburg in 1873, he found as mentor one of the leading historians of philosophy of the day, F. A. Lange, author of the wide-ranging *Geschichte des Materialismus* (1866). Lange was an admirer of Cohen's book, *Kants Theorie der Erfahrung*.[64] Indeed, it was Lange who convinced his Marburg colleagues to accept this book as Cohen's *Habilitationsschrift*. He also lobbied to gain the young scholar an appointment to the Marburg faculty, thus ending Cohen's nearly decade-long search for employment. Lange's chief obstacle was to persuade his colleagues that Cohen, as a Jewish instructor of philosophy in a Protestant university, would not be hostile to Christianity. Lange reportedly asked Cohen if there was "any serious difference between us in regard to Christianity." Cohen's answer reflected his deeply ecumenical beliefs: "No, because what you call Christianity—I call prophetic Judaism."[65] Shortly, thereafter, Cohen was appointed a *Privatdozent* at Marburg in 1873. Three years later, he succeeded the recently deceased Lange as the chair-holder in philosophy.

At first glance, Marburg would seem an unlikely site for a Jewish thinker to expound a philosophical system marked by the quest for a transcendental logic and universal ethics. Home to the oldest Protestant university in Germany (founded in 1527), Marburg was a small provincial town in Hesse in which the winds of romanticism, nationalism, and occasionally anti-Semitism blew during the nineteenth century. It was there that Friedrich Karl von Savigny established the "Historical School of Law," with its conservative-nationalist understanding of the development of German legal tradition. It was also there that the Marburg librarian Otto Böckel campaigned under the slogan "Against Junkers and Jews," becoming the first openly anti-Semitic candidate elected to the German Reichstag in 1887.[66] A year later, Hermann Cohen was called upon to serve as an expert witness in the trial of a local anti-Semitic agitator. Pitted against the hostile Orientalist Paul de Lagarde, Cohen took a page out of the history of medieval disputations by defending the integrity of the Talmud. In fact, his testimony was instrumental in the successful prosecution of the local anti-Semite.

Notwithstanding these unsettling currents, Cohen tended to find in Marburg a hospitable home—perhaps because it reminded him of the small-town intimacy of his native Coswig. He forged friendly relations with a number of Protestant colleagues including the Bible scholar Julius Wellhausen and the theologian Wilhelm Herrmann. Moreover, he attracted to Marburg an impressively diverse roster of students including Ernst Cassirer, Kurt Eisner, Nicolai Hartmann, Jorge Ortega y Gassett, and Boris Pasternak.[67]

But Cohen's affection for Marburg went beyond the level of personal friendship. We have already noted on several occasions that Cohen felt at ease in a Protestant world, to the point that his philosophical, political, and religious perspectives assumed a certain Protestant orientation. His faith in a rational and universal ethical system anchored in biblical sources drew inspiration from the Protestant ideal of returning *sola Scriptura*.[68] As he once declared in 1880, "just as Protestantism has thrown off the yoke of ecclesiastical tradition, so have we [behaved] more or less openly . . . toward the Talmud."[69] On the same occasion, Cohen reformulated what he had earlier conveyed to F. A. Lange—namely, that "with reference to the scientific concept of religion I am unable to discover any distinction between Jewish monotheism and Protestant Christianity."[70]

Still, the task of locating Cohen's precise place in the Protestant intellectual circles of his day has its challenges. Cohen came of age in the midst of the *Kulturkampf* in which German Protestants and Catholics debated, often bitterly, the nature of relations between state and society. Cohen had affinities with those Protestants who marched under the banner of *Kulturprotestantismus*—those who were intent on harnessing the exalted ethical ideals of established religion to the interests of an enlightened state. This turn-of-the-century movement included leading Protestant liberals such as Harnack, Troeltsch, and Herrmann. All shared in the belief that a Christian ethical imperative should "inform and shape the whole of life," even the sphere of politics.[71] But that ethical imperative must not lead to the subordination of state to religion. Rather, the "Christian ethical imperative" should serve as the stimulus for an inspired political organism that was both culturally and morally enlightened—at once a *Kulturstaat* and a *Rechtstaat*.

Hermann Cohen's own Enlightenment-era allegiances make understandable his adoption of language and conceptual models drawn from the world of *Kulturprotestantismus*.[72] In a recent study, Gangolf Hübinger has noted the links between "Culture Protestants" and "Culture Jews" in Germany, united by the shared ideal of "a bourgeois modernity and the universal value of equality of citizenship rights and of life opportunities."[73] Hermann Cohen believed fervently in the goal of an ethically elevated German *Rechtstaat*, vastly preferring it to an ethnically particularist Zionism.[74] From this perspective, he was as passionate an adherent of German-style "bourgeois modernity" as anyone.

And yet, it is not accurate to depict Cohen as a mere Jewish appendage to *Kulturprotestantismus*. Nor is it accurate to assume that Cohen was capable of fully marrying his interests with those of the Culture-Protestants. In a number of instances, he had profound scholarly differences with leading figures in these circles (e.g., Harnack and Troeltsch)—at times over the very function of history. Perhaps more importantly, Cohen's respect for Protestantism was not reciprocated by all liberal Protestants, some of whom harbored deep anti-Semitic sentiments. In light of this, it might be more accurate to cast Cohen as the formulator of a deeply held, uniquely conceived, and subsequently discredited Jewish *Kulturprotestantismus*.[75] This term conveys Hermann Cohen's alternating attempts to trace and then efface the boundary between Jewish and Protestant religious cultures in Germany. To a certain extent, these attempts evoke the early-nineteenth-century call by the legal scholar, Eduard Gans, that Jews should "live on as the river lives on in the ocean."[76] It is easy to conclude, with the benefit of hindsight, that such a vision must of necessity end in conversion, as in Gans's case, or in a more nefarious form of disappearance, as in the case of Cohen's wife, Martha, who perished in a Nazi death camp. But such a tack of "backshadowing" misses the force and sincerity of Cohen's faith in a Jewish-Protestant bond, a link he believed was in the interest of both traditions, and the foundation for a millennial confederation of nations.[77]

## SAVING HISTORY FROM HISTORICISM

Hermann Cohen's affinity for an enlightened Protestant intellectual heritage reaches its pinnacle with his intense engagement with Immanuel Kant. As in other philosophical matters, it was Kant who paved the way for Hermann Cohen's recognition of the "problem" of history. In its simplest form, the question that Kant and a host of successors confronted was whether a universalist rationalism could be reconciled with the notion of temporal and spatial contingency.[78] That Kant did not always admire the fact-driven labors of the historian can be seen in a posthumously discovered note he had written: "I shall not make my head into a parchment and scribble old, half-effaced information from archives on it.[79] His own philosophical labors sought to derive "*a priori* knowledge from concepts." By contrast, history sought a lower—that is, empirical—form of knowledge.[80]

When Kant meditated upon history, he inclined to a discussion of its philosophical properties—or more specifically, to an understanding of it as the unfolding of human reason. A succinct formulation of this understanding came in the eighth thesis of his "Idea for a Universal History" from 1784 according to which "the history of mankind can be seen, in the large, as the realization of Nature's secret plan to bring forth a perfectly constituted state as the only condition in which the capacities of mankind can be fully developed."[81]

In explicating this conception, Yirmiahu Yovel has suggested that Kantian philosophy is informed not only by the famous categorical imperative, but also by a related *historical* imperative that "prescribes a *totalizing* mode of moral action, one which sets the moral progress of the world, not just of the particular individual, as its objectives."[82] As against such a sweeping vision of history, it can be asked: what function exists in the Kantian (and neo-Kantian) scheme for that version of history whose primary focus is the particular or individual? Yovel maintains that Kant never fully resolved the tension between "the empirical and the a priori"—or in the language of the day, between the "historisch" and "geschichtlich"—notions of history.[83]

Throughout the nineteenth century, the distinction between the "historisch" and the "geschichtlich" endured, suggesting that consensus regarding the function and utility of history remained elusive. One place we find this distinction operative is among Protestant theologians and church historians who were sharply divided over the legitimacy of treating Jesus with critical historical methods. As we saw in the last chapter, a widening gap developed from the appearance of David Friedrich Strauss's *Life of Jesus* between approaches focused on the historical personality of Jesus and those on the mythic Christ of faith.[84] By the end of the century, opposition to the "life of Jesus" approach intensified and was sometimes articulated on the basis of the distinction between *Geschichte* and *Historie*. A key example was the Halle theologian, Martin Kähler. In 1892, Kähler published a small volume entitled *Der sogennante historische Jesus und der geschichtliche, biblische Christus* (*The So-Called Historische Jesus and the Geschichtliche Biblical Christ*). At the outset of this book, Kähler declared that "the Jesus of the 'Life-of-Jesus movement' (i.e., the *historische* Jesus) is merely a modern example of human creativity." This subjective impulse was itself a product of modern historicism, which Kähler regarded as "arbitrary," "humanly arrogant," "impertinent," and "faith-lessly gnostic."[85]

We notice a similar concern in Hermann Cohen's friend and colleague, the Marburg theologian Wilhelm Herrmann. Notwithstanding serious differences between them, Herrmann and Kähler both subscribed to the view "that the historical appearance of Jesus . . . cannot be a basis of faith."[86] Indeed, "no historical judgment," Herrmann declared in 1884, "ever attains anything more than probability." But probability did not suffice in matters of faith. What was required was certainty—which, for Herrmann, could only be gained by "a communion of the soul with the living God through the mediation of Christ."[87] This communion was a fundamentally experiential act, neither stimulated nor measurable by human cognition.

On this point, Wilhelm Herrmann could hardly expect affirmation from Hermann Cohen. The two scholars, who arrived at Marburg within three years of one another and remained friends for forty more, shared many intellectual interests. But they differed sharply on a number of core issues. For instance, Herrmann's emphasis on the individual experience of faith was at odds with Cohen's entire philosophical disposition, and especially with his notion of the logically derived *idea* of God as the basis of faith.[88] Moreover, Herrmann's conviction that modern science could never "know anything of a living God" stood in conflict with Cohen's deep faith in the clarificatory powers of the *Geisteswissenschaften*. It is on the basis of such differences that Ernst Troeltsch once wrote that when discussing matters of shared interest, "each meant something completely different."[89]

Curiously, the two Marburgers were of one mind when discussing Ernest Troeltsch. Herrmann and Troeltsch wrote deeply critical reviews of each other's books, in the course of which they staked out clear positions on either side of the history-faith divide in turn-of-the-century Protestant intellectual circles.[90] At the same time, Cohen and Troeltsch engaged in a brief but intense battle along similar lines, as we shall have occasion to see at the end of the chapter. Their shared concern over Troeltsch made Herrmann and Cohen allies in the larger battle against the alternating hubris and naïveté of historicism.

As we recall, Hermann Cohen's concerns surfaced a number of years before he met Wilhelm Herrmann in Marburg. More specifically, the 1871 debate between Adolf Trendelenburg and Kuno Fischer provided him with his first opportunity to address the relationship between empirical and a priori notions of history. Rather than engage in the mere "collection of broken pieces," Cohen believed that historians could most profitably serve the human sciences by exposing "the continuing coherence of philosophical problems within the whole of human culture." Cohen here was articulating what he regarded as a golden rule of the *Geisteswissenschaften*: the more systematically and comprehensively one approached a scholarly problem, the closer one came to a genuinely scientific understanding.[91]

Neither at this stage or at any other moment did Cohen dismiss outright the value of historical study. He shared Kant's ambition of creating "a philosophical historiography of philosophy, written from a 'transcendental,' not an empirical point of view."[92] This meant that historical labor dedicated to the elaboration of the unique and individual fact did not deserve the name history.[93] The kind of historical work that Cohen appreciated—and which accompanied his own efforts to revitalize Kantian philosophy—was *geschichtlich*.[94]

Of course, this notion directly challenged nineteenth-century historicism. At a point of crisis in German academic life, Cohen felt that he must "throw himself brazenly in the midst of a partisan battle." For history was in danger of becoming "perhaps the most dangerous" of the *Geisteswissenschaften*.[95] But to repeat, he did not counsel avoiding history altogether. Rather, he sought to harness its potential to refine and advance philosophy. In particular, history should help philosophy answer not merely *what was* but *what should be*. There was a boldness to Cohen's move. He sought not merely to subordinate history to philosophy in a supremely historicist era. He also sought to transform history from a descriptive enterprise in its own right into a vital complement, a *Hilfswissenschaft*, of a larger prescriptive enterprise. In doing so, Cohen was attempting to rescue history from the debilitating features of historicism itself.

## RETURN TO JUDAISM, FLIGHT FROM HISTORY?

Hermann Cohen's departure from the Jüdisch-Theologisches Seminar in Breslau commenced a nearly two-decade period in which Judaism was largely absent from his scholarly and public activity. By his own admission (per Franz Rosenzweig's report), Cohen "returned" to Judaism only in 1880, the year in which he published a well-known rejoinder to the historian Heinrich Treitschke, who had earlier attacked Heinrich Graetz, his erstwhile teacher from Breslau.[96] Throughout much of his subsequent career, Cohen retained a passionate interest in Judaism that frequently overlapped with his philosophical pursuits. Indeed, Judaism and neo-Kantian philosophy shared, in Cohen's mind, a vital characteristic: both were rational systems devoted to the elaboration and advancement of ethics. As such, both stood guard against the fragmenting tendencies of modern historical research.

Beginning with his public defense of Judaism in 1880, Cohen was giving voice to a newfound sense of responsibility and freedom to express solidarity with his co-religionists. But his chosen mode of expression was not greeted with uniform enthusiasm by German Jews. For Cohen used the occasion of Treitschke's attack to criticize Heinrich Graetz.

Before discussing Cohen's response to Treitschke and Graetz, a few words of historical explanation are required to situate his essay, "Ein Bekenntnis in der Judenfrage." Cohen wrote his article in the midst of a new wave of anti-Jewish activity in Germany that focused on the alleged racial differences and inferiority of the Jews.[97] In fact, it was in 1879 that the term "anti-Semite" was first invented by the German journalist Wilhelm Marr and applied to the Jews. For Marr and others, the Jews appeared as a fundamentally foreign entity within Germany—or in the language of the day, as a distinct and inferior "race." Among the more surprising participants in this new discourse was the Prussian historian and nationalist Heinrich von Treitschke. In 1879 Treitschke read the eleventh and final volume of Heinrich Graetz's *Geschichte der Juden* and reported that he "could scarcely find words to express his disgust."[98] Treitschke discerned in Graetz a deep animus for both Germany and Christianity that, as Michael Meyer has argued, was an exaggerated but not altogether inaccurate representation of the Jewish historian's beliefs.[99]

Treitschke conveyed his aversion for Graetz, as well as for the foreignness of Germany's Jews, in a series of short essays beginning in 1879 and gathered together in 1880 as "Ein Wort über unser Judentum." This pamphlet contains Treitschke's famous epitaph that the Jews are Germany's "misfortune"—a claim that provoked a torrent of response from Jews and non-Jews that filled many pages of Berlin newspapers and journals throughout 1880–81.[100] What is most germane for our purposes is that Hermann Cohen decided to add his voice to the debate not, as he reports, "as a spokesman of a Jewish party, but as a representative of philosophy in a German university and as a confessor of Israelite monotheism."[101] The fact that Treitschke regarded Cohen's response as "the most deeply thought out and most warmly felt among the replies of my opponents" should alert us to its distinctive quality.[102]

Cohen began his retort on a melancholy note. "We young people," the thirty-eight year-old Cohen wrote of his German contemporaries, had been nurtured on the hope of creating a unified body in "the nation of Kant." But "the trust we had has been broken." The new racialist language of the day served to divide rather than unite. Moreover, the anti-Jewish tirade of Treitschke sharply violated Cohen's ecumenical vision, which acknowledged no "difference between Israelite monotheism and Protestant Christianity," or between Kantianism and the "rigor of Israelite ethical teachings."[103]

In light of this ecumenical vision, it is not surprising that Cohen felt compelled to take Treitschke to task. Nor is it surprising that Graetz would also be a target of criticism. But the tenor of Cohen's anger-filled volley against his former teacher is quite striking. Rather than rally to Graetz's defense, Cohen affirmed, in terms that evoked Treitschke, that it was indeed a "misfortune" that his teacher had lately succumbed to a "frightening perversity of emotional judgments." Even more elemental in danger—and revealing to us—was Graetz's "Palestinian" sensibility. Cohen had used this designation a number of years earlier as a point of contrast to his own intellectual and scholarly perspective.[104] In his 1880 essay, he resurrected the term to draw attention to, and take issue with, a form of Jewish particularism that he identified in Graetz.

The vituperative tone of Cohen's response, which spilled over into criticism of other Jews such as Moritz Lazarus, earned him widespread condemnation within the German-Jewish community. Critics accused Cohen of an overzealous hostility toward his own co-religionists, and an unseemly desire to genuflect before the Gentiles.[105] A number of colleagues broke off ties with him following the publication of the essay. We should recall that Cohen subsequently revealed himself to be a vigorous activist on behalf of Jewish self-defense, particularly when he faced down the anti-Semitic Orientalist, Paul de Lagarde, in Marburg in 1888.[106] We should also add that Cohen's fierce resistance to anti-Semitism grew out of his deeply held belief that Judaism was as harmonious with the German spirit as anti-Semitism was antithetical to it.

Underlying this view—and more specifically, Cohen's unflattering opinion of Graetz—was a curious strain of German nationalism to which Cohen professed allegiance to his dying day. Epitomized by Kant, Goethe, and Heine, this strain heralded Germany as an enlightened and humane nation. Such a cosmopolitan and tolerant entity would encourage the integration of Jews without demanding the disappearance of Jewish religious faith.[107] In Cohen's view, Jews would be far more than passive subjects in this process; they would be catalysts in the movement toward the creation of a genuine *Rechtstaat*.[108]

It makes sense then that Cohen would inveigh against Graetz, who, after all, hinted at a fundamental alienation between German Jews and Christians. Cohen's self-proclaimed pain in attacking his former teacher quickly become buried under a scathing assault. There was no more appropriate or, from Cohen's perspective, vengeful epithet to hurl at Graetz than the above-mentioned "Palestinian." Cohen was likely aware of the fact that Graetz had visited Palestine in 1872 in order to prepare himself for the final two volumes of his *Geschichte der Juden*. But, as Hans Liebeschütz has correctly noted, Cohen did not necessarily assign a specific geographic value to the term. Rather, "Palestinianism" connoted a base, material notion of Jewishness that grated against Cohen's more ethereal, Kantian version of Judaism.

There is a curious prescience to Cohen's use of the term, given that it predates the Zionist impulse to return to Palestine. Several years after "Ein Bekenntnis" was published, the first concrete steps were taken toward the creation of a proto-Zionist movement in Eastern Europe. As this movement began to crystallize into a significant force in European Jewish politics, Cohen surfaced as a visible critic. Perhaps the best reflection of his stance emerges in his famous debate with Martin Buber from 1916 in which the two intellectual titans of German Jewry drew clear boundary lines between the ideal of German-Jewish integration and the ideal of Zionism. In a series of critical essays, Cohen assailed the Zionist goal of planting Jewish national aspirations in Palestine. He did not deny that the Jews constituted a distinct ethnic or even national group (*Stamm*). But he made clear that the identity of this group was subordinate both to the authority of the modern state and to the universal force of Judaism the religion. Territorial concentration in the ancestral homeland risked upending this hierarchy and apotheosizing Jewish nationalism at the expense of Judaism. Therefore, Cohen insisted that Diaspora existence, marked by "political integration into the modern nation-state," was the best guarantee of Judaism's survival.[109] And as Cohen had made amply clear in 1915, the union of *Deutschtum* and *Judentum*, Germanness and Jewishness, was the most developed form of this integration—indeed, a model for the broader movement of human progress that Cohen called messianism.[110]

Cohen's foil, Martin Buber, attacked his opponent's assimilationist precepts. That is not to say that Buber's concern was with the political mechanism of a Jewish state in Palestine. But he was concerned with the fate of the dispersed spiritual and cultural resources of world Jewry. Only in the native soil of Palestine, Buber maintained, could "the inner consolidation of the energies of the Jewish people and thereby the realization of Judaism" be effected.[111]

On the face of it, Buber and Cohen held to fundamentally irreconcilable positions, particularly regarding the locus of collective Jewish fulfillment. And yet, they did share a profound concern for the spiritual dimension of Jewish existence. Of even greater interest is that they shared hesitations over the capacity of historical scholarship to grasp the depths of Jewish spiritual creativity. Buber gave a clue to his own disposition as early as 1901 in an essay, "Jüdische Wissenschaft," that appeared in the Zionist journal, *Die Welt*. Lamenting the stale antiquarianism of nineteenth-century *Wissenschaft des Judentums*, Buber expressed the hope that a new *jüdische Wissenschaft*—a Jewish science rather than a science of Judaism—would be able "to collect that which belongs to us, to build up a continuously developing inventory of Judaism, to see what we are, what we have and what we are able to do."[112] To a great extent, this essay was a blueprint for Buber's own work in the first decade of the twentieth century during which he published his popular collections of Hasidic tales.[113] What marked these volumes—*The Tales of Rabbi Nachman* (1906) and *The Legend of the Baal-Shem* (1907)—was Buber's unwillingness "to collect new facts" in typical historicist fashion.[114] Rather, the aim was to recast the Hasidic tales into a readable and vibrant form in order to nourish Jews during their present-day spiritual journey.

Here Buber's anti-historicism converged with his Jewish nationalism to create a mythic reframing of the Jewish past. The fact that Cohen's own hesitations about historicism originated from and led to different places reminds us that anti-historicism assumed different forms in this period. Cohen's goal of reasserting the centrality of philosophy within the *Geisteswissenschaften* coincided with his concern about the function of history. And this concern was no more pronounced than when history narrated the story of the Jewish nation. In such a case, the idiographic nature of history became allied to the narrow particularism of Jewish national identity.

We notice this link in the wake of Cohen's debate with Buber when he returned to the subject of Heinrich Graetz. Following his harsh critique of 1880, Cohen wrote two more articles on Graetz on the occasion of the centenary of his former teacher's birth in 1917; one had a personal and celebratory tone and the other a more analytical focus on Graetz's historiographical principles. Cohen began the latter piece with a broad query: "The major methodological question facing the philosophy of history is whether the centerpiece of history lies in political history or in the collective concept of cultural history." Cohen's answer to this question revealed his own proclivities: The destruction of the Second Temple in 70 C.E. not only spelled the demise of an independent Jewish commonwealth, but also brought to an end the political history of the Jewish people. From this point forward, "a Jewish nation," defined not as a political entity but as the embodiment of "Jewish messianic religion," assumed a key role on the stage of history.[115]

Drawing primarily on Graetz's first major publication, "Die Konstruktion der jüdischen Geschichte" (1846), Cohen depicted his former teacher's view in stark opposition. For Graetz, "Judaism in a precise sense is not at all a religion . . . but rather a political constitution." This politicization of Judaism was offensive in its own right, but doubly so since it was "suspiciously reminiscent of Spinoza's insult of Judaism."[116] Cohen here was referring to Baruch Spinoza's well-known assertion in the *Theologico-Political Treatise* (*TPT*) that Judaism, in its formative context, rested on a political constitution whose validity lapsed with the demise of the ancient Jewish state.[117]

The intellectual fraternity that Cohen suggested between Spinoza and Graetz drew from their apparent agreement on the essentially political-territorial nature of Judaism and, by consequence, on the visceral nature of Jewish history. Indeed, Spinoza implied, at one point in the *TPT*, that Judaism had a legitimate raison d'être only when possessed of a political, territorially based history.[118] Meanwhile, Heinrich Graetz focused in the first part of "Die Konstruktion" on the political capacities of Jews in their ancient commonwealth.[119]

Yet the fraternity that Cohen ascribed to Spinoza and Graetz relied on a fair bit of reductionism. For instance, it is far from clear that Spinoza favored the restoration of political power to the Jews, notwithstanding his famous and enigmatic assertion that it was only the emasculating act of circumcision that prevented it.[120] In the case of Graetz, Cohen collapsed a vibrant and multilayered interpretation into a mono-dimensional, political history. In actuality, Graetz's "Die Konstruktion" divided Jewish history in a fashion quite consistent with Cohen's own understanding—that is, into an earlier period "in which matters of state fully dominated" and a second phase (following the Babylonian Exile) "whose hallmark is that the religious factor now achieves predominance and the social and political concerns assume a subordinate role."[121]

Nonetheless, Cohen's reading was not entirely groundless. He observed that Graetz savored the " 'succulent fruit' [*saftige Frucht*] of national-political Judaism," while dismissing a "sublimated, idealized Judaism [as a] dried-out husk."[122] To be sure, Graetz did not share Cohen's view that Judaism was a rational system of universal and timeless ethics. Rather, he acknowledged both the material and contingent aspects of Jewish history. Moreover, he held out hope at the end of "Die Konstruktion" for a Jewish "religious state which is conscious of its activity, purpose, and connection with the world."[123]

At this point, we can see how Cohen's epistemological concerns about history, voiced as early as 1871, subtly joined with a new set of ontological—and characterological—concerns. The historian's idiographic craft, as Cohen imagined it, suited Graetz's impulsive character perfectly. By contrast, the clear-headed logic of the philosopher suited Cohen's own sober temperament. But even more profoundly, an historian of Graetz's ilk, limited by both method and mindset, could grasp the essence of Jewish history only in partial and distorted terms. The resulting image of a material, particularist, politicized Jewish past—"the 'succulent fruit' of national-political Judaism"—laid bare not only Graetz's "Palestinianism." It also revealed for Cohen the frequent and unfortunate alliance of historicism and nationalism.[124]

FIGURE 2. Hermann Cohen (1842–1918). Courtesy of Bildarchiv Foto Marburg, Philipps-University Marburg.

## TOWARD HISTORICAL ETERNITY

That Hermann Cohen returned to Heinrich Graetz at crucial moments in his life suggests his own unresolved tension with his teacher's personality, discipline, and overall Jewish worldview. It also makes clear that Cohen's vision of an ethical Judaism at home in an enlightened German state had more in common with the ideals of *Kulturprotestantismus* than with those of Graetz or later German Zionists.

The challenges of upholding this vision in a time of crisis were considerable. Bismarck's drive for German national unification unleashed a somewhat schizophrenic conservative spirit, characterized by dismay over the loss of traditional values, on one hand, and the desire to participate in the shaping of a new national order, on the other. Exacerbating the tension between these two sensibilities was the abrupt shift, in the early 1870s, from an inflated sense of national pride following the Franco-Prussian War to the crisis mentality of the *Gründerzeit*, when the economic fate of Germany tottered on the brink of disaster. It is in this period that the *Kulturkampf*, as designated by Rudolf Virchow in 1873, broke out between German Protestants and Catholics over the nature of the state's relationship to organized religion. It is also in this period, indeed in the very throes of the heated debates over the relationship between church and state, that the new racially based anti-Semitism emerged.[125]

Just as the upheaval of this era contributed to a renewed quest for certainty in philosophical, theological, and political realms, so too the unsettling effects of anti-Semitism compelled Jews like Hermann Cohen to clarify the grounds for their existence in Germany. From the time of Treitschke's anti-Jewish attacks, Cohen spent a fair portion of his remaining forty years constructing a spiritual and intellectual genealogy that fused the Jewish and German traditions. This effort was, curiously, a work of intellectual historical reconstruction that aimed for holism rather than fragmentation.

This effort reached a peak of intensity in the last six years of Cohen's life. In 1912, at the age of seventy, Cohen retired from the University of Marburg and took up residence in Berlin, where he taught at the liberal rabbinical seminary, the Lehranstalt für die Wissenschaft des Judentums. In symbolic terms, Cohen was departing a bastion of Protestant culture for the vibrant capital of German-Jewish life.

And yet, Cohen's faith in the compatibility of the Jewish and German spirits had never waned in Marburg. Throughout the fin de siècle period, Cohen sought to meld his philosophical and religious interests—and closely related, the German and Jewish facets of his intellectual personality. Significantly, the point of origin for both was the Israelite prophetic tradition. Cohen's interest in the prophets was manifestly not *historisch*. To the extent that he believed that the Biblical prophets were "the true creators of history," it was, as Steven Schwarzchild observed, in the sense that they transformed history from "a record of the past with a nostalgic, atavistic longing for an idealized golden age of the past into an anticipation of an ideal future."[126]

At the core of this anticipation, Cohen argued in 1901, lay the prophetic rejection of paganism as "the symbol of immorality." By contrast, the prophets "teach and discover the uniqueness of God as the author and guarantor, indeed as the foundation of morality."[127] Through this discovery, the prophets heralded a monumental shift in outlook, from a mythic to an ethically centered worldview in which the moral behavior of human beings marks the fulfillment of God's will. From this perspective, the prophets appear to Cohen as the first socialists—indeed, as the

architects of the moral edifice on which human progress and social per-
fectibility were based.[128]

On one level, Cohen's infatuation with the prophets was an extension
and refinement of mid-nineteenth-century liberal Jewish thought. In writing of the leading figure from that period, Michael Meyer has noted that
"the message of Israel's ancient Prophets, universalized beyond its original context, became for [Abraham] Geiger, as for the Reform movement,
the most viable and important component of Judaism."[129] On another
level, interest in the prophets had become a matter of broad intellectual
concern in Germany, extending well beyond the Jewish community. A
good number of contemporary Protestant thinkers—struggling to define
the "essence of Christianity"—understood the prophets as a vital link in
the chain of Christianity's evolutionary development. Among them was
Hermann Cohen's friend and colleague from Marburg, Julius Wellhausen, the renowned biblical scholar. Cohen was an attentive reader of
Protestant biblical scholarship, especially Wellhausen, for whom the
prophets represented the spiritual heights of Israelite religion.[130] And yet,
Cohen rejected the frequent Christian claim that the prophets represented
the terminal stages of a "late Judaism" whose spiritual embers were rekin-
dled by the new *Verus Israel*, Christianity. Consequently, he cast a disap-
proving eye on the work of Wellhausen, a man whom he otherwise liked
and admired. In eulogizing his colleague in 1917, Cohen expressed appreciation that Wellhausen grasped the "ethical foundation and universalism of the prophets." But he could not understand why Wellhausen's studies "concluded with the political history of Israel and turned just as
quickly to the history of the Arabs." "How could he end the history of
Israel so abruptly," Cohen inquired, "without even devoting attention, as
a philologian, to the language of the Mishna?"[131] The familiar neglect by a
renowned Christian scholar of rabbinic Judaism shook Hermann Cohen's
faith in a genuine dialogue of equals between modern Jews and Christians.

The divergences between Cohen and Wellhausen over the Israelite
prophets offer a fleeting, but revealing glance into the limits of Cohen's
immersion into Protestant intellectual culture. While deeply conversant
with Protestant scholarship, he could not accept the claim that the prophets had passed on the mantle of Israel's spiritual leadership to Christianity.
Rather, he insisted on the ongoing relevance, and even ethical superiority,
of a Judaism rooted in the prophetic tradition. Curiously, though, as
Cohen went about building a lineage of ethical grandeur, he too bypassed
the entire corpus of rabbinic literature.

That is, while the prophets were the progenitors of Cohen's sublime
ethical system, their spiritual heirs were philosophers. Cohen was particularly intrigued by Plato, whom he regarded as the precursor of Kantian
idealism. In fact, in Cohen's scheme, the Israelite prophets and Plato were

"the two most important sources of modern culture," as well as "the spiritual leaders of humanity." Cohen did not regard the message of the prophets as identical to that of Plato, but believed that their complementarity lay the foundation for progress in the modern world. The prophets' social consciousness contained the "pure source of religion." But they knew nothing of scientific thought or reason. It was here that Plato innovated, not merely by introducing scientific perception, but by effecting a synthesis of science and morality (*Wissenschaft und Sittlichkeit*). Without science, Cohen declared, "there could be no perception, no idea, no idealism." It provided the logical framework for ethics, and thus enabled the human quest for the Good. By achieving this epochal fusion of science and ethics, Cohen declared that Plato had gained a measure of "historical eternity" (*geschichtliche Ewigkeit*).[132]

This seemingly oxymoronic phrase suited Hermann Cohen's own intellectual and spiritual ambition. In seeking to construct a grand ethical lineage, Cohen was attempting to locate the timeless moorings of the Judaic—or more accurately, Judeo-German—spirit over and through historical time. After the prophets and Plato in antiquity, the most important medieval link was Moses Maimonides, the great Halakhist and philosopher. Interestingly, Cohen did not emphasize Maimonides' renown as a legal decisor or his acumen as a philosopher operating in the Aristotelian mold.[133] Rather, he argued that the Maimonidean system reflected a strong Platonic thrust, particularly in its preoccupation with ethics. In fact, in Cohen's view, the pinnacle of the Maimonidean system was ethical perfection.[134] Moreover, the process by which one attained this state, embodied in the Hebrew term *hishtalmut*, marked a deep rupture with Aristotelian eudaemonism.[135]

In Cohen's genealogy, Maimonides was not only the heir to Platonic ethics. Remarkably, he was also a leading exponent of the fundaments of Protestantism—indeed, "the standard-bearer of Protestantism in medieval Judaism."[136] In making this claim, Cohen was suggesting that the great Spanish-Jewish philosopher understood the essence of religion to be its ethical ideals rather than its dogmas, prescriptions, or institutions. Maimonides thus adumbrated a far more identifiable Protestant, Martin Luther, who also figured prominently in Cohen's scheme. Luther's rejection of established ecclesiastical authority redirected religious responsibility to the domain of the individual's conscience.[137] Consequently, Cohen identified in Luther and the resulting Reformation core ingredients of the German nation he so admired: particularly, the values of individual autonomy, moral rectitude, and philosophic inquiry.

But the greatest representative of the German nation and its cherished values was Immanuel Kant, who assumed pride of place in Cohen's spiritual genealogy. Notwithstanding Kant's denigration of Judaism as mere "statutory laws," Cohen saw Kant's philosophy as deeply consonant with Judaism. This consonance was reflected, above all, in the shared "rejection of eudaemonism and all its varieties." That is, both Kant and Judaism exhibited steadfast "opposition to egoism, selfishness, and above all the horizon of individualism." By contrast, both acknowledged fealty to the universal force of reason, as well as to a related "social idealism . . . that stands in close connection to messianism."[138] At this point, Cohen's genealogy of ethical grandeur, with its origins in Biblical antiquity, pointed toward the *telos* of history—indeed, toward "historical eternity."[139]

It bears reiteration that Cohen's ethical lineage was relieved of the weight of historicism. For example, in the case of Luther, Cohen exhibited little regard for "the collection of single facts from the life in Wittenberg in the sixteenth century."[140] This disregard for the *historisch* was particularly important when dealing with religion—all the more so in a period in which historical approaches to religion, most notably Harnack's *Das Wesen des Christentums*, had become prevalent. In his essay on Kant and Judaism from 1910, Cohen upheld the superiority of philosophical approaches to religion over historical accounts. Whereas history merely approached the "representation" of the essence of religion, "the philosophy of religion alone can assume the responsibility to distinguish between the essential and the inessential in religion."[141]

Cohen echoed this position at the beginning of his major Jewish book, *Religion der Vernunft* (*Religion of Reason out of the Sources of Judaism*), published posthumously in 1919. After establishing that "the problem of history comes . . . into direct opposition to the problem of the substantive content of religion," Cohen affirmed the importance of understanding Judaism as an historically developing concept. But in a clear departure from the Baden school of philosophers, he hastened to add that "history in itself does not determine the concept of reason." Rather, reason precedes and frames historical knowledge. Consequently, the most pressing methodological obligation belongs to philosophy, for it is "the science of reason."[142]

Here we notice a line of consistency in Cohen's thought. Just as he was intent on asserting the preeminence of philosophy over history in his first appearance as a neo-Kantian in 1871, so too he reiterated the point in his final work. The common thread was his desire to reorder the hierarchy of the *Geisteswissenschaften*, although his motivations varied in the two cases. In the earlier case, and throughout the first decades of his career, concern for the state of philosophical study was paramount. But in the latter case, and more broadly, over the last decade and a half of his life, concern for the state of Judaism and Jewish studies was paramount.[143]

A good example of this concern comes in a 1904 address that Cohen delivered to the Gesellschaft zur Förderung der Wissenschaft des Judentums. There, Cohen recalled that the nineteenth century was not only the century of the natural sciences; it was also the century of history. The twentieth century, he seemed to suggest, must move beyond the methodological poles defined by historicism. Thus, while serious scholarly labor could hardly proceed without history, Jewish scholarship required an infusion of ethics and the philosophy of religion.[144] Cohen's ambition was to overcome a mechanistically empirical approach to Judaism in favor of a substantive approach based on philosophy and ethics. Toward that end, he proposed that chairs in ethics and the philosophy of religion be created in the rabbinical seminaries of Germany. This would provide a necessary corrective to the distorted emphasis on historical studies in *Wissenschaft des Judentums*. It would also provide a more attractive target of support for the Jewish community, whose neglect of intellectual and scholarly matters disturbed Cohen greatly.[145]

Cohen initially held out hope that these correctives—both institutional and intellectual—could be realized within the rabbinical seminaries. Several years later, he refocused his sights on the university as the ideal venue.[146] However, by the end of the First World War, Cohen appeared to have concluded that neither setting was amenable to the kind of scholarship he envisaged. As a result, he embarked on a project to establish a new institution, the Akademie für die Wissenschaft des Judentums (Academy for the Scientific Study of Judaism) in which scholarship and communal interests would coexist.[147] What is especially important to note is that his partner in this important, though short-lived, initiative was Franz Rosenzweig.

Cohen first encountered Rosenzweig in 1913 in his seminar at the Lehranstalt in Berlin. The elder philosopher's effect on the younger Rosenzweig was mesmerizing. Never before, Rosenzweig reports, had he witnessed such a relentless drive to penetrate the core of ideas as in Cohen.[148] Cohen's intellectual passion was "like a volcano smouldering under a smooth surface." Its source was a deep religious piety, and it was precisely the link between this piety and Cohen's intellectual mission, Rosenzweig remarked, that "distinguishes him from the crowd of his contemporaries."[149]

The two men, products of different Jewish backgrounds and generations, formed an extraordinary collaboration that lasted until Cohen's death in 1918. Both were, in a sense, returners to Judaism—the former following the Treitschke-Graetz affair of 1879–80 and the latter following his near conversion to Protestantism in 1913. Both had been deeply immersed in the culture of the secular university, and yet recognized at critical moments in their careers that the revival of Jewish studies, and of Judaism itself, must become a central principle in their professional lives. Finally, both arrived at the conclusion that an important key to revival lay in overcoming the historicist hold over the age.

The outbreak of the First World War placed limits on the new intellectual partnership. Rosenzweig was called to the Balkan front as a soldier; and Cohen was called to political battle in Germany, simultaneously waging combat against Zionism and anti-Semitism. Nevertheless, Rosenzweig maintained epistolary contact with Cohen, as with a number of other important correspondents. In a famous letter from March 1917, Rosenzweig insisted to Cohen that "it is time" to proceed with the task of revitalizing Jewish studies.[150] More specifically, Rosenzweig proposed the creation of a new institution staffed by an elite corps of Jewish teacher-scholars for whom research and communal engagement would be intricately entwined. Hermann Cohen responded with enthusiasm, and worked closely with Rosenzweig in 1918 to devise a blueprint for this new institution, the Akademie für die Wissenschaft des Judentums. Indeed, in one of his last published articles from March 1918, Cohen maintained that only such an Akademie—and not a modern rabbinical seminary or university—could allow for the kind of open-minded, critical, and communally engaged scholarship that he envisaged. But the eventual birth of the Akademie, as we shall see in the next chapter, marked a surprising turn from the direction taken by Cohen and Rosenzweig. For it submitted to the very standards of historicism that they sought to upend.

## History of Prophets or Prophetic History?

The collaboration with Rosenzweig on the Akademie, as well as the work on *Religion of Reason*, reflected Cohen's belief not only in the future of Judaism, but in an illustrious Jewish future in Germany. It is important to add that this labor took place against a background of intense societal pressure. With his customary vigor, Cohen proceeded to combat the accusations of anti-Semites of the day. On related grounds, he saw fit to attack the separatist plans of Zionism. To Cohen's mind, these two causes—anti-Semitism and Zionism—undermined the prospect of a fusion of German and Jewish values.

The same qualities of defense against anti-Semitism and proud allegiance to German culture surface in Cohen's late meditations on the problem of history. Cohen's own attitude toward the problem, particularly when it impinged on Judaism, helps illumine the often evanescent boundary that set him off from his Gentile colleagues. Thus, on one level, he felt compelled to parry the supersessionist thrusts of Christian scholars who regarded their religion as an advanced stage, or even the consummation, of, Judaism. But on another level, he shared the problem of Christian theologians desperate to ward off the assaults of historicism on the mythic Christ of faith.[151] Of course, Cohen was not concerned directly with the historicity of Jesus. But he did manifest a *parallel* concern over the impact of historical research upon those inspired ancients who stood at the center of his universal ethics: the Israelite prophets.

Debate over the function and history of the prophets, which raged throughout the nineteenth century, continued with considerable fervor through the First World War. It occupied some of the leading Protestant intellectuals of the day (Harnack, Troeltsch, and Max Weber) and a good number of Jewish counterparts. An eruption of this debate in 1916–18 revealed that the stakes involved were not only intellectual, but political. The catalyst to the debate was an essay on "The Ethos of the Hebrew Prophets" published by Ernst Troeltsch in 1916.[152] Cohen responded to Troeltsch with anger and scorn. His response, highlighting the universal ethos of the prophets, subsequently incurred the wrath of a number of German Zionists, who derided its denationalized implications.[153]

The exchange between Troeltsch and Cohen pitted two leading scholarly forces in late Imperial Germany. The two shared many cultural and political sensibilities, including the belief in an enlightened German state that was a beacon to humanity. And yet, within the intricate social fabric of German life, one's logical allies did not always become one's close friends. Quite to the contrary, relations between liberal Jews and liberal Christians, as Uriel Tal demonstrated in *Christians and Jews in Germany*, were often deeply strained. The apparent "affinity in their intellectual and theological outlook" often dissolved in the face of social or political pressures.[154] And indeed, Cohen and Troeltsch exemplify the wide chasm between liberal Protestantism and liberal Judaism during the tense war years.

Disagreement between the two revolved around a familiar theme: Cohen's objection to Troeltsch's use of historical method, particularly when applied to the Israelite prophets. But there may well have been an overlay of personal suspicion involved in the relationship between the two, particularly from Cohen's side. In 1913, Troeltsch dedicated the second volume of his collected writings to his mentor, Paul de Lagarde. Lagarde, we recall, was none other than Hermann Cohen's adversary in the 1888 trial of a man accused of defaming Judaism in Marburg. It was Lagarde who was called upon to defend the accuracy of the anti-Jewish defamations. Moreover, he was notorious for his frequent fulminations against Jews as alien and antagonistic to the German nation.[155]

By dedicating a book to Lagarde, Ernst Troeltsch was honoring a man widely regarded by German Jews as an anti-Semite. This act was not destined to win the sympathy of Cohen, who was a vocal opponent of anti-Semitism and was concerned by the growing chorus of anti-Semitic voices during the First World War. Recently, more provocative claims that Troeltsch was himself xenophobic, intolerant, and anti-Semitic have appeared, stemming not only from his regard for Lagarde, but also from his scholarly and public writings.[156] The question of whether Ernst Troeltsch was a self-conscious anti-Semite cannot be resolved here. What we can observe is that when Troeltsch delivered his lecture in 1916 on the subject of the Hebrew prophets, he was staking out a clear position as an historian and a Christian—in a period of rising anti-Jewish agitation. Conversely, Cohen's response reflected his status as philosopher and Jew. The resulting exchange exposed not only important methodological differences between them—Troeltsch as an admirer of the Baden neo-Kantians and Cohen as a founder of the Marburg School.[157] It also exposed deep fissures lurking beneath the surface of Jewish-Christian relations.

Troeltsch's initial salvo in 1916 proclaimed that only an historical approach to religion (*eine religionsgeschichtliche Methode*) could generate serious investigation of the Israelite prophets. Wrapping himself in the cloak of Baden, Troeltsch specifically eschewed an "anthropological-positivist" and, in a swipe at the Marburg School, "a transcendental-rationalist" approach.[158] The goal of the kind of historical inquiry Troeltsch favored was to contextualize the ethics of the prophets. Hence, he maintained that "the ethics of the prophets is not the ethics of humanity, but rather of Israel in the undifferentiated unity of ethics, law, and morality that is particular to all ancient peoples." If there was nothing transcendent about the prophets' ethical message, neither was it equivalent to modern notions of "humanity and freedom or, less, democracy and socialism."[159] Rather, Israelite prophecy was born and bred in the rural ambience of ancient Palestine, an environment markedly distinct from the urban culture of contemporary Canaanites, as well as from the Greco-Roman polis.

What this context yielded, Troeltsch wrote in rather loaded terms, was "an oriental-religious messianic dream" rooted in a particularist concern for the fate of Israel.[160] Troeltsch did not depart from the common distinction of nineteenth-century Christian scholars between ancient Judaism and early Christianity. On the contrary, he insisted that it was in early Christianity that "prophecy lives on again and is rejuvenated." This prophetic impulse in Christianity led to a "profundity and interiority of pure human feeling" unmatched by late Judaism. In fact, it created a universalist sensibility that undergirded "the humane cultural world of the Occident."[161]

When Troeltsch delivered these remarks in 1916, he was immediately challenged by a member of the audience, Benzion Kellermann who was a liberal rabbi and neo-Kantian student of Cohen's. Kellermann attempted to publish his critical response in the same journal, *Logos*, in which Troeltsch published his paper, but was refused. Undeterred, Kellermann produced a seventy-page rebuttal to Troeltsch in 1917 entitled *Der ethische Monotheismus der Propheten und seine soziologische Würdi-*

*gung*.[162] Later in the same year, Hermann Cohen printed a brief reply to Troeltsch—"Der Prophetismus und die Soziologie"—that summarized many of Kellermann's main points.

Despite its brevity, Cohen's retort bristles with disdain. It commences with a strong indictment of contemporary historical scholarship, whose materialist tendencies reduce all cultural achievements to social and economic conditions. In so doing, this scholarship remains blind to the "pure spiritual forces" that guide history. Troeltsch's essay on Israelite prophecy masquerades as sociology, a discipline that Cohen ranked higher than history on the methodological ladder, in large measure due to its attentiveness to spiritual and intellectual forces. But Troeltsch's sociological approach, unlike Max Weber's, failed on the same grounds as history. That is, Troeltsch was able to grasp the ethics of Israelite prophets merely as a function of a rural "peasant mentality" (*Bauernmoral*). This attempt to contextualize the prophetic impulse dramatically transformed "the universalism of the [Israelite] God-teaching into the particularism of a tribal god." "With this," Cohen laments, "Judaism as a religion is destroyed."[163]

Cohen's critique of Troeltsch recalls his sharp essay on Heinrich Graetz from the same year. The misguided perspectives of the two historians obscured the deep spiritual reservoir of Israelite prophecy, as well as the universal character of Israelite monotheism. That Cohen felt particularly agitated in 1917 owed to the fear that his vision of Judaism was under siege. The Great War wreaked havoc on lives and property, but no less on received wisdoms. On one flank, Cohen faced an emboldened camp of Zionists who argued that the time had come to recognize that Jews constituted not a religion, but a nation with its own distinct political aspirations and historical destiny.[164] On the other flank, Cohen felt challenged by conservative German nationalists who insisted in 1916 that Jews were not serving in the German military in numbers proportionate to their size in the general population. In response to these reports, the Prussian minister of war, von Hohenborn, ordered a census of Jewish soldiers (*Judenzählung*) whose results discounted the claims of the anti-Semites.[165]

Nonetheless, the outbreak of this new anti-Jewish sentiment shocked the staunchly patriotic Cohen. His blueprint for a harmonious union of *Deutschtum und Judentum* seemed unsupportable in the current environment. It was not only the national chauvinists of both varieties, German and Zionist, who gave lie to it. It was also the "liberals" like Ernst Troeltsch. Cohen wondered how Troeltsch could dare to present such a flawed perspective on Israelite prophecy, which he dismissively referred to as "supposed scholarship," in an age of rising anti-Semitism.[166] Troeltsch not only *misunderstood* the ethical mission of the prophets; he himself *violated* the ethical mission of the scholar.

We began this chapter with the young Ernst Troeltsch warning his theological elders that many of the leading intellectual values cultivated over the course of the nineteenth century were on the verge of collapse. The "crisis consciousness" of Troeltsch's generation yielded a common sense of urgency, but also a set of intriguing and often contentious differences. In this respect, Troeltsch and Cohen offer a revealing juxtaposition. Troeltsch's aspirations for an ethical Christianity rested on his belief that a critical historical perspective was necessary to reveal the evolving essence of this great world-religion. Meanwhile, his Jewish foil, Cohen, yearned for an ethical Judaism that must resist the ravages of a critical historical (*historisch*) perspective in order to realize its true historic (*geschichtlich*) goal.

In the name of symmetry, it is perhaps appropriate to conclude with the words of Ernst Troeltsch, who acknowledged Cohen's distinctive attitude toward history in his major unfinished study of the historicist idea, *Der Historismus und seine Probleme* (1922). Troeltsch observed that, for Cohen, history was much less a matter of recalling the past than preparing for the future.[167] We might add that it was this kind of future-oriented history that placed Cohen at odds with the dominant historicist ethos of his age. In fact, he was seeking to revive a Kantian ideal of history that sagged heavily under the weight of minute historical data. There is a heroic, as well as tragic, quality to this effort. For Cohen was attempting nothing less than to rescue the ideal of ethical universalism from the ever-advancing reach of historicism that sought to consume it.

## Chapter Three

## FRANZ ROSENZWEIG AND THE RISE OF
## THEOLOGICAL ANTI-HISTORICISM

> The struggle against history in its nineteenth-century sense is at the same
> time the struggle for religion in the twentieth-century sense.
> —Franz Rosenzweig

Even more than his mentor Hermann Cohen, Franz Rosenzweig (1886–1929) has enjoyed a remarkable afterlife, particularly in the recent fin de siècle. Not only has he assumed pride of place within the pantheon of Weimar Jewish intellectuals, whose leading lights include Walter Benjamin, Ernst Bloch, Max Horkheimer, Gershom Scholem, and Ernst Simon. He has also become the focal point of an extraordinary resurgence of interest in modern German-Jewish thought. Dozens of articles, dissertations, and books explore Rosenzweig's complex and vivid restatement of Judaism in his major work, the *Star of Redemption* (1921).[1] These inquiries call attention to Rosenzweig's fluid movement between competing poles rooted in the German and German-Jewish landscapes: those of Zionism and assimilationism, of Jewish particularism and Enlightenment-era ecumenism, and of Hegelian idealism and a new existentialism.

The combination of Rosenzweig's celebrated "return" to Judaism and his agitation toward a *neues Denken* (New Thinking) reflects, above all, a fascinating and multifaceted personality. But it also symbolizes the forceful clash of conservative and progressive impulses that transformed political, intellectual, and artistic life in late Wilhelmine and Weimar Germany. While immersed in this turbulent world, Rosenzweig was able to craft a single-minded mission on behalf of a revitalized Judaism. More impressively, he was able to stake out a position of considerable moral authority—a status based not only on his intellect, but on his personal example as teacher and spiritual guide, as well as on his noble battle against debilitating disease.

Rosenzweig's premature death at forty-three could easily have assured him of posthumous obscurity, especially in light of the subsequent Nazi erasure of German-Jewish culture. However, his legacy has not only survived, but grown, due in no small part to the efforts of his friends and disciples, most prominently Nahum Glatzer. Glatzer's formative encounter with Rosenzweig in Frankfurt am Main left such a profound mark that he devoted a good portion of his own academic career to making Rosenzweig accessible to a wider, and particularly English-reading, audience.[2]

As Rosenzweig's legacy has grown, it has been embraced and adapted in ways that Nahum Glatzer might not have imagined—by historians seeking to recapture the scintillating cultural ambience of Weimar Germany, by philosophers aspiring to repair a shattered moral and philosophical universe after the Shoah, and by cultural theorists intent on upending à la Rosenzweig the binary opposition of particularism and universalism.

Our gaze here will be trained on the problem of history that figured so prominently in Rosenzweig's thought. A long line of scholars including Alexander Altmann, Leora Batnitzky, Bernhard Casper, Robert Gibbs, Peter Gordon, Rivka Horwitz, Steven T. Katz, Ephraim Meir, Stefan Meineke, Paul Mendes-Flohr, Stéphane Mosès, and Elliot Wolfson have already discussed various aspects of this "problem."[3] While each is owed a considerable debt, I will seek to cast a wider contextual net in which to understand Rosenzweig's confrontation with history—as part of the broader phenomenon of anti-historicism in German-Jewish thought in the late nineteenth and early twentieth centuries. Many have noted Rosenzweig's affinity with the young Martin Heidegger, who shared Rosenzweig's impatience with staid philosophical conventions from the nineteenth century. Both thinkers emerged at a time of heightened intellectual agitation that impelled them to make abrupt shifts in their respective career paths. Rosenzeig's *teshuvah* or "return" of 1913 fortified his resolve to abandon the professional study of philosophy and history and commit his energies to forging a vibrant new Judaism. Meanwhile, Heidegger's *Kehre* or "turning" after 1917 emboldened him to undertake a *Destruktion* of the methodological pretenses of the *Geistewissenschaften* in the name of a new emphasis on Being.[4] One of the key points at which the thought of the two converged was their belief that historicism posed an obstacle to the quest for vital existence.

Another important and related point of convergence was their close attention to new currents in Protestant theological circles in early twentieth-century Germany, especially those associated with what came to be known as the "crisis theology." Both Heidegger and Rosenzweig drew great inspiration from their reading of and contact with these theological circles. It is for this reason that I propose to consider Franz Rosenzweig not chiefly in the bold new philosophical context of Weimar Germany epitomized by Martin Heidegger. Rather, I believe that Rosenzweig can and must be understood in another seminal, but lesser known context: in the company of contemporaneous Christian intellectuals whom F. W. Graf calls the "theological anti-historicists."[5] This contextualization is important beyond the individual case of Rosenzweig. For as Allan Megill has perceptively noted, the broader crisis of historicism in Germany evolved largely out of theological concerns rather than philosophical ones.[6]

Permeated through and through with a sense of crisis, Protestant theologians like Karl Barth, Emil Brunner, Rudolf Bultmann, Friedrich Gogarten, and to a great extent, Rosenzweig's closest conversation partners, Eugen Rosenstock-Huessy, and Hans and Rudolf Ehrenberg, were prime protagonists in the "anti-historicist revolution" of the immediate post–World War I period.[7] They were deeply disturbed by the relativizing tendencies of historicism that, to their minds, embodied the most disintegrative features of modernity.[8] More particularly, they were unsettled by the fear that the mist of historical arcana had shrouded authentic religious experience in a cloud. As a remedy, the theological anti-historicists labored to lift this mist and reveal the font of all religious experience: the unvarying factuality of Revelation.

To be sure, this "anti-historicist revolution" of the 1920s had roots in earlier nineteenth-century theological assaults on historicism. But there was a particular intensity to the twentieth-century theological rebellion that was unique to the environment of Weimar Germany. There was also a pronounced generational aspect to the revolt, as the younger theologians discarded the liberal bourgeois truisms of an earlier *Kulturprotestantismus*—much like Heidegger and his philosophical allies ridiculed the epistemological pretenses of the earlier neo-Kantians. In contrast to figures such as Ernst Troeltsch and Adolf von Harnack, the theological young guard was no longer single-mindedly devoted to the establishment of a *Rechtsstaat* founded on the highest ideals of justice. Rather, its energies were focused on the search for a primal religious authenticity.

In this ambience of protest, Franz Rosenzweig came to personify a cohort of young Jewish intellectuals swept up in rebellion against the preceding generation of German Jews. For his generation, both the bourgeois comforts of German-Jewish life and the spiritual aridity of *Wissenschaft des Judentums* led them to rebel against the past. This rebellion emerged out of the same reservoir of discontent that nourished Christian intellectual agitation in Germany. In fact, the lines of dissent represented by Jewish and Protestant (or less frequently, Catholic) contemporaries often overlapped.[9] In the case of Franz Rosenzweig, his theological agenda and terminology bore the traces of a profound encounter with Protestantism.[10] This should not surprise us in the least, since Rosenzweig's closest partners in theological conversation, Rudolf and Hans Ehrenberg and Eugen and Margrit (Gritli) Rosenstock-Huessy, were Protestant.

And yet, these close contacts did not yield an ecumenical theology, a sort of Protestant Judaism à la Hermann Cohen.[11] Instead, they prompted a distinctive vision of Judaism that separated it from all other religions or nations. The measure of eternity that Judaism had earned, Rosenzweig wrote, gives lie "to the worldly and all-too-worldly sham eternity of the historical moments of the nations." Unlike other peoples, the Jews refused to submit to historical contingency; on the contrary, they remained "remote from the chronology of the rest of the world."[12]

The close proximity of German Protestant thinkers to Rosenzweig does not amount to "influence" in the conventional sense of the term. In general, notions of historical "influence" fail to capture the subtle, multidirectional negotiation in which Jews have engaged when living in, adapting to, and transforming Gentile societies.[13] Franz Rosenzweig not only understood the dynamics of this negotiation, but exemplifies the way in which these dynamics produce an identity that can not be summarily reduced to "influence." As Amos Funkenstein once observed, Rosenzweig grasped that Judaism is "a form of existence that, in order to reflect upon itself would have to transgress beyond itself and see itself in Christian eyes." The result of this reflection was not Judaism in the image of Christianity—or, for that matter, in the image of (Christian) anti-Semites per Jean-Paul Sartre. It was Judaism in the image of Christianity *as seen by Jews*—the product of blended optical perspectives. We might describe this condition as *cultural bifocality* and note that it cuts across generational lines within German Jewry. Thus, it can be said to embrace both Hermann Cohen's ecumenism and Franz Rosenzweig's more defiant "post-assimilatory" stance.[14]

Notwithstanding significant differences between them, the two men held to the conviction that the Jews, and Judaism, were not subject to the corrosive effects of historical time. Likewise, they shared a distrust for the fragmenting methods of the modern historian. Here, the student followed the lead of the teacher. For, as Alexander Altmann has written of Hermann Cohen, "it is in no small measure due to his influence that twentieth-century Jewish theology in Germany emancipated itself from a sterile Historicism and recovered the almost lost domain of the Absolute, of Truth and faith in the Truth."[15] As we shall see, Rosenzweig continued and radicalized this quest to emancipate theology from a sterile historicism.

From 1913 to 1918, Rosenzweig cultivated a unique intellectual relationship with Cohen. But in a number of important ways, he diverged from his mentor's path. And this is what makes their relationship so intriguing. In the first instance, the elderly Cohen and the young Rosenzweig met at the crossroads of *teshvuah*—at a point where Judaism assumed an ever-increasing centrality in their lives. This encounter fortified each man's conviction in the path of "return" to Judaism—which interestingly did not lead, in either case, to Zion. Moreover, it predisposed Rosenzweig, then in a state of spiritual turmoil, to regard Cohen with veneration. Some of Rosenzweig's Jewish contemporaries, especially those of a Zionist persuasion, treated Cohen contemptuously, as a bloated icon, a Jew who revealed the folly of Jewish assimilation and a scholar who symbolized the sterility of German *Kathederphilosophie*.[16] Rosenzweig's first meeting with Cohen in a Berlin classroom in 1913 left an entirely different impression:

> I had the surprise of my life. I am used to professors of philosophy who are subtle, acute, lofty, profound, and whatever other attributes are used to praise a thinker—instead, I found something I hadn't expected, a philosopher. In place of the tightrope walkers who execute their leaps on the taut wire of thought more or less boldly, more or less adroitly, more or less nimbly, I saw a man. . . . With Cohen, you felt perfectly convinced that this man must philosophize, that he had within the treasure which the powerful word forces to the surface.[17]

Still, for all of his appreciation for Cohen's philosophical and Jewish passions, Rosenzweig averred in 1916 that the actual content of "his philosophy, his politics, his Judaism are for me quite unimportant."[18] He felt considerable impatience with the neo-Kantian ideals that Cohen held sacred: the steadfast belief in the reign of reason over human consciousness, as well as the abiding faith in the scientific vocation of philosophy. Rosenzweig's rejection of the metaphysical concerns of nineteenth-century philosophy—first and foremost, Hegelianism—had commenced earlier, in 1913, shortly after he completed his dissertation at Freiburg on Hegel and the state. The need to move beyond neo-Kantianism as well, with its epistemological and scientific pretenses, became clear to him during and after the First World War. As a result, the critique of historicism that he would come to express, while drawing from a source of discontent common to Hermann Cohen's, was voiced in a different philosophical register. Whereas Cohen sought to limit the reach of historicism to preserve the integrity of his neo-Kantian method, Rosenzweig firmly believed that both historicism *and* neo-Kantian philosophy obscured the path to genuine vitality in life.

During and after the tumultuous years of the First World War, Rosenzweig—and his generation of intellectual compatriots—urgently sought not the proper method, but the true content, of philosophy and theology. In the process, they began to develop, as Peter Gordon has observed, a "counter-lexicon of religion, vitalism, and *Existenz*."[19] This new language was fueled by the innovative and often subversive spirit that impelled so much artistic, literary, intellectual, and political innovation in the Weimar period. An exemplary contributor to this new language was the scholar of religion Rudolf Otto, who explored the very concept of the holy in his widely known study from 1917, *Das Heilige*. There, Otto declared that his aim was to arrive at a refined understanding of "the contrast between rationalism and profounder religion." In an unmistakable turn away from Kant, he implored the reader of his book "to direct his mind to a moment of deeply-felt religious experience, as little as possible qualified by other forms of consciousness."[20]

It was a similar experiential yearning that impelled young Jewish intellectuals other than Franz Rosenzweig to rebel. For example, Walter Benjamin authored a manifesto in 1918, "On the Program of the Coming Philosophy," in which he labored to escape the shadow of a hyper-rationalist neo-Kantianism. In particular, Benjamin was concerned that the Kantian notion of experience was too formalistic, too beholden to the "scientistic prejudices" of the day.[21] The "task of the coming philosophy," he declared, was to discover a new concept of knowledge "that renders possible not only mechanical but also religious experience." Benjamin was careful to add that this did not imply that "knowledge renders God possible, but rather that it makes the experience and doctrine of God possible."[22]

It was in this period that Benjamin and his close friend Gershom Scholem began their well-known discussions of Kabbalah. One of the chief sources of attraction for Benjamin was the mystical notion of an experience that eluded or preceded cognition. Scholem recalls that this very theme of a noncognitive experience led Benjamin to write his manifesto on the future of philosophy.[23] Meanwhile, Scholem's own intense study of Kabbalah—which, of course, became a lifelong passion—reflected a related quest for a vibrant Jewish experience that was irreducible to an idea. In Scholem's case, the affinity for the mystical was inextricably bound up with his developing Zionist loyalties: "I wanted to enter the world of *kabbalah* out of my belief in Zionism as a living thing."[24] In fact, both Kabbalah and Zionism satisfied his vitalist demands; at the same time, they challenged the old *Bildungsideal* that had accompanied German Jewry from the age of Enlightenment.

Franz Rosenzweig was deeply attuned to this generation's state of rebellious creativity. Even when stationed abroad as a soldier during the war, he was astonishingly prolific in writing about new forms of Jewish education, philosophy, and theology that challenged the existing cultural order. Uniting his efforts was a desire to efface the boundary between the intellectual and spiritual, indeed, between philosophy and theology. Rosenzweig often wrote that after the year 1800, philosophy had become the domain of academic "doctors," who contented themselves with small inquiries into method rather than large questions of existence.[25] His own attempt to revive philosophy—in large measure by crossbreeding it with theological concerns—arose in an ambience of cultural upheaval, punctuated at times by Spenglerian expressions of despair. No longer, Rosenzweig insisted, could standard academic study in a university suffice. Nor could a sense of optimism in the advance of knowledge be sustained. As he wrote to his one-time history mentor, Friedrich Meinecke, in 1920: "Scholarship no longer holds the center of my attention." Rather, he confessed that in the present age of discordant political and cultural vectors, "my life has fallen under the rule of a 'dark drive.' "[26]

It is perhaps not surprising that Rosenzweig manifested in this period a strong sense of identification with the great medieval Spanish-Jewish poet, Judah Ha-Levi (1075–1141). Ha-Levi possessed a passionate artistic temperament that yielded lush elegies to wine drinking as well as heart-aching odes to Zion. Rosenzweig first began to discuss him in letters and writings from 1916, and commenced a translation project of Ha-Levi's verse that culminated in the volume *Sechzig Hymnen und Gedichte des Jehuda Halevi* (1924). As Rivka Horwitz has noted, Rosenzweig's affinity with Ha-Levi stemmed from the fact that both were "poets full of religious fire"—consumed by a spiritual pathos at odds with the rationalist frame of mind.[27] Moreover, commentators have noted the similarities beyond Ha-Levi's and Rosenzweig's views of history, particularly, their shared belief that the Jewish people operated outside the normal flow of historical events.[28]

Rosenzweig's affinity for Ha-Levi presents an illuminating juxtaposition to Hermann Cohen's allegiance to Maimonides (1135–1204), the great rationalist philosopher who was born several years before Ha-Levi's death. Cohen's reverence fits easily into the Haskalah-era veneration of Maimonides as a great proto-Enlightenment paragon.[29] By contrast, Rosenzweig's affection for Ha-Levi points to an emphatically post-Enlightenment disposition in which the rationalist philosopher no longer reigns supreme. In this respect, Amos Funkenstein may well have been right to argue that Rosenzweig spelled "the end of German-Jewish philosophy."[30] Or perhaps we might say that in a period marked by violent rupture, Franz Rosenzweig assumed the mantle of intellectual leadership from Hermann Cohen—thereby signaling the end of the long German-Jewish nineteenth century.

This transfer calls to mind the momentous gathering at Davos, Switzerland, in March 1929. The Davos conference is often portrayed as the site of neo-Kantianism's demise in German philosophy—as an academic prize-fight in which Ernst Cassirer, heir to the legacy of Kant and Cohen, was decisively bested by the upstart Martin Heidegger. In the colloquy between Cassirer and Heidegger, the latter dismissed the inflated claims of the Kantians that consciousness was "universally necessary . . . [and] anticipates all factual experience." Heidegger sought to shift the focus of philosophical inquiry away from consciousness toward Being, while also descending from the plateau of objectivity on which neo-Kantian method (particularly of the Marburg strain) stood. His own mission, he declared in response to Cassirer, was to demonstrate that "truth is relative to *Dasein* (Existence)."[31] For many contemporaries, the move initiated by Heidegger at Davos from epistemology to ontology, from neo-Kantian objectivism to contingent subjectivity, inaugurated a new philosophical era.[32]

What is relevant for our purposes is not only the apparent parallel to the Cohen-Rosenzweig relationship. Nor is it Rosenzweig's resonance with Heidegger's new philosophical language of Existence.[33] It is a far more surprising and counterintuitive point raised by Rosenzweig in one of his last writings before dying from a degenerative disease in 1929. The piece in question, "Vertauschte Fronten," was a brief essay written shortly after the Davos meeting in May 1929 that contains Rosenzweig's impressions of the conference as gleaned from newspaper reports. Rather than cast Martin Heidegger as the initiator of a new philosophical discourse, Rosenzweig performs a remarkable act of genealogical reconstruction that belies some of what he and his generational cohort stood for: none other than Hermann Cohen—often perceived as the last of the great neo-Kantians—emerges as the progenitor of the new philosophical thinking to which Heidegger (and Rosenzweig) contributed so mightily. In particular, Rosenzweig argues that Cohen at the end of his career advanced "a fundamental concept, the idea of Correlation, that . . . leads—to express it in Heideggerian terms—to the 'leap into Existence.' "[34]

It is not our task here to deconstruct this far-fetched intellectual filiation; others have admirably done so.[35] But it is striking to see Rosenzweig sweep his Jewish mentor (Cohen) and his philosophical contemporary (Heidegger) into a single current of intellectual dissent (against the nineteenth century) in which he himself swam. It calls to mind a strong undertow in this current, namely, the rebellion against what Rosenzweig termed in 1914 "atheistic theology." The desire to "leap into Existence," especially through the portal of faith, consumed Rosenzweig's generation of German intellectuals and was present, he insisted, in the work of the "last Cohen" (of *Religion of Reason*).[36] This claim reminds us that, for all their differences, Rosenzweig perceived that he and Cohen shared a critical mission: to "leap into Existence," in large measure by rebelling against the soulless rule of historicism.

It is to a further elaboration of this mission in Franz Rosenzweig that we now turn. As in the previous chapter, we will use our protagonist's intellectual biography to trace the contours of an anti-historicist discourse that traversed the boundary between generations, as well as between Protestant and Jewish cultures.

## "We Are Christian in Everything": The Young Rosenzweig between Judaism and Christianity

It is fitting that Nahum Glatzer commenced his renowned biography/anthology of Franz Rosenzweig with reference to Rosenzweig's great-grandfather, Samuel Meyer Ehrenberg.[37] Ehrenberg was the educator who transformed a small Jewish school—the Samsonschule—in Wolfenbüttel from a traditional *heder* into a modern pedagogic institution. As director of the school, Ehrenberg served as mentor and inspiration to two precocious students, Leopold Zunz and I. M. Jost, who were to achieve fame as leading first-generation practitioners of *Wissenschaft des Judentums*. In this regard, S. M. Ehrenberg merits a special place in the history of modern Jewish studies of which his great-grandson was one of the most unusual representatives.

But Ehrenberg's larger significance lies in the fact that he was the progenitor of two familial branches that followed distinct cultural paths on German terrain.[38] One grandson, Victor, married a woman (Helene von Ihering) who was a descendent of Martin Luther. The couple's children, Hans and Rudolf Ehrenberg, assumed the religion of their mother (one by choice and the other by birth), and Hans would go on to become a prominent Lutheran theologian and pastor. Meanwhile, another grandson, Georg Rosenzweig, married Adele Alsberg, who gave birth to the couple's only child: Franz. Both of Rosenzweig's parents had a rather attenuated connection to Judaism. Coming from such a home, it was quite natural that the young Rosenzweig would contemplate conversion, which he did (apparently with the encouragement of his father).[39] In fact, he engaged in long and detailed discussions with his converted cousins, the Ehrenbergs, over the merits of such an act. And yet, at the brink of the baptismal font, Rosenzweig chose not to follow the route of his cousins, but rather to dedicate himself to the revitalization of Judaism.

On the surface, his fate could not seem more different than that of his cousins. But in fact, the distance between the two family paths emanating from S. M. Ehrenberg—the Ehrenbergs' and Rosenzweig's—was quite close.[40] Not only do we find a great deal of similarity in social status, political disposition, and cultural taste between the converted Ehrenbergs and the assimilated Rosenzweig. We also find that the three cousins were dear friends and intimate conversation partners who shared a spiritual passion and theological language. Indeed, one can hardly resist thinking here of Rosenzweig's image of *Zweistromland*, alluding to the land of two rivers (the Tigris and Euphrates that together created the Fertile Crescent in Mesopotamia). This was the name Rosenzweig gave to his volume of collected Jewish writings; it is often understood to refer to the mutually fructifying realms of Germanness and Jewishness. But the Ehrenberg-Rosenzweig relationship hints at a more narrow and personal understanding of the term: *Zweistromland* as the dense, fertile, and *contested* space between liberal Jews and liberal Protestants, at times even of the same family, that formed the center of Franz Rosenzweig's world.

The symbolic roots of this world extend back to Rosenzweig's birthdate: Christmas Day 1886. They also extend back to his birthplace, Kassel, the city that served as the capital of the Kingdom of Westphalia in the

Napoleonic era. It was there that the first steps toward Jewish emancipation, as well as the reform of Judaism, were taken in German lands. It was also in this milieu that Rosenzweig's parents were raised, met, and married. Rosenzweig's father, who had expanded the small textile business of his father and grandfather, became an affluent and prominent citizen in Kassel. He served on the boards of various Jewish and German organizations, including the local National Liberal party. Neither he nor Rosenzweig's mother was especially concerned with the observance of Jewish ritual; indeed, the family home, like that of many German Jews, was adorned with a Christmas tree. To the extent that Georg and Adele Rosenzweig's only child acquired any knowledge about Jewish practice, it was through contact with his more traditional great-uncle Adam (1826–1908).[41]

As the product of an "economically secure, intellectually and politically liberal, and Jewishly assimilated home," it is curious that the young Rosenzweig developed an interest in religion in general, and Jewish religion in particular.[42] He took pleasure in reading the Bible in German translation, significantly enough, the translation of his great-grandfather's outstanding charge, Leopold Zunz. However, no regular instruction was offered him in the language or history of his ancestors. This led to the unusual request from eleven-year-old Franz that, as a reward for receiving high marks in school, he be provided with a Hebrew teacher.[43]

Traces of Rosenzweig's interest in Judaism, Hebrew, and the Bible periodically surface throughout his letters from the first decade of the twentieth century. But they are only a small portion of the musings of a precocious young adult. The letters abound with meandering philosophical ruminations, interspersed with the predilections of an aspiring bon vivant (in music, dance, and romance). A more sober, but consistent theme in the letters is Rosenzweig's choice of vocation. Rosenzweig commenced university at Göttingen in 1905 with the aim of studying medicine. Shortly thereafter, he drifted to Munich where his commitment to medicine began to wane. In February 1906, he wrote that, after discussions with his cousin Hans Ehrenberg, "a gleam of light" struck him. His true intellectual calling was not medicine but history. "Everything points to that," Rosenzweig declared, noting his habit of "seeing everything historically," as well as his "delight in the individual, the characteristic, the anecdotal."[44] Indeed, through both his formal studies and informal contacts, Rosenzweig had absorbed the historicist sensibility dominant in the German academy. While exclaiming to his parents in March 1906 that "I am no historian!" he nonetheless meditated frequently on problems of historical cognition—surely more than most young students of medicine.[45] For example, in a diary entry from the following month, the twenty-year-old Rosenzweig undertook to address the question of whether there were binding laws of history. This question stood at the heart of the debate instigated by the Baden neo-Kantians over the differences between the *Geistewissenschaften* and the *Naturwissenschaften*. A short while later, Rosenzweig switched institutions yet again, this time going to Freiburg, where he began to take several courses in the natural sciences from professors who were keenly aware of major philosophical questions of the day.[46] This exposure heightened Rosenzweig's own awareness of the pressing methodological questions within the German *Geisteswissenschaften*.

Even before arriving in Freiburg, Rosenzweig was contemplating the differences between history and nature. In his April 29 diary entry, Rosenzweig announced that there was no causal certainty in history. Thus, one could never maintain that "under a certain set of conditions, this and this *must* happen." In fact, "we are incapable of conceiving of any absolute *must* or any notion of pure causality" in history. History, he averred, submitted to the dictates of time and space; nature, by contrast, was "unbounded and unending."[47]

Through this kind of philosophical meditation, Rosenzweig grew more attached to an historicist sensibility—so much so that he believed he had discovered a new calling in life. Conveying the news of this calling to his parents was a delicate affair. His father, with whom he had a tense relationship, wanted Rosenzweig to pursue the more practical (and honorable) profession of medicine. As was often the case in matters of such delicacy, Rosenzweig chose to explain himself first to his mother. His hesitations about medical school, he wrote to her in March 1908, were hardly novel. Despite his desire to succeed, and thereby satisfy his father's expectations, it made no sense for him to continue. He had no passion for the subject. Regarding a "second choice," Rosenzweig did not feel capable of pursuing serious work in philosophy, in which he had begun to dabble in 1906. In a telling if rather unclairvoyant line to his mother, Rosenzweig declared: "I know that I am not suited to be a philosopher, but rather a cultural historian."[48] Consequently, his new plan was to work toward a doctorate in history at Freiburg under the direction of the esteemed Friedrich Meinecke.

Rosenzweig began the formal study of history in the fall of 1908. Over the next two years, he took a wide range of seminars in modern European history with Meinecke. His seminar papers from the period—for instance, his essay devoted to Friedrich Wilhelm V—revealed a newfound interest in the details of nineteenth-century German history, as well as in the historiographical literature of the period.[49] At the same time, Rosenzweig was expanding his intellectual horizons in seminars with the philosopher Heinrich Rickert, who was one of the most important contributors to the debate over the method of the *Geisteswissenschaften*.

Rosenzweig's two mentors represented flip sides of the historicist coin. Meinecke, who published *Nationalstaat und Weltbürgertum* in 1907, was a firm believer in the clarificatory, and therapeutic, powers of history. Historicism, he claimed, was "the highest stage so far reached in the understanding of human affairs" with the potential "to tackle the problems of human history that still confront us."[50] Even while extolling historicism, Meinecke never sought to deny the inevitable subjectivity of historical observation. It was perhaps theoretically possible to write history without a value judgment. But Meinecke believed that "history written without such a valuation is either mere amassing of material and preparation for genuine historical writing or, in claiming to be a genuine history, is insipid."[51]

By contrast, Heinrich Rickert recoiled at the danger of historians succumbing to their own subjective prejudices. Meinecke's historicism was "a form of relativism that can only lead to nihilism."[52] As a devoted neo-Kantian, Rickert maintained that cognition of a given historical object was not a matter of retreating into subjectivity or empathy, but a logical operation governed by formal rules. On this view, the knowing subject could and must transcend the immediacy of time and space in order to achieve a scientifically verifiable stance. In forging this position, Rickert was seeking to fashion, as Charles Bambach has observed, "a philosophical response to the problems generated from out of the historicist tradition" itself.[53]

Like a fellow Freiburg student from this period, Martin Heidegger, Franz Rosenzweig was well aware of Rickert's admonitions. Both he and Heidegger would give voice to their own concerns about historicism's pretenses in their later careers. But in Freiburg, Rosenzweig was compelled by the force of Friedrich Meinecke's intellectual personality, and drew inspiration from Meinecke's approach to *Ideengeschichte*. This was not the kind of mundane history that told the story of "murder and killing." Rather, it was a more exalted history in which philosophical ideas are carefully explicated and situated in context.[54] An important feature of this kind of practice was careful source analysis, which Rosenzweig undertook in the midst of his dissertation research on Hegel's conception of the state. In a letter to Hans Ehrenberg from November 1910, he expressed the exhilaration of the neophyte scholar rummaging through the archives:

> I've joined the philologists. I make excerpts, collate, experience commas, make tracings, graphologize, and like Goethe's Wagner am infatuated with the noble parchment. Especially in the beginning it was very exciting and solemn, and

from time to time I recapture the experience. This feeling of being an eyewitness, a direct observer of Hegel's various attempts to formulate his ideas, is sublime.[55]

But this sense of history as a noble calling was not to survive long. Even in the above-quoted letter to Ehrenberg, Rosenzweig pointed to the episodic quality of his exhilaration. By the peak of his personal-spiritual "crisis" of 1913, few traces of it remained. And yet, already before this letter, there were signs that Rosenzweig was beginning to have doubts about his newly acquired vocation. In January 1910, he joined a group of young scholars of history and philosophy at a conference in Baden-Baden. Animated by the desire to import the energizing spirit of "1800" into the twentieth century, the group heard Rosenzweig lay out a sweeping Hegelian reconstruction of European history according to which the seventeenth, eighteenth, and nineteenth centuries were divided into thesis, antithesis, and synthesis. As Victor von Weizsäcker remembered the event, a number of those present, perhaps motivated by anti-Semitism, dismissed Rosenzweig's sweeping reconstruction as "thoroughly intolerable."[56]

Following the negative experience at Baden-Baden, Rosenzweig was prompted to reassess the wisdom of his historical training, as well as his commitment to the long-standing philosophical tradition that he often referred to in his writings as "Ionia to Jena." As Alexander Altmann has characterized it, this tradition represented to Rosenzweig a "sustained pagan effort of idealist thinking that is gradually neutralized by the impact of the Jewish-Christian tradition, that is, revelation, and spends itself in Hegel."[57] The once-celebrated epiphany of Hegelian idealism now came to represent the end of philosophy—and with it, the belief in History as a progressive and all-encompassing realm of human activity.

We might say that following Baden-Baden, Rosenzweig took his first important steps of intellectual "dissimilation" away from liberal German, and German-Jewish, culture. A brief indication of the direction of his thinking comes in a September 1910 letter to Hans Ehrenberg, who was one of the organizers of the Baden-Baden gathering. While discussing Hegel's tendency to see the hand of God in history, Rosenzweig observed: "God does not redeem man through History, but actually as the God of Religion."[58]

This reference to religion as a realm of experience distinct from, and perhaps superior to, history pointed to a major shift in orientation for Rosenzweig. It also became the key topic in the intense, tumultuous, and revealing conversations that Rosenzweig had with three Protestant intellectuals who were present at Baden-Baden: his cousins Hans and Rudolf Ehrenberg, and most significantly, the legal scholar Eugen Rosenstock (later Rosenstock-Huessy).

Rosenzweig's mentor, Friedrich Meinecke, insisted that it was the tremendous shock of the war that blunted his disciple's passion for history.

But there can be little doubt that Rosenzweig's reservations—about both the inescapability of history and the relativism of historical method—preceded its outbreak.[59] It is also clear that Rosenzweig's doubts were part of a broader "crisis-consciousness" that afflicted young German intellectuals who could no longer tolerate the emptiness of academic study. Within that class of intellectuals was an important subset of thinkers—for instance, Rosenzweig, the Ehrenbergs, Rosenstock, and Karl Barth—hungry for spiritual fulfillment and painfully aware of the widening gap between history and faith.

At this point in his life, Rosenzweig's new consciousness did not entail any positive function for Judaism. His closest conversation partners were Protestant Christians for whom questions of faith—by virtue of their recent conversion from Judaism—arose with almost obsessive frequency. Rosenzweig knowingly operated in an ambience permeated through and through with Christian values. Once in 1909, when justifying Hans Ehrenberg's conversion to his parents, Rosenzweig acknowledged the shallowness of German-Jewish existence in his day:

> We are Christians in everything. We live in a Christian state, attend Christian schools, read Christian books, in short, our whole "culture" rests entirely on a Christian foundation; consequently a man who has nothing holding him back needs only a very slight push . . . to make him accept Christianity.[60]

If one of the major turns in Rosenzweig's life was now to focus his attention on the realm of religion, a closely related and imminent one was to disengage from the ever-present Christian culture and search out a meaningful approach to Judaism. Ironically, that latter step would come about only in the midst of tortured deliberation over whether to convert. Likewise, it was accompanied by Rosenzweig's transformation from a promising historian, contentedly working in the historicist tradition of Friedrich Meinecke, to a critic of historicism, intent on overthrowing the reign of history in German-Jewish thought.[61]

## Against "The Objectivity Swindle": Rosenzweig, Rosenstock-Huessy, and the Roots of Theological Anti-Historicism

Rosenzweig's introduction to Eugen Rosenstock at Baden-Baden was but a foreshadowing of what would become, from 1913, an extraordinarily close as well as trying relationship. What made their relationship so compelling was not only their shared background and interests, but the way in which their profound differences emerged out of and yet remained part of a common cultural fabric. Even more remarkably, this fabric remained intact not only as each man held firm to his own religious tradition, but as Rosenzweig engaged in a passionate love affair with Rosenstock's wife, Gritli (née Huessy)—often under the careful eye of Eugen himself. The newly published volume of letters of Rosenzweig to Gritli sheds light on her central role in Rosenzweig's intellectual and erotic life.[62] Indeed, it suggests that their affair may well have fueled the "dark drive" that animated Rosenzweig's new spiritual and intellectual direction.

Unfortunately, we cannot enter into an extended analysis of that complex relationship here. What is readily apparent and germane for us now is that Rosenzweig's relationship with Eugen Rosenstock-Huessy was one of ceaseless border crossing. In the more platonic realm of ideas, the two seemed to delight in transgressing boundaries—for instance, those separating Judaism and Christianity, history and religion, the old metaphysics and the new (as yet unnamed) existentialism. It is because of this constant boundary crossing that we will derive little benefit from merely stating that one of the two conversation partners ended up a devoted Protestant theologian and the other a devoted Jewish theologian. Mindful of the extraordinary nature of their relationship, Rosenstock-Huessy enigmatically insisted in 1969 that the "arsenals of modern historiography and biography have not yet developed tools" to trace the contours of the intellectual universe he created together with Rosenzweig.[63]

And yet, the following is known about that universe. First, both men were alumni of a German-Jewish *haute bourgeoisie*; like Rosenzweig, Rosenstock-Huessy was born to an affluent Jewish family in 1888. Second, the two were raised in and took flight from a world whose spiritual vacuity and material pursuit they derided. In a letter to Rosenzweig, Rosenstock-Huessy once pointed to the sorry state of their respective families: "My parents' home, like yours, finds itself in a state of self-disintegration, with its good-natured worship of cleverness."[64] Third, this worship of cleverness, which the two men also found in abundance among the academic "doctors" who populated German universities, no longer sufficed. Rosenstock-Huessy, in particular, had little patience for the elaborate intellectual exercises of professional philosophers and theologians. Nor did he derive much succor from Judaism, of which he knew a most diluted version and out of which he converted at the age of seventeen. His life mission was to search for a starker and more immediate truth in Christianity. In time, he would realize and articulate this goal in his *Offenbarungsglaube*, or revelation-based faith.

Franz Rosenzweig, the peripatetic university student, apprehended that Rosenstock was on to something important. In 1913 he made his way to Leipzig where his new friend lectured in medieval law. The two met every day for lunch, conversing about their wide-ranging concerns in history, philosophy, and theology. Rosenstock offered Rosenzweig a compelling response to the deep intellectual and spiritual void into which he had fallen. His embrace of Christianity seemed so passionate and sincere—and so purposive in an age of anomie—that Rosenzweig decided, after a lengthy conversation on the night of July 7, 1913, to follow Rosenstock's course.

The impetus was not only the prospect of spiritual fulfillment, but also a new intellectual probity. The move toward faith hinted at release from the bonds of relativism. As Rosenzweig relates in a letter to his cousin Rudolf Ehrenberg: "In that night conversation in Leipzig [on July 7, 1913], Rosenstock pushed me step by step from the last relativist positions that I held to a thoroughly unrelativist standpoint."[65] Rosenstock, for his part, later explained the frame of mind in which he and Rosenzweig found themselves at the time:

> We both were nearly drowned by a third force, neither Christian nor Jewish, the spirit of nineteenth-century positivism. Our brotherhood consisted in our, both of us, emerging in vigorous swimming from the abyss of this faithless, godless "world" without "star, love, Fortune." So our negation we had in common; and with regard to this negation, I was in the lead.[66]

This negation, which recalls Heidegger's later principle of *Destruktion*, sought to expose the danger lurking beneath the positivist spirit of the *Geisteswissenschaften*. Rosenstock was chiefly incensed at:

> the "objectivity" swindle of the academic class—"swindle" is perhaps too kind a word, since it implies that the culprits at least know what they are doing. . . . A Jew and a Christian momentarily put aside their insoluble antithesis and united against self-styled "humanists" of all descriptions and dispensations. In their enmity towards the idols of relativism (in which not even Einstein believed), "objectivity" (largely spurious at best), abstract and nameless statistics (largely meaningless at best), the Jew and the Christian found a cause in common.[67]

Rosenstock's critique of the emptiness of the *Geisteswissenschaften*, with their hyperscientistic aspiration, riveted Franz Rosenzweig. Rosenstock was certain that the path back from the abyss of objectivity led to Christianity. He had begun to develop his notion of an *Offenbarungsglaube*, a faith based on the factuality and continual reexperiencing of Revelation.[68] This new theological stance was of great appeal to Franz Rosenzweig in the summer of 1913. Having indicated four years earlier that he understood the rationale for a Jew converting, he now felt that baptism was the only viable course for *him* as well. And so, Rosenzweig engaged in the famous, and soon-to-be aborted, act of entering Christianity—in his distinctive way, as a Jew rather than as a pagan.[69]

When Rosenzweig chose to step back from the baptismal font in October 1913, his decision deeply disappointed Eugen Rosenstock and the brothers Ehrenberg. They would persist in their efforts to persuade Franz to convert over the years, testimony not only to their personal theological commitment, but perhaps to their desire for self-legitimation as well. In this regard, it does not suffice to depict Rosenzweig's relationship with them as a battle among unequals—that is, of a Jew (such as Moses Mendelssohn) struggling to enter a "neutral society" only to discover that the "ticket of admission" (à la Heine) was conversion. Rosenzweig's Protestant friends, themselves converts, occupied treacherous theological terrain. Their anxieties and insecurities about the nature of faith were at times as substantial as his—not only because they were converts, but also because of the general sense of crisis pervading Christian culture in their day. In fact, it was the deep existential uncertainty they faced that lent such urgency to their own spiritual quest. And it was this same quality, together with a set of profoundly intimate personal relationships that lent explosive energy to their interaction with Rosenzweig.

As Rosenzweig once wrote to Rudolf Ehrenberg, during the difficult period in 1913 when he was contemplating conversion, "I never for a minute saw before me Christ himself, but always only Eugen [Rosenstock], and next to him you, though first and foremost Eugen."[70] This revealing personalization of his theological meditations did not cease after the tumultuous summer/fall of 1913. He and Rosenstock continued to debate the merits of their respective theological positions in later years, as we know from their published correspondence of 1916. Notwithstanding their theological differences, Rosenzweig had great affection for Rosenstock, which was surpassed perhaps only by his affection for Rosenstock's wife, Gritli. When not in the physical presence of one another, the three wrote letters on a daily basis. This remarkable epistolary output hints at an intimate cultural space inhabited by Franz, Eugen, and Gritli in their shared quest for spiritual—and also sensual—fulfillment.

If Rosenzweig's Christian friends exemplified the allures of their chosen faith, another individual whom Rosenzweig encountered in 1913 personified the virtues of Judaism. In late October Rosenzweig wrote to his mother in still tentative terms that "I hope to have found the path of return."[71] In the next month, he made his way to Hermann Cohen's seminar at the Lehranstalt für die Wissenschaft des Judentums. As he later recalled, his encounter with Cohen there was "the turning point in my Jewish life."[72] For it was Cohen who helped Rosenzweig forge a convincing Jewish response to his overlapping crises of faith and identity. Newly fortified in his decision not to convert, Rosenzweig joined Cohen on the path toward Jewish enrichment—and away from the detritus of historicist fragmentation.

## Between Periphery and Center: The Return to
## Judaism and the Flight from History

Despite Hermann Cohen's reputation as the paragon of German *Kathederphilosophie*, Rosenzweig discovered in the Lehranstalt classroom a thinker for whom ideas were far more than exercises in academic nimbleness. As he recalled of Cohen's lectures in Berlin: "The thing that, disenchanted with the present, I had long searched for only in the writings of the great dead—the strict scholarly spirit hovering over the deep of an inchoate, chaotically teeming reality—I now saw face to face in the living flesh."[73] Cohen's sober recognition of the importance, and real-life consequences, of ideas stood in constructive tension with his volcanic intellectual temperament. Jacques Derrida argues that this volcanic temperament—this "ruptivity" or "dissociative and irruptive power"—not only characterized Cohen's thought but, more broadly, "determines the Jewish in the German."[74] Further, Derrida suggests that it was this quality—quite at odds with Cohen's reputation as the grand harmonizer of *Deutschtum* and *Judentum*—that Rosenzweig apprehended in his new mentor. In fact, Rosenzweig recalled Cohen less as a tired soldier of the German-Jewish old guard than as the very model of Jewish integrity and authenticity.[75] Cohen performed a pair of vital functions for Rosenzweig during the latter's re-formation as a Jew: he was both a guide to the venerable religious and philosophical traditions of classical Judaism and a partner in the spiritual revitalization of a debilitated contemporary Judaism.

In their portentous meeting in 1913, Cohen and Rosenzweig shared a sense of the dangers facing Jewish spiritual life in their day. Foremost among them was the growing attraction that Zionism held for alienated young Jews in Germany. To the extent that Zionism sought to return the Jewish people to history—from its extraterritorial and extratemporal Exile—both Cohen and Rosenzweig found common cause in opposing it. For both believed fervently in the possibility of a rich spiritual and cultural existence for Jews in the Diaspora.[76]

Connected to this shared concern over Zionism was their concern for the hegemonic claims of historicism. As we have seen in the last chapter, these two sources of opposition—Zionism and historicism—merged in Cohen's thinking. Jewish nationalism was the content, and historicism the form, of a base materialism that undermined the ethical grandeur of Judaism. In Rosenzweig's case, Zionism belied the existence of Jews beyond *Geschichte*, whereas historicism bespoke the hubris of a modern discipline—*Historie*—that often misapprehended the nature of religious experience.

Particularly on this latter point, Rosenzweig had much in common with his other major guide from 1913, Eugen Rosenstock-Huessy. In fact, all three—Cohen, Rosenstock, and Rosenzweig—took aim over the next five years at the leading practitioners of the history of Christianity. Hermann Cohen, we may recall, mounted a counterattack to Ernst Troeltsch's attempt in 1916 to situate the great Hebrew prophets in the local context of rural Palestine. In the same year, Rosenzweig and Rosenstock engaged in an intense exchange of letters, one of whose leitmotivs was the historicization of Christianity. In a letter from October 28, 1913, Rosenstock castigated Troeltsch's fellow standard-bearer of *Kulturprotestantismus*, Adolf von Harnack. Rosenstock maintained that Harnack's attempt to understand the "essence of Christianity" through history was doomed to failure. It was not that Harnack lacked piety altogether. In fact, Rosenstock claimed, Harnack was "a man of faith, but also, unfortunately, a man who has more respect for science than he does for God and for God's Word." Franz Rosenzweig responded by suggesting that Ernst Troeltsch was even worse than Harnack. Indeed, he was "the real Antichrist among the theologians" by virtue of his illusory desire to "establish the absolute character of Christianity in temporal terms."[77]

In the midst of this exchange, Rosenstock accused Rosenzweig, the former student of history at Freiburg, of harboring historicist impulses of his own. In one intemperate outburst, he exclaimed to Rosenzweig: "Man, how you treat History! How you see everything as isolated, as individuals, where I see only the branches of a mighty tree! . . . You are, in fact, Troeltsch *plus* Harnack."[78]

Rosenstock's provocation was not entirely groundless. Within the context of their unique intellectual relationship, Rosenzweig was more likely than Rosenstock to acknowledge the benefits of historical scholarship. And as we shall see, Rosenzweig himself engaged in a sort of intellectual history in his various writings, including the *Star of Redemption*. That said, Rosenzweig maintained a deep ambivalence toward history that was evident already from his early encounters with Rosenstock in Leipzig. On one hand, he recognized the epistemic unavoidability of ordering the world in historical terms; on the other hand, he recognized the epistemic artifice involved in such an ordering. In one enigmatic stream of thought from 1916, Rosenzweig captured this double-edged quality:

> Without (historical) scholarship each generation would run away from the preceding one, and history would seem to be a discontinuous series (as in fact it really is) and not (as it ought to appear) the parable of a single point, a *nunc stans* (as history really is in the final moment, but thanks to scholarship, as I have said, appears to be already in advance, here and now).[79]

Here Rosenzweig hints at what might be described later as a Gadamerian respect for the weight of tradition in framing historical understanding.[80] But on many other occasions, Rosenzweig proved less judicious with respect to modern historical scholarship. One of the most interesting and germane occasions was the first essay Rosenzweig wrote after his spiritual upheaval of 1913. This essay, "Atheistische Theologie" ("Atheistic Theology"), was solicited by Martin Buber for a yearbook he started entitled *Vom Judentum*. Rosenzweig's contribution remained unpublished in its day. Not only did Buber refuse to accept the piece (which implicitly criticized Buber's Zionism), but the journal itself never appeared.[81]

Notwithstanding its obscurity at the time, "Atheistic Theology" provides an illuminating lens into Franz Rosenzweig's state of mind in the spring of 1914. The essay is, by turns, terse and dense, lucid and disjointed. It reflects both the bewilderment and emerging direction of a young intellectual recently cast adrift, but slowly making his way to shore. Moreover, it reveals clear signs of Rosenzweig's encounters with Eugen Rosenstock and Hermann Cohen in1913, especially with respect to his growing agitation over historicism and Zionism.

The burden of Rosenzweig's essay was to dissect two forms of "atheistic theologies" prevalent in his day. It is a measure of the centrality of Protestant theological concerns—and of Rosenstock—in Rosenzweig's thinking that he commences his analysis with a discussion of the "Life of Jesus" trend in Christian scholarship. Tracing a trajectory from H. S. Reimarus through D. F. Strauss and Ernest Renan, Rosenzweig notes the tendency of these scholars to equate the essence of Christianity's teachings with the human personality of Jesus. With the sensitivity of a trained historian Rosenzweig calls attention to the Romanticist emphasis on "individuality" in this tradition. And yet, with the steely eye of an astute critic, Rosenzweig also calls attention to the troubling incommensurability of such a perspective—according to which "personality remains locked within the walls of its own individuality." This quality led Rosenzweig to question a core premise of the "Life of Jesus" movement: namely, that a mundane and individualistic historicism could coexist with the universal scope of religion. He readily confessed that he did not share the regnant "confidence with which one believed oneself able to craft the result of critical historical science within faith's holy of holies."[82]

On the contrary, Rosenzweig regarded this confidence as the product of historicism's epistemological audacity. After all, it issued from the modern tendency "to understand the Divine as the self-projection of the human," or what Rosenzweig called a bit later "the monstrous birth of the Divine out of the human."[83] But such an anthropocentric outlook only obscured the deep grounding of faith in the formative experience of Revelation.

This preconscious (and post-Kantian) notion of Revelation found no place in the new Christian historicism. Nor did it find a place in the second case of "atheistic theology" that Rosenzweig examined in his 1914 article: Jewish nationalism. In discussing this latter phenomenon, Rosenzweig insisted that there was no direct Jewish parallel to the nineteenth-century "Life of Jesus" scholarly movement—and in particular, no contemporary parallel to its emphasis on individual personality. Had he been aware of S. R. Hirsch's criticism of Heinrich Graetz's treatment of the Oral Law, he might have thought otherwise. Instead, he made only brief reference to the "flight to detailed historical research" by German Jews in the second half of the nineteenth century—and remarked that Hermann Cohen had already begun to reorient the focus of Jewish scholars back to a more profound philosophical engagement with Judaism.[84]

Rosenzweig's chief concern was the new Jewish quasi-theology of his day that threatened to depart from the centrality of Revelation. This was the "Jewish people" (*Volksjudentum*) movement, clearly associated with the unnamed force of Zionism. Whereas the "Life of Jesus" movement had humanized the Divine (in the form of Jesus), the *Volksjudentum* movement had engaged in the inverse act of deifying the human (in the form of the Jewish nation). Both movements followed a well-trodden historicist path and based their existence on a celebration of the role of personality—individual and collective respectively.

More gravely, both movements—and for that matter, the entirety of humankind—labored under "the curse of historicity." This curse, we might extrapolate from Rosenzweig, had two faces. It was a curse of cognition—of apprehending the world in an unfailingly historicist way. And it was a curse of contingency—of living life within the temporal borders framed by Revelation and the Messianic days.[85] Ultimately, Rosenzweig believed, this two-sided curse would dissipate in the face of Divine omnipotence. In fact, he concluded "Atheistic Theology" with something of a taunt: One could continue to believe in the alliance of theology and science, of faith and history. But one could "never circumvent the notion of Revelation."[86]

This newly emboldened theological stance—inspired by both Rosenstock and Cohen—provided Rosenzweig with an anchor of stability in an increasingly tumultuous world. Several months after writing "Atheistic Theology," the First World War broke out and, shortly thereafter, Rosenzweig was sent to Belgium as a Red Cross nurse. A year later, in September 1915, he enlisted in the German army and served in a variety of locales, including the Balkan front, until his release in December 1918. Throughout the war years, Rosenzweig, and German-Jewish intellectuals more generally, were impelled to revisit the assumptions and allegiances that guided their forebears over the previous century and a half. For Rosenzweig, this reevaluation was less a matter of confronting the staggering physical, psychic, and moral costs of the war. In contrast to other Jews of a more radical political orientation (such as socialists and Zionists), Rosenzweig neither sought deferment from nor inveighed against the immorality of the War.[87] In fact, it is striking to see how thoroughly apolitical his rebellion against the bourgeois sensibilities of his parents was—quite unlike that of other rebels like Gershom Scholem, Walter Benjamin, and Gustav Landauer who diverged from the German-Jewish mainstream by disavowing the war effort.[88]

And yet, if the war per se did not incite Rosenzweig to political activism, it did widen his developing commitment to Judaism in several interesting —and counterintuitive—ways. First, while conditions on the Front were far from ideal, Rosenzweig was able to achieve a remarkable state of concentration and even tranquillity, as demonstrated by his voluminous and rich letters. By his own account, Rosenzweig lived a "hermit's existence" in the Balkans, which afforded him ample time to deepen his knowledge of and write about Judaism.[89] Second, in the course of his wartime travels, Rosenzweig encountered Jews who were quite unlike those he found at home. Both the Sephardic communities of the Balkans and the Jewish communities of Poland revealed a world of ritual comfort, communal solidity, and spiritual authenticity that Rosenzweig had never before witnessed. Rather than express scorn for what others regarded as the cultural primitivity of these communities, Rosenzweig felt pride for the integrity of Jewish life within them. And this sentiment gave force to a third effect of the war upon Rosenzweig: his growing sense that the path to a meaningful Jewish existence lay between the poles of assimilation, on one hand, and Zionism, on the other.[90] Rosenzweig was well aware that there was a pitched struggle for the souls of his generation of disaffected Jews. We may recall that the battle lines had been clearly drawn in the famous polemic between the anti-Zionist Hermann Cohen and the Zionist Martin Buber in 1916. Rosenzweig charted a third path that resisted both the ideal of full social integration and that of Zionist immigration to Palestine.[91] Already at this point, Rosenzweig had arrived at a recognition that would become a cornerstone of his more fully developed thought in the *Star of Redemption*: namely, that the diaspora, which had been the source of Jewish vitality in the past, could remain the locus of a vibrant Judaism in the future. What Rosenzweig now felt was necessary to assure this ongoing vitality was a renewed commitment to—indeed, a revolution in—Jewish education.

Rosenzweig had begun to inquire about existing patterns of Jewish education in Germany in correspondence with his parents from the summer and fall of 1916. A little less than a year later, in March 1917, he proposed a far-reaching set of reforms for Jewish education in Germany. Typically, this proposal was addressed in epistolary form. However, the addressee was no ordinary correspondent. It was Rosenzweig's one-time mentor, Hermann Cohen. Mindful that assimilation more than Zionism threatened the majority of German Jewry, Rosenzweig turned to Cohen as the "intellectual leader" of assimilated German Jewry. His hope was to save those who languished, as he once had, at the periphery of their own tradition.

Rosenzweig's proposal, which was soon published under the title *Zeit ists* (*It Is Time*), had a dramatic effect.[92] According to a close colleague, Ernst Simon, it placed "the previously unknown author all at once at the center of attention of German Jewish culture."[93] With bold precision, the young soldier laid out an agenda for the revival of Jewish learning as part of a larger mission to carve out a discrete "Jewish world" (a term that recurs frequently in *Zeit ists*) within the territorial and cultural boundaries of Germany.[94] The letter's first part included a detailed program for Jewish religious instruction at the primary and secondary school levels. At the core of this program was the demand to move beyond superficial learning to a deeper familiarity with the Hebrew language, the Jewish prayer book, and the classical sources of Judaism, preeminently the Torah.

The second part of the proposal dealt with the mechanism to implement this program. Rosenzweig called for the creation of a new cadre of teacher-scholars (150 in number) who would guide the spiritual and intellectual agenda of the revitalized Jewish community.[95] While receiving training similar to that of rabbis in Germany, the new teacher-scholars would also be conversant in the methods of critical scholarship. Their home would be neither a rabbinical seminary nor, for the time being, a theological faculty attached to a German university. Rather, it would be a new Academy of Jewish Science (Akademie für die Wissenschaft des Judentums) in which the cadre of teacher-scholars could study and research without concern for material sustenance.[96]

Here is a first articulate sign of what Rosenzweig would later call the "New Learning" (*neues Lernen*) required for Jewish cultural revival. Curiously, the institutional framework he favored in 1917 was an Academy of Jewish *Science*, even though he and Eugen Rosenstock had spent a good portion of the previous year assaulting the scientific pretenses of the German humanities. In fact, Rosenzweig wrote in "Zeit ists" that he feared that Jewish scholarship—*Wissenschaft des Judentums*—might go the way of Christian scholarship. This would mean producing "[s]cholars with great sagacity and erudition, but little understanding and sympathy for the peculiarities of Jewish religious thinking."[97] Here, Rosenzweig might well have expected little encouragement from the proposal's initial recipient, Hermann Cohen, who had always been a firm believer in the ameliorative value of *Wissenschaft*. However, he could reasonably expect that Cohen would join him around the point of historicism's exaggerated role in the field of Jewish studies and, more generally, in prevailing conceptions of Judaism.

Rosenzweig recalled several months after writing "Zeit ists" that he consciously desired to "place the (classical) sources in the center and history on the margins." The reason, he wrote, was that history is "a double-edged sword [that] can more easily lead astray than fortify one who has no connection to Judaism other than through it."[98] As we noted in the last chapter, in 1917 Hermann Cohen had also expounded on the theme of historicism's degradation of Judaism by summoning up the legacy of his one-time teacher in Breslau, Heinrich Graetz. But perhaps even more apposite, Cohen gave voice more than a decade earlier to the fear that the philosophical exploration of Judaism had followed the historicist turn of the nineteenth century. That is, the philosophy of religion—here Judaism—had yielded to the *history* of the philosophy of religion.[99] Of course, we must recall that Cohen did not dismiss the value of historical study altogether. He acknowledged its worth, particularly as an auxiliary discipline within the *Geisteswissenschaften*. Moreover, like Rosenzweig, he made recourse to a certain kind of historical labor—the construction of intellectual lineages—in unraveling his philosophical ideas. For a man of Cohen's intellectual breeding, it was simply impossible to avoid altogether the dominant mode of historical cognition.

That said, Cohen was obviously concerned about the corrosive effects of historicism—originally, upon philosophy, and later upon Judaism. Franz Rosenzweig too feared for the integrity of Judaism in the face of historicism. The two men's shared apprehension over historicism is an important, if largely ignored, ingredient in their personal and intellectual relationship. Indeed, if Rosenzweig's goal in "Zeit ists" was, at least in part, to shunt history to the margins, it is not surprising that Cohen responded so favorably. For he too believed that a substantial reorientation of Jewish education was necessary, one that entailed less historicist dissection and more direct engagement with living Judaism. And he concurred with Rosenzweig that the ideal institutional framework for this reorientation was not a rabbinical seminary or a German university, but rather a self-standing Jewish academy.[100]

The upheaval of the war years posed a challenge to sweeping proposals for cultural or spiritual revival such as Rosenzweig's. And yet, it was in the conditions of turmoil that a dizzying array of creative responses both during and after the war surfaced, particularly by Jews. In writing of the Weimar period, Peter Gay notes that the "overflowing plenty of stimuli, of artistic, scientific, commercial improvisations . . . stemmed from the talents of this sector of the population."[101] Shortly before the advent of the Weimar Republic, in the final year of the war, a group of Berlin Jews, emboldened by Hermann Cohen's endorsement of Rosenzweig's proposal, began to meet with the goal of laying the conceptual and institutional foundation for a new center of Jewish learning. Shortly thereafter, in April 1918, the octogenarian Cohen passed away. But the group continued its planning and fund-raising efforts, and in May 1919, the Akademie für die Wissenschaft des Judentums was formally constituted in Berlin.

In the course of the group's deliberations, Rosenzweig's original ideal had been dramatically reformulated. Absent Cohen's inspiration and moral authority, the Akademie became the opposite of the institution that Rosenzweig had once envisaged.[102] Not only had the scale been reduced. Its function was reconceived altogether, and now followed a pattern consistent with trends in German academic culture at the time. Thus, the newly opened Akademie, under the guidance of the ancient historian Eugen Täubler, became a research institute devoted to pure historical scholarship, without any pedagogic or communal responsibilities.[103] In what was surely a cruel turn for Rosenzweig, the Akademie had become the very embodiment of Jewish historicism.

Rosenzweig fought this development in committee meetings, but to no avail. Holding firm to his ambition of revolutionizing Jewish education, he shifted his sights from Berlin to Frankfurt am Main, whose Jewish community was interested in creating a new-style center for Jewish learning. A month before the Akademie opened in Berlin, Rosenzweig visited Frankfurt and met Nehemia Nobel (1871–1922), a philosophically trained Orthodox rabbi who would became a mentor and friend. It was Nobel who arranged the union between Rosenzweig and the Frankfurt Jews intent on enhancing adult Jewish learning in Frankfurt. Out of this union arose, in the summer of 1920, a new institution, the Freies Jüdisches Lehrhaus, which Rosenzweig joined as founding director.[104] It was this institution, and not the Berlin Akademie, that embodied many of Rosenzweig's most valued educational tenets. Concomitantly, it was the Lehrhaus that offered a new mode of Jewish learning, a post-historicist mode that eschewed scholarly convention in the name of a direct encounter with the classical sources of Judaism.

Rosenzweig's guiding motto, as announced in his inaugural address of 17 October 1920, was "[f]rom the periphery back to the center, from the outside in."[105] His intended audience at the Lehrhaus was the large pool of Jewish adults drifting aimlessly in the sea of German culture. Rosenzweig was undaunted by the Jewish ignorance of these people. He sought to transform it into a virtue by arguing that the diverse life experiences of the alienated Jew must be brought back home to enrich the study of

Torah. Rosenzweig went so far as to recommend that teachers at the Lehr-haus, with few exceptions, be devoid of Jewish learning.[106] Herein lay his desire to dig beneath the layers of intellectual fashion and scholarly detachment to gain access to the deepest habits of mind and heart conditioned by experience.[107] This desire came to inform learning at the Lehr-haus, where as many as 1,100 students studied each semester with lay teachers, often in small, intensive seminars.[108]

As Lehrhaus students from various walks of life made their way from the periphery to the center, Rosenzweig and his colleagues acted upon his ambition of pushing history in a reverse direction. The study of Jewish history was not altogether absent, though it paled in comparison to the course hours devoted to the main subjects of Hebrew language and Bible.[109] More importantly, Nahum Glatzer, Rosenzweig's close disciple, reported that at the Lehrhaus, "historicism, so typical of the Science of Judaism, was carefully avoided."[110] This preference followed the path of Franz Rosenzweig's own journey. His passage from the margins of alienation to the center of an integral "Jewish world" was accompanied, perhaps even hastened, by the retreat of history from the center to the periphery of his intellectual worldview.

Rosenzweig brought symbolic closure to his historicist allegiances in a well-known letter to Friedrich Meinecke from this period. While preparing the ground for the soon-to-open Lehrhaus in the summer of 1920, Rosenzweig saw to the publication of his revised doctoral dissertation, *Hegel und der Staat*. His doctoral supervisor, Meinecke, was most impressed with Rosenzweig's philosophical and historical acuity, and offered to arrange a university lectureship for him. In a letter from August 30, 1920, Rosenzweig politely declined. It was here that he wrote to Meinecke of the "dark drive" that had impelled important changes in his life since his studies in Freiburg. In the wake of his "collapse" of 1913, Rosenzweig related that "I suddenly found myself on a heap of wreck-age"—a mound of historical data that exercised his talents more than his passions. Prior to that time, Rosenzweig admitted, his work as an historian satisfied "my hunger for forms, my insatiable receptivity." But after the collapse, he realized that "history to me was a purveyor of forms, no more." Subsequently, he embarked on a search for *content* that led, after several tumultuous turns, to the discovery of "my Judaism." In the process, he was transformed from an eminently employable historian into a proudly unemployable philosopher. He had little doubt that the rewards of this transition far outweighed the detriments. Indeed, he announced to Meinecke with a measure of contentment and resolution about his new direction: "it seems to me that I am today more firmly rooted in the earth than I was seven years ago."[111]

FIGURE 3   Franz Rosenzweig (1886–1929). Courtesy of the
Leo Baeck Institute, New York.

## "BREAKING THROUGH THE SHACKLES OF TIME":
## ROSENZWEIG'S JUDAISM BEYOND HISTORY

Rosenzweig's sense of grounding is curious given the tenuous foundations
of the new Weimar regime (established in November 1918). The ironic
sense of solidity was surely a relief to Rosenzweig, who like many intellectuals of the day, had spent the decade from 1910 to 1920 engaged in an
intense, exhilarating, and enervating self-search.[112] Even as he noticed the
signs of social, political, and intellectual crisis in his midst—and as others
fell victim to a new *Kulturpessimissmus*—Rosenzweig was impelled by
the spirit of innovation in Weimar to push forward with grand solutions

to the problems of Judaism. Both the founding of the Lehrhaus and the publication in 1921 of his *Stern der Erlösung* (though written mainly in 1917–19) represented bold attempts at such solutions, and strengthened Rosenzweig's reputation as one of the leading thinkers on the German-Jewish scene.

In pursuit of one of our narrative trails, it makes sense to situate Rosenzweig's own creative responses alongside a school of Protestant thought that deeply imbibed the Weimar mandate for radical innovation. Assembled under the rubric of the "theology of crisis," this group of thinkers sought new outlets for their simmering discontent with previous modes of theological discourse. Rosenzweig's Protestant friends Rosenstock-Huessy and the Ehrenberg brothers manifested strong hints of this distaste before and during the war. The three formed the nucleus of a study group known as Patmos that was devoted to exploring new pathways of theological inquiry. We hear fleeting mention of Patmos from another Protestant intellectual who met its members in 1920 and was destined to become the most important and influential theologian of his era: Karl Barth (1886–1968).[113]

It was Barth who galvanized the rising chorus of dissent into a coherent call for Protestant theological renewal. Barth's main emphasis, in an age of fierce skepticism, was to assert the absolute transcendence of God—and by consequence, the fundamental incapacity of humans to know God in any meaningful affirmative sense.[114] Central to this stance was a double-edged criticism: first, of the interpretive naïveté of traditional Christian views of faith; and second, of the interpretive hubris of modern philosophers and historians of religion. Barth was particularly unsettled by the latter, who, he argued, revolted against the authority of God through their anthropocentric refashioning of the Christian tradition. Likewise, he objected to the desire of liberal Christians, such as the adepts of *Kulturprotestantismus*, to create a secular culture informed by the ethical values of Christianity. These efforts represented the height of modern arrogance. They also represented a profound category error, for human actions, Barth insisted, were of an absolutely different and lower order than the realm of Divine action.

True faith was only possible through an acknowledgement of the vast gulf between human and God, followed by "the negation of all human aspirations" vis-à-vis God.[115] Through this total negation, and only through it, lay access to Revelation. Some branded this new stance, with its unbridgeable gulf between God and human, a "dialectical theology"; others regarded Karl Barth as the initiator of a "neo-Orthodox" current in Christianity. Although he never fully embraced either term, it is clear that Barth's notion of a stark divide between the human and Divine marked a departure from liberal Protestant theology of the nineteenth and early twentieth centuries.[116]

A signal feature of Barth's teaching was his strong impulse to root theological precepts in a new pastoral praxis. In the first instance, this entailed a new mode of reading Scripture, which Barth sought to instill in himself:

> We tried to learn our theological ABCs all over again, beginning by reading and interpreting the writing of the Old and New Testaments, more thoughtfully than ever before. And lo and behold, they began to speak to us—but not as we thought we must have heard them in the school of what was then "modern theology."[117]

Barth conveyed the importance of the return to the Bible to his parishioners in Switzerland, mainly through carefully sculpted and text-centered sermons. He also set out to develop a new approach to biblical commentary that explicitly abandoned the lens of the enlightened modern reader. To exemplify this method, he undertook a searching commentary upon Paul's Letter to the Romans, the first version of which was published as *Der Römerbrief* (Epistle to the Romans) in 1919, and the second and substantially revised edition in 1922.

Barth's *Epistle to the Romans*, especially the second edition, placed him in the vanguard of "the search for a new paradigm of [Protestant] theology."[118] With unrelenting force, he bore through the thick historical and interpretive soil to reach Paul, whose recognition of the "infinite qualitative difference between time and eternity" was identical to his own. His method required effacing the boundary between author and reader, subject and object, to the point that the present-day observer would be able to claim that "I know the author [of a past text] so well that I allow him to speak in my name and am even able to speak in his name myself."[119] To a great extent, this method signaled what we might call a re-protestantization of scriptural commentary—a renewed attempt at *sola Scriptura*. At the same time, Barth seemed to be approaching a radically historicist hermeneutic that enabled understanding of past texts as their own authors had understood them. Toward that end, he did not hesitate to use history and philology to clear away the interpretive underbrush in the name of a purer "exegetical, dogmatic, and practical theology."[120]

And yet, Barth was the leader not only of a new school of Protestant thought, but of a group renowned for its fierce criticism of historicism. He stated without equivocation that church history did not represent "an independent theological discipline."[121] And he stridently opposed the efforts to historicize inspired religious figures, primarily Jesus, that had consumed modern Protestant scholars before him. At the heart of his objection lay a key distinction between the "historical" and the "non-historical." The first represented an often jumbled "plurality of different and incommunicable elements, of separate individuals, ages, periods, relationships, and institutions." The second was "the veritable substance and quality of all history," the radiant and ultimately incomprehensible source of unity in the world. Barth illustrated these two modes in the *Römerbrief* with reference to the biblical patriarch Abraham:

> In times of spiritual poverty, historical analysis is a method we are bound to adopt. But one day it will itself reach its limit, and must, to take a single instance, pronounce Abraham's personality to be unhistorical; and then it too will stand before the same commanding necessity of a synthesis which is the starting-point of the Book of Genesis.[122]

At the present time, the "non-historical" Abraham was beyond the grasp of the "historical" mindset. Barth was not alone in perceiving this moment of "spiritual poverty." Other Protestant thinkers like Rudolf Bultmann, Friedrich Gogarten, and Emil Brunner believed with equal fervor that a major factor in the current theological crisis was the pernicious influence of historicism. On one hand, its relativist methods afforded the genuine seeker of faith "no absolute standpoint" for his/her quest. On the other hand, history and its sister discipline philology bred, in the vivid image of F. W. Graf, "a kind of pathology of the necrophiliac theological archivist."[123] As a remedy, Barth and a group of fellow "theological anti-historicists" created a new journal in 1922 entitled *Zwischen den Zeiten* (*Between the Times*). The journal took its name from a 1920 essay by Gogarten, in which he declared: "It is the destiny of our generation to stand between the times. We never belonged to the period presently coming to an end; it is doubtful whether we shall ever belong to the period which is to come. . . . So we stand in the middle—in an empty space."[124]

The status of being caught "between the times," between past and future, reflected a vexing predicament for this cohort of new theologians. For all of their interest in achieving a trans-historical state of *Übergeschichtlichkeit*, and for all of their disdain for the atomizing and mind-numbing methods of historians, they were inescapably caught in the current of history. As a function of their own contingency, they made recourse to historicist methods, if only to pry open the passageway to a "post-historical" theology.[125]

I have elaborated on this conundrum in Protestant theology not only because it is key to understanding the early twentieth-century crisis of historicism, but also because it sheds important light on Franz Rosenzweig's own evolution as a critic of historicism. It would be too facile to cast Rosenzweig as a mere appendage to the Protestant anti-historicists of the postwar period. It would be equally facile to insist on total harmony between him and his Protestant contemporaries.[126] And yet, it would be irresponsible to ignore the fact that Rosenzweig belonged to the same cultural-intellectual milieu as his Protestant contemporaries. Insofar as Judaism and Christianity both sought, as he put it, "to overcome the fixity of a religious institution, and to return to the open field of reality," his theological agenda overlapped substantially with that of his Protestant colleagues.[127]

This should not come as a surprise, since we have seen how Franz Rosenzweig confronted the deepest questions of intellectual and spiritual direction in the company of his close Protestant friends from 1910 until 1917. His connections to Barth and the later "dialectical theologians" were less direct, though strong circumstantial bonds linked them. Rosenzweig and Barth were not only born in the same year (1886), but more importantly, both consciously rebelled against the liberal orthodoxies of their parents' generation. Whereas Rosenzweig rejected the rationalist-integrationist creed of the German-Jewish *Bildungsbürgertum*, Barth renounced the critical scholarly ambitions of his theological elders. That is not to say that Rosenzweig and Barth found no common ground with the preceding generation. After all, Rosenzweig shared with Hermann Cohen an aversion for the hegemony of historicism; and Barth developed a similar aversion in the course of his theological studies with Cohen's Marburg colleague Wilhelm Hermann.[128] All four—teachers and students—came to regard Ernst Troeltsch as the personification of the historicist debasement of religious faith. However, the younger pair experienced a far graver crisis of liberal faith than their mentors. And their response was far sharper. Rosenzweig and Barth embarked upon—and advocated for others—a path of return to a religious experience rooted in engagement with classical sources and, above all, in the overwhelming centrality of Revelation. This meant positing a somewhat illiberal vision of a divine power that was not a suitable partner for human dialogue. As Randi Rashkover points out in her recent study of Barth and Rosenzweig, the two held to the view that revelation was the act of a God "who loves humankind in his freedom and who expresses his love by issuing a divine command." This command was not an invitation to conversation, but rather to submission.[129]

Essential to the task of submission was the surrender of academic pretenses and disciplinary tools acquired through years of university study, particularly those of history. The new modes of apprehending the world that Barth and Rosenzweig deemed imperative for spiritual renewal required an abandonment of the fragmenting methods and mundane causal schemes of historicism. This twinning of spiritual renewal and anti-historicism served as a common thread in their theological projects during the last years of the First World War and the early years of the Weimar Republic. With traces of affinity to an earlier, Nietzschean age of discontent, these projects nonetheless emerged out of, and then responded to, what Ernst Troeltsch called *the* crisis of historicism.

The years 1917–21, framed by the conception and publication of the *Star of Redemption*, were an impressively productive era for Franz Rosenzweig. This was a period in which Rosenzweig solidified both his own theological stance and his position as a leader of a new generation of German Jews hungry for intellectual and spiritual sustenance. It was also a period in which Rosenzweig passed from being a skeptic of historicist relativism to a mature critic of historicism. And yet, we must proceed with care lest we cast Rosenzweig's anti-historicism in overly simplistic terms. Like many of his contemporaries, Rosenzweig could abandon neither the overarching concept nor the techniques of history altogether.

This ironic repulsion by and embrace of history, so characteristic of Rosenzweig's era, seems a bit less confounding in light of the thinking of his philosophical contemporary Martin Heidegger. Heidegger's redefinition of Time as a series of continuous movements—rather than as a series of isolated single moments—entailed a clear rejection of the fragmentary nature of *Historie*. As such, Heidegger had little patience either for standard historical practice or for theorizing about history in its turn-of-the-century forms. By contrast, he did advance a sweeping notion of *Geschichte* that not only bound together past, present, and future, but also was equivalent to human existence itself: "History as *Geschichte* signifies a happening that we ourselves are, where we are there present. . . . We *are* history, that is, our own past. Our future lives out of its past. We are carried by the past."[130]

Far from signifying a retreat from the historical, Heidegger's idea of Time contained a radical historicality (*Geschichtlichkeit*), a deep embeddedness in the realm of the temporal. The effect, as Bambach notes, was to transform "the meaning of history from a question of logical method and scientific research to an ontological exploration of the roots of human being in the world."[131]

Franz Rosenzweig did not replicate Heidegger's distinctive language or philosophical mission. But he, along with Karl Barth and the new cohort of Protestant theologians, shared Heidegger's belief that an obsessive concern with the methods of history had obstructed the search for "the roots of human being in the world." Notwithstanding their different philosophical and theological emphases, Heidegger and Rosenzweig both spoke of a vital domain of existence beyond the grasp of historicism.

In Rosenzweig's case, we hear mention of this domain in the letter cum manifesto that he wrote to Rudolf Ehrenberg on November 18, 1917. What is important to note here is that this letter not only served as the blueprint (or *Urzelle*, as it came to be known) for his later *Star of Redemption*. It also served to indicate that Rosenzweig, after years of intellectual turmoil, had found his "long sought after philosophical Archimedean point."[132] Building on his 1914 essay "Atheistic Theology," Rosenzweig identified this point in Revelation, which marked the balance between the termini of creation and redemption. Seen from this perspective, Revelation was "a *center* point, a fixed immovable centerpoint." Revelation was also, in Rosenzweig's lexicon, the source of "pure factuality" (*reine Tatsächlichkeit*)—a phrase that evokes comparison to Heidegger's notion of *Geschichtlichkeit*.[133] Rosenzweig's use of this term likely owes to Friedrich Schelling (1775–1854), the great post-Enlightenment philosopher. Schelling's view that the "pure factuality" of existence precedes thought not only served as a foil to Hegel's Idealism, but proved compatible with Rosenzweig's own push beyond Idealism toward a theology of existence.[134]

It should be clear that the "pure factuality" that Rosenzweig (as well as his friend, Rosenstock) found in Revelation was quite distinct from the factuality of the historian. It signified a plane of existence that was not subject to the continuous, corrosive movement of time. And it was precisely that plane on which Rosenzweig—the theologian and not historian—now sought to locate the Jewish people.

In a series of lectures delivered in his hometown of Kassel in 1919–20, Rosenzweig began to map the Jewish people's path through and beyond history. These lectures reveal his concerted attempt to navigate around the reefs of Protestant theology and contemporary Jewish ideologies in order to assert a singular and inextinguishable Judaism. In a lecture on "Das Wesen des Judentums," he insisted, in defiance of Harnack's omnipresent formulation, that: "The goal is no 'essence' of Judaism, but rather a whole Judaism (*ganze Judentum*); no essence, but rather life."[135] The search for "essence," like the search for an authentic "standpoint" (*Standpunkt*) to grasp Judaism, was but a human effort that could barely comprehend the unique relationship between God and the Jewish people. It was the great error of nineteenth-century Jewish movements—chiefly Orthodoxy, Liberalism (i.e., Reform), and Zionism—to define the "essence" of Judaism in their own image precisely at the point that they were dividing Judaism into sectarian slivers. Indeed, each movement, in its quest for hegemony, was attacking the integrity and vitality of Judaism.

But so too were the historians. The attempt to situate Judaism in space and time—and above all, "within the framework of world history"— deeply disturbed Rosenzweig. It was this impulse that motivated a scholar such as Eugen Täubler, who had so drastically transformed Rosenzweig's plan for an Akademie für die Wissenschaft des Judentums in Berlin.[136] As against the historian's ideal of integrating Jewish history into world history, Rosenzweig declared in another Kassel lecture from 1920: "Jewish history—there really is none." Nor was there a sphere of "world-history"

(*Weltgeschichte*) independent of Jewish history. On the contrary, "world-history *is* Jewish history." Unlike many renderings of the term, Rosenzweig's *Weltgeschichte* did not refer principally to the past. Rather, "it is *now* (*sie ist jetzt*)"—a living present whose inhabitants long ago buried their one-time contemporaries (e.g., the Greeks).[137] In delivering a sweeping panorama of this unique and eternally present "world-history," Rosenzweig revealed to his Kassel audience an outlook quite unlike his earlier historicist stance.

Perhaps the most intriguing manifestation of this new outlook came in an earlier Kassel lecture from the fall of 1919, "Geist und Epochen der jüdischen Geschichte" ("Spirit and Epochs in Jewish History"). Similar to the lecture on *Weltgeschichte*, Rosenzweig began his discussion with a term—*Geist* (spirit)—that was widely used in his day. But he did not interpret *Geist* in a conventional modern sense—as in the "spirit of the time" or the "spirit of the people." Nor did his interest, or for that matter the word's true origins, lie "in Athens or Rome, but in our midst"—in the Hebrew sources, and particularly in the word *ruah*. This Hebrew word connoted the spirit of God, which served as the unifying bond of humanity.[138]

Rosenzweig contrasted this term to *Epochen*, historical periods that have the effect of dividing rather than uniting. But in a curious quasi-historicist move, Rosenzweig claimed that Spirit "creates for itself its existence in *historical epochs*." Moreover, this *Geist*, as the "continuation and heir" of the past, is dependent upon the past for its very self-understanding.[139] How then to make sense of the apparent conflation of *Geist* and *Epochen* in Rosenzweig's lecture?

At one level, Rosenzweig's effort to negotiate between a transcendent Spirit and time-bound periods was an attempt to reconcile his historicist and anti-historicist instincts. But interestingly, when Rosenzweig turned his attention specifically to "our Jewish history," as he called it, the distinction between *Geist* and *Epochen* reappeared—as a line of demarcation between Jews and the nations of the world.[149] Rosenzweig pointed out the centrality of the year 70 c.e.—the year in which the Second Temple was destroyed—in modern Jewish understandings of the past. Both Zionists and German-Jewish assimilationists clung to this date as the boundary between the two main (and hierarchically ordered) halves of Jewish history. For the Zionists, the pre-70 era, marked by territorial concentration in the ancestral homeland, was the font of inspiration for all subsequent Jewish history. For the assimilationists, the post-70 era established the pattern of dispersion among the nations through which Jews realized their most sublime ethical mission.[140] But such a division, Rosenzweig insisted, was faulty in both cases.

In support of this argument, Rosenzweig summoned up the legacy of Heinrich Graetz, the nineteenth-century historian to whom Hermann Cohen (and S. R. Hirsch before him) took such grave exception. Rosenzweig was particularly impressed that Graetz began his multi-volume history of the Jews in medias res, with a volume dealing with the Talmudic era, and not the birth of Israelite monotheism. Underlying this choice was Graetz's recognition that the Talmud served as a bridge between periods—that is, between the era of Jewish territorial centrality in Palestine and the era of rabbinic dominance in the Diaspora. But this perspective suggested to Rosenzweig a far deeper truth: namely, that the Talmudic era, "this high-point of Jewish history," represented the "overcoming of the powerful force of epochal division"—in other words, a manifestation of *Geist* revolting against the modern impulse to periodize and, hence, fragment.[141]

It is striking that Rosenzweig would enlist Heinrich Graetz to make this point. Not only had others castigated him as the arch-historicist. Rosenzweig did not even read carefully Graetz's multivolume history until 1922.[142] Nevertheless, Rosenzweig mobilized Graetz to show, as the latter had intended, that the rabbinic period was an era of glory rather than decline in the annals of the Jews.[143] He also used the cover of Graetz's historical authority to make a decidedly unhistoricist point about the Jews:

> History exercises its power over the nations via epochs, through which they pass from childhood to adulthood to old age and then death. But it is this power of history over the life of nations that is denied here. If the division into epochs is without force, so too is history. The power of history is broken precisely where the instruments of its power—the epochs—are snatched from its hands. And this is what the Talmud has done. It has assumed a place in the (life of the Jewish) nation that the year 70 has otherwise assumed in the history of the nations. A nation—but one that is free from the constraint of time, that same constraint to which all other nations are subject. A nation at once unique and eternal among the nations.[144]

With this forceful statement, Rosenzweig freed himself—and the Jewish people—from the bonds of historical time. Significantly, he also sought to free the Jewish people—and himself—from their historical obligation to the Land of Israel. Indeed, Rosenzweig's vision was of a people born and tested not in its own territory, but in exile, a condition that steeled the Jews for "battle on behalf of the exalted life and against descent into the contingency of land and time." Like Hermann Cohen before him, Rosenzweig now saw fit to combat the alliance of land and time, history and nation, historicism and Zionism. The Zionist ambition to restore the Jews to the normal flow of history badly missed the true nature of Judaism. For, as Rosenzweig concluded: "The Jewish spirit breaks through the shackles of time. Because it is eternal and aims for the Eternal, it disregards the omnipotence of time. Indeed, it walks unperturbed through history."[145]

## UNDER A NEW THEOLOGICAL STAR

Franz Rosenzweig was hardly oblivious to the fact that the image of a people "walking unperturbed through history" implied that history, at least in the case of the Jews, lacked the creative power to mold its bearers. Such an image seemed appropriate in a period in which concerns about the excesses of history reached a new peak. A fair portion of Rosenzweig's own intellectual labor in the period from 1917 until 1921 was devoted to challenging historicism—both as a method and as a broader mode of apprehending the world. The Kassel lectures, for example, allowed him a public forum to air his concerns about historicism and its relationship to the Jewish people. At the same time, they also allowed him to rehearse ideas central to the grand project on which he started working in 1917, and which was published in 1921 as the *Star of Redemption*.

This is not the place for a full analysis of the *Star*, which has garnered an impressive and ever-expanding array of commentators from the time of its publication to the present. This dense book can be read on many different levels, as Rosenzweig himself indicated in various scattered remarks on the subject.[146] Among the ways in which it can be read, I would suggest, is as a spiritual autobiography that relates the author's tortuous but ultimately uplifting journey from unbelief to belief, from Christianity to Judaism, from Idealism to "pure factuality," from historicism to theology—each of which emanated from the grandest of passages noted at the very beginning and the very end of the book, namely from spiritual death "INTO LIFE."[147]

Strikingly, Rosenzweig's return to spiritual life came amid the pervasive culture of death of the First World War. The mere fact that he was able to write the text while a soldier at the front and in various locales in Germany was an extraordinary feat. But for all his powers of concentration, Rosenzweig was unable—and probably unwilling—to resolve the deep tensions inhering in the book, and by extension in his life. For example, one does not have to read between the lines of the *Star of Redemption* to see its competing ecumenical and particularist strands.[148] The careful and sustained attention that he gives Christianity in the *Star*, particularly in Part III, follows these two divergent strands. The ecumenical strand refers to the "Church of love" as an "exemplary human brother" that obediently follows a temporal path on the way to eternity. The more particularist, Judeocentric strand admonishes Christians that "they have inherited naught but lies from their fathers," specifically regarding the messiahship of Jesus. Even more centrally, Rosenzweig upends the prevailing assumption of modern Protestant theology that a vibrant Christianity effectively superseded an expired Judaism. "Only we," Rosenzweig asserted of his fellow Jews, "live a life in the eternity of redemption and thus can celebrate it." By contrast, "Christianity is only on the way." Thus, the true bearer of the "Eternal Truth"—or in Rosenzweig's idiosyncratic scheme, the "fiery nucleus of the Star"—was Judaism out of which "the rays [i.e., Christianity] shoot forth."[149]

While denying the deeply entrenched supersessionism of Christianity, Rosenzweig engaged in a rather extended excursus on the history and sociology of the Church. In fact, this discussion relates to one of the most interesting and counterintuitive features of the *Star*: its reliance on the techniques of intellectual history, sociology, and comparative religion to trace the distinct paths of Judaism and Christianity. At this point, the tension between historicism and anti-historicism in Rosenzweig's thought assumes new form. Not only does Rosenzweig speak of an ontological realm of "pure factuality" between Creation and Redemption, but he, a declared critic of historicism, also sees fit to use the very tools of the historian's trade, of *Historie*, in his most important work.

For instance, in the first part of the *Star*, Rosenzweig attempts to contextualize his own rebellion against the philosophical truisms of the past. He discusses the flight of his nineteenth-century forebears (chiefly Schopenhauer and Nietzsche) away from Idealism as part of a more exhaustive survey of the history of Western ideas (though with forays to the East) from antiquity to modernity. In the course of this broad review, Rosenzweig identifies three great moments of enlightenment: (1) the ancient philosophical movement against pagan mythology; (2) the Renaissance drive against Scholasticism; and (3) the modern historical enlightenment that was directed against "the gullibility of experience."[150] It was the last of these three that shaped the intellectual world in which Rosenzweig lived. Indeed, his own analysis in the *Star* was the beneficiary of the very mode of thought that this "historical enlightenment" spawned.

And yet, Rosenzweig did not consider the effects of this third enlightenment entirely salutary. One of its most distressing byproducts was the modern (and mainly Protestant) enterprise of "historical theology," against which Rosenzweig had inveighed already in "Atheistic Theology" of 1914. The goal of historical theology, he intimated, was at cross-purposes with the quest for knowledge: "Historical theology is commissioned to intercept what has transpired, and partly to pigeonhole it, partly to clothe it anew, that is, in essence, to erect a Chinese wall against knowledge."[151]

The relativism of this enterprise, fueled by a bald subjectivity, stood in glaring contrast to the scientific aspirations of its purveyors. The result was devastating. Under the weight of early twentieth-century criticism (chiefly from opponents of the Historical Jesus trend), "the edifice of historical theology collapsed without hope of reconstruction." And the consequences were not limited to the field of Protestant theology. "The *auctoritas* of history" itself, he asserted, "has broken down."[152] Consequently, the present crisis of historicism spelled the demise of the great historical enlightenment of modern times.

Rosenzweig's rendering of the rise and fall of this historicist moment in Part I of the *Star* paved the way for his discussion in Part III of the "Eternal People" of Israel. No matter how refined or scientific modern historical methods were, they invariably failed to grasp an entity that resisted contextualization—indeed, that "remains remote from the chronology of the rest of the world." Unlike Christianity, the Jewish people bore no imprint of the ravages of time. Nor did it succumb to historicism's ironclad laws of growth and development. Rather, in the case of Jews, Rosenzweig boldly declared that "eternity has already come—even in the midst of time!"[153]

Just as the notion of eternity within time recalls the strivings of Rosenzweig's philosophical and theological contemporaries, it also evokes the legacy of his medieval poetic hero, Judah Ha-Levi. But while Ha-Levi desperately yearned for the return of the Eternal People to its homeland, Rosenzweig disagreed, amplifying a central theme of his Kassel lecture on "Geist und Epochen." Exile was the ideal habitat for the Jews. For it served to remind them that "home never is home in the sense of land." Whereas other nations become enslaved to the idol of land, the Jew maintains an "untrammeled freedom" to traverse the world, alternately soaring through and beyond history.[154]

Rosenzweig hints in the *Star* at a close link between the ahistorical journey of the Jewish people and its extraterritoriality. In this respect, his critique of historicism went hand in hand with his critique of the Zionist project of territorial reclamation. Herein lies a key affinity with his elderly teacher and friend Hermann Cohen. Of course, many differences in temperament and outlook separated the two, chiefly Rosenzweig's impatience with the old neo-Kantian system of which Cohen was such a proud representative. But we should recall that it was Rosenzweig himself who, in the wake of the famous philosophical gathering at Davos in 1929, pointed to Cohen as the leader of a *new* philosophical movement—indeed, as the first to take a bold "leap into Existence." Somewhat paradoxically, this "leap into Existence" was, for both thinkers, a "leap out of history." It is equally paradoxical—and a bit poignant—that this paradox led Cohen and Rosenzweig to fashion visions of Judaism rooted in the very historical contexts they sought to escape.

## Chapter Four

## ANTI-HISTORICISM AND THE
## THEOLOGICAL-POLITICAL PREDICAMENT IN
## WEIMAR GERMANY: THE CASE OF LEO STRAUSS

Both Franz Rosenzweig and Hermann Cohen evince—each in his own way—a curious but common enough position in German intellectual culture after Nietzsche: an articulated skepticism or outright disdain for *historicism* coupled with an irrepressible and often unacknowledged use of *history*. This position was a function of the ubiquitous "historical-mindedness" of European intellectual culture from the nineteenth century. But it was precisely the ubiquity of the historicist habit of mind that upset a wide range of European thinkers in the early twentieth century. Historicism had become for many in this era a term of opprobrium, signaling the grinding down of grand ideals or events into minute contextual shards.

Dismay over the impact of historicism on German intellectual life gathered momentum in the late nineteenth century, continued throughout the early decades of the twentieth, and reached a peak in the wake of the Great War. The postwar era was a time of social and political instability, as well as of cultural and intellectual innovation. As we have already noted, systems of thought and methods that had long held sway in German intellectual life succumbed to withering criticism. Historicism remained a dominant presence in this age of upheaval, summoned both as an argument for change and as a symptom of decline.

It is instructive to follow the trail, once again, of Ernst Troeltsch, who observed in 1922 that modern culture had been thoroughly overrun by historicism: "State, law, morality, religion, [and] art all disappear into the current of historical being and are understandable only as components of historical development." One particularly noticeable consequence was that the relativism of historicism "shakes all eternal truths."[1]

For decades Troeltsch had vigorously defended historicism in the face of theological attack. But now in a period of political and intellectual

chaos, he felt besieged by a "crisis of historicism," as he entitled his essay
in 1922. This crisis was, in fact, a front in the broader battle that broke
out after the First World War itself and pitted

> [c]ulture and progress, skepticism and aesthetics against Christianity, and above
> all against the long-standing association of culture and Protestantism; realists,
> modernists, Völkists, expressionists against antiquity, venerators of Christianity
> with one another and against modern culture, the Dionysian and Apollonian
> renewers of antiquity against Christianity and modernity together.[2]

Squarely in the midst of these oppositions stood historicism. Whereas
Troeltsch earlier relished the explosive capacity of history as "a leaven
transforming everything," he was now mindful of its destructive impact.[3]
His own attempt to make sense of the crisis of historicism in the Weimar
years was ineluctably historicist. Thus, he undertook—in what turned out
to be the last year of his life—a wide-ranging study of the passage of
historicism from a force of "liberation" to a source of "perplexity" and
"burden:" *Der Historismus und seine Probleme*.[4] His aim was to salvage
the project of historicism, in large measure by overcoming the century-
old antagonism between the disciplines of history and philosophy.[5]

The Troeltsch of 1922 was quite distinct from the young scholar who
had warned his theological elders in 1896 of the imminent collapse of
their world. He was now an elder facing the collapse of his own. His
theological juniors—Barth, Gogarten, and Brunner—inveighed against
the atomizing force of the historical method that he treasured.[6]

Unlike Troeltsch, the younger generation sought answers to the crisis
of historicism outside of historicism itself. Their quest to discover a realm
of experience outside of history bespoke a measure of hope, but also a
profound dissatisfaction with present-day intellectual and cultural norms.
This combustible mix of sensibilities characterized the Weimar regime
that took rise in the embers of the Great War: On one hand, the rise of a
new progressive government under the socialist Friedrich Ebert fueled
expectations for radical change; on the other, the political and economic
weakness of the regime created a culture of chaos marked by violence and
fears of cataclysmic decline. As a result, the forces of hope and of the new
*Kulturpessimismus* clashed without cease in the early years of the regime.
And yet, the competing flanks of intellectuals and cultural activists shared,
as Steven Aschheim has shown, an important trait: Both held the Enlightenment project—the rationalist ideal of old—in utter contempt.[7] A jarring
symbol of the death of this ideal was the assassination in 1922 of the
Jewish foreign minister of the nascent Weimar Republic, Walter Rathenau. The fact that Rathenau was able to accede to the pinnacle of
political power without formally renouncing Judaism seemed to fulfill the

grandest ecumenical hope of the Enlightenment. His subsequent murder dashed this hope with brutal immediacy.

Even before Rathenau's death, the younger generation of German intellectuals, born in the last decade and a half of the nineteenth century, had begun to move beyond the promise of Enlightenment. Franz Rosenzweig, for example, called for a thorough reorientation of German-Jewish cultural and educational norms through the Frankfurt Lehrhaus. But there was a more peculiar quality to the dissent of Rosenzweig and his generation. Michael Löwy has written of the powerful messianic impulses among Jewish intellectuals of this generation, and he follows Gershom Scholem (a participant-observer of the phenomenon) in distinguishing these impulses from the Enlightenment vision of a "rational utopia of eternal progress."[8] Anson Rabinbach has shed further light on the neo-messianism of this Jewish generation, noting, among other effects, its wholesale "abandonment of the Enlightenment."[9]

To this messianic moment we might add another familiar ingredient: forceful resistance to mundane historicism. For a good number of intellectuals like Rosenzweig, historicism came to be seen as a sticky tar, staining and weighing down any object with which it came into contact. The new messianic impulse sought to dissolve this recalcitrant agent, thereby liberating both the historical moment and the present—the *Jetztzeit*—from their contextual bonds.

Some of the most prominent exemplars of this kind of new redemptive thinking—such as Ernst Bloch and Gustav Landauer—were affiliated with the progressive or radical politics emblematic of the early Weimar years (e.g., 1918–1923). But a similar impulse to slip out of the shackles of history can be found among conservative thinkers in Weimar culture, both Jewish and non-Jewish. These adepts of the so-called Conservative Revolution, while allied against the Weimar left, nonetheless harbored their own version of a mythic-mystical thinking that was unbound by time. Indeed, they were, as one contemporary noted, "oriented toward the eternal *ordre du coeur*, not toward the changing ideal of *Ratio*."[10]

Although the term "Conservative Revolution" extends back to the mid–nineteenth century, it is in the Weimar period that it assumes particular focus and power.[11] Its adherents—an odd assembly of secular, Protestant, and Catholic thinkers—were stimulated by the explosive discharge of cultural and political energy after the First World War. On one hand, they saw their movement as a clear refutation of the liberal and progressive ideologies unleashed in the wake of the French Revolution that were now on prominent display in Weimar political culture. On the other, they imagined themselves not merely as restorers of a status quo ante bellum, but as revolutionaries intent on creating a society anchored by traditional norms, and unparalleled in its unity and holism.[12]

This cohort of thinkers, whom Armin Mohler has exhaustively catalogued in *Die Konservative Revolution in Deutschland*, reminds us of the ample discursive space in Weimar Germany in which radical critiques of the Enlightenment project—from both left and right—abounded. The "inhabitants" of that space included more than the leading lights of Weimar Jewish thought such as Rosenzweig, Scholem, and Walter Benjamin. They also included thinkers who find no place on the familiar list of Weimar Jewish progressives. In the next two chapters, we will study two such Jewish thinkers—Leo Strauss (1899–1973) and Isaac Breuer (1883–1946)–who themselves present a fascinating study in contrasts. The former was an unconventional and, at the end of the day, atheist political philosopher with deep sympathies for both religious thought and the weight of tradition. The latter was a university-trained lawyer, an urban cosmopolite, and a vocal proponent of a politically active ultra-Orthodoxy. While neither figure is normally mentioned among the renowned "conservative revolutionaries" of Weimar times, each embraced largely illiberal solutions to the enduring modern predicament known as the "Jewish question." That is not to say that either submitted to a chauvinistic German nationalism or to a harsh and intolerant Zionism. It is to say, however, that both chose routes that diverged from the leftist drift of Weimar Jewish culture.

Thus, in concert with the "conservative revolutionaries," Strauss harshly attacked the political and intellectual flaccidity of liberalism, preferring a return to a pre-modern medieval rationalism. And Breuer, in parallel to contemporaneous neo-Orthodox currents within Protestantism, favored a renascent Orthodoxy that was conservative in the Mannheimian sense (that is, both reactive to and absorbing of a modern secular sensibility).[13] Strauss's and Breuer's respective visions converge at three points that reveal instructive affinities between them, as well as with the larger theme of this book: First, both give voice to a "theological-political" crisis in their midst; second, both perceived that historicism was an important contributor to that sense of crisis; and third, both regarded Zionism as incapable of resolving the crisis, in part because of its naïve and misguided ambition to restore the Jewish people to history. It is the task of this chapter and the next to demonstrate the links among these points by exploring Strauss and Breuer, two of the more innovative and unusual Jewish thinkers of the Weimar setting. But first we begin with a brief genealogy of the "theological-political" predicament that has exercised modern intellectuals from the seventeenth century to the present.

## The "Theological-Political" Predicament and the Advent of Modernity

In his study of anti-democratic currents in Weimar, Kurt Sontheimer pointed to the "politicization of the irrational" as a prime characteristic of conservative thought.[14] In fact, this form of politicization cut across the spectrum, implicating virtually every party or school of thought in the Weimar milieu, including theologians and religious thinkers.

The openness afforded by the new regime, along with Enlightenment fatigue, provided fertile ground for a reconsideration of the relationship between religion and a modern, nominally secular, society. This reconsideration overlapped with the ever-present political questions of the day, and together they assumed a new hybrid form: "theological-political" discourse. We see clear evidence of this conjunction in Carl Schmitt (1888–1985), the Catholic legal scholar and later Nazi theorist who published a small volume in 1922 entitled *Politische Theologie*. Schmitt's main concern in this book was to understand the nature of political sovereignty, particularly as it assumed form in response to emergency situations (e.g., Weimar itself). In the course of the book, Schmitt set out to show that modern notions of the state, anchored by the idea of sovereignty, were but "secularized theological concepts."[15] He was particularly agitated by liberal notions of governance, which rested on a fundamental belief in the goodness of man. As against these notions, Schmitt recalled with reverence a trio of nineteenth-century Catholic counterrevolutionaries—de Maistre, Donoso Cortés, and Bonald. Fearful of the perils of secular liberal nihilism, they preferred regimes of a dictatorial character, in large measure due to their pessimistic and religiously inflected view of the evilness of man.[16] Schmitt's recovery of these thinkers provided him, as one scholar has noted recently, with "certain strands of Catholicism" that could provide fodder for a "radical counteroffensive" to the degenerating cultural and political universe around him.[17]

Schmitt's desire to fuse time-honored theological principles with politics grated against the pervasive modern confidence that secularization was not only a salutary feature of modernity, but that it could ultimately escape its own theological origins. But politics could not escape the clutches of theology. Nor could anything ever escape politics. As Schmitt declared, "any decision about whether something is *unpolitical* is always a *political* decision."[18]

This view of the continued potency—and inextricability—of the political and theological in contemporary society was shared by Schmitt's erstwhile Jewish friend and correspondent, Leo Strauss. Strauss recalled that, as a young German Jew in Weimar, he "found himself in the grip of the *theologico-political* predicament." This phrase not only recalls, if in inverted fashion, Schmitt's "political theology." It also summons up the memory of the towering early modern figure who was the subject of Strauss's first book: Baruch Spinoza.[19] It was Spinoza, the excommunicated Jew of Amsterdam, who addressed and attempted a solution to the "theological-political" predicament in early modern Europe, and who would continue to occupy Strauss's attention throughout the latter's career. And yet, the theological-political predicament of Strauss's day was different than in Spinoza's. To gain a sense of this difference, we would do well to recall some of the main elements of Spinoza's *Theologico-Political Treatise* (1670).

Spinoza was engaged in a double act of liberation. First, he imagined a political regime that no longer relied on irrational religious authority for legitimacy. "Despotic statecraft," he wrote, was inclined "to hoodwink the subjects, and to mask the fear, which keeps them down, with the specious garb of religion."[20] Conversely, regimes that no longer cloaked themselves in this garb were at greater liberty to cultivate an ambience of free discourse for their subjects, which was one of Spinoza's cardinal desires. But a second task, and one that was no mere surrender to convention, was to liberate religious belief from the strictures of ecclesiastical authority. Freedom of belief was not only possible; it was indispensable—and for religion itself: "[N]ot only can such freedom be granted without prejudice to the public peace, but also . . . without such freedom, piety cannot flourish nor the public peace be secure."[21]

In advancing this set of claims, Spinoza was laying down guidelines for a redefined relationship between theology and politics in his day. It is important to note that even while pushing toward a more modern separation of church and state, he did not abandon the view that "the outward observance of piety" (e.g., ritual performance) should be "in accordance with the public peace and well-being," and hence subject to the approval of the temporal power.[22] But he contrasted this realm of "outward observance" to the realm of thought—be it religious or philosophical—which must never be constrained. It is in this respect that Steven Smith considers Spinoza's stance in the *Theologico-Political Treatise* a "theology of the liberated individual." Indeed, it was the free-thinking individual whom Spinoza had in mind when he proclaimed at the end of the *Theologico-Political Treatise* that "the true aim of government is liberty."[23]

Writing at a vital point of transition in European history, Spinoza charted a course toward a modern liberal order, secular in nature, but respectful of the private religious predilections of its subjects. In forging this path, he felt compelled to analyze the source from which ecclesiastical authority drew its legitimacy: the Holy Scripture. It is this line of inquiry that earned Spinoza excommunication, as well as posthumous contempt, from fellow Jews.[24]

Spinoza's forays into scriptural criticism relied on an intimate familiarity with the Hebrew Bible, gained as a precocious student in Amsterdam's Jewish academies. This knowledge was utilized to question the most fundamental claims about the Bible's origins. "It is . . . clearer than the sun at noonday," he wrote, "that the Pentateuch was not written by Moses, but by someone who lived long after Moses."[25] This refutation of Mosaic authorship of the Hebrew Bible resulted from a bold interpretive method that recalls our discussion on the rise of historicism in chapter 1. Thus, the "universal rule" proclaimed by Spinoza was "to accept nothing as an authoritative scriptural statement which we do not perceive very clearly when we examine it *in the light of its history*."[26] History became the new measure of Scriptural veracity. By its light, Spinoza uncovered linguistic and historical incongruities (most famously, mention of Moses' death) that cast doubt on—in fact, rendered altogether implausible—Mosaic authorship of the Bible.[27]

It was a related historicist understanding that prompted Spinoza to upend the traditional Jewish conception of Revelation. Significantly (and contrary to his image as an unreconstructed heretic), Spinoza *did not* call into question the occurrence of Revelation itself. He *did* cast doubts on the eternal validity of Revelation, as well as on the claim that the Jews were chosen to receive Revelation because they possessed some unique moral gifts. In fact, Spinoza argued that "the laws of the Old Testament were revealed and ordained to the Jews [only because of] the special constitution of their society and government"—that is, due to their relatively stable social and political organization, and not to any exalted ethical bearing.[28] On this reading, Revelation was revealed legislation, a body of laws that would serve, for all intents and purposes, as the constitution of the Jews' ancient commonwealth. When the ancient Jewish commonwealth ceased to exist—following the destruction of the Second Temple—the validity of these revealed laws lapsed.

In suggesting that Revelation was temporally circumscribed and that the Bible was not the exclusive result of Mosaic authorship, Spinoza was deliberately violating the traditional view. His early historicist approach required him to undertake a critical examination of the past precisely in order to lift its burdens. Indeed, the more Spinoza investigated the ancient source of religious claims to temporal power, the more he came to believe that these claims were inapplicable to his day. History thus served a vital task in disentangling theology and politics, and helped Spinoza imagine a new equilibrium of power that would guide individuals and regimes alike into the modern age.

It is not surprising that Spinoza's daring made him both a celebrated and reviled figure in subsequent eras. During the eighteenth century, various advocates of Enlightenment looked to Spinoza as the paragon of philosophical lucidity and innovation. Among them was the renowned *juif de Berlin*, Moses Mendelssohn, who privately admired the acuity of his excommunicated co-religionist and shared his ambition of carving out a space for free thought and belief unrestrained by temporal authority. The similarity between the two thinkers—the latter of whom remained a scrupulously observant Jew—led Gotthold Ephraim Lessing to declare in 1754 that Mendelssohn's "honesty and his philosophical mind make me anticipate in him a second Spinoza equal to the first in all but . . . his errors."[29]

By the last decades of the eighteenth century, such an association spelled serious trouble. A band of forceful counter-Enlightenment thinkers transformed "Spinozist" into an epithet that connoted a fanatical belief in the infallibility of reason that resembled, ironically, the worst kind of religious superstition (which, often enough, meant Catholicism).[30] One of the leading members of this group, F. H. Jacobi, accused Lessing of embracing "Spinozism" shortly before dying in 1781. In fact, Lessing's affection for the Amsterdam philosopher had developed much earlier. But now in the midst of a counteroffensive by the likes of Jacobi and Johann Georg Hamann, Spinoza came to be seen as the progenitor of a rigid rationalism that stifled the spontaneity of life experience.[31]

The story of Spinoza's reception hardly ends with this counter-Enlightenment critique. Rather, his struggle against religious obscurantism and on behalf of freedom of thought struck a positive chord among nineteenth-century novelists and scholars, particularly Jews in search of a distinguished precursor to illuminate their path from the margins to the center of European society.[32] But if this image of Spinoza inspired the lingering Enlightenment allegiances of German Jews, it should not surprise us that when this sensibility later came under attack, as it did by Leo Strauss and others, Spinoza's reputation suffered proportionately. That is not to say that every Jewish critic of Spinoza necessarily abandoned the Enlightenment dream; Hermann Cohen, for example, stands in defiance of that proposition. Nor is it to say that the twentieth-century figures who coupled criticism of Spinoza with criticism of the Enlightenment project were exact replicas of earlier Counter-Enlightenment thinkers like Hamann or Jacobi.[33]

Nevertheless, an important thread must be identified. The eighteenth- and twentieth-century critics of Enlightenment were united in believing that Spinoza had failed to resolve the "theological-political" predicament of modernity in satisfactory fashion. Neither his hopes for a benign liberal regime nor his iconoclasm toward religious authority appeared warranted. Consequently, in the charged ambience of the Weimar Republic, intellectuals began to ponder afresh the legacy of Spinoza and redefine the terms of their own theological-political predicament.

## THE "THEOLOGICAL-POLITICAL" PREDICAMENT OF WEIMAR

We have emphasized that the Weimar moment was one in which competing political and cultural vectors grated against each other, producing a friction that was both vitalizing and menacing. We must also emphasize that the rise of a new progressive regime—whose constitution proclaimed the principle that "personal liberty is inviolable"—unleashed a flurry of attacks from left and right upon the Enlightenment ideals of rationalism and liberalism.[34]

This critical spirit went hand in hand with a deepening spiritual desire on the part of many intellectuals. The new language of yearning they created bespoke a significant reframing of the theological-political predicament—one that was quite different from the dilemma faced by Spinoza. For Weimar intellectuals, the challenge was not to loosen the grip of religious authority upon individual thought or belief. After all, by the twentieth century, religious authorities no longer held the power to grant or bar free thought as they had earlier. Rather, the task was to release the grip of liberal Enlightenment values upon religious sentiments. In parallel, it was to release the grip of historicism upon received tradition. Liberal rationalism and historicism—once regarded as the antipodes of Enlightenment and Romanticism—were now seen as central and interlocking symptoms of the malaise of modernity.

Among Jewish thinkers of the age, Walter Benjamin offered an unusual diagnosis of the malady. Historicism, he observed, had become a technique of stringing together events like "beads of a rosary."[35] As such, it abandoned its true mission of bestowing distinctiveness upon the individual event. This resulting neglect of the individual was not only a methodological lapse; it was also a moral lapse.

This point becomes clear in Benjamin's well-known recourse to the image of the "angel of history," inspired by Paul Klee's painting *Angelus Novus*. In the ninth of his "Theses from the Philosophy of History," written shortly before his suicide in 1940, Benjamin depicted the angel of history as fixated upon an event, a "single catastrophe," from the past. "The angel," he observed, "would like to stay, awaken the dead, and make whole what has been smashed." But the storm from Paradise, representing the onrushing tide of liberal progress, pushes the angel "into the future to which his back is turned."[36]

Benjamin's evocation of the angel was an attempt to recapture the true individualizing thrust of historicism, and thereby give voice to the forgotten and disenfranchised in the past.[37] In fact, his differentiation between moral and amoral versions of historicism entailed a reworking of the terminological distinction employed by Hermann Cohen and other German thinkers extending back to Kant. Thus, *Historie* represented the historicist fashioning of a seamless "continuum of events"; *Geschichte* was the less tidy historical repository from which the neglected and oppressed could be excavated.[38]

This distinction—along with his "Theses on the Philosophy of History"—was crafted at a later stage of Benjamin's career. But the kernel of his views about a disruptive and potentially redemptive kind of history was formed in the Weimar environment. As is well known, Benjamin was extremely close to Gershom Scholem, whose own fascination with Jewish messianic aspirations was gaining momentum in this period.[39] Like Scholem, Benjamin maintained a sense of the liberating possibilities of rupture, as exemplified by the Weimar experiment itself. He also came to believe à la Franz Rosenzweig that a productively disruptive history "creates a sort of eternity in the middle of time."[40] It is just this kind of redemptive quest, so unlike prior teleological schemes, that typified Weimar thinkers. Stéphane Mosès has designated this quest in Benjamin as his "theological politics"—signaling an agenda for unsettling classic nineteenth-century notions of "temporal continuity," "historical causality," and the "ideology of progress."[41]

The payoff for such agitation, as Benjamin attempted to show in his massive and uncompleted *Passagen-Werk* (begun in 1927), was not a glorious utopian future. Rather, it was recovery of a messy *Urgeschichte*, a primal history comprised not of rarefied ideas, but of the "refuse" and "detritus"—indeed, the forgotten voices—of history.[42]

At the other end of the political spectrum, another Weimar Jew, Leo Strauss, was excavating his own "eternity in the middle of time." Strauss's version of an *Urgeschichte* mandated a search for grand philosophical ideals, and thus was altogether distinct from Benjamin's. And yet both thinkers were intent on understanding the vexed relationship between theology and politics in their time. In this joint endeavor, they serve to remind us that the boundary between left and right, like that between Protestant and Jew, was far more permeable than it might have appeared in the unique intellectual climate of Weimar Germany.

## LEO STRAUSS'S "THEOLOGICAL-POLITICAL" CRISIS

Of late, scholars have come to recognize that Leo Strauss was a good deal more than the godfather of American neo-conservatism.[43] For a variety of reasons, most notably the desires of his own students, Strauss had long been depicted as the revered master of a tight coterie of disciples intent on preserving tradition against the naïve or, worse, nihilistic advances of liberalism. The content of this "tradition" was rooted in firm natural rights principles whose timeless virtue was appreciated only by a select fraternity of great thinkers scattered over time and place. To add further intrigue to the story, these thinkers, according to Strauss's own "hermeneutics of suspicion," often had to disguise their profound engagement with grand philosophical principles in an esoteric style of writing.[44] Often enough, the principles to which they were devoted were too subversive of religious or political convention to be tolerated in overt form.

Strauss's distinctive understanding of the history of philosophy rested on a healthy skepticism of the benefits of modernity. He was especially concerned about the role of modern historicism in upending the timeless norms and values that great philosophers knew to appreciate. The destructive wake of historicism, Strauss once asserted, guaranteed that "[t]he only standards that remained were of a purely subjective character, standards that had no other support than the free choice of the individual."[45] Indeed, the historicist creed demanded that "all principles of justice [e.g., natural right principles] are mutable," and hence "culminated in nihilism."[46]

This critical perspective on historicism and, more broadly, on the project of modernity, burnished Strauss's reputation as a leading Cold War intellectual whose rise to prominence came in the midst of the great enmity between the United States and the Soviet Union from the 1950s through the 1980s. But the more discerning among Strauss's readers recognize that many of his deepest intellectual instincts were forged well before this time, indeed, in advance of his arrival in New York in 1938.

Already as a young scholar in the turbulent Weimar years, Strauss began to address the problematic aspects of modernity, historicism, and liberalism. As with many of his contemporaries, the question of faith in a modern world riven by claims of scientific certainty, on one hand, and historicist relativism, on the other, stood at the heart of his concerns. Strauss was much preoccupied with this tension, and all the more so because of the precarious condition of German Jews. To his mind, they were locked in a state of political and spiritual dependence, alternately seduced and debilitated by the prospect of liberal democracy. This predicament was different from, but still causally linked to, the earlier "theological-political" crisis faced by Spinoza in the seventeenth century. In that earlier case, the Spinozistic assault on "the kingdom of darkness"—the world of traditional medieval society—had eviscerated the foundations of Judaism, leaving it unprepared to fend for itself in the freewheeling liberal marketplace.[47]

The Weimar-era crisis was a reflection of that eviscerated Judaism. To address it, Leo Strauss believed that a new path—or perhaps an old path long obscured—was required. His impulse was to immerse himself in the

sources of pre-modern philosophical and theological writings. In this regard, he was clearly energized by the "New Thinking" of figures such as
Barth, Heidegger, and Rosenzweig. And yet, the result was neither a Barth-
ian neo-Orthodoxy nor a Rosenzweigian existentialism. Rather, it was an
iconoclastic position that congealed over time into what might be described as "orthodox unorthodoxy." On one hand, Strauss would gain
great renown for his belief that only a single and relatively narrow body
of inspired texts was worth reading. On the other hand, his decades-long
effort to bore through layers of interpretive accretions—especially those
imposed by the "modern Enlightenment"—yielded a canon of great *philosophical*, not theological, works. Indeed, the highest ideal for Strauss was
a "noble atheism" quite distinct from the modern version contained in
Spinoza's critique of the Bible. This "noble atheism," which was itself "a
descendent of Biblical morality," approached religious orthodoxy with a
mix of "gratitude, rebellion, longing and indifference."[48] Among other
merits, it was the philosophical stance best suited to Exile—that dangerous but liberating state that Strauss came to recognize as vital for genuine
"intellectual probity."[49]

## Against Enlightenment: Strauss as a Weimar Jewish Conservative

Regrettably, we do not possess an abundance of biographical knowledge
about Leo Strauss. Strauss might well have delighted in—and perhaps
deliberately contributed to—this predicament, given his predilection for
secrecy and esotericism and his concerns over historicist misreadings.
Risking the latter, we can suggest that the roots of Leo Strauss's lifelong
quest for "intellectual probity" extend back to his hometown of Kirchhain, where he was born on September 20, 1899.[50] Located in the state
of Kurhessen, Kirchhain is a small rural town near the University of Marburg, which during Strauss's early years was home to Hermann Cohen
and the neo-Kantian school that bore its name. Like Franz Rosenzweig,
Strauss came to reject the premises of neo-Kantianism and did not sub-
scribe either to Cohen's equation of Judaism and philosophy or to his
unwavering liberal enthusiasm. But he was a great admirer of the Marburg philosopher. Part of this admiration resulted from the combination
of Cohen's prominence and his physical proximity to young Strauss's
hometown.[51] Part may also have resulted from a sense of shared Jewish
origin. Both Strauss and Cohen were born into traditional—which is to
say, observant—Jewish homes in rural German towns. The decidedly un-
cosmopolitan ambiences of Coswig and Kirchhain fostered in both a textured feeling for Judaism that was never vanquished; nor was it acquired

at a later stage of life, as in the case of Franz Rosenzweig.[52] Needless to say, this common small-town origin did not yield a monolithic cultural or political position. But it does help explain Strauss's deep appreciation of Cohen, whom he remembered as "a Jew of rare dedication, the faithful guide, defender and warner of German Jewry."[53] In this last regard, Strauss may have recalled Cohen's lifelong defense against anti-Semitism, including his 1888 testimony in Marburg against an anti-Jewish agitator.

In his excellent recent study, Eugene Sheppard has pointed to a set of countervailing environmental forces that forged Strauss's emerging intellectual personality: "Kurhessen's conservative and antisemitic ambience, on one hand, and the enlightened university of Marburg, on the other."[54] Sheppard follows Steven Lowenstein's important corrective to the "urbanist" bias of German-Jewish historiography by noting the mix of "[r]eligious orthopraxy and political conservatism" among rural German Jews such as the Strauss family. Strauss himself recalled that he "was brought up in a conservative, even orthodox Jewish home somewhere in a rural district of Germany."[55] Values such as traditionalism and patriotism—in pointed contrast to the ethos of innovation and internationalism found among urban Jews in the fin de siècle period—were prevalent in this milieu, and helped lay the foundation for Strauss's political orientation.

At the same time, Strauss studied in the local gymnasium, where he read widely in the classics and imbibed "the message of German humanism." He also began to read, "furtively" by his own admission, two important critics of the modern German humanistic tradition, Schopenhauer and Nietzsche.[56] This last allusion is significant, and hints at a significant relationship that earned Laurence Lampert's close attention in *Leo Strauss and Nietzsche* (1996). At one level, Nietzsche would appear to exemplify the very philosophical nihilism that Strauss reviled in modern thought.[57] On another level, Nietzsche's attack on the façade of modern Enlightenment—as well as on the stultifying effects of modern historicism—resonated with Strauss. Indeed, the two men had little tolerance for the hubristic and misguided claims of modern historians.[58] In fact, both aspired toward what Strauss once noticed in Nietzsche: a "radical historicism"—that is, an historicism that refused to succumb to the atomizing and subjective tendencies of modern scholars, but rather sought to grasp the historical object in its full vitality and presence.[59] It is precisely this kind of historicism that the mature Strauss would mobilize from the 1940s on as part of his renowned hermeneutical program of understanding the great philosophers. But the source of this view rested in an earlier period, when Strauss first encountered Nietzsche. As he once confided in a letter to Karl Löwith: "Nietzsche so dominated and charmed me between my 22nd and 30th years that I literally believed everything I understood of him."[60]

Strauss's affections must be seen as part of the broader fascination with Nietzsche that swept through German intellectual culture during and after the First World War.[61] And yet, we should not overstate the case. We know that Strauss had begun to drift away from his moderately observant Jewish home and had embraced the cause of political Zionism at the age of seventeen. But we also know that in 1918 he headed off to the university in Marburg, in no small measure due to the legacy of the recently deceased Herman Cohen. Moreover, when Strauss subsequently switched to the University of Hamburg, in the peripatetic fashion of German students, he went to work on a dissertation under the supervision of the preeminent Jewish disciple of Hermann Cohen, Ernst Cassirer.

It is conceivable that Strauss had once dreamed of continuing the distinguished chain of Jewish neo-Kantianism. But his actual scholarship revealed, from the first, a fundamental resistance to the guiding premises and aims of that scholarly tradition. There was nothing of the spirit of *Versöhnung* (reconciliation) that so animated Cohen's philosophical and cultural writings—indeed, no attempt to equate Judaism and philosophy or Jewishness and Germanness. Rather, Strauss's earliest scholarly inquiries were devoted to the roots of dissent from Enlightenment rationalism.

We see this most clearly in his 1921 dissertation on the problem of knowledge in F. H. Jacobi. On the face of it, this study was a continuation of the multivolume inquiry into modern notions of knowledge undertaken by his *Doktorvater*, Ernst Cassirer. But in fact, Strauss's sympathetic interest in Jacobi marked an abrupt detour from the path of Cassirer and previous neo-Kantians.[62] Indeed, what Strauss found so compelling in Jacobi was that he upheld, in contrast to "idealism and rationalism . . . the transcendence and the irrationality of God."[63]

This "celebration of 'belief' at the expense of critical reason," as Michael Zank calls it, grated against the veneration of Enlightenment and *Bildung* that defined German Jews in the nineteenth century. Strauss himself declared that the era of Judaism in which Hermann Cohen was a representative figure "definitely belonged to the pre–World War I world."[64] A new set of figures appeared in the postwar world to redefine the intellectual horizons of German culture. Ranging across the religious spectrum, they included Karl Barth, Martin Heidegger, Rudolf Otto, Franz Rosenzweig, and Max Scheler. All of these thinkers shared an intense desire to move beyond the moribund state of German philosophical study. In parallel all were critical of the inflated ambitions of modern historicism. Their critical stance toward both philosophy and history translated into a shared yearning for the immediacy of experience that became a hallmark of Weimar intellectual life—indeed, that cut across denominational, disciplinary, and political boundary lines.

FIGURE 4  Leo Strauss (1899–1973). Courtesy of the Joseph Regenstein Library, University of Chicago.

## THEOLOGY AND SCIENCE "BETWEEN THE TIMES"

Strauss was at a most impressionable age when Barth, Heidegger, and Rosenzweig came to prominence in the early 1920s.[65] Having distanced himself in his dissertation from a naïve Enlightenment optimism, Strauss was still in a phase of considerable transition, seeking to clarify whether his critique of Enlightenment permitted or foreclosed a return to religious tradition. Indeed, Strauss recalled that at this point—in the immediate aftermath of his dissertation—"my predominant interest was in theology."[66] As would become clear over time, he was too much a modern to cast his lot fully with traditional orthodoxy. Conversely, he was too much a skeptic to embrace the facile truisms of modernity. In the Weimar milieu, this ironic stance—as a modern skeptic of modernity—led him, and others, to theology. As he reminisced some forty years later:

> The reawakening of theology, which for me is marked by the names of Karl Barth and Franz Rosenzweig, appeared to make it necessary to investigate how far the critique of orthodox theology—Jewish and Christian—deserved to be victorious. Since then the theological-political problem has remained *the* theme of my investigations.[67]

While it is not our task to follow the course of Strauss's life after the Weimar years, it suffices to say that after leaving Germany in 1932, Strauss devoted much of his scholarly career to figuring out how the quest for ultimate truths—theological or philosophical—fared under various political regimes.[68] What first intrigued and disturbed him in the Weimar years was the sense that the liberal proclivity for Enlightenment rationalism crowded out traditional theological concerns. Like Rosenzweig and Barth, Strauss took aim at the modern enterprise of *Religionswissenschaft*, as distinct from pre-modern theological inquiry or from simpler religious expressions that he took to calling "orthodox." Strauss had not yet elaborated the idea of a medieval Enlightenment that was superior to its modern successor; this notion would figure prominently in his book *Philosophie und Gesetz* (1935) in which he sharply criticized the modern bias of his fellow scholar of Jewish philosophy, Julius Guttmann.[69]

But Strauss's antipathy for the bold impiety of the modern Enlightenment and its intellectual heirs was evident already in the early 1920s. Curiously, he found a pillar of support in the Protestant theological journal that Karl Barth coedited: *Zwischen den Zeiten*. As we noted in the last chapter, the journal's title hinted both at a rupture of historical time and at the prospect of a timeless present. As he groped around for his own theological standpoint, Strauss identified with the efforts of the new journal's founders to establish an Archimidean point even while "between the times." Thus, he lauded the *Zwischen den Zeiten* group in 1925 as "the able ones [who] have already cleared away the path."

What they cleared away, Strauss implied, was the weighty obstacle of modern historical scholarship in the guise of *Wissenschaft*. This critical historical undertaking prevented a genuinely "new Biblical theology, a theological exegesis of the Bible."[70] Barth and his colleagues from *Zwischen den Zeiten* had shown the way. Their goal was not, as Barth declared in the journal's opening issue, "another substantive contribution to positive, liberal Ritschlian theology in its history of religion guise."[71] That is, it was not to establish or dispute the historicity of the text. Rather, it was to approach Scripture with a mix of reverence, curiosity, and faith in its edifying value. Friedrich Gogarten sounded a similar theme in the same issue of the journal, targeting not the nineteenth-century Ritschl but the twentieth-century Ernst Troeltsch. It was Troeltsch, he declared in a telling statement, who did a grave disservice to the Christian faithful by upending their "naïve claims of absoluteness."[72]

In his subsequent career, Leo Strauss would himself eschew "naïve claims of absoluteness." He came to believe that pre-modern philosophers developed a highly complex and encoded mode of writing in order to conceal their subversive views from the eyes of the simple "orthodox" masses. And yet, in the 1920s, Strauss had not fully "cracked" this code of esoteric writing. Nor had he drawn up the idiosyncratic canon of great philosophic thinkers with which his name later became so identifiable. But he had begun to pave the way toward these more mature positions by challenging, à la Barth and his colleagues, critical "scientific" approaches to past texts. Like them, Strauss identified a clear connection between the crisis of modern theology and the crisis of the *Geisteswissenschaften* in his day. In the process, he evinced considerable empathy for the modern theological seeker adrift in a turbulent sea of historicist undertows. The remedy, as he noticed in Barth, was to be "concerned exclusively with the subject matter as distinguished from *historical interpretation*."[73]

Strauss amplified this perspective in a series of essays written from 1923 through the end of the decade. Already in his 1923 review of Rudolf Otto's *Das Heilige*, he applauds the author's preference for "religion" over "theology." The "secondary character" of theology is itself the result of a major shift in orientation occasioned by modernity: whereas "once God was the primary fact . . . now [it is] world, man, and religious experience." Struggling against this anthropocentric current, Otto redirected the focus of inquiry away from "the rational moment in religion [toward] the transcendence of the religious object.[74]

Strauss's appreciation of this shift is echoed in an essay from 1924. Here Strauss challenged not only the avatars of a Protestant *Religionswissenschaft*, but the late Jewish eminence Hermann Cohen. He took particular exception to Cohen's belief that modern scholarship and religion were reconcilable and mutually reinforcing. It was not true, as Cohen claimed, that the "*wissenschaftlich* critique of religion is at the end of the day an immanent critique"—that is, it operates within the religious system as a tool of clarification (in Cohen's case, of a rational religion).[75] Rather, modern *Wissenschaft* had confronted and bested religion in a fight to the finish. Its victory had the effect of shattering any coherent image of a transcendent divine. Moreover, it subjected every religious experience, myth, or dogma either to the logical explanatory categories of philosophy or to the empirical standards of history. With respect to Judaism, *Wissenschaft* sowed dissension by creating denominational fissures based on the degree of adherence to it. Thus, Orthodox and Liberal Jews in Germany waged a battle with one another over their attitude to *Wissenschaft* that often surpassed in intensity their respective confrontations with Zionism.[76]

Conflict was especially heated on the battleground of biblical studies. Strauss could hardly avoid extending his critique of *Wissenschaft* to the Bible, for the stakes were nowhere so high. In "Biblical History and *Wissenschaft*" (1925), he reviewed the work of the Russian-Jewish historian resident in Berlin, Simon Dubnow, who had published in that year the first volume of his *Weltgeschichte des jüdisches Volkes*. Strauss's essay offers an illuminating demonstration of his conservative instincts, but no less so of a deep ambivalence that would characterize him throughout his career. Thus, Strauss set himself up as a rigorous defender of tradition against overzealous researchers like Dubnow, who were intent on liberating "tradition" from its own errors. Critical historical method or *Wissenschaft*, he asserted in tones evocative of Karl Barth, really knows nothing of the central tenets of Judaism: God's existence, God's presence in the world, and God's presence in Jewish history. Nor does it speak of God except as an object of historical or psychological interest. In this regard, its goal is to subvert "the theological interpretation of Biblical history" which posits "a strong conception of God as Master of the entire world, not only of the human world."[77]

Such a critical tenor drew Strauss into league with neo-Orthodox critics of historicism (from the Jewish S. R. Hirsch to the Protestant *Zwischen den Zeiten* cohort).[78] It is striking, then, to see Strauss also describe Dubnow's program as "necessary" and "not revolutionary." It is even more striking to hear him dismiss traditionalist reverence for the inspired figures of the Bible—for example, the Patriarchs, Judges, and Kings—as "homiletic *Schmalz* [sop]." This perspective hints at the ambivalent strains of Strauss's intellectual personality; while desperately seeking to escape the excesses of secular modernity, he at times chose to stand squarely in its midst.

This ambivalent quality appears in Strauss's various writings on Spinoza's biblical scholarship from the period, beginning with his essay on Herman Cohen's treatment from 1924. It is ironic that Cohen, who was no admirer of Spinoza's historicizing impulses, became for Strauss the exemplar of an historicist approach to Spinoza.[79] Thus, in "Cohen's Analysis of Spinoza's Bible Science," Strauss asserts that Cohen availed himself of extraneous biographical data—specifically, the *herem* (excommunication) issued against him by the Amsterdam Jewish community—to explain Spinoza's unorthodox stance toward the Bible in the *Theologico-Political Treatise*. Strauss found little merit in this "appeal to the facts of the life history of a thinker." As far as he was concerned, "the contents [of the book] *precede* the ban."[80]

Up to this point, Strauss would seem to be a fairly predictable critic of the "contextualist fallacy"—the belief that a text or actor can be explained exclusively by recourse to the surrounding historical environment.[81] But in fact, what Strauss objected to in Cohen was not the act of contextualization per se, but rather an incorrect contextualization. That is, it was not internal Jewish communal politics, but the broader struggle of philosophers to gain freedom from ecclesiastical authority (who also had access to temporal power) that impelled Spinoza to write his controversial *Treatise*. Thus, according to Strauss, the appropriate context in which to consider Spinoza's "theological-political" predicament was not the Amsterdam Jewish community, but Protestant Holland on the brink of dramatic change in the seventeenth century.[82]

Strauss's discussion of Spinoza veers between the poles of historicism and anti-historicism—an impulse that should be familiar from our previous discussions of Cohen and Rosenzweig. In coming years, Spinoza would continue to provide Strauss with a prism through which to reflect on historicism, as well as on his own "theological-political" crisis in the Weimar years. Indeed, in the latter half of the 1920s, Strauss thought and wrote a great deal about Spinoza, eventually producing a full-length study of the Dutch philosopher's approach to Biblical criticism, *Die Religionskritik Spinozas als Grundlage seiner Bibelwissenschaft* (1930).

Strauss undertook this work while employed as a *Mitarbeiter* (staff researcher) at the Akademie für die Wissenschaft des Judentums in Berlin. The Akademie, we recall, was the successor to Franz Rosenzweig and Hermann Cohen's original scheme for a center of Jewish intellectual rejuvenation. However, under the directorship of Eugen Täubler, and later Julius Guttmann, the Akademie assumed a much narrower scholarly path.[83]

Strauss was hired by the Akademie in 1925, and began to work with an impressive team of researchers including Fritz Bamberger, Simon Rawidowicz, and Bruno Strauss on a large collaborative project: a comprehensive edition of the collected writings of Moses Mendelssohn.[84] Whatever ambivalence he may have felt toward the Akademie's turn away from its original mission was muted.[85] After all, employment was a precious enough commodity for a young Jewish researcher, especially in the wake of the devastating German inflation of 1923. Strauss was fortunate to receive an additional subvention from the Akademie for his ongoing Spinoza research.[86] And it was the Akademie-Verlag that published his book on Spinoza's critique of religion.

And yet, a central premise of that book stood in direct conflict with the underlying rationale of the Akademie. In name and deed (though not in original conception), the Akademie für die Wissenschaft des Judentums was devoted to a purely "scientific" understanding of Jewish history and thought. By contrast, Strauss was attempting to delineate in his Spinoza book the point at which "science"—that is, critical biblical scholarship—subverted Scripture.[87] Far from celebrating this momentous transition, Strauss was deeply skeptical about "the superiority of the scientific mind" that Spinoza and other moderns claimed for themselves vis-à-vis Scripture. "But is it not the case," he asked in *Die Religionskritik Spinozas*, "that Scripture itself calls science into question?" His question pointed toward "an end of life, a task of life quite different in kind from science, namely, obedience to God's revealed Law."[88]

The persistent paradox of this stance—and of his intellectual existence more generally—was that Strauss never professed "obedience to God's revealed Law." It is this paradox that makes Strauss such an intriguing personality and distinguishes him from other "neo-traditionalists" of his day (e.g., Barth, Rosenzweig, Schmitt). Strauss never reached the point of affirming faith as they did, but he shared, and even sharpened, their criticism of liberal critics of religion. Those critics blithely dismissed the core premises of religious faith without realizing that "religion and science by their inherent intent [are] so basically different that they cannot come into conflict with one another."[89] Intoxicated by the power of their newly honed scholarly tools, the critics of religion developed a faith in science that was no less naïve than that of simple-minded believers in their respective traditions.

First among equals in the adulatory stupor was Spinoza, whose method of scriptural interpretation was couched, Strauss observed, in the objectivist terms of science. Accordingly, the first task was to render the words of the Bible meaningful based on a firm grasp of Hebrew and "without . . . introducing our views or convictions on the truth of the matter contained." Only after attaining a precise sense of meaning should the text be placed in its proper historical context. This approach, according to Strauss, was the foundation of Spinoza's belief in his biblical criticism as "objective" science.[90]

But such a view of "science" was no longer tenable, especially after the challenges and critiques of late nineteenth-century intellectuals. Accordingly, Strauss took it upon himself to expose the inflated ambition and faulty logic of some early architects of the "scientific" assault upon religion (e.g., Uriel da Costa, Isaac de la Peyrère, Thomas Hobbes, and Spinoza). For instance, he argued that Spinoza was not actually interested in Scripture. Rather, the true aim of critical historical method was to subvert the authority of Revelation.[91]

In advancing this position, Strauss appears not only as a fierce critic of the arrogance of the modern outlook, but as a sensitive student of the allure of religion. Indeed, one of the chief goals in *Die Religionskritik*

*Spinozas* was to offer a path of escape to religious orthodoxy from the clutches of science (in the guise of history). He does so by cleverly shifting the grounds on which religion stands from knowledge to belief:

> If orthodoxy claims to *know* that the Bible is divinely revealed, that every word of the Bible is divinely inspired, that Moses was the writer of the Pentateuch, that the miracles recorded in the Bible have happened and similar things, Spinoza has refuted orthodoxy. But the case is entirely different if orthodoxy limits itself to asserting that it *believes* the aforementioned things, i.e., that they cannot claim to possess the binding power peculiar to the known. For all assertions of orthodoxy rest on the irrefutable premise that the omnipotent God whose will is unfathomable, whose ways are not our ways, who has decided to dwell in the thick darkness, may exist.[92]

This distinction moves Strauss close to the position of the theological anti-historicists of the 1920s, with whom he shared an evident distrust for modern historical method. But, as we have already noted, one insurmountable difference separated them: they were unabashed believers, and Strauss, for all his sensitivities, was not. Even before leaving his hometown of Kirchhain, Strauss had begun to escape the confines of a traditional Jewish lifestyle. That said, Strauss maintained a respectful attitude toward traditional Judaism, impelled by the same antipathy toward modern liberalism that he shared with many philosophers and theologians of his day. Liberalism, after all, had eroded the distinctive features of religious tradition in the name of a shallow ecumenism. Moreover, liberalism's agent of social change—assimilation—had created "the illusionary surrogate of trust in the humanity of civilization."[93] This unwarranted trust was, at best, a palliative, and, at worst, a prod to the theological-political crisis of the day. As such, it threatened the integrity of *Judaism* the religious tradition. But at the same time, it risked dissolving *Jewishness*, the often diffuse compound of cultural and ethnic allegiances that comprised the modern Jew.

This distinction undergirds one of the most compelling aphorisms ever uttered about the modern Jewish condition. Hannah Arendt once asserted that "Jews had been able to escape from Judaism into conversion; from Jewishness there was no escape."[94] True to this aphorism, Leo Strauss abandoned the faith and rituals of Judaism, but never surrendered his Jewishness. As evidence, we notice his flirtation with Zionism as a late teen. For a good number of contemporaneous Jewish intellectuals, the experience of the First World War—particularly, the anti-Semitic claim that Jewish soldiers were not serving in sufficient numbers—shook their confidence in the prospect and value of Jewish acculturation into German society. They embarked on a new route, the path of "dissimilation," that in fact trailed off in various directions, including most prominently, Zionism.[95] Strauss's own infatuation with Zionism can be seen as a product of this dissimilatory movement. One of the movement's virtues, he wrote in a 1923 essay on Max Nordau, was that it did not suffer from the false hope of seamless integration. Rather, it sought to extricate the Jewish people from its ethereal diaspora existence as a *Luftvolk*. But in the course of its critique of the Jewish condition, Strauss noticed, Zionism "continues and increases the dejudaizing tendency of assimilation." And here we see yet again the other, paradoxical side of Strauss. Notwithstanding his personal disengagement from Judaism, he chided Zionism for disdaining the religious and intellectual tradition on which Jews had been nurtured hitherto. In fact, he opined that Zionism's "virile causalism"—the belief that its adherents could actually seize control of their own fate—was as unappealing as the "helotry of assimilation" against which he also inveighed.[96]

Strauss thus arrived at a position similar to that of a number of prominent Jewish intellectuals in Weimar—neither committed fully to assimilation nor Zionism. Even more interestingly, Strauss resembled Franz Rosenzweig in his appreciation of the status of *Galut* or Exile. *Galut* was reviled by assimilationists as the locus of Jewish insularity and by Zionists as the provenance of Jewish passivity. But for Rosenzweig, it was an ideal condition—one in which Jews could do "battle on behalf of the exalted life and against descent into the contingency of land and time." Strauss's sense of the necessity of *Galut* was no less great than Rosenzweig's. Yet his depiction was not nearly as fulsome or idyllic. Thus, *Galut* was the space created at the juncture of internal Jewish will and external constraints. At such a crossroad, Strauss wrote in his Nordau essay, Jews found the "maximum possibility of existence by means of a minimum normality."[97]

What kind of Jews could survive and flourish in these conditions? One might imagine various groups, including a small circle of philosophical elites who not only accepted but were inspired to creativity by the condition of "minimum normality." It was this class about whom Strauss wrote in *Persecution and the Art of Writing*, as well as in his famous introduction to Maimonides' *Guide of the Perplexed* (1963).[98] A somewhat more obvious and contemporary group was Orthodoxy Jewry. As we have seen, Strauss had a good deal of empathy for religious orthodoxy, even though he did not follow the ritual or dogmatic strictures of *Jewish* Orthodoxy. In particular, he was intrigued by Orthodox Jews' rejection of the competing paths of assimilation and Zionism. It was they who seemed to comprehend best that a life of "minimum normality"—via steadfast adherence to Halakhah within an insular communal framework—assured the "maximum possibility of survival."

In meditating on his own "theological-political crisis" in Weimar, Strauss turned his gaze to the phenomenon of Orthodoxy—and particularly to the separatist Orthodox community of Frankfurt, founded by Samson Raphael Hirsch in 1876 and led by his son-in-law, Salomon Breuer. The Breuer community's well-known openness to secular culture rested uneasily alongside its strong stand against interaction with less pious members (i.e., the overwhelming majority) of the German-Jewish community. But this tension would seem to embody the *Galut* posture that Leo Strauss found so compelling. So too did the Frankfurt community's opposition to Zionism as a solution to the lingering "Jewish problem."

Strauss addressed this opposition in a 1925 essay "Ecclesia militans." This title harks back to the rallying cry of sixteenth-century Roman Catholics—particularly the German theologian Johannes Eck (1486–1543)—who invoked martial metaphors in preparing the Church for battle against Martin Luther.[99] Transposing the Reformation-era battle lines to his own day, Strauss saw an Eck-like figure in his midst, a Jew true to his tradition who aggressively fought any intra-Jewish effort to reform or replace Orthodoxy. This standard-bearer of a Jewish "militant church" was Isaac Breuer, the leading intellectual figure of the Frankfurt community and son of the community's leader, Rabbi Salomon Breuer. In his 1925 essay, Strauss expressed intrigue with Breuer's fiercely antagonistic attitude toward Zionism. While he had not altogether abandoned hopes for a Zionism that aspired to create more than "a nation of merchants and lawyers," Strauss showed sympathy with Breuer's anxiety over the mundane political claims of Zionism. In reviewing Breuer's anti-Zionist pamphlet, *Das jüdische Nationalheim*, Strauss describes it as "an oasis for the Jewish heart languishing in the desert of politics."[100] Although he would later take Breuer to task in this essay, he did share Breuer's concern that Zionism was seeking to replace the traditional theological foundation of Jewish existence.[101] And like Breuer, he too found little merit in the Zionist program of normalization, which was yet another sorry product of the "shallowness of the Enlightenment" (or the later "soullessness of the 19th century").[102]

This 1925 essay reveals, among other interesting themes, the sharply divided intellectual personality of Leo Strauss. Simultaneously attracted and repelled by both Zionism and Orthodoxy, Strauss seemed to take refuge in the precarious realm of Exile. Little did he know that Exile would assume a far more perilous and personally consequential form a little more than a decade later. Shortly before Hitler's rise to power, Strauss left Germany, seeking employment in France and England before settling permanently in the United States in 1938.

But before his departure, Strauss seemed drawn to the realm of *Galut*—to a world caught between the poles of normality and abnormality in a postwar state of rupture. From such a position of temporal and spatial suspension, Strauss could resist the ever-present temptations of modern historicism. But this position would also afford him the opportunity to venture forth later in his career as a "radical historicist," seeking out the true intent and content of great philosophical minds from another time.

As the case of Franz Rosenzweig reminds us, Strauss's embrace of Exile was not unique among Weimar Jews. Nor was his critique of historicism. Nevertheless, his "orthodox unorthodoxy" points to a stance that few of his fellow Jewish—or, for that matter, non-Jewish—intellectuals could replicate. The same could be said of the stance of his polemical target, Isaac Breuer, who presents a fascinating source of comparison to Strauss.

For both men, the challenges posed by Zionism were related to the challenges posed by historicism. Each of these modern innovations threatened to upend a noble tradition worthy of veneration. While Strauss and Breuer agreed on the nature of the threat, they articulated their concerns in different tones: one sounded in the voice of a restless skeptic and the other in the voice of a true believer. Between Strauss's "noble atheism" and Breuer's unbending Orthodoxy lay much common ground, but also much diversity. It behooves us now to traverse some of this territory— fertile terrain for the study of German-Jewish anti-historicism—by focusing our attention on Isaac Breuer.

# Chapter Five

## ISAAC BREUER AND THE JEWISH PATH
## TO *METAGESCHICHTE*

At first glance, Isaac Breuer (1883–1946) seems to mark a dramatic departure from the lineage of thinkers whom we've examined to this point. He does not belong to the pantheon of celebrated Weimar Jewish intellectuals, and consequently has received a good deal less scholarly attention than the others studied in this book. This situation has begun to change of late, as researchers demonstrate new interest in his life and thought. Nevertheless, we are still far from the point, longed for by one admiring scholar, at which Breuer is "studied by every student who is specializing in the Jewish thought of modern times."[1]

Breuer is less known because he inhabited a narrower intellectual universe than that of Cohen, Rosenzweig, and Strauss. Whether in Frankfurt or Jerusalem, he remained within the confines of a tightly knit and exclusive religious community. Moreover, whereas Cohen, Rosenzweig, and Strauss varied greatly in their levels of ritual observance, Breuer proudly and unwaveringly accepted the strictures of Halakhah from childhood to death.

An important exception to Breuer's chosen state of social insularity was the formative period he spent as a student in various German universities (1902–13). Notwithstanding his steadfast ritual observance, he avidly pursued secular knowledge as a living testament to the philosophy of his grandfather, Samson Raphael Hirsch. Indeed, Breuer was a voracious consumer of philosophy, history, and literature—subjects on which he would later write voluminously. He was also a scholar and practitioner of law, the field in which he received his doctorate in 1912.

Still, for all his exposure to the academic world, and despite his fervent intellectual passions, Breuer spent the bulk of his life outside of the university. Perhaps as a result, his thinking and writing in German never took the form of a systematic philosophical treatise (à la Cohen's *Religion of Reason* or Rosenzweig's *Star*).[2] Nor did Breuer, for all his commitment to Torah study, share Rosenzweig's aim of building a new institution of Jewish learning. In general, he was much less an institution builder than an agitator and activist—a *Gemeindepolitiker*, as a recent biographer has put it—intent on guarding his community's boundaries from the relentless waves of hostile modern threats.[3]

Significantly, Breuer was raised and lived much of his life in Frankfurt am Main. Of course, Berlin was the acknowledged center of Jewish intellectual life, extending back to the age of Moses Mendelssohn. By contrast, Frankfurt, the second largest Jewish city in Germany, lacked the cultural cachet of Berlin. But it was an important hub of commerce and finance, home to the first stock exchange in Germany (founded in 1585). Moreover, it was a bastion of Jewish affluence and philanthropy, boasting such leading families as the Rothschilds and Schiffs.[4] This affluence permeated the city's large Orthodox population, which exercised a powerful role in the local Jewish community.[5] In fact, Isaac Breuer, in his various novelistic forays, repeatedly called attention to the wealth—and vacuous materialism—of his own community, which had formally seceded from the mainstream Jewish *Gemeinde* (community) in 1876. On these grounds, he found common cause with a recent Jewish arrival to Frankfurt, Franz Rosenzweig, who came in 1919 to direct the Jüdisches Lehrhaus. In the same vein, he evinced surprising affinities with the notable collection of socialist and Marxist intellectuals, many Jewish, affiliated with the Institut für Sozialforschung in Frankfurt. It was this group—out of which emerged the renowned Frankfurt School—that produced some of the most sustained and incisive critiques of bourgeois culture in the twentieth century.[6]

The very notion that Breuer shared in the critique of bourgeois materialism already complicates our first impression of him as a separatist Orthodox Jew. But so do the overlapping strands of thought between him, on one hand, and Franz Rosenzweig and Leo Strauss, on the other. With the former, he shared contempt for the bourgeois staidness of German Jewry (from its assimilated to Orthodox poles). With the latter, he shared a sense of a rapidly escalating "theological-political" crisis. All three were trenchant, though not uncomprehending, critics of Zionism. And all three held distinctly critical views of modern historicism. Of the three, Rosenzweig and Breuer were serious students of history in university and contemplated at various points—Rosenzweig far more seriously than Breuer—professional careers as historians.[7] At the same time, all three regarded historicism as capable of degenerating into pedantry, or worse—of exceeding its authority by challenging sacred values and texts. Moreover, both Breuer and Rosenzweig contended that the Jewish people could resist the pull of historicism and, in fact, rise above the plane of history on which the rest of the nations of the world operated. Here the two drew inspiration from the medieval rabbi and poet Judah Ha-Levi. As mentioned in chapter 3, adulation for Ha-Levi signaled, in the German-Jewish context, a form of dissent from the ideal of Enlightenment rationalism, whose celebrated prototype was Maimonides. Ha-Levi was, at once, deeply immersed in the cultural and literary life of Muslim Spain and a fiercely particularistic Jew. His notion of a divinely guided realm of Jewish history distinct from the history of the nations of the world resonated with a number of Weimar-era Jewish intellectuals like Rosenzweig and Breuer.[8] Their embrace via Ha-Levi of a unique Jewish course that deviated from the pathways of conventional history was a form of dissimilation, a rebellion against the historicist bearings of modern German Jews, as well as against the integrationist pressures of the surrounding society. Breuer's own debt is reflected in his novel, *Der Neue Kusari*, whose title, dialogic style, and thinking about history consciously evoke Ha-Levi's most renowned work.

From the belief in a unique historical path to messianism was a short leap, and Breuer took it with great gusto. Many of his early twentieth-century Jewish contemporaries—from Hermann Cohen to Ernst Bloch and Walter Benjamin—made use of messianic motifs in their writing. But few had as concrete a sense of messianic immediacy as Breuer did in the final months of the First World War. In his pamphlet *Messiasspuren*, Breuer interpreted the war, and a number of other significant events in history, as pieces of a well-rehearsed divine plan to introduce the messianic era. Here messianism was no mere metaphor for social progress, but rather an unmistakable case of divine intervention in the course of history.

In light of this, it makes sense to locate Breuer at the margins of the Weimar Jewish intellectual milieu—not fully inside, but not fully outside either. Like many other notable Jewish intellectuals of the era, he experienced the World War as a soldier. Like them, he fully grasped the calamitous nature of the war, as well as the profound sense of political and cultural crisis that it induced. And like them, he shared in the heady messianic optimism that the war's end seemed to mark.

And yet, his voice carried in a different key. It did not herald the emerging *Existenz* philosophy, with its emphasis on being rather than knowledge. Instead, it resonated with the fading echoes of Kantian epistemology, on one hand, and the timeless standards of classical Judaism, on the other. Particularly in the latter case, it expressed an unbroken faith in the inviolability of Torah (Written and Oral), as well as in the promise of divine redemption.

Given that uncommon and decidedly unmodern point of departure, Breuer was a curious kind of conservative revolutionary. He insisted on bringing Jewish tradition to bear on contemporary issues, but frequently tested the boundaries of that tradition through his university-inspired intellectual pursuits. And he did so in a cultural ambience that was markedly open to such inversions and innovations. One prominent example, as we've explored in previous chapters, was Protestant neo-Orthodoxy, whose postwar adherents arrived at their position after years of absorbing and critiquing historicist norms of the day. Similar to adepts of that tradition, Isaac Breuer, the heir of Hirschian neo-Orthodoxy, sought to elaborate a view of Judaism that was insulated from but not ignorant of critical scholarly attitudes.

The affinities between Jewish and Christian neo-Orthodoxy in this regard are less personal than structural; unlike Strauss and Rosenzweig, Breuer had no contact with nor expressed any sustained interest in Weimar-era dialectical theology. Nonetheless, in the midst of a swirling sea of chaos, both Breuer and his Protestant theological contemporaries imagined and willed their respective communities beyond history—to a realm known as *Metageschichte* (Metahistory) in the former case, and *Übergeschichtlichkeit* (Trans-historicality) in the latter.

The task ahead in this chapter is to provide a thick contextual description of Isaac Breuer's quest for *Metageschichte*. We will take note of the way in which he used and then subverted prevalent terms such as community, nation, and history—deeming them modern shells to be filled with traditional content. This terminological subversion points to the intriguing contradictions and tensions that defined Breuer's intellectual personality. These tensions will shed light, in turn, on an important strand of anti-historicist discourse among Weimar Jews, one that stands at the border between secular and traditionalist communities. In examining this strand, we will gain glimpses of the process of cultural osmosis that continually reshaped even the most self-contained of German-Jewish worlds.

## ISAAC BREUER AND THE HIRSCHIAN LEGACY

Consistent with a long line of German-Jewish intellectuals extending back to Solomon Maimon, Isaac Breuer was in fact not German by birth. Rather, he was born in the western Hungarian town of Pápa on September 19, 1883. Even after the family moved to Frankfurt in 1890, Hungary remained an important cultural presence in the Breuer household. Not only was Isaac's father, Salomon, of Hungarian birth. But many of the young men who came to study at the new yeshivah founded by Salomon Breuer in 1890 were also Hungarian.[9] In fact, there were few German students at the yeshivah. Over the course of the nineteenth century, German Jewish men had abandoned traditional Torah learning, choosing to study either in the modern-style rabbinical seminaries or, far more commonly, in universities.

To supplement his own sons' Talmudic education, Salomon Breuer often hired visiting Hungarians (e.g., the future historian, Jacob Katz) as tutors. These foreign students brought to Frankfurt their characteristic

Hungarian stringency in Jewish ritual matters—similar to what Salomon Breuer had brought with him when he came to Frankfurt. As a general rule, they were also far less enamored of the surrounding Gentile culture than German Jews. Characteristic of this Hungarian reserve, Salomon Breuer, according to his son, rarely if ever picked up a "secular book" after completing his own university studies.[10]

What makes this all the more remarkable is that Salomon Breuer was the successor to his father-in-law, Samson Raphael Hirsch, as head of the Israelistische Religionsgesellschaft (IRG) in Frankfurt. The intellectual foundation of the IRG was Hirsch's well-known credo of *Torah 'im derekh erets*, according to which familiarity with the norms and culture of the land was seen as complementary to the primary obligation of strict observance of the laws of the Torah.[11] For Hirsch, the connection between the two realms was not contradictory, but mutually fructifying. As a warrant for his own unreserved love for German culture, Hirsch insisted that the "more a Jew is a Jew, the more universalist will his views and aspirations be, the less aloof will he be from anything that is noble and good, true and upright, in art or science, in culture or education."[12]

Since Hirsch's time, his followers have argued over whether the ideology of *Torah 'im derekh erets* was principled and enduring or a mere concession to the exigencies of the day. Advocates of the latter position have cast the Hirschian stance as a temporary decree ("hora'at sha'ah") designed to lure the disaffected back to the tradition through secular learning—simply put, to render Orthodoxy more appealing.[13] On the other hand, Rabbi Joseph Breuer, grandson of Hirsch, asserted in 1965 that the validity of his grandfather's position was not ephemeral: "Anyone who has but a fleeting insight into the life and work of Rabb. Hirsch will realize that his Torah im Derech Eretz formula was never intended by him as a *hora'at ha-sha'ah* [temporary decree]."

Joseph Breuer went on to argue that the logic of his grandfather's position was "more acute and far more pressing" one hundred years after his death—that is, as the process of Jewish acculturation into mainstream society continued apace.[14] Isaac Breuer shared his brother Joseph's perspective, though it seems that their understanding of *Torah 'im derekh erets* was a good deal more liberal than their father's. For in Salomon Breuer's home, the sons were fed an educational diet comprised largely of Talmud. Outside of it, they proved to be voracious in their intellectual passions.

On one important Hirschian tenet, there was no difference of opinion across the generations. All adhered to the "Frankfurt principle" according to which members of the IRG were compelled to reject contact with any synagogue or Jewish organization that did not uphold the inviolability of the Torah, Written and Oral. It was this principle that provided a measure of internal cohesion to Samson Raphael Hirsch and his followers, who formally seceded from the established Jewish community in Frankfurt in 1876. And it was this principle that led Hirsch and his followers to regard other forms of Jewish practice not only with contempt, but as heretical. Isaac Breuer was keen to admit that his grandfather had never meant to brand *individual Jews* as sinners, but rather to hold the Judaism they practiced as sinful.[15] Nonetheless, Isaac Breuer was steadfast in his commitment to an exclusionary community segregated from the larger Jewish population.

We can begin to gain a sense both of the distinctive legacy that Isaac Breuer inherited from his grandfather and of the powerful tensions emerging from it. On one hand, he was enjoined from participating fully in the larger communal and cultural life of German Jewry. On the other, he was encouraged to swim in the vast sea of German and European culture—though this encouragement came more from his grandfather's example than his father's desire. The formative environment in which this dual legacy was transmitted was rather circumscribed. Young Isaac's companions were either Hungarian yeshivah students or fellow Frankfurt Jewish children of the Breuer community. While the former were unschooled in *derekh erets*—the ways of the world—the latter were largely unschooled in Torah. This must have been somewhat alienating for the young Breuer, who had few real peers with whom to share his intellectual curiosity. He also felt himself at odds with the affluent materialism of the Breuer community, whose members were part of the busy commercial life of Frankfurt. In his parents' home, Breuer recalls, there was "no love of money whatsoever." On the contrary, there was a decidedly "anti-capitalistic" spirit that Breuer absorbed from childhood, and that would resonate with the social criticism voiced by Frankfurt intellectuals in Weimar times.[16]

The sense of social disaffection that Breuer experienced as a youth within his own segregated world would develop over time into a combative and polemical voice. But it did not diminish the fiercely loyal and proprietary attitude toward the community founded by his grandfather. He believed that this community not only bore the imprint of an inspired religious sage, but more importantly, was the torchbearer of the unique truths of the Torah. Indeed, according to his distinctive causal understanding, the foundation of the Frankfurt community had been laid hundreds of years earlier as an act of God—well before the advent of Reform Judaism in the nineteenth century, whose appearance he perceived as a grave threat to communal unity.[17] Preserving the fabric of the community in his own day was not only a social necessity, but a sacred obligation. In fact, Breuer once proclaimed that "whoever denies the unity of the Jewish community also denies the [ancient Jewish] State and the Holy Temple, denies Sinai, denies the family line of our Patriarch Abraham—indeed, denies God's Law."[18]

Breuer's powerful communal commitment was a hallmark of his own notion of *Torah 'im derekh erets*. So too was his engagement with the world of secular learning. Here too his experience was refracted through a separatist lens. Breuer recalls that in more than a decade of study in the university, he befriended almost no Gentile students and felt himself "a guest, a foreigner." He was similarly disconnected from mainstream Jewish student organizations such as the Kartell-Convent deutscher Studenten jüdischen Glaubens (KC). But this provided him with an opportunity to help establish, following the family pattern, a new organization specifically for Orthodox students, the Bund jüdischer Akademiker. From the ranks of the Bund's membership, Breuer found a most hospitable and embracing circle of friends with whom he spent his university years—and to whom he would remain close for the rest of his life.[19]

Breuer's university career began in the last years of study at his father's yeshivah (1902–1904), when he took courses in German literature and philosophy at Giessen. Like many university students of the day, Breuer did not stay long at the first institution. He moved on to Strasbourg in 1904, and from there to the universities of Marburg and Berlin before receiving a doctorate in law.

Clearly, the university provided nourishment to a hungry young consumer whose exposure to secular subjects had been somewhat limited hitherto. And yet, Breuer was careful to note in his autobiography that he always approached his university studies "as a Jew."[20] One wonders whether this is more a statement of intent than fact—a kind of apologia directed at an audience skeptical of the virtues of university study. But actually Breuer exhibited a constant tendency to marshal and modify secular subjects—history, philosophy, law—to fit his Jewish worldview.

The course was set early in this life. Breuer describes how as a youngster, he would ferret out the few secular history books in his father's library (such as K. F. Becker's popular *Weltgeschichte*). Reading these books made clear to him that "history, when it is understood and taught correctly, is the most important element in any education." For this reason, Breuer continued to study history in the more formal setting of the university, enjoying in particular G. F. Knapp's lectures on economic history at Strasbourg.[21] Through his study, he came to the realization that history represented "the most important means of linking the individual to the whole."

This principle served Breuer's evolving conception of Jewish history. That is, it not only paralleled the relationship between the individual Jew and the Jewish community. In the tradition of his revered predecessors (from Judah Ha-Levi to S. R. Hirsch), it also made manifest the link between the Jewish people and God. It is only in this sense that Breuer could declare that "one should not detach Judaism from history or grasp it without historical understanding."[22]

What we notice here is an interesting transformation, or transvaluation, of historicist norms. Breuer asserts the significance of the study of history, but does not rest content with the historicist charge to understand the past on its own terms. Rather, history's value lies in illuminating the present. In fact, *true* history reveals the course of a vital people (the Jews), as distinct from a history of dead objects strewn about the past. While such a view stands in contrast to Walter Benjamin's anti-triumphalist counter-history, it echoes the exceptionalist stance of the medieval Ha-Levi. In the *Kuzari*, the King of the Khazars admits to the Rabbi that "[m]any nations which arose after you have perished without leaving a memory."[23] Breuer shares Ha-Levi's sense that what is worth recording for posterity is that Jews survive and flourish on a plane of history distinct from the ephemeral plane on which the rest of the nations of the world rise and fall. It is this former plane that Breuer designated *Metageschichte* (Metahistory) and to which we will return later.

For now, it is important to note the connections between Breuer's views on history and his growing interest in philosophy. He began to read in the latter subject in his last years of yeshivah and gained a strong foundation in ancient and medieval philosophy at Strasbourg with Clemens Baeumker (Gershom Scholem's dissertation advisor in Munich). However, the most powerful philosophical encounter he had was with Immanuel Kant, whose work he came to know largely on his own.[24] Interestingly, Breuer spent two semesters at Marburg, home of Hermann Cohen and a major center of neo-Kantianism. But he never attended a single lecture of Cohen's. While he admired Cohen's proud defense of Jews against anti-Semites, he had a far less favorable impression of him than either Franz Rosenzweig or Leo Strauss did. In particular, he resented the fact that the Marburg professor did not approach his philosophical mission "as a Jew," but rather "took from Kant the foundations of his Jewish world-view."[25]

By contrast, Breuer believed that he was using Kant to reinforce a number of extant pillars in his own Jewish worldview. As he remembers, "from the first moment, I knew that it would be from his [Kant's] arsenal that I would take the weapons with which to defend the holy ground of the Torah." This meant, of course, ignoring Kant's dismissive reference to Judaism as an ossified *statutarisches Gesetz* (statutory law).[26] More substantively, it meant using Kant's theory of perception as a bulwark against the misguided truth claims of modern scholarship. Breuer was well aware that biblical critics in the nineteenth century had begun to call into question some of the most basic tenets of Judaism, including belief in Mosaic authorship of the Pentateuch and the veracity of miracles. He mobilized Kant not to herald the powers of human perception or illuminate the bounds of human consciousness, but, on the contrary, to demarcate the limits of what can be known from human experience. Thus, what modern scholars claimed to know, he argued, touched only upon their experience of the *phenomenal* world, the world of appearances—not upon the unknowable *noumenal* world of God's creation.[27] In making this argument, Breuer insisted that Kantianism was perfectly consonant with the Torah, as he asserted in the following gloss on a well-known biblical verse: " 'And do not go after your own heart and your own eyes' (Num. 15:39). In Kant's language: Do not follow your internal or external experience, for in following this course, you will be betraying Me."[28]

On this reading, Kant, the erstwhile critic of Judaism's statutory rigidity, became a herald of truth, the one to "lead us back to the Talmud, to the national law of Judaism." Kant's view that human consciousness frames the external world was buried under the weight of a more important position: namely, skepticism over the value of sensory experience. It is this latter point that most suited Breuer's purpose. Not even Revelation, he asserted, can be "the object of experience, because it breaks through experience."[29]

Such a perspective, which Breuer began to develop in his university years, was thoroughly compatible with his historical—or more accurately, ahistorical—view. Thus, the Jewish people, and the major events that defined it, were not susceptible to the kind of causal explanations that historicism attempted of human experience. In his view, God stands guard over the Jewish people, intervening at critical junctures in its history. Breuer attests to this supervision in a fascinating comment that affirms the uniqueness of Kant to the Jewish people:

> I am convinced in the depths of my soul that the God and King of Israel from time to time causes the appearance of enlightened men among the nations of the world, people whose destiny is to intervene in Jewish Metahistory and play a redemptive part in it. Not only Nebuchadnezzar and Titus are the scepter and rod of God. God also anointed Cyrus. Gutenberg too made a seminal contribution to the preservation and dissemination of the Oral Torah. And in a time of great struggle . . . God raised up among the nations a great man, far surpassing any other, Immanuel Kant. . . . Blessed is God who gave of His wisdom to Kant!

This near apotheosis of Kant is of a different order from the reverence usually accorded the Königsberg philosopher by his admirers, including Hermann Cohen. It is particularly uncommon given that Kant had fallen out of favor in many philosophical circles of the day. But Breuer was not completely out of step with contemporary intellectual trends. In the wake of Adolf von Harnack's lectures on the "essence of Christianity," Breuer can be said to belong to a loose grouping of neo-traditionalist thinkers intent on affirming the timeless essence of their respective religions. Without mentioning either Harnack or other Christian theologians by name, Breuer acknowledged as much. In an article from 1910, he wrote that the great battle of his day was "the struggle for the essence of Judaism."[30] His own definition of "essence" tended to be legal, as befitted his training, his Orthodox orientation, and, particularly, his fear of a Reform assault on the integrity of the *Halakhah*.

As with philosophy, law was a discipline that Breuer marshaled to solidify his core Jewish worldview. Both from his father's home and his grandfather's legacy, he developed the conviction that the Oral Torah was the unyielding anchor of Jewish group identity. Meanwhile, he began the formal study of law while at Strasbourg, and continued at Marburg and Berlin before receiving his doctorate in the field. If Kant served to confirm Breuer's belief in a God beyond experience, then his legal studies fulfilled an important comparative function. They allowed him to juxtapose Jewish and modern European notions of law, with the ultimate goal of "penetrating to the core of the Divine laws."[31] Modern law, Brewer contended, is "expedient," always seeking to balance the interests of society's members and the need for "coercive regulations for maintaining order."[32] Jewish law, by contrast, "does not serve the balance of personal interest." Nor does it redefine itself in response to shifting ethical norms. Rather, it is a fixed, God-given body of law that bestows duties and obligations. Only within the boundaries of those duties and obligations are human beings at liberty to pursue their own moral course.[33]

Similar to his distinctive embrace of Kant, Breuer's comparison of Jewish and modern law suited his evolving metahistorical vision. The Jewish people possessed a unique, indeed transcendent, legal birthright that lifted it above the Gentile nations. Not surprisingly, Breuer felt most comfortable nurturing this exclusivist vision of Judaism within the insular community to which he returned in 1913. This is not to suggest that his encounter with the secular academy was unimportant. It was indispensable to his formation and self-presentation as an Orthodox theorist and political leader. On a more practical level, it prepared him for a professional career as lawyer and notary in which he was compelled to engage the broader social milieu around him. Nevertheless, Breuer felt most at home in the company of other Jews, and like-minded ones at that. Even with the latter—for instance, his fellow Orthodox activist from Frankfurt, Jacob Rosenheim—Breuer did not always live peaceably. For he was a sharp polemicist who had little patience for dissent from his clear-cut view of Orthodoxy.

It is partly Breuer's polemical ferocity that led Leo Strauss to invoke the image of the combative Counter-Reformation Church, "Ecclesia militans," in writing of him in 1925. But it was also the fact that Breuer was facing what he believed to be a Jewish reformation in his day—heralded by religious reformers, as well as Zionists.[34] Against these new modes of Jewish expression, Breuer was unswerving in his defense of the uniqueness and immutability of Torah Judaism. Perhaps Leo Strauss recognized something of his own conservative, or counterrevolutionary, instincts in Breuer—though, of course, they were expressed in a far more traditional form in Breuer's case.

Breuer, for his part, believed that he was following the path of the true revolutionary of modern Jewish history: S. R. Hirsch. In a lecture in Frankfurt, he once declared that revolutionaries in the Gentile world possessed a strong antinomian impulse to overturn laws and norms that were humanly derived and hence transitory. This same impulse to upend existing laws and norms characterized the "illegitimate revolutionaries" in Jewish history, from the rebellious king of antiquity, Jeroboam, to the nineteenth-century Reformers Abraham Geiger and Ludwig Philippson. By contrast, what made a Jewish revolutionary *legitimate* was the knowledge that Jewish law was Divine Law, and thus eternal. And what made such a figure *revolutionary*, according to Breuer, was not the desire to surrender to a "new [historical] reality" like the illegitimate revolutionaries. Rather, it was the willingness "to demand the right of the complete domination of that new reality by the Divine Word . . . until it conformed entirely to the Torah." It was the goal of a world in conformance with Torah toward which the true revolutionary of the modern age, Samson Raphael Hirsch, aspired. It was also this goal that coincided with Hirsch's grand messianic plan of "restor[ing] the Jewish nation to the heart of its history, which has no objective other than to prepare anew for a Divine State."[35]

## "I AM A NATIONAL JEW"

In his close study of Isaac Breuer, Matthias Morgenstern frequently refers to his subject as "Enkel Hirschs" (Hirsch's grandson) rather than by his own name. The implication is that Breuer so deeply imbibed the ideals and dreams of his grandfather that his own identity merged with the latter's. There is a good deal to be said for this point, since Breuer revered Hirsch as a figure of prophetic stature and clairvoyance.[36] Moreover, his own lifestyle and system of thought were proudly derivative of the Hirschian path. At the same time, Breuer deviated from Hirsch's model, as even the most reverential of heirs tend to do.

A good case in point for the former is Breuer's elaboration of Hirsch's view regarding the divine supervision of Israel's history. Breuer fully concurred with Hirsch that "the Jewish people and the Torah are different from any other people and any other set of laws."[37] Indeed, both believed that Israel was, at once, beyond the plane of mundane history and yet "*the* people of history."[38] The meaning that the two bestowed upon the term "history" was much different than that used by most practicing historians—and is most accurately rendered as *Metageschichte*.

And yet, Breuer did a good deal more than amplify Hirsch's ideas. He shifted their focus, and in rather substantial fashion. Perhaps the most notable instance pertains to their respective views of the land of Israel. Hirsch was opposed to attempts to settle large numbers of Jews in the Holy Land, as he made clear throughout his career and particularly in rejecting Rabbi Zvi Hirsch Kalischer's call for a return to the land of Israel in *Derishat Zion* (1862). Breuer, by contrast, advocated Jewish settlement in Palestine and saw it as an indication of progress toward the creation of a genuine Torah state there. In this sense, he was proposing a significant innovation over Hirsch. For Breuer, it was not merely the ways of the land that must be reconciled with Torah (*Torah 'im derekh erets*). It was the ways of the land *of Israel* itself that must be reconciled with Torah (*Torah 'im derekh erets Yisrael*!).[39]

The seeds of Breuer's creative adaptation of Hirsch, as well as of his distinctive Jewish nationalism, were planted in an early article, "Lehre, Gesetz und Nation" ("Doctrine, Law and Nation") from 1910. This essay offers an illuminating glance at the ideological and intellectual currents guiding Breuer, the university student, as he was beginning to formulate his philosophy of history. He commenced the essay by discussing the swirling debate in Germany over the nature of the *Geisteswissenschaften*, and particularly over the nature of historical understanding. He was mindful that some preferred to understand history according to the hard-and-fast scientific norms of the *Naturwissenschaften*, while others tended to regard historical knowledge as a willful surrender to the subjective impressions of the individual observer. Neither approach satisfied Breuer. In general, he eschewed the historicist interest in the fleeting individual event, focusing instead on an enduring Idea—indeed, an Idea "that is destined to emerge victorious over all temporal changes . . . in its original form."[40] This notion echoed Samson Raphael Hirsch's own ahistorical vision of Judaism, although it was presented in a far more sophisticated philosophical idiom.

Breuer's intent in affirming the atemporality of great ideas was to establish a timeless foundation on which Judaism could stand. This was not a mere academic exercise, but a vital weapon in the intra-Jewish battle between Orthodox and Liberal (or Reform) camps over the "essence of Judaism." Indeed, the same question that Harnack had introduced into modern Christianity a decade earlier now animated Breuer: to what extent could a sacred tradition be understood in historicist terms? Breuer followed his grandfather in maintaining that the Divine Law was not subject to change over time, which is why it became the stable anchor of identity for the Jewish people. By contrast, he argued that Reform Jews tended to understand Judaism as a series of context-bound episodes, each of which was as meaningful as the next. In this way, they could choose the form of Judaism most palatable to them. But Judaism, Breuer countered, was not a matter of individual choice. It required absolute submission to the eternal authority of the Divine Law.[41]

In the same essay from 1910, Breuer introduced another criterion that distinguished him even further from his Jewish opponents. Whereas Orthodoxy "acknowledge[s] the Jewish nation, [liberal Judaism] does not believe in the existence of the national will." So as to leave no doubt, Breuer declared: "I am a national Jew."[42] Just what he meant by this declaration is worth considering. He clearly did not intend it as a profession of loyalty to Zionism, which, to his mind, had altogether abandoned the centrality of the Divine Law.

Nevertheless, Breuer's self-definition reveals the extent to which he operated within the turn-of-the-century nationalist discourse of which Zionism was a leading component. Breuer relates in his memoirs that while "the word 'Palestine' was foreign to me" as a child, the name "Erets Yisrael" was near and dear to him; it signified "our homeland that connects the future with the past." In fact, a large map of the country hung on the wall of the family's home.[43] Perhaps even more surprising was Breuer's attitude toward the founding father of political Zionism, Theodor Herzl (1860–1904), who himself led a decidedly secular life. As Breuer proudly recalled, Herzl was the veiled hero of the first article that he wrote at the age of twenty in 1903 (published in the Orthodox journal, *Der Israelit*). In the following year, Breuer wrote a remarkable encomium to Herzl on the occasion of the latter's death. Herzl's soul, Breuer wrote, had "roamed the countries," looking for a stable and welcome haven. After years of self-delusion and lack of fulfillment, Herzl's soul then "turned in upon itself completely and listened attentively to its inner chords." At that point, Herzl "found his way back to Judaism," discovered the downtrodden Jewish masses, and began to labor on their behalf for a revived Jewish nation. In the process, he "became the first conscious *national* Jew."[44]

Much of Breuer's eulogy rings with praise for Herzl's abiding love of his people. The sole note of dissonance, and it is a powerful one, comes at the end of the essay. After declaring that Herzl "paced the earth like the king of the Jews," he observed that "even today the crown of the king of the Jews is still a crown of thorns!"[45] With this final sentence, Breuer engaged in the ultimate act of Jewish delegitimation by comparing the recently departed Herzl (and his Zionist creed) to the fallen Jesus.

But this last expression is so discordant with the rest of the text as to expose Breuer's deep inner conflicts over Herzl and Zionism.[46] He emphasized that he was eminently appreciative of Herzl's "genius," particularly his recognition that "there is no solution to the Jewish problem other than the return of the Jewish people to the land of the Jews." And yet, for all his Jewish pathos, Herzl did not—and as a secular Jew, could not—grasp the true significance of Zion for Jewish national consciousness. Judah Ha-Levi's aching odes to the Promised Land did not echo in his ears, as they did for Breuer. One consequence was that Herzl was prepared to surrender the prospect of a Jewish homeland in Erets Yisrael, as he did when the British offered territory in Eastern Africa to the Zionists in 1903.[47]

The so-called Uganda proposal was thoroughly unacceptable to Breuer. Like many Zionist critics of Herzl, he demanded that Erets Yisrael stand at the center of Jewish national aspirations. After all, he felt himself a foreigner in Germany—not a surprising frame of mind given the insular communal life that he and his family lived. Moreover, when Breuer chose to define his Jewish affiliation, interestingly, he eschewed the category of "religious" in favor of "national."[48] But this choice did not amount to Zionism. On the contrary, Breuer's national Jewish identity was fiercely anti-Zionist. To his mind, the Zionist gambit rested on a bold new belief in the power and efficacy of human agency, embodied in the will of Jews to reclaim their ancestral homeland. Such an anthropocentric approach, he maintained, undermined the faith of the Torah-true Jew in the omnipotence of the Divine Hand.

To combat the growing appeal of Zionism, Breuer and other like-minded Jews set out to create an organizational framework of their own less than a decade after Herzl's death. The founding conference of Agudat Israel (otherwise known as the Agudah) took place in the German town of Kattowitz, Germany (today Katowice, Poland) on May 27–28, 1912. The goal of the group was to bring together the diverse and often competing elements of the Orthodox Jewish world in a united front under Torah and against Zionism. Its founders recognized, as Breuer himself was keenly aware, that to succeed in the twentieth century was to establish a sound organizational infrastructure. And yet, the initial efforts at achieving organizational and broader communal harmony were hampered by internal dissension, chiefly (and ironically) between the leading lights of the Frankfurt Orthodox community: Jacob Rosenheim, on one hand, and Salomon and Isaac Breuer, on the other. As against Rosenheim's more tolerant attitude, the Breuers were adamant in their insistence that only members of separatist Orthodox communities like their own, as opposed to those who worked with non-Orthodox Jews under a single communal roof, be permitted to serve in leadership positions in the Agudah.[49] The resulting dispute injected a bitter note into the early discussions surrounding the organization. Further polluting the environment were serious differences of opinion over the role of Erets Yisrael. Whereas Rosenheim believed that the question of Palestine should be subsumed under the larger goal of unifying Orthodox Jews worldwide (most of whom lived in Europe), Isaac Breuer pushed the Agudah to shape its agenda around the centrality of Erets Yisrael in Jewish life. As he would explain in 1921, the very idea of "Agudism demands that the divine people and the divine land be prepared and rendered fit to become united once more under the rule of the divine law as a State of God."[50]

These ideological fissures were but one obstacle in the path of the newly founded Agudah. An even more sizable one was the outbreak of the First World War in 1914, which prevented the actual physical assembly of Orthodox Jews from throughout Europe in order to ratify the new organization's mission. As a result, the meeting at which ratification was planned, known as the Kenesiah Gedolah, was not held until 1923!

The intervening period of institutional paralysis did not prevent Isaac Breuer from developing and refining his thinking. In fact, Jacob Levinger is correct to point out that the War "left a considerable mark upon Breuer's personality, his speculative labors and his practical ideology."[51] In general, we think of the war as a vast and bloody battlefield in whose trenches millions died. And it surely was that. But for Breuer, as well as for Franz Rosenzweig, the war afforded large chunks of unstructured time during which they could read, think, and write. Freed from combat duty because of vision problems, Breuer worked as a military censor for the Red Cross and later as an advocate for the German army. He wrote a steady stream of articles and pamphlets during and immediately after the war. Especially noticeable in this body of writing is Breuer's belief that the war was not just the source of untold suffering. It was also "an unmistakable symptom of the birth-pangs of the Messiah."[52] God was actively at work in this period, propelling Jews closer to redemption in Erets Yisrael. Breuer's language in describing this extraordinary moment was quite explicit. Historical events became props in a grand messianic drama.[53] At the same time, Breuer shared in the apocalyptic spirit so characteristic of German intellectuals during and after the war. Consistent with their hopes, he clung to the idea that out of the depths of destruction would emerge a new social, political, and spiritual order.

## THE "MESSIANIC NATION" BETWEEN HISTORY AND METAHISTORY

In the final year of the war, Isaac Breuer found himself in a state of tumult, acutely aware of the massive destruction it had wrought.[54] This prompted a feverish fit of literary activity in which he called for a "new orientation" in Jewish life. Close in time and impetus to Franz Rosenzweig's New Thinking, Breuer understood this new orientation as a necessary by-product of his time: "The War is not merely an episode. Rather, it inaugurates a new era, an era that places on our people a totally new mission, which we have not known for two thousand years of Exile, indeed, which needs to be carried out as a unified people."[55]

He elaborated on the task at hand in a small pamphlet from 1918, *Judenproblem*. We notice here a feature of his thought that has often surfaced in our discussion: a tendency to borrow, and then infuse with new meaning common terms of reference. In *Judenproblem*, Breuer ponders and then dismisses conventional categories of Jewish identity in ways that would make a Zionist proud.[56] For instance, in a chapter entitled "The Essence of Judaism," Breuer writes: "The Old Testament is not the recorded source of a *religion*, but the history of a still living Jewish *national* consciousness, of the divine founding of a *nation*."[57]

This recasting of the Hebrew Bible issued from Breuer's belief that the "nation is the most distinctive and finest work of history."[58] But, as earlier, Breuer departs from the standard Zionist understanding. To his mind, the Jewish nation requires neither a state nor sovereignty to survive and flourish. Its unbending collective will, anchored in an eternal relationship with God, makes it unique among the nations. "Despite its dispersion," Breuer wrote, the Jewish people "is a nation in a more exalted sense than all the other nations on earth."

Breuer's co-option of the term "nation" in *Judenproblem* is best seen in conjunction with his appropriation of the term "history." As we noted at the outset, the link between history and nation was a common feature of aspiring national movements in the nineteenth and twentieth centuries, especially as they sought to ground their legitimacy in the ancient past. Zionists of the early twentieth century embarked on their own quest for historical legitimacy by attempting to demonstrate the antiquity of Jewish settlement in the land of Israel.[59] Breuer too sought to grasp the Jewish national collectivity "on the grounds of history," but not necessarily by digging up the first traces of Jewish settlement in Palestine. His notion of history was less etiological—and, for that matter, territorial—than his Zionist contemporaries'.[60] Thus, the fact that Jews, even after the loss of their state, "have never ceased to be historical" meant something quite different than we might expect. To be "historical," in Breuer's sense, was to maintain a timeless (and extraterritorial) bond with God.[61]

If, as Matthias Morgenstern suggests, Breuer formulated an "alternative Zionism," then it is also fair to say that he formulated an alternative or counter-history to the unfolding Zionist narrative.[62] Just as the Zionists wanted to return the Jews to the realm of what he called "visible" history, he aimed to situate the Jews in the less visible and more sublime domain of "Metahistory." To enable this task, Breuer reconstrued the long period of Exile from a source of ignominy, as in the Zionist narrative, to a necessary phase in the unfolding drama of Jewish national history. Breuer thus recalls Franz Rosenzweig and Leo Strauss, both of whom understood *Galut* (or *Golus* in Breuer's Ashkenazic locution) as the incubator of a unique Jewish group identity. Moreover, Breuer shared with Rosenzweig the desire to assert the historicity of the Jews, provided that the term be understood in an almost ironic noncontingent sense (i.e., what he called *Metageschichte* and Rosenzweig *Weltgeschichte*).

The affinity between Rosenzweig and Breuer was hardly accidental. Not only did the two criticize the Zionist version of Jewish history without surrendering their own particularist vision of that history. They also thought and wrote about the relationship among Jews, God, and history in the same period: Breuer in the final year of the war when he published two booklets, *Judenproblem* and *Messiasspuren*; and Rosenzweig in the first years after the war when he delivered a series of lectures on Jewish history in his hometown of Kassel.

At a more direct level, Breuer and Rosenzweig knew of each other's work. Both lived after the war in the same city, Frankfurt. The respective worlds they inhabited—that of the Lehrhaus and the Breuer community—were quite distinct. But Rosenzweig hinted at Breuer's intellectual presence when he reported that he read *Judenproblem* several weeks before starting to write the *Star of Redemption*.[63] Breuer, for his part, responded with enthusiasm when Rosenzweig sent him a copy of the *Star*. He was deeply impressed by Rosenzweig's insights into Judaism, particularly when compared to recent Zionist writers.[64]

To be sure, Breuer and Rosenzweig differed on a number of key points, including the imperative of Halakhic observance and, most germane for us, the imminence of messianic fulfillment. It is this last point that fuels Breuer's *Messiasspuren* (Messianic Traces) from December 1918. Breuer commences his pamphlet by reaffirming the uniqueness of the Jewish people as a "God-nation" (*Gottesnation*).[65] This designation differentiates the Jewish nation from other nations, which occupy the prosaic plane of human history. By contrast, the Jewish nation soars above the realm of the "every-day" (*Alltag*).[66] Whereas *Alltag* connotes history from the bottom up, Breuer's instinct is exactly the opposite. God is the prime causal mover in Jewish history, prompting Breuer to exclaim: "What a special history! No state or military history, nor cultural or economic history in the usual sense. It is messianic history."[67]

Similar to Rosenzweig and, to a lesser extent, Strauss, Breuer insists that the condition of Exile is not only unavoidable, but in fact the "salvation" of the Jews. Its chief attributes, powerlessness and dispersion, liberate the Jews from an unhealthy and obsessive reliance on land and state. Indeed, it was in Exile that the "messianic nation" learned to "abjure the path of sovereignty, the striving for political power." And thus, Breuer proclaimed, "Golus became the school of the messianic nation," as well as "the most creative epoch that the Jewish nation ever had."[68]

Breuer's conflation of time and space in his depiction of Exile is hardly the product of a confused mind. On the contrary, it signifies a concerted assault on the modern nationalist project, as symbolized by Zionism. Rather than reify the existence of the Jews through a return to history, Breuer sought to sacralize their path by projecting it beyond the time and space of "visible history." But even as he made this point, Breuer could not escape the imagery and language of contemporary nationalism. His anti-Zionist counternarrative in *Messiasspuren* illustrates this well. Arguing that "the cultural epoch of the Enlightenment is long over by now," Breuer averred that "[w]e are in the age of nationalism."[69] But he quickly qualified this claim, insisting that the "sovereign national (model) of the pre-War period" no longer held sway. Rather, a new form of nationalism, focused on humanity far more than the single nation, was on the verge of realization. And the standard-bearer of this new nationalism was the "messianic nation," the Jewish people, whose very extraterritorial status exemplified the eroding boundary between national and transnational aspirations.[70]

The real force of this text emanates from Breuer's unabashed insertion of messianic significance into the events of the day. The World War, with all its destruction, was a clear sign of the Messiah. Even more remarkably, Zionism, which Breuer excoriates as "pseudo-Judaism" and "crass politicization," also signaled the coming of the Messiah. It represented the *yetser ha-ra'* of the Jewish nation—a term common in rabbinic parlance to describe the human inclination to evil, often in the form of sexual temptation.[71] In Breuer's dialectical scheme, this nationalist *yetser ha-ra'* stood in opposition to a previous evil, the excessive individualism borne of the Enlightenment. Both were to be overcome, or exhausted, by the messianic nationalism of the *Gottesnation.*

Breuer's language points in an interesting direction. As Alan Mittleman has discussed in *Between Kant and Kabbalah*, Breuer was familiar with and indebted to the thought of the sixteenth-century Jewish mystic from Safed, R. Isaac Luria (1534–1572). Mittleman notes the resemblance between a core principle of Breuer's, *Willenskontraktion* (the contraction of the individual will at the limit of its perceptual powers) and the central Lurianic doctrine of *tsimtsum* (the contraction of the Divine infinity, leading to the creation of the world).[72] In fact, two other fundaments of the Lurianic system may help explain Breuer's view of the instrumental function of Zionism qua *yetser ha-ra'.* According to Luria and his disciples, evil enters the world when the energizing light of God shatters the vessels that contain it (a process known as *shevirat ha-kelim*). The subsequent mission of the human race is to retrieve the shattered fragments of the vessels, now embodying evil, and restore them to completed form.[73] In this way, the elimination of evil becomes an indispensable part of the messianic process of *tikkun olam*, repair of the world.[74]

At the peak of his own messianic fervor in 1918, Breuer developed a strikingly similar and, consequently, magnanimous attitude toward Zionism. Its growing strength, while hardly beneficial on its own terms, nonetheless served a salutary function: to refocus the spiritual energies of the Jewish people on Erets Yisrael. In this respect, it brought closer the approaching redemptive moment.[75] In fact, the Divine Hand was evident not only in the form of Zionism, but, as Breuer later wrote, in the Balfour Declaration of 1917 in which the British government voiced support for a Jewish "national homeland" in Palestine. It was present as well in the subsequent Mandate establishing British control over Palestine.[76] Taking his cue from these messianically charged events, Breuer intensified his Palestine-centered activities, particularly within the Agudah immediately after the war.[77]

The rising prominence of Erets Yisrael in Breuer's thought gives us an indication not only of his palpable messianic excitement, but of the bedrock principle of divine causality in which his view of history took hold. Like his medieval hero, Judah Ha-Levi, as well as other Jewish chroniclers up through David Gans of Prague, Breuer grasped large historical events as signs of God's active intervention in history. These events were invested with salvific meaning in a way that defied the modern historicist imagination. Breuer thus developed an approach to history that we might call neotraditionalist, and that characterizes the attitude of many Orthodox thinkers in the modern age.[78] In his particular case, the roots of this approach can be traced back to his grandfather. At the same time, they extend forward throughout the entire Hirschian tradition—reaching as far as the late-twentieth-century Shimon Schwab, whom we mentioned in chapter 1.

## Between Philistine and Shlemiel: Breuer and the Critique of Bourgeois Judaism in Frankfurt

Breuer's passion for Erets Yisrael, present already in childhood, was fanned by the powerful messianic winds blowing after the war. But it is necessary to ponder another source of this passion in the postwar period: his increasing disillusionment with the Breuer *Kehilah* of Frankfurt in which he had been raised and to which he returned after university. With an eye already turned toward Zion, Breuer looked on with disgust when his older brother Raphael (1881–1932) was passed over in a bruising succession battle for the post of *Kehilah* rabbi in 1924. At that point, the chain of familial transmission that commenced with S. R. Hirsch and descended to Breuer's father, Salomon, was broken.[79] This development only reinforced Breuer's apprehension that the community was adrift. The grand era of Hirsch's leadership, combining spiritual intensity and intellectual rigor, had passed. In its place came rule by an unlearned bourgeoisie, more at home as bankers than scholars.

The historian Mordechai Breuer (son of Isaac) notes that an air of malaise hovered over Orthodox Jews in Germany after the war. Like many other disaffected Jews, they too yearned for a "new orientation" in life: "Growing cultural pessimism, lack of trust in authorities, uncertainty about the merits of the present condition, the expectation of an approaching new world, a shift toward the irrational–all these components of the generally prevailing mood of crisis at that time can also be detected within Orthodox Jewry."[80]

There were few Orthodox Jews more mindful of this "mood of crisis"—or sharply critical of the status quo—than Isaac Breuer. In that he saw himself as heir and continuator of his grandfather's legacy, it is nothing short of remarkable that Breuer adopted, as his son has observed, "an astonishingly radical standpoint in his criticism of Orthodox Jewish society."[81] It is true that Breuer developed a strong dose of skepticism toward capitalism. It is also true that Breuer, the strictly devout Jew, was an admirer of Karl Marx, whose work made clear to him the centrality of economic factors in understanding human experience.[82] And yet, the depth of his animus toward the comfortable merchants and financiers of his own community is striking. As far back as 1907, when the twenty-four year-old Breuer was a university student, he decried the "Philistinism" (*Philistertum*) of his fellow Jewish students. This epithet recurs frequently throughout his polemical and novelistic writings. It stands in contrast, as Matthias Morgenstern notes, not to a model of proletarian virtue, but to an eminently Jewish figure: the "Shlemiel," the Yiddish term for an innocent, hapless, and tragicomic soul.[83]

The opposition between Philistine and Jewish values receives clear expression in *Ein Kampf um Gott* (1920) and *Falk Nefts Heimkehr* (1923), two of Breuer's novels that reflect well "the author's abhorrence of the bourgeois-capitalistic atmosphere that prevailed in the Orthodox Judaism of Germany."[84] The protagonists of these two novels, as well as the later *Der Neue Kusari*, are young men, raised in affluent, but spiritually arid Jewish homes, who are in search of something richer than material fulfillment. In *Falk Nefts Heimkehr*, the eponymous hero makes his way back to a meaningful life of Torah observance, but only by challenging his father's bourgeois and Zionist commitments.[85]

These two commitments were closely linked in Breuer's worldview. Both represented misguided attempts at accommodation to the prevailing norms of Gentile society—in other words, surrender to *Philistertum*. The *material* appetites of the Jewish bourgeoisie were distractions from the main tasks of rigorous study and devout observance on which Torah Judaism rested. Zionism, for its part, advanced the fallacy that a prosaic *material* existence—life as a nation like other nations—marked the ultimate goal of Jewish nationhood. These two forms of (non-Marxist) materialism had a similar effect: forcing the "God-Nation" down from the elevated plane of *Metageschichte*. Fearful of this consequence, the fictional Falk Neft hastened to explain to his father why he opted to be a Jew rather than a Zionist:

> Zionism means: affirmation of the historical life of the nations. Judaism means: denial of the historical life of the nations. Zionism means: denial of the God-King of Zion and Jerusalem. Judaism means: affirmation of the God-King of Zion and Jerusalem. There is no meeting, no reconciliation. It is Yes and No.[86]

The resistance of Breuer (via Falk Neft) to the historicizing impulse of Zionism belongs to the current of dissent that we have been following in this book. We may recall that Hermann Cohen strenuously objected to Heinrich Graetz's pre-Zionist "Palestinianism"—the code word for a misguided material framing of Jewish history. Likewise, Franz Rosenzweig suggested that the "power of history over the life of nations" dissolved in the face of the extraterritorial Jewish people. All three identified an unholy alliance between a base form of Jewish nationalism and a base historicism that reduced all objects in its path to equally sized fragments. Concern over this alliance was a signal feature of the anti-historicist trend in German-Jewish thought in the early twentieth century.

We have seen that for Breuer and Rosenzweig, the sense that Judaism was under siege and in need of rescue was particularly pronounced after the war. Confronted by a mountain of physical and psychological rubble, they both felt it imperative to renounce the excesses of "Philistinism." It is no coincidence that they both resided in Frankfurt, which was in the midst of substantial intellectual and ideological ferment in the postwar period. Indeed, the city had become a major center of social theory—home to an outstanding sociology department at the city's university, and more importantly to the Institut für Sozialforschung. It was the Institut, many of whose leading members were Jews, that set the agenda for a wide-ranging critique of bourgeois society—initially through a somewhat unreflexive Marxism and later through a substantial revision of Marxist theory.[87]

Frankfurt's ambience of anti-bourgeois criticism also left an imprint on Franz Rosenzweig's Lehrhaus, which opened four years before the Institut. The Lehrhaus's goal of reinvigorating Judaism was to be achieved, to a great extent, by weaning German Jews away from their closely held bourgeois affections. For example, its declared aim of erasing the boundary between teacher and student held considerable appeal for those in rebellion against the social stratification of bourgeois society. In light of these impulses, it is not surprising that some Jewish intellectuals in Frankfurt—among them the psychoanalyst Erich Fromm and the economist Leo Löwenthal—moved between the somewhat parallel (and largely Jewish) worlds of the Lehrhaus and the Institut.

Isaac Breuer belonged to neither of these worlds; nor did he have extensive contacts with them. Nevertheless, his own anti-bourgeois disposition resonated deeply with Weimar (and Frankfurt) intellectual culture. In step with social critics from across the political spectrum, Breuer inveighed against the liberal celebration of the individual, whose self-indulgence he loathed.[88] The antidote to this modern malady was retreat to the confines of a holistic community, whose members would stand as one in reverent submission to the Law. In Breuer's parlance, this ideal community bore the name "Knesset Yisrael," a term that abounds in biblical, rabbinic, and kabbalistic literature and usually connotes, as E. E. Urbach notes, "the unique, sanctified, and chosen people of Israel."[89] Fully cognizant of the classical resonances of the term, Breuer spoke with an almost mystical reverence of the *Knesset Yisrael*, describing it as "the metahistorical name of the Jewish people . . . in its full and eternal unity."[90] But as always, Breuer's understanding was framed by more modern inspirations. In his crowning novelistic achievement, *Der Neue Kusari* of 1934, the main character, Alfred Roden delivers an interesting neo-Kantian gloss on community. The *Knesset Yisrael*, he argues, was "the a priori of the Jewish people, the cognitive framework for the comprehension of its unique history."[91] That is, membership in the Jewish community—as expressed through adherence to the Divine Law *and* belief in the divinity of the Oral Law—opened the epistemological portal through which to grasp the Jewish historical experience.

The central role of community in Breuer's vision of Judaism points in another interesting direction: the robust communitarian spirit in German and German-Jewish life from the end of the nineteenth century. An important impetus in creating the resonant language of community came from the late nineteenth-century sociologist Ferdinand Tönnies, who posed a stark distinction between a traditional organic community and a mechanistic modern society in *Gemeinschaft und Gesellschaft* (1887). Tönnies's work undergirded later critiques of the ills of modernity from both left and right—that is, from socialist utopians to conservative revolutionaries.

In the case of German Jewry, the new communitarian impulse intersected with the rise of Zionism.[92] Throughout the early decades of the twentieth century, advocates of Zionism advanced the view that Jewish identity dwelt not in an incorporeal spiritual unity, but in a concrete communal body (*Volksgemeinschaft*). Paradoxically, Martin Buber saw the First World War as an impetus to the new communitarianism. Writing weeks after the war broke out, he insisted that "in the catastrophic events that he experienced with his neighbors, the Jew discovered with shock and joy the great life of *Gemeinschaft*."[93] This patriotic German expression would be channeled over time into a more particular Jewish idiom. Following the war, a bevy of new political parties and ideologies—including Zionism—emerged on the German-Jewish landscape speaking the language of community.[94] At the crowded juncture of communitarian and nationalist discourses in Weimar times stood Isaac Breuer. Caught in the wake of Zionism, but forever swimming against it, he craved anew the embrace of an organic Jewish community.

Community, we recall, was a major concern of S. R. Hirsch. It was he who oversaw the birth of the separatist Frankfurt *Kehilah*. His grandson never renounced support for the *Kehilah*. But he did shift the locus of his communal desires from Frankfurt to Jerusalem; and he would rename his grandfather's guiding program from *Torah 'im derekh erets* (TIDE) to *Torah 'im derekh erets Yisrael* (TIDEY). It is difficult to measure the relative weight of strictly personal motives (e.g., the defeat of his brother for *Kehilah* rabbi) as against more ideologically grounded convictions in explaining this shift. Both sets of factors point in the direction of Zion. And it is to Zion that Breuer now directed his energies. He first visited Palestine in 1926 and opted to settle there permanently in 1936. By 1925, he had outlined his vision of a non-Zionist Jewish community in Erets Yisrael. The chief aim of Jewish settlers in Palestine, he wrote in *Das Jüdische Nationalheim*, should be to establish a "legitimate corporate body in the Holy Land [guided by] the Torah as revealed by God, and handed down by their Fathers, its written and traditional laws as recorded in the 'Shulchan Aruch.' "[95] As against the comfortable Jewish bourgeois and the Philistine Zionist, the déclassé Schlemiel—outwardly hapless and inwardly aflame with love for Judaism—would make an ideal and principled settler in this new community.

## SELF-CRITICISM AND THE PATH TO ZION

"If Hirsch had inaugurated the bourgeois era of German-Jewish Orthodoxy," Matthias Morgenstern writes, "it was now the task of the generation of his grandson to analyze, critique, and overcome it."[96] Isaac Breuer readily assumed the role, casting a critical eye upon his own community.

FIGURE 5  Isaac Breuer (1883–1946). Courtesy of
the Leo Baeck Institute, New York.

The *embourgeoisement* of Orthodox Jews in Germany was, by many accounts, a mark of considerable social success and adaptability. But Breuer
saw the underside, the pedestrian tastes and acquisitive passions of his
fellow Orthodox. In this regard, his perspective differed little from that
of less traditional Jewish intellectuals of his generation whose disaffection
from German-Jewish life found an outlet in the intense ferment during
and after the First World War. Like a number of prominent members of
this intellectual class, Breuer eventually surrendered the illusion of a vibrant Jewish community in the Diaspora and decided to move to Palestine. Unlike them, the vehicle that bore him to Erets Yisrael was not Zionism, but rather its sworn enemy, Agudism.

Herein lies one of the defining paradoxes of Isaac Breuer. The man who once branded Zionism "the most dreadful enemy that has ever arisen against the Jewish nation" embarked on the most Zionist of paths—and in an age of feverish Zionist activity.[97] Once in Palestine, he lashed out at the organized Agudah leadership in Europe for denying the profound link between "the people of the Torah and the land of the Torah."[98] This makes all the more curious Breuer's version of Agudism, which replicates Zionism in institutional form and geographic focus. One might speculate that this mimetic act was the result either of a remarkable opacity or a secret envy.

Even if we accept one of these explanations, we would not have an accurate portrait of Isaac Breuer. He was anything but a limp marionette, bending and bowing in response to external manipulation. Breuer thrived on the energy of a vibrant marketplace of ideas, honing his own proposals and polemics through exposure to others. There was always a fearless intellectual quality to him, visible not only in his openness to ideas, but in his attitude toward his own community. Operating within a world in which submission to authority was expected, Breuer had the right mix of family pedigree, unquestioned piety, and intellectual restlessness to extend his attitude to the farthest reaches of legitimacy. His agitation was present in virtually everything he wrote, but received its fullest expression in the heroes of his novels—and above all, in the figure of Alfred Roden in *Der Neue Kusari*.

It is curious and telling that Breuer often used the novelistic form, hardly the most traditional of Jewish literary genres, to offer detailed exposition of his ideas. Indeed, while his fiction may have lacked artistic merit, it did not suffer from a dearth of interesting insights.[99] On the contrary, it provided Breuer with an opportunity to do what he might have regarded as indulgent or even decadent in essay form: to expose and explore his own religious psyche.

Alfred Roden was, in this respect, an interesting mirror of Breuer. Roden was typical of the Weimar-era Jewish intellectuals who could no longer tolerate the bourgeois tedium of their parents' homes. Neither could he accept what Franz Kafka called in the famous letter to his father "the insignificant scrap of Judaism you yourself possessed."[100] But as a probing young man, Roden was not prepared to surrender the legacy of his ancient forebears. In the tradition of Ha-Levi's Khazar king or S. R. Hirsch's Benjamin in *The Nineteen Letters of Ben Uziel*, Roden sought answers to a wide range of religious and philosophical questions. Mindful of his own ignorance, he solicited advice from a representative sampling of experts drawn from the diverse ideological and denominational camps in the Jewish community. Not surprisingly, Roden ended up, after a long journey, in a separatist Orthodox community, which he believed to be a microcosm of the *Knesset Yisrael*. But even in that community, his fervor was inexplicable to the more established members, many of whom had long ago ceded spiritual passion to material comfort. Over time, Roden the neophyte injected new energy into the community, and even went on to develop the novel ideological program of *Torah 'im derekh erets Yisrael* (known by its German acronym, *Thedaismus*).

Roden's impassioned advocacy of this stance tracked Breuer's own conviction that the time was approaching to move to Palestine. Shortly before the book's publication, in the winter of 1933–34, Breuer visited the country again. The rise of Hitler a year earlier provided substantial incentive to exit Europe. Even more portentously, it hinted, like the First World War before it, at the possibility of Divine redemption. In anticipation of that reward, Breuer wrote in the final line of *Der Neue Kusari*: "And so the year of the German-Jewish catastrophe became a [new] epoch in the Metahistory of the God-State."[101]

While many imagined the return to Palestine as a conclusive return to history, Isaac Breuer saw Erets Yisrael as the ultimate station in the Jewish people's long journey to *Metageschichte*. On this point, Breuer differed not only from Zionists and Agudists. He also stood apart from those German-Jewish thinkers whom we've studied in previous chapters, and with whom he had a number of other important affinities. Like Cohen, Rosenzweig, and Strauss, Breuer was acutely aware of the twin ills of historicism and nationalism. Unlike them, he sought refuge not in the comforting netherworld of *Golus*, but in the national homeland in Palestine.

It was perhaps Baruch Kurzweil (1907–1972), the brilliant and irascible literary scholar at Bar-Ilan University, who best understood Isaac Breuer. As a young man, Kurzweil was one of the Jews who came from abroad, in his case Moravia, to study at the yeshivah of R. Salomon Breuer in Frankfurt. Kurzweil recalled Isaac Breuer's charismatic presence at the yeshivah with great fondness and respect.[102] He also came to recognize the later Breuer as one of the most incisive and underappreciated figures in modern Jewish thought. But what made Breuer truly compelling to Kurzweil—and what resonated so deeply with his own restless temperament—were the deep and unresolved tensions in Breuer. "Huge contradictions," Kurzweil wrote in 1943, "swim around in the depths of his soul." We have touched upon some of them in the preceding pages, yet it was Kurzweil who knew to identify the biggest of them all. For all of his invective against the hyperindividualism of modern bourgeois society, Isaac Breuer was himself an unmistakable individualist, idiosyncratic in his preferences and iconoclastic in his convictions.[103]

It was this bold individualism that fueled Breuer's critical spirit. It enabled him to bound confidently over the chasm of contradictions and forge clear ideological stances and existential choices. As he moved from Frankfurt to Jerusalem, Breuer sensed that he was inching ever closer to the true metahistorical *Knesset Yisrael*. For better or worse, few followed him along his tortuous path, strewn, as it was, with "dangerous landmines."[104] Solitude was the price to be paid for his radical individualism.

Interestingly, one who did pursue a similar path was Baruch Kurzweil. Kurzweil moved from Frankfurt to Palestine armed with his own deep reservations about both Zionism and historicism.[105] While the two hardly constitute a school, they nonetheless attest to the continuous flow of Jewish anti-historicist currents through time and space—across the great abyss of the Shoah, and from Exile to Zion.

## Chapter Six

## FROM CONCLUSION TO OPENING: A WORD
## ON INFLUENCE, GERMAN JEWS, AND THE
## CULTURAL HISTORY OF IDEAS

> Because to influence a person is to give him one's own soul. He does not
> think his natural thoughts, or burn with his natural passions. . . . He
> becomes an echo of someone else's music, an actor of a part that has not
> been written for him.
> —Oscar Wilde, *The Picture of Dorian Gray*

The affinity between Isaac Breuer and Baruch Kurzweil extends
from Frankfurt, the site of their first encounter, to Palestine,
where both decided to move despite deep reservations about the
Zionist project. Indeed, neither believed nor hoped that the return to Zion
would mark a return to mundane history. In this regard, the pair belonged
to the ranks of vocal Zionist critics. At the same time, both belonged
to a distinctive strand in the fabric of modern Jewish anti-historicism:
Orthodox thinkers intent on engaging, rather than resisting, modern secular culture.[1] Well into the twentieth century, many traditionally observant
Jews expressed little desire to engage secular culture, even if they had
unwittingly absorbed elements of it over time. By contrast, for those Orthodox Jews who consciously desired such engagement (e.g., S. R. Hirsch
and his disciples), historicism posed as great a challenge as any modern
intellectual pursuit. For its commitment to contextualization eroded the
boundary between sacred and profane, and thus upset the delicate balance
between Torah and secular culture.

Given the seriousness of this problem, it is no surprise that Orthodox
malaise with history survived well beyond the Weimar period. Baruch
Kurzweil's strident attacks on historicism, for example, found their clear-
est target not in interwar Europe, but in post-WWII Israel. They were
directed at his intellectual nemesis, Gershom Scholem, who, according to
Kurzweil, had assembled a cast of adoring acolytes around him at the
Hebrew University. In a series of critical essays in *Ha-arets* from the
1960s, Kurzweil accused Scholem and friends of bowing to "the god of
historicism, the same god of the science of the normalization and historici-

zation of Judaism." So as to leave no doubt, Kurzweil declared that "the god of historicism and normalization is not the God of Israel."[2]

Kurzweil's resistance to the "science" of history, as well as to the Zionist impulse to "normalize" the Jewish condition, is echoed in another Orthodox thinker in Israel: Yeshayahu Leibowitz (1903–1994). Over the course of his long career as professor of chemistry, neurophysiology, and philosophy in Jerusalem, Leibowitz gave voice to a unique set of positions on Judaism and Zionism that earned him a large, attentive, and often hostile audience. The unvarying point of departure for Leibowitz was his belief that to be a Jew was to submit totally to the dictates of Halakhah. In that the obligation to perform commandments was a function of individual human will, he was loath to ascribe religious significance either to external historical events or their recollection. "Religious faith," Leibowitz maintained, "is not a matter of knowledge of events that occurred, but rather of man's decision to take upon himself the burden of the kingdom of Heaven."[3] And just as an individual's faith did not depend on knowledge of the past, neither was Jewish peoplehood determined by the events of the past: "If there is uniqueness to the Jewish people, it is not as a result of the conquest of the land [of Israel] nor of settlement in it . . . but rather in what it is required to do in this land: in the obligations placed upon it and not placed upon other peoples."[4]

Leibowitz's sense of "divine supervision" (hashgahah 'elyonah) was manifestly at odds with the Zionist goal of freeing the Jewish people from the paralyzing grip of such supervision—indeed, from what Scholem called "a life lived in deferment."[5] Contra Scholem, Leibowitz appeared willing to live a life of *historical* deferment—that is, an observant life apart from the fast-moving current of history. What makes him so intriguing is that his worldview was forged not only out of a rich web of Jewish learning and Halakhic commitment, but also out of deep philosophical and scientific erudition. Leibowitz skillfully and provocatively navigated amid these diverse realms. But he always remained immune to the allures of historicism in modern intellectual discourse.

The same might well be said for another contemporary of Leibowitz's and Kurzweil's, Rabbi Joseph B. Soloveitchik (1903–1993), the towering figure of modern Orthodoxy in twentieth-century America. Soloveitchik was both a vastly learned Halakhic sage and a trained philosopher who wrote a dissertation on Hermann Cohen.[6] In the course of his career, he did not discuss historicism in extended or systematic fashion. But he did address the theme in at least one of his renowned Talmudic lectures (shiurim). There Soloveitchik distinguished between two approaches to history. The first, or etiological, approach rested on the assumption that "universal (non-Jewish) history is governed by causality" and is best understood as a search for origins. The second, or teleological, approach referred to the unique "covenantal" history of the Jews. It pointed not only to the past, but also to the future. As Soloveitchik explained: "What happens to Jews emanates from a Divine promise foretold about the future, rather than by events impelling from the past. Jewish history is pulled, as by a magnet, towards a glorious destiny; it is not pushed by antecedent causes. This is the meaning of the Patriarchic Covenant; it is a goal projected, a purpose pursued, a destination to be reached."[7]

To grasp the meaning of this Covenant is decidedly not to subject the glorious annals of the Jewish past to base contextualization. Soloveitchik insisted, for example, that Zionism can not be understood solely as a function of nineteenth-century European nationalism. Here he represented a sharp departure from Kurzweil and Leibowitz. Whereas they opposed any ascription of messianic import to Zionism, he suggested that the creation of the state of Israel was an important point along the eschatological pathway of Jewish history.[8]

In asserting the primacy of "destiny" over "cause" in Jewish history, Soloveitchik not only reversed the normal order of historicist operation. He also revived the classic dichotomy, which we have noticed in thinkers ranging from the twelfth-century Judah Ha-Levi to the twentieth-century Isaac Breuer, between the divine history of the Jews and the mundane history of the Gentiles. We might do well to translate Soloveitchik's dichotomy into the Kantian terms familiar to us from earlier chapters: purposive Jewish history was *Geschichte*; contingent Gentile history was *Historie*. Soloveitchik's version of *Geschichte* was unperturbed by the erratic intrusions of *Historie*. This vision of a Divinely supervised Jewish history was shared by the other thinkers whom we've mentioned so far in this chapter—and is, in fact, a hallmark of Orthodox attitudes toward history up to the present.[9]

In thinking about the fate of historicism in contemporary intellectual life, it is readily apparent that not only Orthodox Jews expressed skepticism. A diverse array of European and American intellectuals have given voice to their own concerns over the effects of historicism in the aftermath of the Holocaust. For some of these thinkers, the Holocaust assumed a scale of destruction so vast as to shatter all existing forms of historical measurement.[10] For others like the French Jewish philosopher Emmanuel Lévinas, the Holocaust exposed the frailties of the project of modernity, one of whose destructive effects was to "denounce the eternity of Israel by placing in question its very inner life."[11] Meanwhile, for Yosef Yerushalmi, the Shoah cast a long shadow over the world and triggered the desire for a "new, metahistorical myth"—one that historians, wedded to their cautious methods, have little hope of erecting.[12]

These varied ruminations and reservations about historicism from the latter half of the twentieth century continue, in many ways, the story told in this book about the first half. Taken together, they remind us that historicism has posed serious theological and philosophical problem up to our own day. At the same time, they remind us that the Second World War, like the First, wrought far more than physical destruction; it violently shook the pillars of Western society, and in the process, inspired a quest for a spiritual and moral standard untouched by the corrosive forces of history.

Our mission here is not to explain the impact of either war on Western society. Nor is it to produce a genealogy of anti-historicism that snakes its way in a thin current from the turn of one century to the turn of another. While these are worthwhile projects, this book has attempted a somewhat different and more modest task: to record an important moment of anti-historicist expression in the late nineteenth and early twentieth centuries. In analyzing this moment, we have not aimed for an ethereal history of ideas whose prized possessions, like in a good hunt, are plucked from their native environment, cleansed of contextual residue, and then placed on display in a rarefied taxidermic setting. On the contrary, the variations of the anti-historicist idea that we have traced are embedded in overlapping, but still rather circumscribed biographical and historical contexts. Within that complex web of texts, personalities, and social norms, the variations of anti-historicism become part of what we might call a *cultural* history of ideas.

The adjective "cultural" is doubly important here. In the first instance, it suggests to us that ideas can best be explained within the larger cultural *milieu* in which they arise. Stated otherwise, these ideas make sense only within "a system of symbols and meanings" that might best be called culture.[13] But the term also refers to a dynamic form of *activity*—negotiation, translation, adaptation, and modification—in which Jew meets non-Jew, if not as political and social equals, then as partners in ceaseless interaction (e.g., of ideas, practices, values).[14] Throughout this study, we have generally avoided describing that interaction as the triumph of a dominant host group (e.g., German society) over a passive recipient group (e.g., German Jewry).[15] This is hardly to suggest that culture qua activity is removed from contests of power. On the contrary, struggles between groups over ideas, practices, and values are constant—and rarely, if ever, pit contestants of equal strength. In this vein, many German Jews aspired to place German culture at the core of their souls—only to be repelled by repeated torrents of anti-Semitism.

And yet, it is essential to note that the aspiration to assimilate was invariably mediated and transformed by particular Jewish sensibilities. This results in the "cultural bifocality" that was mentioned in chapter 3—a blending of optical perspectives and perceptions that joins the German and Jewish experience into one, at times seamlessly and at other times disjointedly. The notion of bifocality argues against the view that Jews, even in the most acculturated contexts, were absorbed en masse into the cultural mainstream to the point of disappearance. Rather, while absorbing from the surrounding culture, they did so by retaining a distinct (if sometimes faint) Jewish tint to their lenses.

Equipped with these lenses, German Jews interacted with non-Jews, molding ideas and social norms in common and in response to one another. We have explored here one instructive point of interaction: growing discontent with historicism in German culture. Not long after historicism began to assert its dominance in the nineteenth century, criticism of its perceived excesses was sounded. Both Jews and Christians in Germany, struggling to find their way in the new secular era, shared in this criticism. Both were siblings of the same Enlightenment parent; both were alternately attracted to and unsettled by their inheritance, of which historicism was an indispensable part.

Among the post-Enlightenment generations, we notice different waves of criticism, each defined in its own philosophical or theological key: neo-Kantianism, existentialism, conservative traditionalism, neo-Orthodoxy. We also notice that Jews absorbed these new trends as readily as any other group of Germans. Concomitantly, they played a creative and often leading role in forging new conceptual horizons within these trends. Hermann Cohen, for example, was the intellectual father of an influential school of German philosophy: Marburg neo-Kantianism. Insofar as he was a philosopher of great stature and originality, we do no service by depicting him either as a slave to German culture or as a mere borrower. He constantly sought to negotiate between *Deutschtum* and *Judentum*, believing in the depth of his soul that their intersection was a meeting of equals. More to the point, his reservations about historicism issued from the unique blend of Kantian and Jewish ideals that he so assiduously cultivated.

In discussing Cohen and those who followed him, we have sought to avoid the "fallacy of origins," the very etiological impulse to which J. B. Soloveitchik took exception.[16] This does not mean that we are endorsing Soloveitchik's alternative, a teleological view of history. But we are mindful of the fact that there are certain risks to burrowing back into the past, like an archaeologist, in search of the earliest traces of a phenomenon. While a hallmark of historicist practice, this impulse is often accompanied by a value judgment that rewards the early and disdains the late. As against that impulse, we have tried to resist establishing Jewish—or Christian—primacy for a given idea or movement. Likewise, we have tried to avoid declaring a winner in the perennial historiographical contest of who influenced whom, for here too value judgments can be and often are misapplied. If our goal then is not *archaeological*, we might say that it is *cartographic*: to plot the multiple and multidirectional historical vectors operating in a dense intellectual field.[17] Within such a field, it is the dynamics of exchange and negotiation, more than the extent of influence, that interests us.

## INFLUENCE AND ITS DISCONTENTS IN JEWISH HISTORIOGRAPHY

I recall a memorable dinner that my wife and I had with two visiting colleagues at a restaurant in Los Angeles about a decade ago. In the midst of our conversation, I was startled by the comment of one of the guests, a most creative and audacious Jewish studies scholar, to the effect that the search for influence in history was overrated, even misguided. Although I argued vigorously at the time that one could hardly make sense of history without influence, I have been bedeviled by the comment ever since.

Indeed, I think back to the restaurant in which this conversation took place. It was a rather eclectic affair, a kosher eatery that served both Chinese and Mexican food. At first glance, it would seem to be a cheap knock-off of more authentic versions of those two cuisines. And yet, on second glance, the question of culinary *authenticity* becomes less and less relevant. More intriguing is the juncture of cultural vectors that marked the spot. The Chinese food symbolized the well-known American Jewish affinity for that cuisine. The Mexican food highlighted the prominence of Chicano culture in Los Angeles. And the roast chicken, brisket, and cholent on the menu, hardly standard fare at Chinese or Mexican restaurants, were a nod to the traditional Eastern European Jewish kitchen. To the restaurant's clientele, there seemed nothing odd or inauthentic about the mix of these distinct cuisines under one kosher roof. Rather, it represented a tasty, if jumbled, fusion of cultures, eminently familiar to them as American Jews.

The lesson to be learned is a seemingly banal, but nonetheless important, one: any given cultural moment is comprised of competing and complementary vectors. The case of the restaurant offers a cautionary note against the stigma of inauthenticity that often results from the search for singular influence. Usually, the winners in the game of influence are those who influence, the losers those who are influenced. Or conversely, the heroes are those who resist the onslaught of external influences, while the traitors are those who succumb to it. What is common to both depictions is the moral measure invoked. For example, in writing of the first generations of Jewish Enlightenment figures, Heinrich Graetz wrote contemptuously of "the Jewish youth [who] ravenously flung themselves upon French literature." "The clever daughters of Israel," he continued, "also ardently devoted themselves to this fashionable folly."[18] For Graetz, succumbing to French influence was clearly an act of betrayal.

In the case of a small diaspora group such as the Jews, the challenge of preserving a distinct collective identity without disappearing has been considerable. When Jewish historians attempted to chronicle this struggle, they often regarded the absorption of cultural norms from the broader society (e.g., names, language, dress) with suspicion or disdain. This trend is particularly prevalent among those for whom Jewish history is propelled by a powerful immanent drive—for example, among the small but steady stream of traditionalist Orthodox Jewish writers who have turned to the historical genre to reveal the hand of God. From the *Toldot Yisrael* of Ze'ev Jawitz (1895) to the *Toldot Yisrael* of Chaim Dov Rabinowitz (1979) this stream forms a kind of counternarrative to the presentation of Jewish history by authors who rely on prosaic external forces to explain the historical path of the Jews.[19]

A rather different source of this "immanentist" impulse can be found among historians operating under the ideological and institutional aegis of Zionism. In his multivolume anthology *Yisrael ba-golah*, the prolific scholar, educator, and political figure, Ben-Zion Dinur, described the Jewish people as a "special organic unit [whose] unique life processes" prevented its total assimilation in the diaspora.[20] Meanwhile, Gershom Scholem sometimes sought to ward off claims that early forms of Jewish mysticism in antiquity were the product of Christian or other non-Jewish influence.[21] And their colleague in Jerusalem, Yitzhak Baer, lauded the steadfast resistance of Ashkenazic Jewry to the allures of Gentile culture.[22] In all three cases, the fear of external influence went hand in hand with an immanentist impulse. As such, this impulse identifies one pole on the value-laden spectrum of historical causality.

The opposite pole marks the surfeit, rather than dearth, of influence. Here too, the Jerusalem scholars weighed in. While depicting the premodern opponents of external influence as valiant nationalists *avant la lettre,* they often regarded those who "succumbed" to influence in censorious terms. Baer's assault on the cultural promiscuity of medieval Spanish Jews is a clear example of this tendency.[23] So too is Scholem's argument against the idea of a "German-Jewish dialogue." On his view, the notion of a "dialogue" between the two cultures was but an illusion. Jews in Germany were so anxious to soak up the surrounding cultural norms that they abandoned their own. As a result, the German-Jewish experience was a one-sided and unrequited love affair by Jews for Germans.[24]

These examples hardly do justice to the complex historiographical legacy of Scholem, Baer, and Dinaburg. They were each accomplished—and in some cases, seminal—scholars who laid the foundation for the most important center of Jewish studies in the world. It is a mistake to cast them as beholden to a monolithic Zionist view of the past. In fact, their disciplinary instinct to contextualize often clashed with and even trumped their Zionist commitments and immanentist impulses. For example, Baer at times acknowledged the "influence"—even the relatively benign influence—of "Christian concepts and definitions" on medieval Ashkenazic culture.[25] Scholem, for his part, acknowledged the formative influence of non-Jewish currents on ancient Jewish mysticism.[26] The point then is not that they understood Jewish history as immune to environmental influence. They recognized influence when they saw it, but tended to regard it as moving in only one direction. Moreover, they often enough affixed moral judgments both to the influencers and the influenced. The resulting picture of the past was a bifurcated one, divided into distinct realms of assimilation and insularity.

But history, and surely Jewish history, operate in the large gray area between assimilation and insularity. Assigning unidirectional influence— and attaching moral judgments in the process—are not always the best ways to chart that gray area. This is important to bear in mind, because it is natural enough for the historian to seek out influence in the course of historical reconstruction. The problem arises when this search fails to appreciate the dynamic process of negotiation, mediation, and translation that defines interaction between groups.

An interesting foil to the first-generation Jerusalem scholars is the contemporaneous Jewish philosopher Simon Rawidowicz (1896–1957). It may be no accident that a thinker like Rawidowicz, who lived in the Diaspora—where Jews have interacted with the host society as a clear minority—developed a critical view of the idea of influence. It should be noted that his main concern was not the relationship between Jews and their non-Jewish hosts, but rather that between Diaspora Jewry and the newly created Jewish state. Speaking at a symposium in 1949, Rawidowicz declared:

> We speak too much of *hashpa'ah* [Hebrew for "influence"]; and that results in what might be called in English "hashpaitis." This is a long-standing axiom in our world, but it now requires a fundamental revision. The point, in my opinion, is not the question of whether or how the State of Israel will influence the Diaspora. The first question is: what will Diaspora Jewry do—for itself, and then for all of [the people of] Israel, including the State of Israel?[27]

Rawidowicz's belief that the Jewish world of his day was divided into two equal halves—the State of Israel and the Diaspora of Israel, or as in the title of his posthumous work, *Babylonia and Jerusalem*—formed the core of his diasporist stance.[28] What is most germane for us here is not that ideological stance, but rather his diagnosis of *hashpaitis*: the tendency to assert the dominant influence of one body (e.g., the State of Israel) upon a second (e.g., the Diaspora of Israel). In depicting the latter as a vital and independent force in its own right—and as an equal partner with the former—Rawidowicz was suggesting that the scholarly and ideological regime of *hashpaitis* had outlived its usefulness.

Others have applied this critique of influence to diverse areas of the Jewish past. For example, a later American scholar, the historian Gerson Cohen (1924–1991), wrote in 1966 one of the most incisive, penetrating, and underappreciated essays in twentieth-century Jewish scholarship, "The Blessing of Assimilation."[29] Cohen did not address directly the concept of "influence" or *hashpaitis* in this article. But he did reveal a subtle grasp of the cultural interaction between Jews and non-Jews. Cohen's essay is a brilliant elegy to assimilation—understood not as a quick route to self-negation, but as a means of assuring cultural survival. It rejects the traditional midrashic admonition against Jews absorbing the names, language, and dress of the land in which they resided. When considering a figure such as Philo of Alexandria, Cohen points out that cultural integration—even in pre-modern times—was not only unavoidable, but enriching to Jewish culture. Indeed, "in a profound sense," Cohen declared, "this assimilation and acculturation was [*sic*] a stimulus to original thinking and expression and, consequently, a source of renewed vitality." If "properly channeled and exploited," assimilation "*can* become a kind of blessing."[30]

More recently, Amos Funkenstein (1937–1995) analyzed the stigma of assimilation with characteristic breadth and theoretical sophistication. In "The Dialectics of Assimilation" (1995), he took note of the fact that "[a]ll too often, Jewish historians operate with a family of dichotomies" ill equipped to assess the subtleties of the past. For example, the common assumption that Jewish history was a battle between "endogamous" and "exogenous" forces was mistaken. These categories were too rigid to account for the fluid nature of Jewish cultural absorption. As we noted briefly in his discussion of Franz Rosenzweig, Funkenstein was keenly attuned to the way in which Jews continually refashioned their identity in the midst of (and in response to) the broader society. Thus, he argued that "even the self-assertion of Jewish culture as distinct and different is articulated in the language of the surrounding culture," prompting the conclusion that "assimilation and self-assertion are truly *dialectical* processes."[31]

The insights of Rawidowicz, Cohen, and Funkenstein hint at an alternative to the regnant influence-based model of historical explication. Culture, on their view, is the product neither of hegemonic imposition nor of heroic resistance, but rather of a more confluent mingling of intellectual, aesthetic, religious, social, and political sensibilities between groups in a given milieu.

This important insight resounds in different intellectual quarters. The French philosopher, Paul Ricoeur, once observed that "only a living culture, at once faithful to its origins and ready for creativity on the levels of art, literature, philosophy, and spirituality, is capable of sustaining the encounter of other cultures."[32] A similar sentiment stands at the center of some recent postcolonial thinking. A prominent train of thought, extending back to C.L.R. James, and represented in our day by scholars such as K. A. Appiah, Homi Bhabha, Stuart Hall, and Edward Said, holds that the culture of the colonizer was not absorbed in unmediated form by the colonized.[33] On the contrary, the colonized (or the putatively influenced) often appropriated, transformed, or subverted the culture of the colonizer (here the influencer).

Bringing this insight back to the study of Jewish history seems wholly appropriate given the long-standing status of the Jews as a politically dependent and culturally innovative diaspora group.[34] The motivation to do so is surely not to dismiss all scholarship, past and present, in which the criterion of influence was central. It is rather to acknowledge the constant need to recalibrate the scales of historical measurement, in this case by shifting away from the organizing principle of influence to the criterion of interaction and exchange. This shift is hardly an innovation of the twenty-first century, as we have seen in our brief survey of Rawidowicz, Cohen, and Funkenstein. But what *is* interesting and noteworthy about the present is that there is a growing cohort of Jewish studies scholars who have begun to organize their work around the criteria of interaction and exchange. Their shared labor challenges the influence-based model of explanation and presents the formation of Jewish culture as a rich, multidirectional process.

## AGAINST *HASHPAITIS*: NEW TRENDS IN JEWISH HISTORIOGRAPHY

Setting the tone for this approach, Peter Schäfer attempts in his recent *Mirror of His Beauty: Feminine Images of God from the Bible to the Early Kabbala* to reclaim the late antique astrological connotation for the term "influence." The term signified an " 'inspiration,' emphasizing the active participation of the 'influenced' during the process of 'influencing.' " There were no clearly designated "active" and "passive" partners in this process, but rather "a dynamic relationship in which the influenced actively and creatively 'digests' what it receives, creating something that is new, no longer identical with its 'origin.' " This kind of understanding—which Schäfer elaborates in his book's final chapter, "How Much

'Origins,' or: The Anxiety of Influence"—comports with our own attempt to move beyond winners and losers in the game of historical influence.[35]

The fact that Professor Schäfer's stance is close to the one adopted here reflects less—to put an exclamation mark on the point—any mutual influence than a shared intellectual-cultural universe in which sensitivity to the deficiencies of an influence-based model is growing. Schäfer applies his insights to the realm of mysticism, and more particularly to Jewish and Christian notions of the feminine side of God. In the course of this application, he illuminates the way in which the history of religion can be understood as a series of lateral, and not merely vertical, movements.

Although Schäfer's book marks a culmination of sorts, scholars in a number of different areas of Jewish history have begun to adopt this new perspective. A good case in point is research on the Hellenistic world during and after the Second Temple period. Recent books by Lee Levine, Erich Gruen, Shaye Cohen, and John Barclay seek to situate Hellenistic Judaism *between* the poles of assimilation and segregation—in a sense, beyond "influence," in a space marked by multidirectional cultural exchange.[36] Their work focuses more on the synchronic processes of osmosis and symbiosis than on diachronic influence. As such, this body of work recommends a novel way of describing Jewish encounters with diverse world cultures.[37]

An adjacent field in which we notice alternatives to the influence model is that dealing with Judaism and Christianity in late antiquity and the Middle Ages. For some time, scholars have regarded rabbinic Judaism and early Christianity as overlapping historical entities—or to borrow the familiar (and familial) metaphor, as competitive siblings rather than as overbearing parent and rebellious child. This image is reflected, for example, in the title of Alan Segal's important book from 1986, *Rebecca's Children*, and surfaces again in Yisrael Yuval's *Shne goyim be-vitnekh* (*Two Peoples in Your Womb*) from 2000. In between the appearance of Segal's and Yuval's books, a number of scholars have attempted to explain the relationship between rabbinic Judaism and early Christianity without assuming the influence of one on the other. Most prominent among them is Daniel Boyarin, who depicts Judaism and Christianity in late antiquity "as a single circulatory system within which discursive elements could move from non-Christian Jews and back again, developing as they moved around the system."[38]

This perspective makes sense in the intense social and religious context of Palestine in the early centuries of the Common Era—that is, in a space in which the social and religious worlds of Jews and Christians constantly intersected. But what of a later period in which the social and religious boundaries between Judaism and Christianity were far less permeable? For instance, can the relationship between medieval Ashkenazic Jews and their Christian contemporaries be described as one of "dialogue"? On the surface, it would seem not. However, scholars have recently pointed to subterranean currents of cultural, ritual, and even theological exchange between medieval Jews and Christians that amount to an unacknowledged dialogue.[39] One of these scholars, Jeremy Cohen, conjures up the vision of a shared cultural space and calls upon scholars "to take note no less of that which is common to Jewish and Christian culture in the Middle Ages than of overtures that members of these cultures make to foreign values outside of their own."[40]

Cohen's call has been joined by researchers of early modern Jewish history, particularly those who study Renaissance-era Italy. Representing a milieu of great cultural energy and openness, on one hand, and considerable social restraints on Jews, on the other, Italy is an historical enigma. But it is clearly a fruitful site to investigate the fluidity of Jewish-Christian relations. Recently, Kenneth Stow has offered a nuanced reading of these relations in *Theater of Acculturation: The Roman Ghetto in the Sixteenth Century.* Acculturation, he notes, was "a two-way street" in early modern Rome. That is, Christians were aware of and absorbed Jewish cultural and legal norms, just as Jews did Christian norms.[41] Stow's important book builds upon the work of other scholars—Robert Bonfil and David Ruderman come immediately to mind—who have explored with great subtlety the complex negotiation between Jews and Christians in early modern Italy.[42]

Much of the above-mentioned work, on subjects ranging from ancient Hellenism to Renaissance Italy, acknowledges the fluid nature not only of cultural interaction, but of the very category of Judaism. It resists the claim of Jewish insularity as readily as that of unidirectional external influence. Moreover, it stands in opposition to monochromatic "lachrymose" depictions of Jewish history. Taken as a whole, this body of scholarship has succeeded in galvanizing prescient insights from the past into a new perspective—not yet fully coherent or crafted into a seamless narrative, but with the potential to force us to rethink, in the midst of an everdynamic interpretive process, the way in which we write Jewish history.

## GERMAN-JEWISH HISTORY BETWEEN ASSIMILATION AND INSULARITY

A centerpiece of this new framing is surely the field of German-Jewish history. With its high degree of cultural achievement and persistent antiSemitism, the German-Jewish experience has often lent itself to either of two extremes on the explanatory spectrum. On one hand, the experience can be summarized per Gershom Scholem as a failed symbiosis in which

Jews willingly surrendered their cultural distinctiveness only to be greeted with animosity and violence by their German hosts. On the other hand, the experience can be narrated per George Mosse as the story of German Jewry's passionate romance with the ideal of *Bildung*. Here too, German Jews shed their traditionalist cloak, but in this case, they received considerable cultural and educational benefits.[43]

It is a mistake to reduce the rich German-Jewish experience to either of these interpretive poles. The divergent perspectives of Scholem and Mosse—two towering giants of twentieth-century scholarship and themselves embodiments of the German-Jewish experience—have had a long reign in the field both as historical explanations and cultural visions. But an impressive roster of historians has begun in recent decades to agitate for a perspective that avoids the extremes of unrestrained assimilation and rigid separation.[44] This list includes well-established scholars such as Steven Aschheim, Gary Cohen, Marion Kaplan, Paul Mendes-Flohr, Anson Rabinbach, David Sorkin, and Shulamit Volkov, as well as younger researchers like Peter Gordon and Samuel Moyn. Faced with the gap between "Liberal" and "National" (i.e., Zionist) renderings of German-Jewish history, Volkov counsels that a "radical new beginning may be the order of the day."[45] In a long series of essays, she has heralded that beginning, observing with a keen eye that the Jewish encounter with modernity did not spell the demise of Judaism, but rather led to an existence that was "modern, not traditional, but nonetheless Jewish."[46]

Managing this encounter with modernity was hardly the Jews' burden alone. As Peter Gordon aptly notes in his study of Rosenzweig and Heidegger, "Germans and German Jews moved through the very same philosophical waters, pursuing a common course that, in a sometimes unsettling fashion, carried them in a common direction."[47] This aquatic image allows us to take stock of shifting perceptions of the German-Jewish experience. At the beginning of the nineteenth century, the young legal historian, Eduard Gans made the enigmatic claim that the integration of Jews into German society would allow them to "live on as a river lives on in the ocean."[48] A century later, Franz Rosenzweig spoke of Jews as dwelling in the fertile terrain created by two great rivers of culture. Today, some seventy-five years later, scholars speak of German Jews as having traveled the same cultural byways as non-Jews, sometimes calmly and at other times turbulently. What results is the image of a joint, but uneasy, passage—one that holds out the prospect of a "shared history" of Jews and Christians in Germany, as F. W. Graf has recently proposed. Such an approach that integrates the experience of the two groups would enable scholars not only to avoid polar extremes in narrating the German-Jewish experience.[49] It would also allow them to escape the long shadow of the

Holocaust that often shrouds in darkness past interaction between Jews and non-Jews in Germany.[50]

The goal of producing a meaningful shared history—coinciding with Shulamit Volkov's call for a "radical new beginning"— is a demanding one toward which scholars will be striving over the next generation. It would be an act of hubris to claim that the present volume achieves this goal. After all, its primary objective has been to trace the contours of a *Jewish* discourse of anti-historicism through the prism of four *Jewish* intellectuals. But it endeavors to contribute to an eventual shared history in two regards: first, it portrays the Jewish crisis of historicism as part of the broad legacy of historicism itself—understood here as a method and worldview that left a profound imprint on European intellectuals of *all* religious and ethnic stripes from the nineteenth century on. Second, it seeks to analyze anti-historicist expression by Jews without assuming the domineering influence of one cultural group upon another. This means depicting Jewish anti-historicists not as derivative of non-Jewish intellectuals, but as drawing from a shared discursive and conceptual well.

We have seen the extent to which Hermann Cohen initially immersed himself in the "return to Kant" movement, but then developed his own neo-Kantian system that provided a framework for his abiding Jewish commitments. While Cohen had no reason to abandon the Kantian notion of *Geschichte*, his neo-Kantian perspective made him wary of *Historie* insofar as it might inflict damage upon his intertwining philosophical and Jewish passions. For this reason, he sought to assure that history not displace philosophy at the methodological foundation of the human sciences. By contrast, Cohen's student Franz Rosenzweig found little satisfaction in the neo-Kantian tradition. He and his circle of intimate friends—first, Jewish-born Protestants and later, fellow "returnees" to Judaism in Frankfurt—dispensed with the scientific aspirations of Marburg neo-Kantianism, as well as with the extended debates over the *Geisteswissenschaften* of the Baden school. Rosenzweig and friends preferred a new kind of philosophical endeavor—unburdened by the weight of historicism—that could lead to intellectual and spiritual renewal.

Meanwhile, Leo Strauss took aim at the enterprise of historicism as part of a Weimar-era backlash against the Enlightenment. Unlike those intent on philosophical innovation, he tried, in line with conservative thinkers of his day, to salvage an authentic, if submerged, pre-modern tradition. In Strauss's view, the irreverence of modern historicism devalued the grand philosophical ideals that constituted this tradition—and that he hoped to recover. The fourth figure in our study, Isaac Breuer, was another kind of conservative critic, deeply committed to tradition, but hardly to the noble philosophical atheism of Strauss. Breuer followed the example of his grandfather, Samson Raphael Hirsch, by propelling Judaism and the Jewish people beyond the realm of prosaic history.

Taken as a group, these four thinkers illuminate a fascinating moment of anti-historicist anxiety in modern European and Jewish history. As products of an intellectual culture permeated through and through with historicism, they were all exposed to the study of history from an early age. Over the course of their respective careers—and at times coinciding with their "return" to Judaism—each came to apprehend that danger lurked in an excess of history. They did not arrive at this awareness in isolation, but at a time in which historicism symbolized the dangerous atomizing impulse of modernity.

As we have seen throughout this book, the last decades of the nineteenth century and the first decades of the twentieth witnessed mounting dissatisfaction with the ills of modernity. In response, new philosophical and political programs, as well as bold new agendas for art, architecture, and literature, were offered. These initiatives reached a peak of intensity in the Weimar period, whose spirit of new beginnings clashed with a strong dose of postwar gloom. As a microcosm of that predicament, the academic study of history met up with a rising chorus of anti-historicist dissent, leading to a veritable "crisis of historicism." The thinkers we've explored here were not only parties to the crisis, but combatants in the battle to overturn the hegemony of historicism. They believed that instead of preserving Judaism, historicism reduced it to a mound of minute factual shards.

The methods of the modern historian were grounded in an overarching Weltanschauung that demanded that everything be situated and thus understood *within* history. Each of the figures we have studied struggled against that worldview, especially against the gravitational pull of contingency that dragged down their visions of a transcendent Judaism. It is this struggle that recalls, for a final time, the affinity between anti-historicism and hesitations over Zionism.

One of Zionism's wagers was that it would restore the Jewish people to history. Its advocates argued—and lamented—that Diaspora life was somehow beyond history. But it was this very point that the Jewish anti-historicists applauded. They were in search of a life beyond history's quotidian grind—a distinctive Jewish path that flowed beyond the boundaries of nation-states. In this regard, they occupied the middle ground between two main ideological poles of the day: Zionism and assimilationism. They fell comfortably into neither camp nor, for that matter, into the ethnic and religious categories these ideologies championed.

There was another kind of middle ground occupied by the central actors of this book. Their view of historicism harked back to a traditionalist frame of mind according to which Jews, uniquely, inhabited the realm of sacred history. And yet, all four of this book's protagonists were university-trained intellectuals who found it impossible to avoid the methods and logic of historicism. They invariably constructed historical narratives in order to chart their own theological or philosophical course. And thus, their best anti-historicist intentions were tempered by deeply ingrained—and ultimately inescapable—historicist impulses.

To be sure, this paradoxical condition was not theirs alone. Historicism permeates our very mode of cognition, our way of ordering and explaining the past. Reaction against this mode—as manifested in the desire to soar above the current of mundane history—has animated many moderns in search of spiritual or philosophical holism. The bulk of our discussions has centered on the early twentieth century. But as we noted at the outset of the chapter, adverse reactions abounded in the latter half of that century too—especially in the wake of the catastrophe that befell European Jewry. In fact, the lack of confidence in old intellectual wisdoms that afflicted thinkers after the Holocaust has carried over into the current postmodern age, an age of great skepticism and equally great spiritual seeking.

Anti-historicism then remains with us, finding refuge in the academy and the place of worship alike. Indeed, the impassioned debate over the Exodus story in Los Angeles in 2001 reminds us that the tension between history and faith has not yet been resolved. Nor is it likely to be resolved soon. For historicism and anti-historicism have endured into the present not only as foils, but as partners in a complex codependent relationship.[51]

A final illustration of this point: the story of anti-historicism in this book has been told from an unmistakably historicist perspective. I empathize with—and hope I have treated empathically—those who yearn for an experience or belief system that defies historical gravity. But like Ernst Troeltsch, I am faced with the recognition that such an experience or belief is almost always refracted through an historicist lens—and will continue to be unless or until a vast epistemological paradigm shift occurs. This may mean that our most treasured ideals—those that have been eroded by the lapping waves of modern historicism—are destined to be fortified and reconstructed only by historicism itself. If this be true, perhaps the best consolation to offer is, again, an eminently historicist one: to know not that we can escape the clutches of historicism, but that we have not been alone in our despair.[52]

# NOTES

## INTRODUCTION

1. See Kierkegaard's attempted reclamation of a true Christianity in his 1850 *Training in Christianity*, included in Robert Bretall, ed. *A Kierkegaard Anthology* (Princeton: Princeton University Press, 1946), 388–89.

2. Ibid., 392.

3. Albert Schweitzer, *The Quest of the Historical Jesus: A Critical Study of Its Progress from Reimairus to Wrede*, introduction by James M. Robinson (New York: Macmillan, 1968), 401. For an excellent survey of the state of research on the "historical Jesus," see E. P. Sanders, "In Quest of the Historical Jesus," *New York Review of Books*, November 15, 2001, 33–36.

4. Friedrich Nietzsche's 1874 essay, "Vom Nutzen und Nachteil der Historie für das Leben," has been translated as *On the Advantage and Disadvantage of History for Life*, translated by Peter Preuss (Indianapolis: Hacket Publishing, 1980), 28.

5. Troeltsch, "Die Krisis des Historismus," *Die Neue Rundschau* 33 (1922), 573.

6. See Karl Heussi, *Die Krisis des Historismus* (Tübingen: J.C.B. Mohr, 1932), 102.

7. On the link between historical knowledge and relativism, see Maurice Mandelbaum, *The Problem of Historical Knowledge* (New York: Liveright, 1938), passim.

8. Heussi, *Die Krisis des Historismus*, 13–14.

9. Troeltsch, *Der Historismus und seine Probleme* (Tübingen, 1922), 104.

10. Georg G. Iggers discusses this moment in "The Dissolution of German Historism," in Richard Herr and Harold T. Parker, eds. *Ideas in History: Essays Presented to Louis Gottschalk by His Former Students* (Durham, N.C.: Duke University Press, 1965), 296.

11. Heussi's small book was an expanded version of a lecture delivered in Saxony and Jena in the fall of 1929. See *Die Krisis des Historismus*, 104.

12. As Iggers notes, "[t]he break with political and historiographical traditions was much deeper and more real after 1945 than it had been after 1918." Iggers, "The Dissolution of Historism," 310.

13. See, for instance, Saul Friedländer's introduction to his important edited volume, *Probing the Limits of Representation: Nazism and the "Final Solution"* (Cambridge, Mass.: 1992).

14. See Mark Poster, "Cultural History and the Discipline," *Litteraria Pragensia* 1 (1991), 5.

15. Teresa Watanabe, "Doubting the Story of Exodus," *Los Angeles Times*, April 13, 2001, 1.

16. Rabbi Steven J. Leder, "Torah Truths," *Los Angeles Jewish Journal*, April 20, 2001, 10.

17. Dennis Prager, "Faith in Exodus," *Los Angeles Jewish Journal*, April 20, 2001, 11.

18. Felice Maranz, "Did the Exodus Really Happen?" *The Jerusalem Report*, April 8, 1993, 16.

19. See, for example, Israel Finkelstein and Neil Asher Silberman, *The Bible Unearthed : Archaeology's New Vision of Ancient Israel and the Origin of Its Sacred Texts* (New York: Free Press, 2001).

20. "A Message from David Wolpe," *Los Angeles Jewish Journal*, April 20, 2001, 11.

21. According to Wolpe, "the most important part of it (i.e., the Exodus story) is it is true—even if it is not literal, even if it is not factual—it is true and Jews for millennia have seen the truth of it." See the interview with Gustav Niebuhr in "Religion Journal: A Rabbi's Look at Archaeology Touches a Nerve," *New York Times*, June 2, 2001.

22. See Lutz Niethammer, *Posthistoire: Has History Come to an End?* trans. Patrick Camiller (London and New York: Verso, 1992), 3.

23. See the intriguing recent attempt by Shubert Spero to argue that the meaning of history (i.e., Jewish history) can be rendered intelligible and meaningful through a regime of double causation—that is, by recourse to both natural and divine causes. Spero, *Holocaust and Return to Zion: A Study in Jewish Philosophy of History* (Hoboken, N.J.: 2000), 246–49.

24. For a discussion of the history-memory divide in recent Jewish historiography, see my essay, "Neuere jüdische Geschichtsschreibung und der Diskurs über Geschichte und Gedächtnis," and Yosef Yerushalmi's response in Michael Brenner and David N. Myers, *Jüdische Geschichtsschreibung heute: Themen, Positionen, Kontroversen* (Munich: Beck, 2002), 55–94.

25. Carole Fink mentions this epithet in her discussion of the French sociological critique of German historicism in *Marc Bloch: A Life in History* (New York: 1989), 29–33.

26. Scholem, "Mi-tokh hirhurim 'al Hokhmat Yisra'el," *Luah ha-arets* (1944), and republished in Paul Mendes-Flohr, ed. *Hokhmat Yisra'el: Hebetim historiyim u-filosofiyim* (Jerusalem: Merkaz Shazar, 1979).

27. Yosef Hayim Yerushalmi, *Zakhor: Jewish History and Jewish Memory* (1982; rpt. New York: Schocken, 1989), 92–99.

28. See, for example, Jacques Ehrenfreund, *Mémoire juive et nationalité allemande: Les juifs berlinois à la Belle Époque* (Paris, 2000), Shmuel Feiner, *Haskalah ve-historyah: Toldoteha shel hakarat-'avar yehudit modernit* (Jerusalem, 1995); Susannah Heschel, *Abraham Geiger and the Jewish Jesus* (Chicago, 1998); Christian Wiese, *Wissenschaft des Judentums und protestantische Theologie im wilhelminischen Deutschland: Ein Schrei ins Leere?* (Tübingen, 1999); Perrine Simon-Nahum, *La cité investie: la "science du judaïsme" français et la République* (Paris, 1991); Amnon Raz-Krakotzkin, "Yitsuga ha-le'umi shel ha-galut: Ha-historyografyah ha-tsiyonit ve-yehude yeme ha-benayim," Ph.D. diss., Tel Aviv University, 1996; and David N. Myers, *Reinventing the Jewish Past: European Jewish Intellectuals and the Zionist Return to History* (New York, 1995).

29. Sylvie-Anne Goldberg has undertaken a searching analysis of Jewish conceptions of time, largely in antiquity, in *La Clepsydre: Essai sur la pluralité des temps dans le judaïsme* (Paris: Albin Michel, 2000); meanwhile, Tamar M. Rudav-

sky has studied the interrelated notions of time and cosmology in medieval Jewish thought in *Time Matters: Time, Creation, and Cosmology in Medieval Jewish Philosophy* (Albany: SUNY, 2000).

30. For a discussion of some of these contributions, see chapter 6.

31. An exception is Josef R. Lawitschka's study, "Metageschichte: Jüdische Geschichtskonzeptionen im frühen 20. Jahrhundert: Franz Rosenzweig, Isaac Breuer und das Echo," Ph.D. diss., Berlin: 1996.

32. Troeltsch's essay from 1898, "Über historische und dogmatische Methode in der Theologie," has been translated as "Historical and Dogmatic Method in Theology" in idem, *Religion in History*, translated and introduced by James Luther Adams (Minneapolis, 1991), 12, 16.

33. See Konrad Jarausch, "The Institutionalization of History in Eighteenth-Century Germany," in Hans Erich Bödeker, Georg Iggers, Jonathan B. Knudsen, and Peter Hanns Reill, eds. *Aufklärung und Geschichte: Studien zur deutschen Geschichtswissenschaft im 18. Jahrhundert* (Göttingen, 1986), 46, 48.

34. See Howard's excellent study, *Religion and the Rise of Historicism: W.M.L. de Wette, Jacob Burckhardt, and the Theological Origins of Nineteenth-Century Historical Consciousness* (Cambridge, 2000), 14.

35. Perhaps the locus classicus of the equation of historicism and modernity is Friedrich Meinecke's *Die Entstehung des Historismus* (Munich and Berlin, 1936). More recently, Donald R. Kelley describes history as "an advocate and conveyor of modernity" in his *Faces of History: Historical Inquiry from Herodotus to Herder* (Yale, 1998), 274. See also Carl Schorske, *Thinking with History: Explorations in the Passage to Modernism* (Princeton, 1998).

36. As I. A. Akinjogbin notes, the African historian "is no longer sure to which world he belongs"—the Western historiographical tradition or the rich fabric of African culture. Meanwhile, Ranajit Guha and more recently, Vinay Lal, have written of the tensions between critical historiographical currents and traditional Bengali or Indian views of the past. See Guha, *An Indian Historiography of India: A Nineteenth-Century Agenda and Its Implication* (Calcutta, 1988), and Lal's review of books by Guha, Peter Heehs, Sumit Sarkar, and Achin Vanaik in *History and Theory* 41 (February 2001), 135–48. There Lal argues that "India did at one point make a civilizational choice of forsaking discourses of history, [preferring myth] by means of which the past is often accessed." Lal, 148.

37. Armed with a healthy dose of disdain, Ibn Warraq has recently called attention to the reticence of Muslim scholars to undertake critical study of Muhammad and early Islamic sources. See Ibn Warraq, *The Quest for the Historical Muhammad* (New York: Prometheus, 2001), 15–24. But cf. J.M.S. Baljon, *Modern Muslim Koran Interpretation (1880–1960)* (Leiden: E. J. Brill, 1961).

38. Delumeau's comment from *Le Monde* of December 15, 1992 is included in an essay in a fascinating volume produced under his direction that explores the boundaries historians draw between their scholarly mission and faith commitments. See Alexandre Faivre, "Des histoires en théologie: conflit de méthodes ou de croyance?" in Jean Delumeau, *L'historien et la foi* (Paris: Fayard, 1996), 101.

39. The most textured study of "the multiplicity of temporal registers" in Judaism is now Goldberg's *La Clepsydre*, 11ff.

CHAPTER ONE
JEWISH HISTORICISM AND ITS DISCONTENTS: AN INTRODUCTION

1. See Tamar M. Rudavsky, *Time Matters: Time, Creation, and Cosmology in Medieval Jewish Philosophy* (Albany: SUNY, 2000).

2. Based on an intriguing reading of Eliyahu Capsali's sixteenth-century *Seder Eliyahu Zuta*, Robert Bonfil argues that there may well be a lost or suppressed "tradition of medieval Jewish historical writing closely related to the Christian tradition." Robert Bonfil, "Jewish Attitudes Toward History and Historical Writing in Pre-Modern Times," *Jewish History* 11 (Spring 1997), 21. Still, Bonfil argues elsewhere that the writing of history by medieval Jews was "scanty," but that the same obtained for medieval Christians as well. See his "How Golden Was the Age of the Renaissance in Jewish Historiography?" in *History and Theory*, Beiheft 27 (1988), 86.

3. This holds especially true for the Askhenazic realm, in which, as Bonfil notes, the bulk of medieval Jewish historiography was produced. See Bonfil, "Jewish Attitudes," 26–27.

4. Yosef Hayim Yerushalmi, *Zakhor: Jewish History and Jewish Memory* (1982; rpt. New York: Schocken, 1989), 31.

5. Against Salo Baron and Yosef Yerushalmi, Robert Bonfil argues that during the sixteenth century, "Jewish historiographical writing [was] much less than exceptionally rich." Bonfil's chief source of comparison is not medieval Jewish historical writing, but rather early modern *Christian* historiography. While Bonfil's comparative frame is helpful to bear in mind, his perspective dilutes somewhat the density of Jewish historiographical production in the sixteenth century relative to the previous four centuries. Bonfil, "How Golden Was the Age of the Renaissance in Jewish Historiography?" 86.

6. See now the exceptional critical edition of de Rossi's *Me'or 'Enayim* produced by Joanna Weinberg, *The Light of the Eyes* (New Haven: Yale, 2001), xxvii.

7. Anthony Grafton, *Joseph Scaliger: A Study in the History of Scholarship II: Historical Chronology* (Oxford: Oxford University Press, 1993), 5.

8. See Pocock's chapter on "The Varieties of Early Modern Historiography" in his *Barbarism and Religion* (*Narratives of Civil Government*, vol. 2) (Cambridge: Cambridge University Press, 1999), especially 20–25.

9. Bonfil, "How Golden Was the Age of the Renaissance in Jewish Historiography?" 90.

10. Gans (1541–1613) was a German-born Jewish savant with wide-ranging intellectual interests, especially in mathematics and astronomy. After moving to Prague by the age of twenty, Gans established close contact with the leading rabbinic figure of the city, Judah ben Bezalel Loew (known as the MaHaRaL). At the same time, he developed intellectual ties with leading Gentile scientists of the day, including a pair of renowned mathematicians and astronomers resident in Prague: Johannes Kepler and the "Noble Dane," Tycho Brahe. For a discussion of these contacts, see André Neher, *Jewish Thought and the Scientific Revolution of the Sixteenth Century: David Gans and His Times* (Oxford: Oxford University, 1986), 216–28.

11. See Breuer's introduction to his critical edition of *Tsemah David le-Rabi David Gans (1592)* (Jerusalem: Magnes, 1983), xxiii–xxvi.

12. *Tsemah David*, 7.

13. Ibid., xiv.

14. *Shulhan Arukh*, Orah Hayim, 307, 16. Cf. Bonfil's interesting gloss on this prohibition in "Jewish Attitudes toward History," 12–16.

15. One thinks in this context of the various recreations, especially gambling, of Gans's near contemporary from Italy, R. Leon Modena (1571–1648). See the translation of Modern's engaging autobiography, *Haye Yehudah*, with accompanying commentaries in *The Autobiography of a Seventeenth-Century Venetian Rabbi: Leon Modena's "Life of Judah,"* edited by Mark R. Cohen (Princeton: Princeton University, 1988).

16. This criterion is the ninth virtue, and Gans claims, somewhat disingenuously to my mind, that he may have included it only to get to ten virtues. *Tsemah David*, 167.

17. The term "historical sense," as applied to sixteenth-century Jewish thinkers, connotes here (a) recognition of Gentile history as a domain worthy of attention and study and (b) growing appreciation for history as a literary genre worthy of production. These connotations bear some relation to, but are nonetheless distinct from, Amos Funkenstein's law-centered notion of "historical consciousness." See Funkenstein's "Collective Memory and Historical Consciousness" in *Perceptions of Jewish History* (Berkeley: University of California, 1993), 16–17.

18. Baron outlines his classic position in "Azariah de Rossi's Historical Method," in *History and Jewish Historians: Essays and Addresses* (Philadelphia: Jewish Publication Society, 1964), 239.

19. Funkenstein, *Perceptions of Jewish History*, 14–15.

20. Amos Funkenstein, *Theology and the Scientific Imagination* (Princeton, 1986), 207.

21. Perhaps the most explicit example is Solomon ibn Verga's notion of "natural cause" (*ha-sibah ha-tiv'it*) in his *Shevet Yehudah* from 1554. See Yerushalmi's nuanced and qualified reading in *Zakhor*, 65.

22. Spinoza, *A Theologico-Political Treatise*, translated by R.H.M. Elwes (New York, 1951), chapters 3 and 8.

23. See Steven B. Smith's account in *Spinoza, Liberalism, and the Question of Jewish Identity* (New Haven, 1977), 87.

24. A translation of the writ of 27 June 1656 can be found in Paul R. Mendes-Flohr and Jehuda Reinharz, eds. *The Jew in the Modern World* (New York: Oxford, 1995), 57.

25. John E.A.D. Acton, *A Lecture on the Study of History, delivered at Cambridge, June 11, 1895* (London: Macmillan, 1895), 58.

26. I have relied here on Alexander Altmann's translation in his monumental *Moses Mendelssohn: A Biographical Study* (Philadelphia, 1973), 108.

27. *Moses Mendelssohn's Gesammelte Schriften*, V:268, as cited in Hans Liebeschütz, "Mendelssohn und Lessing in ihrer Stellung zur Geschichte," in Siegfried Stein and Raphael Loewe, *Studies in Jewish Religious and Intellectual History Presented to Alexander Altmann on the Occasion of His Seventieth Birthday* (Tuscaloosa, Ala., 1979), 168.

28. Cassirer's *Die Philosophie der Aufklärung* from 1932 has been translated as *The Philosophy of the Enlightenment* (Princeton: Princeton, 1951), 197.

29. Emphasis added. On the historicity of Sinai, see Mendelssohn's "Gegenbetrachtungen" in the most recent version of Mendelssohn's *Gesammelte Schriften. Jubiläumsausgabe* 7: 86–88, as cited in David Sorkin, *Moses Mendelssohn and the Religious Enlightenment* (Berkeley, 1996), 83–84.

30. Sorkin elaborates that "Mendelssohn embraced history as a basis of faith, yet he rejected a historicism that subjected faith and the sources of faith to notions of process and development." David Sorkin, *Moses Mendelssohn and the Religious Enlightenment* (Berkeley, 1996), 85, 87.

31. Hans Liebeschütz, "Mendelssohn und Lessing in ihrer Stellung zur Geschichte," 179.

32. Kant, *The Critique of Pure Reason*, quoted in Yirmiahu Yovel, *Kant and the Philosophy of History* (Princeton, 1980), 247.

33. J. G. Herder, "Ideas toward a Philosophy of the History of Man," excerpted in Patrick Gardner, ed. *Theories of History: Readings from Classical and Contemporary Sources* (New York: Free Press, 1959), 39.

34. See the still valuable discussion of Herder in Friedrich Engel-Janosi, *The Growth of German Historicism* (Baltimore: Johns Hopkins, 1944), 23.

35. Meinecke's *Die Entstehung des Historismus* (Munich and Berlin, 1936), was translated as *Historism: The Rise of a New Historical Outlook*, translated by J. E. Anderson (London, 1972), 380–81, liv.

36. See, for example, Erich Rothacker, "Das Wort 'Historismus,' " *Zeitschrift für deutsche Wortforschung* 16 (1960), 4, as well as Georg G. Iggers, "Historicism: The History and Meaning of the Term," *Journal of the History of Ideas* 56 (1995), 130. See also Dwight E. Lee and Robert N. Beck, "The Meaning of 'Historicism,' " *American Historical Review* 59 (1954), 568–77.

37. Iggers, "Historicism: The History and Meaning of the Term," 130.

38. Carl Menger, *Die Irrthümer des Historismus in der deutschen Nationalökonomie* (Vienna, 1884). See Maurice Mandelbaum's brief discussion in "Historicism," *Encyclopedia of Philosophy* (London and New York: Macmillan, 1967), III–IV: 22.

39. For an excellent account of the concept and attendant critique of historicism, see Annette Wittkau, *Historismus: Zur Geschichte des Begriffs und des Problems* (Göttingen: Vandenhoeck and Ruprecht, 1992).

40. Meinecke, *Historism*, lv.

41. Most distinctive may be Karl Popper's strange inversion of the conventional view of historicism. In *The Poverty of Historicism* (London, 1957), Popper holds that the essence of historicism is *not* its idiographic, but rather its nomothetic inclination—that is, its search for general laws of development.

42. Rand, "Two Meanings of Historicism," *Journal of the History of Ideas* 25 (1965), 505, 507–513.

43. Troeltsch, "Die Krisis des Historismus," 573.

44. This statement can be found in the prospectus of *Ha-Me'asef*, entitled "Nahal besor." See the English translation in Paul R. Mendes-Flohr and Jehuda Reinharz, eds. *The Jew in the Modern World* (New York, 1995), 80.

45. This is the judgment of Shmuel Feiner in his study of Haskalah attitudes to history, *Haskalah ve-historyah* (Jerusalem, 1995), 46.

46. Yerushalmi's discussed the gap of a "biblical" generation between the Maskilim and the first university-trained Jewish historians in the fourth chapter of *Zakhor*.

47. The juxtaposition between the two is spelled out more fully in D. N. Myers, *Reinventing the Jewish Past: European Jewish Intellectuals and the Zionist Return to History*, 25–37.

48. Still, it should be noted that the first-generation *Wissenschaft* scholars did not emerge out of a linguistic vacuum. They themselves were proficient in Hebrew, and even occasionally wrote in it. Moreover, they were preceded by a cohort of historical writers such as Peter Beer, Markus Fischer, and Solomon Löwisohn who produced narrative accounts of the Jewish past in both Hebrew and German in the late eighteenth and early nineteenth centuries. See, for example, Michael A. Meyer, "The Emergence of Modern Jewish Historiography: Motives and Motifs," *History and Theory* 27 (December 1988), 160–75, and Reuven Michael, *Ha-ketivah ha-historit ha-Yehudit mi ha-renasans 'ad ha-'et ha-hadashah* Jerusalem, 1993), 121–59.

49. In the early twentieth century, Gershom Scholem warned that the Zionist-inspired attempt to create a modern Hebrew neglected the possibility that "the language [might] turn against its speakers." See Scholem's letter to Franz Rosenzweig in *Franz Rosenzweig zum 25 Dezember 1926* (New York, 1987), 47–48.

50. Horst Walter Blanke carefully chronicles the shift in German historical thought from "Enlightenment history" to historicism in his study, *Historiographiegeschichte als Historik* (Stuttgart-Bad Cannstatt, 1991). A parallel shift occurs from a Jewish Enlightenment history in Hebrew to a German-Jewish historicism. But cf. the ingenious perspective of Amnon Raz-Krakotzkin who argues that the founder of modern Jewish historical scholarship, perhaps even historical consciousness, wrote in a language other than Hebrew and was not even a Jew— i.e., Jacques Basnage, who authored the first multivolume history of the Jews in the early eighteenth century (1706–11). See Raz-Krakotzkin, "Yitsuga ha-le'umi shel ha-galut: Ha-historyografyah ha-tsiyonit ve-yehude yeme ha-benayim," Ph.D diss., Tel Aviv University, 1996.

51. Although established under the banner of educational innovation, the Freischule held to a very traditional Jewish curriculum until the appointment of Samuel Meyer Ehrenberg as director in 1807. Ehrenberg sought to modernize the school curriculum, and in the process exerted a powerful and lasting influence on Zunz. See Zunz's recollections of his time at the Freischule in the diary excerpts included in Ludwig Geiger, "Zunz: Mein erster Unterricht in Wolfenbüttel," *Jahrbuch für jüdische Geschichte und Literatur* 30 (1936), 131–40. See also Michael Meyer's insightful account of Zunz in *The Origins of the Modern Jew: Jewish Identity and European Culture in German, 1749–1824* (Detroit, 1967), 144–82.

52. See the brief biography by Nahum N. Glatzer in his edition, *Leopold and Adelheid Zunz: An Account in Letters, 1815–1885* (London, 1958), xv.

53. For a close analysis of de Wette's views and career, see Howard, *Religion and the Rise of Historicism*, 65–71.

54. Zunz, "Etwas ueber die rabbinische Literatur," *Gesammelte Schriften* (Berlin, 1875), vol. 1: 4; see the abbreviated English translation in Paul Mendes-Flohr and Jehuda Reinharz, *The Jew in the Modern World*, 197.

55. For a discussion of *Wissenschaft* in the work of Zunz and his Jewish colleagues, see my "The Ideology of *Wissenschaft des Judentums*," in Daniel Frank and Oliver Leaman, eds., *History of Jewish Philosophy* (London: Routledge, 1997), 706–21.

56. On Zunz's resistance to superstition, see Luitpold Wallach, "Über Leopold Zunz als Historiker: Eine Skizze," *Zeitschrift für die Geschichte der Juden in Deutschland* 5 (1935), 249.

57. Zunz, "Etwas ueber die rabbinische Literatur," 4 (English, 197).

58. "Etwas ueber die rabbinische Literatur," 4 (English, 196, 197).

59. See Luitpold Wallach's discussion of Wolf's and Boeckh's efforts at systematization in *Liberty and Letter: The Thoughts of Leopold Zunz* (London, 1959), 77–79.

60. "Etwas ueber die rabbinische Literatur," 17 (English, 200), 19 (English, 200–201).

61. As Blanke notes, history was a recognized field in the German university system from the mid–eighteenth century. See *Historiographiegeschichte als Historik*, 126ff. See also Herbert Butterfield, *Man on His Past: The Study of the History of Historical Scholarship* (Cambridge, 1955), 32–61.

62. Like philology, statistics in the early nineteenth century signified wide-ranging study focused on the political, social, and economic conditions of a group. Zunz outlined his view on the need for a "statistical" study of the Jews in "Grundlinien zu einer künftigen Statistik der Juden," *Zeitschrift für die Wissenschaft des Judentums* 2 (1822), 523–32. See the comments of Reuven Michael in his *Ha-ketivah ha-historit ha-yehudit*, 210–11.

63. According to Sinai Ucko, Zunz proposed the following names: Verein für Literaturfreunde, Verein für Beförderung unter den jüdischen Glaubensgenossen, Academia, Philagathia, and Symposion. See Ucko's study of the formation of the Verein, "Geistesgeschichtliche Grundlagen der Wissenschaft des Judentums," *Zeitschrift für die Geschichte der Juden in Deutschland* 5 (1935), 19.

64. Leon Wieseltier, "*Etwas über die jüdische Historik*: Leopold Zunz and the Inception of Modern Jewish Historiography," *History and Theory* 20 (1984), 138.

65. According to Nipperdey, this "Wissenschaftsglaube" became "the new measure for the question of meaning in life and happiness." See Nipperdey, *Deutsche Geschichte, 1800–1866* (Munich, 1983), 445, cited in Howard, *Religion and the Rise of Historicism*, 103. Nipperdey gives a lucid summary of the rise of historicism in Germany, noting the early nineteenth-century proliferation of fields of inquiry reliant on historical method (e.g., philology and legal scholarship). While this development finds close parallels among German–Jewish scholars, the emergence of history per se in an early century figure like B. G. Niebuhr does not; as we shall see, it surfaces more explicitly in the second generation of *Wissenschaft des Judentums*. See Nipperdey, *Deutsche Geschichte*, 513ff.

66. Ismar Schorsch, "Breakthrough into the Past: The *Verein für Cultur und Wissenschaft der Juden*," in his *From Text to Context* (Hanover, N.H.: University Press of New England, 1994), 220.

67. "Etwas ueber die rabbinische Literatur," 5.

68. See the still reliable account of Georg Iggers on the origins of German national historiography in *The German Conception of History: The National Tradition of Historical Thought from Herder to the Present* (Middletown, Conn.: 1983), 44–89.

69. As Michael Meyer notes, the question of Savigny's influence on Zunz has been the subject of debate. Meyer himself discounts a strong direct influence on Zunz, pointing to Savigny's anti-Jewish animus among other reasons. See Meyer, *The Origins of the Modern Jew*, 158, especially n. 45. Nonetheless, it is clear that Zunz was familiar with Savigny and his work from the University of Berlin—and even more so, with the new nationalist currents in German historical scholarship of his day.

70. See Iggers, *The German Conception of History*, 70–71.

71. Most egregiously for them, this rollback entailed exclusion from the professorial ranks of German universities. In August 1822, a Prussian *Kabinettsorder* was issued that barred Jews from professorial appointments, prompting some (most notably Eduard Gans) to convert.

72. Zunz did, however, make explicit use of the term history in his later collection, *Zur Geschichte und Literatur* (Berlin, 1845). Of the first-generation Verein members, it was Eduard Gans who most frequently used the rubric of "history" in his research. See, for example, his "Vorlesungen über die Geschichte der Juden im Norden von Europa und in den slavischen Ländern," *Zeitschrift für die Wissenschaft des Judentums* 1 (1822), 95–113.

73. Wallach, *Liberty and Letters*, 105–106.

74. Quoted in Meyer, *The Origins of the Modern Jew*, 152. See also Michael, *Ha-ketivah ha-historit ha-Yehudit*, 241. Ismar Schorsch labeled "indefensible" Jost's "decision to call his work a history of the Israelites," while noting his deep distaste for the term "Juden." Schorsch, "From Wölfenbüttel to Wissenschaft: The Divergent Paths of Isaak Markus Jost and Leopold Zunz," *Leo Baeck Institute Year Book* 22 (1977), 121.

75. Jacques Ehrenfreund argues that German-Jewish historical researchers throughout the nineteenth century were beset by the problem of an "impossible nationalization"—that is, by their inability to shape Jewish historical research according to the contours of the nation. In this regard, they were at a marked disadvantage vis-à-vis their non-Jewish counterparts in Germany. See Ehrenfreund, *Mémoire juive et nationalité allemande*, 169–71.

76. See Ismar Schorsch, "Ideology and History," in *From Text to Context*, 272.

77. Riesser's remarks are drawn from his debate with the Heidelberg Orientalist, Heinrich Paulus, and are quoted in Mendes-Flohr and Reinharz, *The Jew in the Modern World*, 131.

78. See Michael A. Meyer, "Jewish Religious Reform and Wissenschaft des Judentums: The Positions of Zunz, Geiger and Frankel," *Leo Baeck Institute Year Book* 16 (1971), 19–41.

79. See Ismar Schorsch, "The Emergence of Historical Consciousness in Modern Judaism," originally published in *Leo Baeck Institute Year Book* 28 (1983), and reprinted in *From Text to Context*), 191.

80. See Frankel's "Einleitendes" in *Monatsschrift für Geschichte und Wissenschaft des Judentums* 1 (1851/52), 5.

81. Frankel's "positive historical" position, as it came to be called, drew upon German legal scholars who balanced the organic development of law against the authoritative role of tradition in shaping it. See Jay M. Harris, *How do we know this?: Midrash and the Fragmentation of Modern Judaism* (Albany, 1995), 193–97.

82. This essay, "Die Construktion der jüdischen Geschichte," was first published in an earlier journal edited by Frankel, the *Zeitschrift für die religiösen Interessen des Judenthums* 3 (1846), and translated and commented upon by Ismar Schorsch in his edition of Heinrich Graetz's *The Structure of Jewish History and Other Essays* (New York, 1975), 64.

83. Schorsch, "Historical Consciousness in Modern Judaism," 192.

84. Jacob Katz discussed the educational diet of the early modern Askhenazi rabbinical student in *Tradition and Crisis*, translated by Bernard Dov Cooperman (New York, 1993), 167. On the modern transformation of the rabbi, particularly focused on Germany, see Ismar Schorsch, "Emancipation and the Crisis of Religious Authority: The Emergence of the Modern Rabbinate," in *From Text to Context*, 9–50.

85. A quarter century before in 1829, the Collegio Rabbinico of Padua opened its doors to students with a course of study devised by the Italian-Jewish savant, I. S. Reggio; in the same year, the École Rabbinique of Metz welcomed its first class with the goal of creating an enlightened French rabbinate. See the helpful article on the Padua seminary by Nikolaus Vielmetti, "Die Gründgeschichte des Collegio Rabbinico in Padua," in *Kairos* 12 (1970), 1–30, especially 24–26.

86. Frankel wrote a detailed memorandum in 1835 that discussed his ideas on modern rabbinical training. See Schorsch, "Emancipation and the Crisis of Religious Authority," 13.

87. Graetz's course offerings during his time at the Breslau seminary (1854–91) are listed in Beilage III in M. Brann, *Geschichte des Jüdisch-Theologischen Seminars (Fraenckel-sche Stiftung) in Breslau. Festschrift zum fünzigjährigen Jubiläum der Anstalt* (Breslau, 1904), xix–xxiv.

88. Franz Rosenzweig recounts this story in his introduction to Hermann Cohen's Jewish writings, *Jüdische Schriften* (Berlin, 1924), 1: xxii.

89. Max Wiener offered a detailed treatment of the process of "historicization" of Judaism, with particular reference to Graetz's "nationalist" perspective, in his *Jüdische Religion im Zeitalter der Emanzipation* (Berlin, 1933), translated into Hebrew as *Ha-dat ha-Yehudit bi-tekufat ha-emantsipatsyah* (Jerusalem, 1974), 250–55.

90. As Ismar Schorsch notes, "[t]hough major consumers of *Wissenschaft*, Jews were denied the chance to become its producers and purveyors" in the German university system. See Schorsch, "The Religious Parameters of *Wissenschaft*: Jewish Academics at Prussian Universities," in *From Text to Context*, 62.

91. On the idea of a German-Jewish "subculture," see David J. Sorkin, *The Transformation of German Jewry, 1780–1840* (New York, 1987), 5–8.

92. With the stakes so high, it is no wonder that Ludwig Philippson, the prominent Jewish author and editor, lamented in 1863: "It is really a shame how the dozen Jewish scholars devour each other and forcibly crush the scarcely reviving

respect of the Jewish and Christian public." Philippson's letter of 1 May 1863 to Meir Wiener is quoted in Michael A. Meyer's essay, "Jewish Religious Reform and Wissenschaft des Judentums: The Positions of Zunz, Geiger and Frankel," *Leo Baeck Institute Year Book* 16 (1971), 40.

93. In the well-known formulation of Yosef Yerushalmi, "[f]or the first time it is not history that must prove its utility to Judaism but Judaism that must prove its validity . . . by revealing and justifying itself historically." Yerushalmi, *Zakhor*, 84.

94. Nathan Rotenstreich, *Tradition and Reality: The Impact of History on Modern Jewish Thought* (New York, 1972), 50.

95. Carl E. Schorske, *Thinking with History: Explorations in the Passage to Modernism* (Princeton, 1998), 4.

96. To take one visual example, synagogue architecture in Germany, beginning in the 1830s, effected a "Moorish style," marked by grandiose structures, elaborate façades, ornate curves, and distinctive cupolas that were intended to recall the magnificent edifices of Muslim Spain. The image that the new Moorish-style synagogues conjured up was of a dignified and culturally advanced Judaism at peace with its surroundings, and thus free to create its own elegant and imposing house of worship. The fact that the actual models on which the new synagogues were based were North African and not Spanish is a remarkable illustration of the malleability of historical images in the formation of cultural identity. See Schorsch, "The Myth of Sephardic Supremacy," 79. Harold Hammer-Schenk has carefully traced the rise of Moorish-style synagogues in Germany, first in small towns in the 1830s and then in larger cities in the mid-1850s. See his *Synagogen in Deutschland: Geschichte einer Baugattung in 19. und 20. Jahrhundert (1780–1933)*, (Hamburg, 1981), 259–309.

97. Ignoring the biblically grounded inhibition against figural representation, European Jewish artists in the nineteenth century—e.g., Simeon Solomon, Moritz Oppenheim, Eduard Moyse, Alphonse Lévy, and Isidor Kaufmann—returned to the Jewish past in search of serviceable motifs for their painting. See Richard I. Cohen, *Jewish Icons: Art and Society in Modern Europe* (Berkeley, 1998), 165.

98. Scholars have argued that the proliferation of historical fiction from the 1830s reflected the appetite of German Jews for a past in whose image their present could be forged. Marking this fiction was the combination of a critical view of tradition (e.g., fascination with figures like Spinoza), a newfound respect for contextual detail, and a willingness to use history as a vital instrument in the work of communal self-definition. See, for example, Nitza Ben-Ari, *Roman 'im he-'avar: ha-roman ha-histori ha-Yehudi-ha-Germani min ha-me'ah ha-19 vi-yetsiratah shel sifrut le'umit* (Tel-Aviv, 1997) or Jonathan Skolnik, "Writing Jewish History between Gutzkow and Goethe: Auerbach's Spinoza and the Birth of Modern Jewish Historical Fiction," *Prooftexts* 19 (May 1999), 101–26.

99. The anonymous article in a special fiftieth anniversary *Beilage* to the *Allgemeine Zeitung des Judentums* 51 (1887) is quoted in Hans Otto Horch, *Auf der Suche nach der jüdischen Erzählliteratur: Die Literaturkritik der "Allgemeinen Zeitung des Judentums" (1837–1922)* (Frankfurt and New York, 1985), 14. Horch studies a number of central literary motifs discussed in the pages of the Allgemeine Zeitung, two of which are the "historical-heroic" and "village and ghetto annals" types.

100. See Ehrenfreund, *Mémoire juive et nationalité allemande*, 133–48.

101. See the figures compiled in Jacob Borut, "Vereine für Geschichte und Literatur at the End of the Nineteenth Century," *Leo Baeck Institute Year Book* 41 (1996), 89.

102. See Jacob J. Schacter's multidimensional study, "Facing the Truths of History," *Tora U-Madda Journal* 8 (1998–99), 202.

103. Schwab's essay, "Jewish History," is included in idem, *Selected Writings: A Collection of Addresses and Essays on Hashkafah, Jewish History and Contemporary Issues* (Lakewood, N.J., 1988), 234.

104. Hirsch's perspective recalls that of the noted Italian-Jewish scholar, Samuel David Luzzatto (1800–1865). Writing of German-Jewish scholars in his day, Luzzatto observed in 1860: "For them, Goethe and Schiller are greater and more venerable than all the Prophets, Tannaim, and Amoraim. They study the ancient Jewish past as others study the ancient past of Egypt, Assyria, Babylonia, and Persia—that is, for the love of science, or for the love of honor." See Luzzatto's letter to S. Y. Rapoport from June 5, 1860, in S. D. Luzzatto, *Igrot ShaDaL*, ed. Eisig Graeber (Cracow, 1894), 1367.

105. See Hirsch, "Der Jude und seine Zeit," in *Jeschurun* 1 (1854) 17.

106. The review, "*Geschichte der Juden* von Dr. H. Graetz," was published in *Jeschurun* 2 (1855–56), and has been translated in Samson Raphael Hirsch, *The Collected Writings*, vol. 5 (New York, 1988), 35.

107. In a diary entry during his time in Oldenburg, Graetz accused Hirsch of a "bornierter Schulchan-Aruchanismus." In a later entry around the time of his departure from Oldenburg, Graetz wrote of Hirsch in French: "Il a peu de connaissance hors de ses enormes livres poskim." Both entries are quoted in Noah H. Rosenbloom, *Tradition in an Age of Reform: The Religious Philosophy of Samson Raphael Hirsch* (Philadelphia, 1976), 73, 75.

108. Quoted in Schorsch, "Ideology and History," in *The Structure of Jewish History*, 36.

109. Ibid, 48.

110. Hirsch's review of Graetz's fourth volume, scattered over four years of *Jeshurun* issues, is found in volume 5 of Hirsch, *The Collected Writings*, 6. For further discussion of Hirsch's opposition to Graetz, see Jay M. Harris, *How do we know this?* 187–88.

111. Hirsch, *Collected Writings*, 74–75 (my emphasis).

112. Ibid., 75.

113. Jay M. Harris, *Nachman Krochmal: Guiding the Perplexed of the Modern Age* (New York: NYU Press, 1991), 135.

114. Hirsch quickly added: "But thank God, this is not the case." See *Jeschurun* 7 (1861), 357, quoted in Mordechai Breuer, *Modernity within Tradition: The Social History of Orthodox Jewry in Imperial Germany* (New York: Columbia University Press, 1992), 178. Breuer offers an extended analysis of Hirsch's attitude toward *Wissenschaft des Judentums*, juxtaposing it with the more affirmative stance of Esriel Hildesheimer and the scholars associated with the Berlin rabbinical seminary he founded. Ibid., 173–93.

115. A recurrent source of misunderstanding and contention in the Orthodox reception of the legacy of Rabbi Hirsch is the principle of "Torah 'im derekh

erets." For instance, Rabbi Schwab, who was once a member of the Hirsch community in Frankfurt before moving to New York, insists (as do others) that Hirsch intended this principle only as a "temporary decree" (*hora'at sha'ah*). See his *Heimkehr ins Judentum* (Frankfurt, 1934). Schwab's position was refuted by a young Jacob Katz, writing in the Hirsch community's journal, *Nach'lath Z'wi* 5 (1935), 92. For a discussion of recent debates over Hirsch's true intentions, see J. J. Schacter, "Facing the Truths of History," 241.

116. See Strauss, *The Life of Jesus Critically Examined*, edited by Peter C. Hodgson and translated by George Eliot (Philadelphia, 1972), 72–74. Albert Schweitzer surveys critical scholarship on Jesus prior to Strauss, *The Quest of the Historical Jesus*, introduced by James M. Robinson (New York, 1968), 13–47. See also the discussion in Susannah Heschel, *Abraham Geiger and the Jewish Jesus* (Chicago, 1998), chapters 4–5.

117. *The Quest of the Historical Jesus*, 96. For a good synthesis of the reactions to Strauss's first edition, see also Colin Brown, *Jesus in European Protestant Thought, 1778–1860* (Durham, N.C., 1985), 197–202.

118. Heschel notes that the focus of critical Christian scholarship following the first edition of Strauss's *Life of Jesus* "shift[ed] to apostolic and postapostolic Christianity," especially during the heyday of the Tübingen school of theological research. Heschel, 128.

119. Quoted in Van Harvey's still incisive study, *The Historian and the Believer: A Confrontation between the Modern Historian's Principles of Judgment and the Christian's Will-to-Believe* (New York, 1966), 6.

120. Geiger wrote this in a letter to M. A. Stern on March 31, 1836. See *Abraham Geigers Nachgelassene Schriften*, ed. Ludwig Geiger (Berlin, 1878), 5: 87–90, quoted in Heschel, *Abraham Geiger*, 108.

121. Graetz was discussing the French edition of the third volume of his *History* in a letter to Hess from November 21, 1865, in Graetz, *Tagebuch und Briefe*, ed. Reuven Michael (Tübingen, 1977), 263.

122. Mordechai Breuer notes that Orthodox Jews in late nineteenth-century Germany undertook a campaign of apologetics in order to combat the rampant atheism of the surrounding society, with particular aim directed at the perceived godlessness of *Wissenschaft des Judentums*. Breuer, *Modernity within Tradition*, 203ff.

123. Baron's essay, "The Historical Outlook of Maimonides," originally published in the *Proceedings of the American Academy for Jewish Research* 6 (1935) was republished in idem, *History and Jewish Historian* (Philadelphia, 1964), 109. It is interesting to note that Baron had modified his views by 1963 when he observed that "the problem of history versus faith, which has so deeply agitated Christian theologians in recent generations, has also affected some thinking of Jewish students." Baron, "Newer Emphases in Jewish History," ibid., 106.

124. In contemplating the transition from the nineteenth to the twentieth centuries, Hermann Heimpel observed that "das 19. Jahrhundert war überladen mit Geschichtswissenschaft, das 20. Jahrhundert ist überbürdet mit Geschichte." See Heimpel, "Geschichte und Geschichtswissenschaft," *Vierteljahrshefte für Zeitgeschichte* 5 (1957), 3.

CHAPTER TWO
HERMANN COHEN AND THE PROBLEM OF HISTORY
AT THE FIN DE SIÈCLE

1. See Walter Köhler, *Ernst Troeltsch* (Tübingen, 1941), 1. For further discussions, see Hans-Georg Drescher, *Ernst Troeltsch: His Life and Work* (Minneapolis, 1993), 86, and more generally, H. Stuart Hughes, *Consciousness and Society: The Reorientation of European Social Thought, 1890–1930* (New York: Knopf, 1958), 229–30.

2. See, for instance, K. Nowak, "Die 'antihistoristische Revolution': Symptome und Folgen der Krise historischer Weltorientierung nach dem Ersten Weltkrieg in Deutschland" in H. Renz and F. W. Graf, eds., *Troeltsch-Studien: Umstrittene Moderne*, vol. 4 (Gütersloh, 1987), 133–71.

3. Troeltsch, "Die Krisis des Historismus," *Die neue Rundschau* 33 (1922), 572–90.

4. Numerous scholars have pointed to the 1890s as the beginning of a concentrated period of painful meditation over the intellectual norms of European society—indeed, as an era marked by frequent expressions of "crisis." See, for example, Hughes, *Consciousness and Society*, 229–48, Robert J. Rubanowice, *Crisis in Consciousness: The Thought of Ernst Troeltsch* (Tallahassee: University Presses of Florida, 1982), and Charles R. Bambach, *Heidegger, Dilthey, and the Crisis of Historicism* (Ithaca: Cornell, 1995).

5. This is the subtitle of his *Consciousness and Society*.

6. See Troeltsch, "The Dogmatics of the "religionsgeschichtliche Schule," *The American Journal of Theology* 17 (January 1913), 2, and republished in Troeltsch, *Religion in History*, translated and introduced by James Luther Adams (Minneapolis: Fortress Press, 1991), 88.

7. While Troeltsch was among the leading theoreticians and practitioners of the history of religions approach in Germany, he was not certain that an actual "school" existed. See "The Dogmatics" in *Religion in History*, 90.

8. Nietzsche uses this description in a letter from October 1868 to his friend, Paul Deussen; quoted in Peter Levine, *Nietzsche and the Modern Crisis of the Humanities* (Albany, NY: 1995), 72.

9. See "On the Advantage and Disadvantage of History for Life," translated by Peter Preuss (Indianapolis, 1980), 2, 39.

10. See Lamprecht, *Moderne Geschichtswissenschaft: Funf Vorträge* (Freiburg im Breisgau, 1905), 28, quoted in Fritz Ringer, *Max Weber's Methodology: The Unification of the Cultural and Social Sciences* (Cambridge, Mass.: Harvard, 1997), 23.

11. According to Georg Iggers, these late-nineteenth-century advocates of positivism belittled the methodological naïveté of the discipline and, instead, sought to show "that the methods of the natural sciences would reveal the lawful structure of physical and social reality alike." Georg G. Iggers, *The German Conception of History: The National Tradition of Historical Thought from Herder to the Present* (1968; rpt. Middletown, Conn.: Wesleyan University Press, 1983), 124

12. See Dilthey, *Introduction to the Human Sciences: An Attempt to Lay a Foundation for the Study of Society and History*, translated and introduced by Ramon J. Betanzos (Detroit: Wayne State, 1988), 105 (my emphasis).

13. Ringer, *Max Weber's Methodology*, 32.

14. See Windelband, *Geschichte und Naturwissenschaft: Rede zum Antritt des Rektorats der Kaiser-Wilhelms Universität Strassburg* (Strasbourg: Heitz & Mundel, 1904).

15. See Henri Dussort, *L'école de Marbourg* (Paris, 1963), 37. According to Hans-Georg Gadamer, by the mid–nineteenth century, "philosophy as a whole had gone bankrupt and the breakdown of the Hegelian domination of the world by spirit was only a consequence of the bankruptcy of philosophy in general." See his *Reason in the Age of Science* (Cambridge, Mass.: MIT Press, 1981), 24, quoted in Bambach, *Heidegger, Dilthey, and the Crisis of Historicism*, 23.

16. Although the philosopher Otto Liebmann is often regarded as the first to sound the call in his *Kant und die Epigonen*, Eduard Zeller uttered the cry "back to Kant" in his inaugural address upon accepting the chair in philosophy at Heidelberg in 1862. For an excellent account of the history of early history of neo-Kantianism, see Judy Deane Saltzman, *Paul Natorp's Philosophy of Religion within the Marburg Neo-Kantian Tradition* (New York: Georg Olms, 1981), 35.

17. Bambach, *Heidegger, Dilthey, and the Crisis of Historicism*, 28ff.

18. In the case of Hermann Cohen, neo-Kantianism entailed a "transcendental method [that] does not seek the principles of reason but the principles of science." See Steven S. Schwarzschild, "Two Modern Jewish Philosophies of History: Nachman Krochmal and Hermann Cohen," D.H.L. thesis, Hebrew Union College, Cincinnati, Ohio, 1955, 88.

19. See Betanzos's introduction to Dilthey, *Introduction to the Human Sciences*, 22. Bambach, *Heidegger, Dilthey, and the Crisis of Historicism*, 140.

20. Bambach, 146. See also the discussion of Dilthey's intermediate position between neo-Kantians and the "Historical School" of Ranke. Ibid., 148.

21. Quoted from Dilthey, *Gesammelte Schriften*, V: xliii, in Betanzos's preface to *Introduction to the Human Sciences*, 16.

22. Cohen's professional career spans virtually the entire period in which neo-Kantianism exerted a powerful influence on German philosophy—from the time of the mid-nineteenth-century crisis of philosophy to the rise of existentialism in the early decades of the twentieth century. On the dominance of neo-Kantianism in philosophical circles in Wilhelminian Germany, see Helmut Holzhey's introduction to *Hermann Cohen*, ed. H. Holzhey (Frankfurt: Peter Lang, 1994), 15.

23. Indeed, Cohen was neither a "pure methodologist" of history like Heinrich Rickert nor a practicing historian. See Thomas E. Willey, *Back to Kant: The Revival of Kantianism: German Social and Historical Thought, 1860–1914* (Detroit: Wayne State, 1978), 139.

24. Charles Bambach has shown that while the Baden neo-Kantians directly addressed questions of historical method, a number of prominent Marburgers undertook, without any programmatic announcement, "significant historical interpretations of the philosophical tradition." Bambach, *Heidegger, Dilthey, and the Crisis of Historicism*, 59.

25. See Cohen's lecture from 1910, "Innere Beziehungen der Kantischen Philosophie zum Judentum," published in his *Jüdische Schriften*, edited by Bruno Strauss and introduced by Franz Rosenzweig (Berlin, C. A. Schwetschke: 1924), I: 284–305. I have also consulted an abridged English version, "Affinities between the Philosophy of Kant and Judaism," in *Reason and Hope: Selection from the Jewish Writings of Hermann Cohen*, trans. Eva Jospe (New York: Norton, 1971), 83, 88. One observer has recently argued that "no philosopher in modern times had as profound an effect on Jewish self-understanding as Immanuel Kant." Kenneth Seeskin, "Jewish Neo-Kantianism: Hermann Cohen," *The Routledge History of Jewish Philosophy* (London, 1997), 786. Indeed, a diverse array of Jewish thinkers in the nineteenth and twentieth centuries were attracted to the great Enlightenment philosopher, though rarely for the same reasons. For example, nineteenth-century Orthodox Jews transformed a negative feature of Kantian thought, the idea that statutory laws are the "pure quintessence" of Judaism, into a validation of their own denomination's adherence to ritual commandments. See Kant, *Die Religion innerhalb der Grenzen der blossen Vernunft, Gesammelte Schriften*, vol. 6: 224. David Ellenson provides a fine analysis in "German Orthodoxy, Jewish Law, and the Uses of Kant" in his *Between Tradition and Culture: The Dialectics of Modern Jewish Religion and Identity* (Atlanta: Scholars Press, 1994), 15–26.

26. Cohen, "Affinities," 88.

27. Henri Dussort, *L'école de Marbourg* 87.

28. Hermann Cohen, "Zur Kontroverse zwischen Trendelenburg und Kuno Fischer," in idem, *Schriften zur Philosophie und Zeitgeschichte*, vol. I (Berlin: Akademie Verlag, 1928), 274–75, quoted in Andrea Poma, *The Critical Philosophy of Hermann Cohen*, trans. John Denton (Albany: SUNY Press, 1997), 5.

29. It is in this sense—ironically, as a "timeless source"—that Simon Kaplan argued in 1930 that "history is, for Cohen, a guiding principle of his very method." Kaplan's dissertation is the first treatment of Cohen's notion of history, though it takes little note of Cohen's resistance to historicism. See Simon Kaplan, *Das Geschichtsproblem in der Philosophie Hermann Cohens* (Berlin: Reuther & Reuther, 1930), 46.

30. Cohen, "Zur Controverse zwischen Trendelenburg und Kuno Fischer," in his *Schriften zur Philosophie und Zeitgeschichte*, edited by Albert Görland and Ernst Cassirer (Berlin: Akademie Verlag, 1928), I: 270.

31. The most sustained discussions remain a pair of older dissertations: Simon Kaplan's *Das Geschichtsproblem in der Philosophie Hermann Cohens* from 1930 and Steven Schwarzchild's "Two Modern Jewish Philosophies of History: Nachman Krochmal and Hermann Cohen" from 1955.

32. Hans Liebeschütz makes this point in noting that since Cohen "had established his own position as a philosopher, he saw himself as a champion of truth, which is essentially eternal and not dependent on circumstances." Liebeschütz, "Herman Cohen and His Historical Background," *Leo Baeck Institute Year Book* 13 (1968), 4.

33. As against J.G.A. Pocock and Quentin Skinner, Mark Bevir tries to revive, not fully successfully, the "myth of coherence" in intellectual history. See his

"Mind and Method in the History of Ideas," *History and Theory* 36 (May 1997), 167–89.

34. Cf. Cohen's volumes *Kants Theorie der Erfahrung, Kants Begründung der Ethik*, and *Kants Begründung der Aesthetik*, published between 1871 and 1889, as noted by Bambach, *Heidegger, Dilthey, and the Crisis of Historicism*, 59. Meanwhile, Franz Rosenzweig noted that the kind of history of philosophy in which Cohen engaged was not devoted to "precise monographs arranged one after another," but to the more systematic task of elaborating "the history of the single human reason." Introduction to *Jüdische Schriften* (Berlin: C. A. Schwetschke, 1924) I: xvii.

35. Adolf Harnack, *Das Wesen des Christentums* (Leipzig, 1900), translated by T. B. Saunders as *What Is Christianity?* (London and New York, 1901).

36. For a discussion of theological and philosophical divisions within the Christian intellectual world in Germany, see Brent Sockness, *Against False Apologetics: Wilhelm Hermann and Ernst Troeltsch in Conflict* (Tübingen, 1998), 11, 13.

37. On Jewish reactions to Harnack, see Uriel Tal, *Christians and Jews in Germany: Religion, Politics, and Ideology in the Second Reich, 1870–1914*, translated by Noah J. Jacobs (Ithaca: Cornell, N.Y., 1975), 202ff., as well as his "Theologische Debatte um das 'Wesen' des Judentums," in Werner E. Mosse, ed., *Juden in Wilhelminischen Deutschland, 1890–1914* (Tübingen: J.C.B. Mohr, 1976), 599–632. See also the recent discussion by Christian Wiese, *Wissenschaft des Judentums und protestantische Theologie im wilhelminischen Deutschland* (Tübingen: J.C.B. Mohr, 1999), 131–40. For discussions of Leo Baeck's response to Harnack, see Albert H. Friedlander, *Leo Baeck: Teacher of Theresienstadt* (New York: Hold, Rinehart and Winston, 1968), 51–60, as well as Aharon Shear-Yashuv, "Ha-mahloket shel Leo Baeck 'im 'mahut ha-Natsrut' shel Adolf Harnack," *Da'at* 23 (1989): 111–20. For Baeck's own incisive criticism of (Christian) historicist assaults on theology, see his essay "Theologie und Geschichte" in idem, *Aus drei Jahrtausenden: Wissenschaftliche Untersuchungen und Abhandlungen zur Geschichte des jüdischen Glaubens* (Tübingen: J.C.B. Mohr, 1958), 28–41.

38. See the account of Dr. Steinthal, "Aus Hermann Cohens Heimat," *Allgemeine Zeitung des Judentums* 82 (1918), 222.

39. On Luther's derogatory attitudes toward Jews, see the entry on him in the *Encyclopedia Judaica*, 11: 584–86. See also Gerhard Falk, *The Jew in Christian Theology: Martin Luther's Anti-Jewish Vom Schem Hamphoras* (Jefferson, N.C.: McFarland, 1992).

40. See Cohen's famous essay from 1915, "Deutschtum und Judentum," reprinted in his *Jüdische Schriften*, II: 242ff. See also the illuminating comments in Liebeschütz, "Hermann Cohen and His Historical Background," 13.

41. Quoted in Rosenzweig's introduction to Cohen, *Jüdische Schriften*, I: xxviii.

42. Liebeschütz argues that Cohen's reading of Luther reflected the influence of the school of Protestant theology associated with Albrecht Ritschl, the teacher of both Friedrich Nietzsche and Ernst Troeltsch. Both the Ritschlian school and Cohen sought to immunize theological truths against the advances of historicism, in large measure by resorting to Kant. Liebeschütz, "Hermann Cohen and His Historical Background," 13.

43. Jacques Derrida, "Interpretation at War: Kant, the Jew, the German," *New Literary History* 22 (1991), 54. Cohen's essay, *Deutschtum und Judentum* reinforced the author's long-held belief that there was a complete union of interests between German and Jewish identities.

44. See Cohen's essay from 1916, "Der polnischer Jude," republished in *Jüdische Schriften*, II: 163.

45. Steinthal, "Aus Hermann Cohens Heimat," 223.

46. Rosenzweig's introduction to *Jüdische Schriften*, I: lxiv.

47. Steinthal, "Aus Hermann Cohens Heimat," 223.

48. See Mosse, *German Jews beyond Judaism* (Bloomington: Indiana University Press, 1985). For critical perspectives on Mosse's view of the dominance of *Bildung* in German-Jewish culture, see *The German-Jewish Dialogue Reconsidered: A Symposium in Honor of George L. Mosse*, ed. Klaus L. Berghahn (New York, 1996).

49. My emphasis. See Cohen's recollection, "Ein Gruss der Pietät an das Breslauer Seminar," *Jüdische Schriften*, II: 421.

50. Ibid., 420.

51. Jay Harris discusses Frankel's historical perspective on the history of Halakhah, and calls attention to the strong influence of Heinrich Graetz on Frankel. See Jay M. Harris, *How do we know this? Midrash and the Fragmentation of Modern Judaism* (Albany: SUNY Press, 1995), 190–202.

52. Cohen's letter defending Frankel is referred to by Hirsch in his journal, *Jeschurun* 7 (1861), 297.

53. Cohen, "Ein Gruss der Pietät," 423.

54. Cohen's essay "Über die Psychologie des Plato und Aristoteles" already reveals the traces of Heymann Steinthal's teaching. See Andreas Poma, *The Critical Philosophy of Hermann Cohen*, 21.

55. See Lazarus's and Steinthal's long programmatic essay in the opening issue of the *Zeitschrift für Völkerpsychologie und Sprachwissenschaft* 1 (1860), 5.

56. Ingrid Belke offers a helpful summary in *Moritz Lazarus und Heymann Steinthal: Die Begründer der Völkerpsychologie in ihren Briefe* (Tübingen: J.C.B. Mohr, 1971), vol. 1, lii. The comprehensive nature of this new method recalls the encyclopedic mission of philology earlier in the century, as outlined by Leopold Zunz in his 1818 essay "Etwas ueber die rabbinische Literatur." In fact, philological analysis remained an important component of Völkerpsychologie, especially in the work of Heymann Steinthal.

57. One recent scholar has written of "the shared identity of philosophy and psychology" in Cohen's early thought. Poma, *The Critical Philosophy of Hermann Cohen*, 22.

58. "Die platonische Ideenlehre psychologisch entwickelt," reprinted in Cohen's *Schriften zur Philosophie und Zeitgeschichte*, I: 51–52.

59. See "Philosophorum de antinomia necessitatis et contingentiae doctrinae," *Schriften zur Philosophie und Zeitgeschichte*, 29.

60. Information on Cohen's university studies is based on the archival materials collected in *Hermann Cohen: Kantinterpret, Begründer der "Marburger Schule," Jüdischer Religionsphilosoph: Eine Ausstellung in der Universitätsbibliothek Marburg vom 1. Juli bis 14. August 1992* edited by Franz Orlik and intro-

duced by Reinhard Brandt (Marburg: Universitätsbibliothek Marburg, 1992), 28–34.

61. See, for instance, Cohen's 1867 essay, "Heinrich Heine und das Judentum," *Jüdische Schriften*, II: 11. This essay was originally published in serialized form in the Berlin Jewish weekly, *Der Gegenwart*. See also "Der Sabbat in seiner kulturgeschichtlichen Bedeutung." Cohen, *Jüdische Schriften*, II: 66–72. The article was originally delivered as a lecture before a group of German-Jewish intellectuals on January 19, 1869. However, it only appeared in 1881 in the German-American journal, *Der Zeitgeist*, in 1881. See the editor's notes in Cohen, *Jüdische Schriften*, II: 469.

62. A short time before, Cohen confided to a close friend that "my Kant stands before me and I am attempting to grasp a glance of him." See Cohen's letter of August 2, 1870, to Hermann Lewandowsky in *Hermann Cohen: Briefe*, eds. Bertha and Bruno Strauss (Berlin: Schocken, 1939), 24.

63. As noted, Cohen's own efforts to comprehend Kant betrayed a certain historicist ambition. Indeed, he admitted in the introduction to the first of his major neo-Kantian books, *Kants Theorie der Erfahrung*, also from 1871, that he "felt the urgent need to present the historical Kant again." Hermann Cohen, *Kants Theorie der Erfahrung* (Berlin, 1918; rpt. 1871), iii–iv, quoted in Poma, 7.

64. Notwithstanding the fact that Cohen criticized him in *Kants Theorie der Erfahrung*, Lange called the book "one of the most significant achievements to emerge in the field of philosophy in the last years." Quoted in *Hermann Cohen: Kantinterpret*, 54.

65. Cohen expressed gratitude to Lange "without whose aid I would not have been able to became a university lecturer." Ibid., 54. For an account of Cohen's exchange with Lange, see Jehuda Melber, *Hermann Cohen's Philosophy of Judaism* (New York: Jonathan David, 1968), 82 (quoting *Jüdische Schriften*, II: 97).

66. On Böckel's activities, see Richard S. Levy, *The Downfall of the Anti-Semitic Political Parties in Imperial Germany* (New Haven: Yale University Press, 1975), 39–48.

67. See the recollections of Pasternak, who studied philosophy with Cohen in Marburg, in *Safe Conduct* (New York, 1949), 61.

68. On the affinity between the Protestant Reformation and the nineteenth-century "Jewish Reformation" of which Cohen was a legatee, see Gabriel Motzkin, "Hermann Cohen's Integration of Science and Religion," *Archives de sciences sociales des religions* 60/1 (1985), 44.

69. Cohen's essay, "Ein Bekenntnis in der Judenfrage," is included in Walter Boehlich, *Der Berliner Antisemitismusstreit* (Frankfurt: Insel-Verlag, 1965), 148, and quoted in Uriel Tal, *Christians and Jews in Germany: Religion, Politics, and Ideology in the Second Reich, 1870–1914*, translated by Noah J. Jacobs (Ithaca: Cornell University Press, 1975), 62.

70. Tal, *Christians and Jews*, 60 (Boehlich, 127).

71. See George Rupp, *Culture-Protestantism: German Liberal Theology at the Turn of the Twentieth Century* (Missoula, Mont., 1977), 9.

72. For the most sustained discussion of the origins of the term, see F. W. Graf, "Kulturprotestantismus: Zur Begriffsgeschichte einer theologiepolitischen Chiffre," in *Archiv für Begriffsgeschichte* 28 (1984), 214–86.

73. Gangolf Hübinger, *Kulturprotestantismus und Politik: Zum Verhältnis von Liberalismus und Protestantismus im wilhelminischen* Deutschland (Tübingen, 1994), 267.

74. In one of the few notable discussions of "Protestant Judaism," Akiva (Ernst) Simon portrays it as decidedly resistant to Jewish nationalism. See Simon, *Ha-im 'od Yehudim anahnu?* (Tel Aviv: Sifriyat Po'alim, 1982), 9–30.

75. On this point, see my essay, "Hermann Cohen and the Quest for Protestant Judaism" *Leo Baeck Institute Year Book* 46 (2001), 195–214.

76. Gans offered this famous formulation in his 1822 presidential address to the Verein für Cultur und Wissenschaft der Juden. See S. Rubaschoff, "Erstlinge der Entjudung: Drei Reden von Eduard Gans in 'Kulturverein,' " *Der jüdische Wille* 2 (1919), 112. For commentary, see my article " 'The Blessing of Assimilation' Reconsidered: An Inquiry into Jewish Cultural Studies," in David N. Myers and William V. Rowe, *From Ghetto to Emancipation: Historical and Contemporary Reconsiderations of the Jewish Community* (Scranton, 1998), 17ff.

77. We must note that a good number of German Jews regarded *Kulturprotestantismus* not as a benign force, but rather as a recipe for the obliteration of Jewish distinctiveness. See Uriel Tal's discussion in "Liberal Protestantism and the Jews in the Second Reich, 1870–1914," *Jewish Social Studies* 26 (January 1964), 26.

78. In his study of Kant's view of history, Yirmiahu Yovel asks the question: "Is rationalism compatible with the modern historical outlook?" Yovel, *Kant and the Philosophy of History* (Princeton, 1980), 3. Hermann Cohen offered his own version of an answer to this question, when he declared that "die Geschichte muss mit der Vernunft anfangen." See *Die Religion der Vernunft aus den Quellen des Judentums* (Leipzig: G. Fock, 1919), 98.

79. Quoted in Lewis White Beck's introduction to *Kant on History* (Indianapolis: Bobbs-Merrill, 1963), vii.

80. See Beck's introduction to *Kant on History*, xviii.

81. See Kant's "Idea for a Universal History from a Cosmopolitan Point of View" in *Kant on History*, 21. This essay reflects Kant's understanding of history as distinct from "the work of practicing empirical historians" (25).

82. Ibid. 138.

83. Yovel, *Kant and the Philosophy of History*, 240.

84. See the classic articulation of the problem in Albert Schweitzer, *The Quest of the Historical Jesus* (New York: Macmillan, 1968), 3ff.

85. Martin Kähler, *The So-Called Historical Jesus and the Historic Biblical Christ*, translated by Carl Braaten (Philadelphia, 1964), 43.

86. For a concise discussion of their differences, see Carl Braaten's introduction to *The So-Called Historical Jesus*, 15–17.

87. Wilhelm Herrmann's *Der Verkehr des Christen mit Gott, im Anschluss an Luther dargestellt* of 1884 has been translated as *The Communion of the Christian with God* (New York, 1906), 70, 72, 9.

88. As William Kluback notes, Herrmann maintained that "Cohen did not comprehend" that it was the self, rather than an a priori Idea, that enabled the encounter with God. See Kluback, "Friendship without Communication: Wilhelm Herrmann and Hermann Cohen," *Leo Baeck Institute Year Book* 31 (1986), 326.

89. Troeltsch's comment on the Cohen-Herrmann relationship in *Theologische Literaturzeitung* 4/5 (1918), 62, is quoted in Kluback, "Friendship without Communication," 335.

90. Brent Sockness offers a thorough analysis of the Herrmann-Troeltsch exchanges in *Against False Apologetics*, passim.

91. Cohen, "Zur Controverse zwischen Trendelenburg und Kuno Fischer," 270, 271. Cohen took Kuno Fischer to task for asserting that history was "the most important of the philosophical *Wissenschaften*." Ibid., 274, 272.

92. See Yovel, *Kant and the Philosophy of History*, 247. The idea of a "philosophical history" was shared by adepts of the various Enlightenment movements across Europe in the late eighteenth century. The great Englishman Edward Gibbon once quipped that "if philosophers are not always historians, it were, at any rate, to be wished that historians were always philosophers." One of Gibbon's most astute recent students, David Womersley, comments that the "intellectual eminence of the philosophic historian prevents him from being overwhelmed by the minutiae of historical facts." See Womersley's introduction to Gibbon, *The History of the Decline and Fall of the Roman Empire* (1776; rpt. New York: Penguin, 1995), I: xx, xxi. Meanwhile, Cohen discusses the function of such a philosophical historiography in "Zur Orientierung in der Losen Blättern aus Kants Nachlass," *Schriften zur Philosophie und Zeitgeschichte*, 434ff.

93. Simon Kaplan, in his dissertation on the problem of history in Cohen's philosophy, argued that for Cohen, "the idea of history cannot be derived from the historical empirical; rather it must be based on an Eternal that must be searched for outside of all temporal/sensual and historical experience." Kaplan, *Das Problem des Geschichte*, 50.

94. Or as one important scholar of Cohen described it, "only those facts deserve the dignity of that name which are consciously ordered with an eye toward a rational, i.e., ideal, end." See Schwarzschild, "Two Modern Jewish Philosophies of History: Nachman Krochmal and Hermann Cohen," 96–97. It is helpful to bear in mind Michael Frede's distinction between "doxological" and "chronological" history. The former, which held sway at least through the age of Kant, did not seek to clarify the precise etiology of philosophical ideas, but rather to explore "whether the views of the past are still worth considering philosophically or not." Cohen clearly held to a doxological view of history. See Frede, "The History of Philosophy As a Discipline," *Journal of Philosophy* 85 (1988), 667–68. I would like to thank Abe Socher, who called my attention to this article.

95. "Zur Controverse zwischen Trendelenburg und Kuno Fischer," 272, 274.

96. See Rosenzweig's reference in the introduction to *Jüdische Schriften*, I: xxvi. Treitschke's essay, "Unsere Aussichten," originally published in the *Preussische Jahrbücher*, is included in Boehlich, *Der Berliner Antisemitismusstreit*, 5–12.

97. On this wave of anti-Semitism and Jewish responses to it, see Michael A. Meyer, "Great Debate on Antisemitism: Jewish Reactions to New Hostility in Germany, 1789–1881," *Leo Baeck Institute Year Book* 11 (1966), 137–70.

98. See Michael A. Meyer, "Heinrich Graetz and Heinrich von Treitschke: A Comparison of their Historical Image of the Modern Jew," *Modern Judaism* 6 (1986), 8.

99. For example, Meyer notes that Graetz wrote a letter to Moses Hess in 1868 in which he said of his forthcoming volumes: "I am looking forward with pleasure to scourging the Germans and their leaders—Schleiermacher, Fichte, and the whole wretched Romantic school." Ibid., 9.

100. Many of these sources are collected in Boehlich, *Der Berliner Antisemitismusstreit*.

101. Cohen, "Ein Bekenntniss in der Judenfrage," originally published as a separate pamphlet in Berlin in 1880, and reprinted in *Jüdische Schriften*, II: 74.

102. Quoted in Meyer, "Great Debate on Antisemitism," 151.

103. Cohen, "Ein Bekenntnis," 73, 75, 76.

104. See Cohen's letter to F. A. Lange from September 5, 1874, discussed in Hans Liebeschütz, "Hermann Cohen and his Historical Background," 3–4, n. 2.

105. See Meyer, "Great Debate on Antisemitism," 152. The claim of disloyalty issued from Cohen's comment in "Ein Bekenntnis" that "we wish we had an absolutely German-Germanic appearance." Cohen's one-time teacher, Steinthal, broke off relations with him following this essay, in part because Cohen also attacked Steinthal's collaborator, Moritz Lazarus. See Rosenzweig's introduction to *Jüdische Schriften*, I: xxx, as well as Dieter Adelmann, "H. Steinthal und Hermann Cohen," in *Hermann Cohen's Philosophy of Religion*, ed. Stéphane Moses and Hartwig Wiedebach (Hildesheim: Georg Olms, 1997), 2–3

106. See Melber's extended discussion of Cohen's encounter with Lagarde in a Marburg courtroom in *Hermann Cohen's Philosophy of Judaism*, 216–34.

107. Uriel Tal speaks of the "double aim" of German Jewry in the period under discussion: "to integrate completely into their environment as full-fledged Germans and at the same time preserve their separate Jewish existence." See Tal, *Christianity and Jews in Germany*, 17.

108. Cohen, "Deutschtum und Judentum (I)," *Jüdische Schriften*, II: 286–87.

109. The exchange between Cohen and Buber from July–September 1916 is translated in Paul Mendes-Flohr and Jehuda Reinharz, *The Jew in the Modern World*, 574.

110. Cohen, "Deutschtum und Judentum," in *Jüdische Schriften*, II: 290.

111. Quoted in Mendes-Flohr and Reinharz, *The Jew in the Modern World*, 575.

112. Buber, "Jüdische Wissenschaft," *Die Welt* 41–43 (October 11 and 25, 1901), reprinted in Mendes-Flohr and Reinharz, 242.

113. According to Paul Mendes-Flohr, these volumes assumed a "unique authority among Central European intellectuals." See Mendes-Flohr, "Fin de Siècle Orientalism, the *Ostjuden*, and the Aesthetics of Jewish Self-Affirmation," in *Divided Passions: Jewish Intellectuals and the Experience of Modernity* (Detroit, 1991), 88.

114. Buber clarified this point in a letter to the Russian-Jewish scholar Shmuel Horodetzky in 1908. He averred that his interest was not in historical differences between earlier and later Hasidim, but rather in "the commonality of the entire subject" of Hasidism. See Buber, *Briefwechsel aus sieben Jahrzehnten*, vol. 1 (Heidelberg: L. Schneider, 1972). More than a half-century later, Buber admitted, in response to Gershom Scholem's criticism, that his "presentation of Hasidism is not a historical one." See Buber, "Interpreting Hasidism," *Commentary* 36 (September 1963), 218.

115. See "Grätzens Philosophie der jüdischen Geschichte," *Jüdische Schriften*, II: 203.

116. "Grätzens Philosophie," 205, quoting Heinrich Graetz, *Die Konstruktion*, 88.

117. Benedict de Spinoza, *Theologico-Political Treatise*, translated and edited by R.H.M. Elwes (New York: Dover, 1941), 45, 55–56.

118. Spinoza makes clear that the survival of the Jews in exile is neither "marvelous" nor salutary, but rather a function of their stubborn adherence to outmoded rituals and the attendant hatred of Gentiles. *Theologico-Political Treatise*, 55.

119. See Ismar Schorsch's English edition of *Die Konstruktion*, published as *The Structure of Jewish History and Other Essays* (New York: Jewish Theological Seminary, 1975), 74ff.

120. "Nay, I would go so far as to believe that if the foundations of their religion have not emasculated their minds they may even, if occasion offers, so changeable are human affairs, raise up their empire afresh, and that God may a second time elect them." *A Theologico-Political Treatise*, 56.

121. See "The Structure of Jewish History," in Graetz, *The Structure of Jewish History*, 84. As a further cautionary note, we need only recall the lament of Simon Dubnow, the great Russian-Jewish historian of the early twentieth century, that Graetz's approach was plagued by its excessive attention to the history of Jewish learning and suffering. See Dubnow's introduction to *Weltgeschichte des jüdischen Volkes* (Berlin, 1925), translated in *Nationalism and History*, edited by Koppel S. Pinson (Phildaelphia: Jewish Publication Society, 1958), 337.

122. Cohen, "Grätzens Philosophie," 205.

123. "The Structure of Jewish History," 124.

124. In the posthumous *Religion of Reason*, Cohen observes: "National history . . . is in general not yet history. It cannot even be a methodological foundation, because it cannot be the point of departure for scientific orientation." Ibid., 205. In light of our discussion, one must regard skeptically Erwin I. J. Rosenthal's attempt to minimize the "difference in method and approach" between Cohen and Graetz. See Rosenthal, "Hermann Cohen and Heinrich Graetz," in *The Salo Wittmayer Baron Jubilee Volume* (Jerusalem: American Academy for Jewish Research, 1975), 725. See also Reuven Michael, "Cohen contra Graetz," *Bulletin des Leo Baeck Instituts* 4 (1961), 301–322.

125. Tal, *Christians and Jews in Germany*, 143, 120. Tal demonstrates that the Jews, or more accurately the Jewish question, "served as a convenient standard of comparison in evaluating the political and moral character" of the struggle between German Catholics and Protestants.

126. Schwarzschild, "Two Modern Jewish Philosophies of History," 120.

127. Cohen, "Der Stil der Propheten," in *Jüdische Schriften*, I: 263.

128. Cohen, "Religion und Sittlichkeit," *Jüdische Schriften*, III: 124. See also the concise presentation in Hans Liebeschütz, "Hermann Cohen and His Historical Background," 21.

129. See Michael A. Meyer, *Response to Modernity: A History of the Reform Movement in Judaism* (New York, 1988), 95–96. It is interesting to note that Heinrich Graetz, foil to both Geiger and Cohen, shared in the praise for Israelite prophecy, calling it "the glory of the Jewish spirit." Nonetheless, Graetz empha-

sizes less the universalist message of the prophets than their fortification of Judaism from within. See Graetz, "The Structure of Jewish History," 80–82.

130. According to Hans Liebeschütz, "it was the work of Wellhausen and his school, which gave the prophetic message its definite place in Cohen's interpretation of Judaism." Liebeschütz, "Hermann Cohen and His Historical Background," 21–23.

131. See Cohen's eulogy, "Julius Wellhausen: Ein Abschiedsgruss," in *Jüdische Schriften*, II: 464.

132. See Cohen's posthumously published lecture from 1916, "Das soziale Ideal bei Platon und den Propheten," in *Jüdische Schriften*, I: 306, 330, 310, 309. For elaboration, see Pierfrancesco Fiorato, *Geschichtliche Ewigkeit: Ursprung und Zeitlichkeit in der Philosophie Hermann Cohens* (Königshausen, 1993), especially chapter 3.

133. See, for instance, Isadore Twersky's remarks in *Introduction to the Code of Maimonides* (New Haven: Yale, 1980), 465.

134. According to Cohen, Maimonides' "God is not a God of metaphysics, of the substance of the world, but is rather the God of ethics." "Characteristik der Ethik Maimunis," *Jüdische Schriften*, III: 289.

135. See "Characteristik der Ethik Maimunis," *Jüdische Schriften*, III: 275 (including note 1). In making this claim, Cohen creatively misread Maimonides, upending the carefully delineated hierarchy of perfections set out in the last chapter of the *Guide of the Perplexed*. Thus, Cohen seems to transpose the fourth and final perfection of the Maimonidean system, rational virtues, and the penultimate perfection, moral virtues. See the Pines/Strauss edition of Moses Maimonides, *The Guide of the Perplexed*, vol. 2 (Chicago, 1963), 635.

136. Cohen, "Deutschtum und Judentum (I)," *Jüdische Schriften*, II: 244.

137. See Liebeschütz, "Hermann Cohen and His Historical Background," 13.

138. Cohen, "Innere Beziehungen der Kantischen Philosophie zum Judentum," *Jüdische Schriften*, I: 290, 292, 301.

139. In eulogizing his teacher, Ernst Cassirer wrote of Cohen that "[w]e encounter three fundamental moments in the thought of this great rationalist: Plato, Kant, and prophecy." See Cassirer's comments in the *Vossische Zeitung*, May 18, 1920, quoted in *Hermann Cohen. Kantinterpret*, 156. Jacques Derrida, meanwhile, writes of the "Platonico-Judeo-Protestant axis" in Cohen's thought. Derrida, "Interpretations at War," 61.

140. Derrida, Interpretations at War," 61.

141. Cohen, "Innere Beziehungen der Kantischen Philosophie zum Judentum," *Jüdische Schriften*, I: 304.

142. Cohen, *Religion of Reason out of the Sources of Judaism*, translated by Simon Kaplan and introduced by Leo Strauss with new essays by Steven S. Schwarzchild and Kenneth Seeskin (1972; Atlanta: Scholars Press, 1995), 1, 5.

143. In both cases, Cohen pushed philosophy and ethics to the center of the agenda. His 1904 address, "Die Errichtung von Lehrstühlen für Ethik und Religionsphilosophie an den jüdisch-theologischen Lehranstalten," was republished in *Jüdische Schriften*, II: 115.

144. "Die Errichtung," 110–11. Avi Bernstein-Nahar elaborates on this point in his insightful essay, "Hermann Cohen's Teaching concerning Modern Jewish Identity (1904–1918)," *Leo Baeck Institute Year Book* 43 (1998), 29.

145. "Die Errichtung," 113. Bernstein-Nahar, 41–43.

146. In this regard, he was giving new voice to Leopold Zunz's famous claim that the emancipation of Wissenschaft des Judentums was an essential precondition of the emancipation of the Jews in general. See his 1907 essay, "Zwei Vorschläge zur Sicherung unseres Fortbestandes," *Jüdische Schriften*, II: 140.

147. See D. N. Myers, "The Fall and Rise of Jewish Historicism: The Evolution of the Akademie für die Wissenschaft des Judentums (1919–1934)," *Hebrew Union College Annual* 63 (1992), 107–44.

148. See Rosenzweig's notebook entries on Cohen in Nahum Glatzer, ed. *Franz Rosenzweig: His Life and Thought* (New York: Schocken, 1953), 29.

149. Quoted in Derrida, "Interpretations at War," 45–46.

150. Rosenzweig's letter bore the title "Zeit ists" (It is time). See Myers, "The Fall and Rise of Jewish Historicism," passim.

151. In fact, it has been argued that Cohen exercised an important influence on post-WWI dialectical theologians (particularly Karl Barth) for whom opposition to historicism was quite pronounced. See John Lyden, "The Influence of Hermann Cohen on Karl Barth's Dialectical Theology," *Modern Judaism* 12 (1992), 167–83.

152. Troeltsch, "Die Ethos der hebräischen Propheten," *Logos* 6 (1916/17), 1–28.

153. See Moses Glückson's essay, "Hermann Cohen und das nationale Judentum," *Neue Jüdische Monatshefte* 3 (March 1919), 231–35, cited in Jörg Hackeschmidt's helpful essay, "Die hebräischen Propheten und die Ethik Kants: Hermann Cohen in kultur- und sozialhistorischer Perspektive," *Aschkenas* 1 (1995), 129. See also the discussion in Hackeschmidt, *Von Kurt Blumenfeld zu Norbert Elias. Die Erfindung einer jüdischen Nation* (Hamburg: Europäische Verlagsanstalt, 1997), 96–101. I would like to thank Ofer Nur for bringing Hackeschmidt's work to my attention. We might add that Cohen was engaged in this period in his famous polemic with Martin Buber over Zionism; likewise, he was coming under attack from his student, the dedicated Zionist Jacob Klatzkin, over his Jewish universalism. See Wendell S. Dietrich, *Cohen and Troeltsch: Ethical Monotheistic Religion and Theory of Culture* (Atlanta: Scholars Press, 1986), 36

154. Tal, *Christians and Jews in Germany*, 220.

155. See Jacob Katz's discussion of Lagarde in *From Prejudice to Destruction: Anti-Semitism, 1700–1933* (Cambridge: Harvard, 1980), 305–306, or George L. Mosse, *Toward the Final Solution: A History of European Racism* (Madison: Wisconsin, 1975), 100–101.

156. For the most sweeping brief against Troeltsch, see Constance L. Benson's controversial book *God and Caesar: Troeltsch's Social Teaching as Legitimation* (New Brunswick, N.J.: Transaction, 1999).

157. See Willey's discussion of Troeltsch's affinities for and critique of the Baden School in *Back to Kant*, 156–61.

158. Troeltsch's critique of the latter revealed his fealties to the historically oriented Baden tradition of neo-Kantians as distinct from Hermann Cohen's Mar-

burg School. See Troeltsch, "Das Ethos der hebräischen Propheten," *Logos* 6 (1916–17), 28. See also Dietrich's discussion of the distinction between Troeltsch's Baden neo-Kantianism and Cohen's Marburg version in *Cohen and Troeltsch*, 56–57.

159. Troeltsch, "Das Ethos der hebräischen Propheten," 15, 18.

160. Ibid., 24–25. See also Dietrich, *Cohen and Troeltsch*, 38–39.

161. Troeltsch, "Der Ethos der hebräischen Propheten," 26, 28.

162. Benzion Kellermann, *Der ethische Monotheismus der Propheten und seine soziologische Würdigung* (Berlin: Schwetschke, 1917).

163. Cohen, "Der Prophetismus und die Soziologie," in idem, *Jüdische Schriften*, II: 398, 399.

164. Cohen attempted to answer the claims of Zionism in a 1916 essay entitled "Religion und Zionismus." There he offers a terminological distinction between "nations" and "nationalities," maintaining that the Jews qualify as the latter but not the former. This essay was originally published in *K.-C. Blätter* 11 (May/June 1916), and reprinted in *Jüdische Schriften*, II: 322.

165. See Israel Elbogen, *A Century of Jewish Life* (Philadelphia: Jewish Publication Society, 1966), 457.

166. Cohen, "Der Prophetismus und die Soziologie," 400.

167. Troeltsch, *Der Historismus und seine Probleme*, vol. 1 (Tübingen, 1922), 542.

CHAPTER THREE
FRANZ ROSENZWEIG AND THE RISE OF THEOLOGICAL ANTI-HISTORICISM

1. For a comprehensive survey of literature published on Rosenzweig until 1990, see L. Anckaert and B. Casper, eds. *Franz Rosenzweig: A Primary and Secondary Bibliography* (Leuven, 1990). Since that time, a large stream of publications has appeared dealing with Rosenzweig. Among those I have consulted here are Leora Batnizky, *Idolatry and Representation: The Philosophy of Franz Rosenzweig Reconsidered* (Princeton, 2000), Richard A. Cohen, *Elevations: The Height of the Good in Rosenzweig and Levinas* (Chicago, 1994), Robert Gibbs, *Correlations in Rosenzweig and Levinas* (Princeton, 1992), and Ephraim Meir, *Kokhav mi-Ya'akov: Hayav ve-yetsirato shel Franz Rosenzweig* (Jerusalem, 1994). Peter Gordon has recently undertaken a wide-ranging *Rezeptionsgeschichte* that surveys the Rosenzweig revival in recent philosophical and literary circles. See Gordon, "Rosenzweig Redux: The Reception of German-Jewish Thought," *Jewish Social Studies* (new series) 8 (Fall 2001), 1–57.

2. See, for instance, Glatzer's two seminal editions, *Franz Rosenzweig: His Life and Thought* (New York, 1953), and *On Jewish Learning* (New York, 1955).

3. See Altmann, "Franz Rosenzweig on History" and Mendes-Flohr, "Franz Rosenzweig and the Crisis of Historicism," in Mendes-Flohr, ed., *The Philosophy of Franz Rosenzweig* (Hanover, N.H., 1988), 124–37, 138–61. See inter alia Bernhard Casper, *Das dialogische Denken* (Freiburg, 1967), 69–89, Robert Gibbs, *Correlations in Rosenzweig and Levinas*, 114–23, Peter Eli Gordon, "Under One Tradewind: Philosophical Expressionism from Rosenzweig to Heidegger," Ph.D. diss., Berkeley, 1997 (or in the revised book *Rosenzweig and Heidegger: Between Judaism and German Philosophy* [Berkeley: University of California, 2003]),

Rivka Horwitz, "Tefisat ha-Yahadut be-mahshevet Franz Rosenzweig," *Proceedings of the American Academy for Jewish Research* 37 (1969), passim, Steven T. Katz, "On Historicism and Eternity: Reflections on the 100th Birthday of Franz Rosenzweig," in idem, *Historicism, the Holocaust, and Zionism* (New York, 1922), 1–26, Ephraim Meir, *Kokhav mi-Ya'akov*, 120–33, and Stéphane Mosès, *System and Revelation: The Philosophy of Franz Rosenzweig* (Detroit, 1992), 201–209. Cutting against the grain, Leora Batnitzky concurs with Leo Strauss (in *Spinoza's Critique of Religion*) that "Rosenzweig's thought is fundamentally historicist in character." While there is much with which I agree in Batnitzky's analysis, I nonetheless find her assessment a bit too unequivocal. I will depict Rosenzweig here as driven by competing impulses—the first rooted in his immersion in an historicist culture and the second relating to his desire to liberate the Jewish people from the shackles of historical contingency. See Batznitzky's interesting essay, "On the Truth of History or the History of Truth: Rethinking Rosenzweig via Strauss," *Jewish Studies Quarterly* 7 (2000), 224. Meanwhile, Elliot Wolfson adds an insightful and intriguing twist to the consideration of Rosenzweig's historical thinking. He notes that Rosenzweig "ascribes messianic significance to the task of the historian, for the recollection of the past fosters a sense of continuity in time that is inherently lacking in the sequential flow of temporality." See Wolfson's essay, "Facing the Effaced: Mystical Eschatology and the Idealistic Orientation in the Thought of Franz Rosenzweig," *Zeitschrift für neurere Theologiegeschichte* 4 (1997), 46.

4. See Bambach's helpful discussion in *Heidegger, Dilthey, and the Crisis of Historicism*, 201–203.

5. Friedrich Wilhelm Graf, "Die 'antihistorische Revolution' in der protestantischen Theologie der zwanziger Jahre," in Jan Rohls and Gunther Wenz, eds. *Vernunft des Glaubens: Wissenschaftliche Theologie und kirchliche Lehre* (Göttingen, 1988), 377–405. Peter Gordon has done a fine job of considering Rosenzweig and Heidegger as part of that new philosophical moment in *Rosenzweig and Heidegger: Between Judaism and German Philosophy*. Samuel Moyn has followed a somewhat parallel path, situating Rosenzweig in the new theological moment of Weimar in "Weimar Revelations: Rosenzweig, Barth, and the Theological Other" from his forthcoming book *Origins of the Other: Emmanuel Levinas and Interwar Philosophy*.

6. See Megill, *History and Theory* 36:3 (October 1997), 419.

7. For an early diagnosis of this anti-historicist sentiment, see Hermann Heimpel's 1956 essay, "Geschichte und Geschictswissenschaft," reprinted in *Vierteljahrshefte für Zeitgeschichte* 1 (1957), 1–17. An excellent survey of the concept can be found in Kurt Nowak, "Die 'antihistorisiche Revolution': Symptome und Folgen der Krise historischer Weltorientierung nach dem Ersten Weltkrieg," in H. Renz and F. W. Graf, eds. *Umstrittene Moderne: Die Zukunft der Neuzyeit im Urteil der Epoche Ernst Troeltsch (Troeltsch-Studien Band 4)* (Gütersloh, 1987), 133–71.

8. Graf, "Die 'antihistorische Revolution,' " 384.

9. Leonore Siegele-Wenschkewitz argues that Protestant theologians evinced a new understanding of and sympathy for Judaism in Weimar times in "The Relationship between Protestant Theology and Jewish Studies during the Weimar Re-

public," in Otto Dov Kulka and Paul R. Mendes-Flohr, eds. *Judaism and Christianity under the Impact of National Socialism* (Jerusalem: Shazar Center, 1987), 133–50.

10. In describing his own turn to a decidedly Jewish orientation, Rosenzweig wrote in 1913 that "I no longer borrow my concepts from Christianity (*linguistically and terminologically I still do, but no movement can be autonomous in these matters*)." Emphasis added. See Rosenzweig's diary entry, translated in Nahum N. Glatzer, ed. *Franz Rosenzweig: His Life and Thought* (New York, 1953), 28.

11. See my "Hermann Cohen and the Quest for Protestant Judaism," *Leo Baeck Institute Year Book* 46 (2002), 195–214.

12. *The Star of Redemption*, translated by William W. Hallo (Notre Dame, 1970), 334, 331.

13. For attempts to move beyond this model, see, for example, Gordon, "Under One Tradewind, xi, 14, and Paul Mendes-Flohr's recent study of Rosenzweig and German-Jewish identity, *German Jews: A Dual Identity* (New Haven, 1999), especially chapters 1–3.

14. Amos Funkenstein, "An Escape from History: Rosenzweig on the Destiny of Judaism," in idem, *Perceptions of Jewish History*, 301. In a related essay, Funkenstein notes the paradox that in Rosenzweig, "the uniqueness and eternity of Israel is described in a language saturated with Christian images and terms." See "Franz Rosenzweig and the End of German-Jewish Philosophy," ibid., 269, 270.

15. Altmann, "Theology in Twentieth-Century German Jewry," *Leo Baeck Institute Year Book* 1 (1956), 194.

16. For example, Gershom Scholem and Walter Benjamin had a somewhat dismissive attitude toward Cohen, whose work they read together in 1918. Benjamin inveighed against the "transcendental confusion" of Cohen's rationalist system, and concluded after reading Cohen that "I might as well become a Catholic." See Gershom Scholem, *Walter Benjamin: The Story of a Friendship* (Philadelphia, 1981), 60.

17. Quoted in Glatzer, *Franz Rosenzweig: His Life and Thought*, 29.

18. See Rosenzweig's letter to Eugen Rosenstock-Huessy in Rosenstock-Huessy, ed. *Judaism despite Christianity: The "Letters on Christianity and Judaism" between Eugen Rosenstock-Huessy and Franz Rosenzweig* (University, Alabama, 1969), 97.

19. Gordon, "Under One Tradewind," 66.

20. Rudolf Otto, *The Idea of the Holy* (London and New York, 1958), 2, 8.

21. See the discussion of this essay in Richard Wolin, *Walter Benjamin: An Aesthetic of Redemption*, revised edition (Berkeley, 1994), 34.

22. The essay "Über das Programm der kommenden Philosophie" is reprinted in Benjamin's *Gesammelte Schriften* 2(1): 164, and quoted in Wolin, 35.

23. According to Scholem, Benjamin posited a concept of experience in his 1917 essay that "encompassed man's intellectual and psychological connection with the world, which takes place in the realms not yet permeated by cognition." Scholem, *Walter Benjamin: The Story of a Friendship*, 59.

24. See "With Gershom Scholem: An Interview," in Gershom Scholem, *On Jews and Judaism in Crisis*, edited by Werner J. Dannhauser (New York, 1976), 18.

25. See Rosenzweig's letter of June 8, 1916 in his *Briefe und Tagebücher*, 194, as well as in the English version of the Rosenzweig-Rosenstock correspondence, *Judaism despite Christianity*, 83. For a helpful and careful analysis of the year 1800 in Rosenzweig's thought, see Paul Frank's comments in Franz Rosenzweig, *Philosophical and Theological Writings*, edited by Paul W. Franks and Michael L. Morgan (Indianapolis, 200), 25–47.

26. Glatzer, *Franz Rosenzweig*, 96. See also Stefan Meineke's helpful discussion of Rosenzweig's anti-university sentiment in "A Life of Contradiction: The Philosopher Franz Rosenzweig and His Relationship to History and Politics," *Leo Baeck Institute Year Book* 36 (1991), 464.

27. This is the view of Rivka Horwitz in her "Tefisat ha-Yahadut be-mahshevet Franz Rosenzweig," *Proceedings of the American Academy for Jewish Research* 37 (1969), 7. Horwitz recalls that Rosenzweig had once declared that "my correct [Hebrew] name should be Judah ben Samuel, which is exactly the name of the great man whose middle-sized reincarnation upon the road of transmigration I am: Judah ha-Levi." See Rosenzweig's letter to his mother from June 5, 1929 in Glatzer, *Franz Rosenzweig: His Life and Thought*, 167.

28. Horwitz, "Tefisat ha-Yahadut," 14, as well as Amos Funkenstein's discussion in his *Perceptions of Jewish History* (Berkeley, 1993), 293.

29. See James H. Lehman, "Maimonides, Mendelssohn and the *Measfim*: Philosophy and the Biographical Imagination in the Early *Haskalah*," *Leo Baeck Institute Year Book* 20 (1975), 87–108.

30. See Funkenstein's chapter, "Franz Rosenzweig and the End of German-Jewish Philosophy," in *Perceptions of Jewish History*, 257–305. Schalom Ben-Chorin extends the point even further by arguing that "Franz Rosenzweig was the last" of German Jews. Ben-Chorin, "Franz Rosenzweig und das Ende des deutschen Judentums," in the first volume of the conference proceedings on Rosenzweig's centenary held in Kassel, *Der Philosoph Franz Rosenzweig: Die Herausforderung jüdischen Lernens*, edited by Wolfdietrich Schmied-Kowarzik (Munich, 1988), 58.

31. Heidegger's comments in his exchange with Cassirer are found in the comprehensive collection of texts from the Davos conference, *Débat sur le kantisme et la philosophie*, translated by P. Aubenque, J. M. Fataud, and P. Quillet (Paris, 1972), 35, 36.

32. See Peter Gordon's excellent discussion of Davos in chapter 5 of "Under One Tradewind," especially 425.

33. In observing Heidegger's emphasis on *Dasein*, Gordon notes that "Rosenzweig too was deeply committed to the meaning of this word in the lexicon of religion and modern philosophy, and, much like Heidegger, he was acutely aware of how the idealist tradition bore a heaving responsibility for having 'forgotten' its precise meaning in favor of various other, more ethereal alternatives." Gordon, "Under One Tradewind," 406–407.

34. Written in 1929 and published in *Der Morgen* in April 1930, "Vertauschte Fronten" is reprinted in Rosenzweig, *Der Mensch und sein Zeit: Zweistromland*, edited by Reinhold and Annemarie Mayer, vol. 3 (Dordrecht, 1984), 237. The affinity between Cohen and Rosenzweig has been noted by a host of commenta-

tors, including Batnitzky, *Idolatry and Representation*, 54–60, and Gibbs, *Correlations in Rosenzweig and Levinas*, 17–23.

35. See Gordon's discussion of Rosenzweig's linkage of Cohen and Heidegger, which he calls "one of the most provocative specimens of intellectual history written in the twentieth century." "Under One Tradewind," 441.

36. Rosenzweig, "Vertauschte Fronten," 237.

37. Glatzer, *Franz Rosenzweig: His Life and Thought*, xi–xiii.

38. See most recently Mendes-Flohr, *German Jews: A Dual Identity*, 66–70.

39. See Rivka Horwitz's discussion of Rosenzweig's parents' attitude toward the prospect of their son's conversion in her introduction to the Hebrew edition of Franz's letters and diary, *Mivhar igrot ve-keta'e yoman* (Jerusalem, 1987), xxiv.

40. So too the cultural distance between the Rosenzweig family and the family of Rosenzweig's close friend, Eugen Rosenstock-Huessy, was quite close. Like Rosenzweig, Eugen Rosenstock was raised in an affluent and assimilated Jewish ambience in Hamburg-Altona. To tighten the cultural knot even further, Rosenstock's mother (Paula) was the daughter of the director of the Jewish school in Wolfenbüttel that was founded by the great-grandfather of Franz Rosenzweig and the Ehrenbergs.

41. Glatzer, xxxvi–xxxvii.

42. See the editor's introduction to Rosenzweig, *Briefe und Tagebücher*, 1.

43. Quoted in Glatzer, xxxviii.

44. See Rosenzweig's diary entry of 12 February 1906 in *Briefe und Tagebücher*, 27.

45. See Rosenzweig's letter to his parents of 1 March 1906 in ibid., 30.

46. Bernhard Casper, *Das dialogische Denken*, 71.

47. Diary entry of 29 April 1906 in *Briefe und Tagebücher*, 41 (emphasis added).

48. Rosenzweig conveyed his decision in a letter to his mother from March 4, 1908. *Briefe und Tagebücher*, 77.

49. Rosenzweig's forty-eight-page paper on Friedrich Wilhelm V, focusing particularly on Heinrich von Sybel's representation of him, is found in the Franz Rosenzweig Collection, ms. 1a, AR 4193, Leo Baeck Institute Archives (New York).

50. See Meinecke's *Historism: The Rise of a New Historical Outlook* (London, 1972), lvii, quoted in Bambach, *Heidegger, Dilthey, and the Crisis of Historicism*, 113.

51. This sharp comment, delivered in response to Rickert, came in Meinecke's 1928 essay, "Kausalitäten und Werte," translated in Fritz Stern, ed. *Varieties of History* (New York, 1958), 68.

52. Rickert, *Die Probleme der Geschichtsphilosophie* (Heidelberg, 1924), quoted in Bambach's excellent discussion, 115.

53. Bambach, *Heidegger, Dilthey, and the Crisis of Historicism*, 108.

54. See Rosenzweig's letter to Hans Ehrenberg from fall 1908 in *Briefe und Tagebücher*, 88. See also the discussion of Meinecke in Alexander Altmann, "Franz Rosenzweig on History," 124–25, and Paul Mendes-Flohr, "Franz Rosenzweig and the Crisis of Historicism," 140–42, in Mendes-Flohr, ed. *The Philosophy of Franz*

*Rosenzweig.* Robert Gibbs also offers perceptive insights into Meinecke's historiographical style in Gibbs, *Correlations in Rosenzweig and Levinas,* 114–17.

55. Glatzer, *Franz Rosenzweig: His Life and Thought,* 20–21. See also Otto Pöggeler, "Between Enlightenment and Romanticism: Rosenzweig and Hegel," in *The Philosophy of Franz Rosenzweig,* 113.

56. See von Weizsäcker's recollections quoted in *Briefe und Tagebücher,* 96,

57. Altmann, "Franz Rosenzweig on History," 126.

58. *Briefe und Tagebücher,* 112–13.

59. Casper notes that up to the completion of his dissertation in 1913, Rosenzweig was perched between "dem Anspruch Hegels, die absolute Wahrheit zu erkennen, und dem Relativismus der historischen Methode." *Das dialogische Denken,* 75.

60. See Rosenzweig's letter of November 6, 1909, in Glatzer, *Franz Rosenzweig: His Life and Thought,* 19.

61. See Casper's discussion of the two related *Wenden* in Rosenzweig's life in this period: toward religion and away from history. *Das dialogische Denken,* 76–77.

62. Harold Stahmer first revealed the intense intellectual, as well as erotic, connections among Franz, Eugen, and Gritli in nearly 1,500 unpublished letters in "The Letters of Franz Rosenzweig to Margrit Rosenstock-Huessy: 'Franz,' 'Gritli,' 'Eugen,' and the Star of Redemption," delivered at the international congress in Kassel on the occasion of Rosenzweig's centenary (1986) and published in Wolfdietrich Schmied-Kowarzik, ed., *Der Philosoph Franz Rosenzweig,* vol. 1 (Munich, 1988), 123. Rivka Horwitz followed in Stahmer's footsteps and analyzed this same body of material anew, calling attention to the passionate love affair between Franz and Gritli in her lecture of December 19, 2000, at the Association for Jewish Studies meeting in Boston. More recently, some 1,000 letters written by Rosenzweig, and Rosenstock, but not by Gritli herself, have been published as *Die "Gritli" Briefe: Briefe an Margrit Rosenstock-Huessy,* edited by Inken Rühke and Reinhold Mayer (Tübingen: Bilam Verlag, 2002). Gritli's letters were destroyed by Rosenzweig's widow, Edith. The publication of these letters occasioned a scathing response from F. W. Graf, who lamented inter alia their incomplete nature, in the Frankfurter Allgemeine Zeitung from June 3, 2002.

63. Rosenstock-Huessy, *Judaism despite Christianity,* 172.

64. See Rosenstock-Huessy's letter to Rosenzweig from October 4, 1916, in *Judaism despite Christianity,* 104.

65. See Rosenzweig's letter to Rudolf Ehrenberg from October 31, 1913, in *Briefe und Tagebücher,* 133. See also Alexander's Altmann's discussion of the Rosenzweig/Rosenstock-Huessy correspondence in *Judaism despite Christianity,* 32.

66. Rosenstock-Huessy's comments were made to Dorothy M. Emmett and are published in her essay "The Letters of Franz Rosenzweig and Eugen Rosenstock-Huessy," reprinted in *Judaism despite Christianity,* 48.

67. Rosenstock-Huessy, "Prologue/Epilogue to the Letters—Fifty Years Later," in *Judaism despite Christianity,* 71.

68. See Paul Mendes-Flohr's introduction to *The Philosophy of Franz Rosenzweig,* 5.

69. Glatzer, *Franz Rosenzweig: His Life and Thought,* 24–28.

70. See Rosenzweig's letter to R. Ehrenberg of August 25, 1919, in *Mivhar igrot*, 174.

71. See Rosenzweig's letter to his mother from October 23, 1913, informing her of his decision to remain a Jew in *Briefe und Tagebücher*, 131.

72. Rosenzweig's letter to Eduard Strauss from September 14, 1919, is found in *Mivhar igrot*, 177.

73. Glatzer, *Franz Rosenzweig: His Life and Thought*, 29.

74. Derrida, "Interpretation at War: Kant, the Jew, and the German," *New Literary History* 22 (1991), 44.

75. Later, in 1916, Rosenzweig defended Cohen to Rosenstock, arguing that he is "the first full-blown professor I have seen whom, without mockery, I would call a philosopher. And it is the same with his Judaism." *Judaism despite Christianity*, 97.

76. That said, it would be inaccurate to describe Rosenzweig as vehemently anti-Zionist. As Stéphane Mosès shows, Rosenzweig at various points in his life, particularly in the 1920s, appeared quite comprehending of the Zionist impulse, and even sympathetic to Jewish settlement in Palestine. For instance, Mosès recalls that Rosenzweig once wrote in his diary in 1922 that "the Jew who lays down roots in the diaspora loses his creative Jewish and religious powers." See Mosès, "Franz Rosenzweig mul ha-Tsiyonut," in *Ha-Tsiyonut u-mitnagdeha ba-'am ha-Yehudi* eds. Haim Avni and Gideon Shimoni (Jerusalem, 1990), 324. For a broader review of Rosenzweig's ambivalence toward Zionism, see also Ephraim Meir, *Kokhav mi-Ya'akov*, 105–19.

77. *Judaism despite Christianity*, 121; and Rosenzweig to Rosenstock-Huessy from November 30, 1916, 161.

78. Rosenstock-Huessy to Rosenzweig from October 30, 1916, in ibid., 127.

79. Rosenzweig to Rosenstock-Huessy (undated) in ibid., 168.

80. Batnitzky has noted the affinity between Rosenzweig and Gadamer on tradition in her *Idolatry and Representation*, 44–46, as well as in "On the Truth of History or the History of Truth," passim.

81. The essay was published posthumously in Rosenzweig's *Kleinere Schriften* (Berlin, 1937), and republished in the third volume of the recent edition of his collected writings, *Der Mensch und sein Werk: Zweistomland*, 687–97.

82. Rosenzweig, "Atheistische Theologie," 689, 688. I have also consulted here the translation in the Franks/Morgan edition of Rosenzweig's *Philosophical and Theological Writings*, 14.

83. Rosenzweig, "Atheistische Theologie," 692, 696 (Franks/Morgan, 17, 23).

84. Ibid., 690.

85. Rosenzweig's view here resembles that of the German theologian, Franz Overbeck. In his posthumously published book *Christentum und Kultur* from 1920, Overbeck presents history as that plane in which humans operate between the poles of *Urgeschichte* and death. As Thomas Ogletree explains, "[t]hese two points, 'primal history' (*Urgeschichte*) and death, are the 'last things' between which lies our life in this world, the given world, our world, the understandable world." See his *Christian Faith and History: A Critical Comparison of Ernst Troeltsch and Karl Barth* (New York and Nashville, 1965), 86.

86. Rosenzweig, "Atheistische Theologie," 697 (Franks/Morgan, 24).

87. In fact, in a letter to his parents from August 17, 1916, Rosenzweig declared without the slightest irony that "[w]ar is no more immoral, i.e., irreligious, than peace. It is the *men* who are good or evil." Glatzer, *Franz Rosenzweig: His Life and Thought*, 38. See also Meineke, "A Life of Contradiction," 469.

88. Rivka Horwitz includes Rosenzweig among her roster of Jewish opponents of the war in her "Voices of Opposition to the First World War among Jewish Thinkers," *Leo Baeck Institute Year Book* 32 (1988), 233–59. But see Meineke's trenchant criticism of Horwitz's claim that Rosenzweig was a pacifist in "A Life of Contradiction," 469, n. 39. There Meinecke offers an extended analysis of Rosenzweig's attitude to politics, linking his detached stance to his anti-historicism.

89. See Rosenzweig's letter to Rudi Ehrenberg from October 1916, in which Rosenzweig admits that in the conditions of the front, he "developed a great taste for writing and write[s] endless letters." Glatzer, *Franz Rosenzweig: His Life and Thought*, 42.

90. For an early articulation of this mapping, see Rosenzweig's letter of May 1, 1917, to Gertrud Oppenheim in Glatzer, *Franz Rosenzweig: His Life and Thought*, 53. See also Rosenzweig's Kassel lecture from 1919, "Geist und Epochen der jüdischen Geschichte," reprinted in *Der Mensch und sein Werk: Zweistromland*, 527–38.

91. Shulamit Volkov has discussed the impulse toward "dissimilation" that affected a number of prominent German-Jewish intellectuals in this period. For some, dissimilation led to Zion; for others, like Rosenzweig, it led to a renewed commitment to Diaspora culture. See Volkov, "The Dynamics of Dissimilation: *Ostjuden* and German Jews," in Jehuda Reinharz and Walter Schatzberg, eds. *The Jewish Response to German Culture from the Enlightenment to the Second World War* (Hanover, N.H., 1985), 195–211.

92. *Zeit ists* (Berlin and Munich, 1918); the letter cum proposal is reprinted in Rosenzweig, *Der Mensch und sein Werk: Zweistromland*, 461. Its title comes from Ps. 119:126: "It is time to work for the Lord; they made void Thy teachings."

93. Simon, "Franz Rosenzweig und das jüdische Bildungsproblem," *Korrespondenzblatt des Vereins zur Gründung und Erhaltung einer Akademie für die Wissenschaft des Judentums* 11 (1930), 2.

94. "Zeit ists," *Der Mensch und sein Werk*, 463. In Rosenzweig's lexicon, the term "Jewish world" connoted a cultural sphere that was undeniably surrounded by, but not subsumed under, a non-Jewish world.

95. "Zeit ists," 463. The following discussion of "Zeit ists" and the efforts to establish the Akademie für die Wissenschaft des Judentums borrows from my article, "The Fall and Rise of Jewish Historicism: The Evolution of the Akademie für die Wissenschaft des Judentums (1919–1934)," *Hebrew Union College Annual* 63 (1992), 107–144.

96. Funds to provide for this cohort would be raised through an educational tax levied on German-Jewish communities. "Zeit ists," 463.

97. "Zeit ists," 474. I have also consulted here Nahum Glatzer's English version in Franz Rosenzweig, *On Jewish Learning* (New York, 1965), 45.

98. See Rosenzweig's letter to Richard Ehrenberg, father of Hans and Rudolf, from December 28, 1917, in *Briefe und Tagebücher*. 1 502.

99. Cohen delivered his remarks in 1904 at a meeting of the Gesellschaft zur Förderung der Wissenschaft des Judentums. They were published as "Die Errichtung von Lehrstühlen für Ethik und Religions-Philosophie an den jüdisch-theologischen Lehranstalten," *Monatsschrift für Geschichte und Wissenschaft des Judentums* 48 (1904), 2–21.

100. Cohen, "Zur Begründung einer Akademie für die Wissenschaft des Judentums," *Neue Jüdische Monatshefte* 2 (10 March 1918), 254–59. Cohen's endorsement of Rosenzweig's proposal may have signaled not only his concerns over the state of Jewish education, but his own incremental alienation from the very intellectual culture that he cherished so dearly. In particular, his apparent belief that the university was no longer the most appropriate venue for Jewish intellectual and cultural activity violated a long-standing article of faith articulated by Leopold Zunz—namely, that the full emancipation of German Jewry would only follow the full integration of Jewish studies into the German university. That Rosenzweig would surrender this ideal is consistent with his critique of German academic culture. Cohen's surrender, however, is far more noteworthy.

101. Peter Gay, *The Berlin-Jewish Spirit: A Dogma in Search of Some Doubts* (15th Leo Baeck Memorial Lecture) (New York, 1972), 3–4.

102. The story of this reversal of fortune is told more fully in my "The Fall and Rise of Jewish Historicism," especially 116ff. Nahum Glatzer also notes that Rosenzweig's plan in "Zeit ists" to combine reform of primary and secondary education with a reorientation of Jewish scholarship ran afoul of pedagogic experts within the Jewish community. See *Franz Rosenzweig: His Life and Thought*, 89.

103. Indeed, the idea of discrete research institutes became a popular form of what has been called the "research imperative" within the German university in the turn-of-the-century period, replacing in many instances the more integrated research seminar. See Björn Wittrock, "The Modern University: The Three Transformations," in Sheldon Rothblatt and Björn Wittrock, *The European and American University since 1800: Historical and Sociological Essays* (Cambridge, 1993), 330. For a discussion of the emergence of research institutes in Germany, see Hans-Juergen Panel, "Von der Teegellschaft zum Forschungsinstitut: Die historischen Seminare vom Beginn des 19. Jahrhunderts bis zum Ende des Kaiserreichs," in Horst Walter Blanke, ed. *Transformation des Historismus: Wissenschaftsorganisation und Bildungspolitik vor dem Ersten Weltkrieg* (Waltrop, 1994), 1–31.

104. For an excellent discussion of the Lehrhaus (and of related educational developments in Germany), see Michael Brenner, *The Renaissance of Jewish Culture in Weimar Germany* (New Haven, 1996), 69–90.

105. Rosenzweig's opening address from 1920, "Neues Lernen," is reprinted in *Der Mensch und sein Werk: Zweistomland*, 508.

106. Brenner, *The Renaissance of Jewish Culture in Weimar Germany*, 79–84.

107. In his oft-noted letter to Friedrich Meinecke from August 30, 1920, Rosenzweig vividly describes how, in the wake of his "collapse" of 1913, he commenced an excavation of his self that yielded great treasures. See Glatzer, *Franz Rosenzweig: His Life and Thought*, 95–96.

108. Brenner, *The Renaissance of Jewish Culture in Weimar Germany*, 71.

109. See the list of courses in Nahum Glatzer's still valuable article, "The Frankfort Lehrhaus," *Leo Baeck Institute Year Book* 1 (1956), 119, as well as in Brenner, *The Renaissance of Jewish Culture in Weimar Germany*, 234, n. 20.

110. Emphasis added. See Glatzer's introduction to Rosenzweig, *On Jewish Learning*, 17.

111. Rosenzweig to Meinecke from August 30, 1920 in Glatzer, *Franz Rosenzweig: His Life and Thought*, 95–96.

112. Hans Ehrenberg gives a fine sense of the psychic turmoil of the period, especially from 1910 to 1914. Ehrenberg describes these years, which were also immensely repercussive for Rosenzweig, as "the most concentrated which I have ever known; I realize this now when I recall the intensity of the spiritual mood in which I was living. Sometimes I was almost physically exhausted, so great was the inner tumult." Ehrenberg, *Autobiography of a German Pastor*, translated by Geraint V. Jones (London: Northumberland, 1943), 114.

113. Barth makes reference to the group, whose members he met in a visit to Germany in February 1920, in the volume compiled by his student Eberhard Busch, *Karl Barth: His Life from Letters and Autobiographical Texts*, trans. John Bowden (Philadelphia: Fortress, 1976), 112.

114. See the entry on Barth by Zdravko Kujundzija in the *Dictionary of Modern Western Theology*, and found at *http://people.bu.edu/wwildman/WeirdWildWeb/courses/mwt/dictionary/mwt_themes_750_barth.htm*.

115. See Van Harvey's lucid treatment in *The Historian and the Believer*, 133.

116. Barth objected to the fact that liberal theology had "at any rate in all its representative figures and trends . . . become *religionist* and thus *anthropocentric*; in this sense it had become *humanist*. Busch, *Karl Barth: His Life from Letters and Autobiographical Texts*, 119.

117. Ibid., 97.

118. See F. W. Graf, "Die 'antihistorische Revolution' in der protestantischen Theologie der zwanziger Jahre," 380.

119. Barth, *The Epistle to the Romans*, trans. Edwyn C. Hoskyns (London, 1933), quoted in Harvey, *The Historian and the Believer*, 26.

120. Barth, *Kirchliche Dogmatik*, (Munich, 1932), I/1, 3, quoted in Graf, "Die 'antihistorisiche Revolution,' " 390. It is important to note that Barth later wrote a comprehensive intellectual history of nineteenth-century Protestant thought, *Die Protestantische Theologie im 19. Jahrhundert* (Zurich: Evangelischer Verlag, 1952).

121. Graf, "Die 'antihistorisiche Revolution,' " 390.

122. Barth, *The Epistle to the Romans*, 145, 147.

123. Graf, "Die antihistorische Revolution," 387, 390.

124. See Gogarten, *Die Christlichle Welt* 34 (1920), 377–78, quoted in Bambach, *Heidegger, Dilthey, and the Crisis of Historicism*, 192. For a meticulous description of the origins and development of the journal, see also Peter Lange, *Konkrete Theologie? Karl Barth und Friedrich Gogarten "Zwischen den Zeiten" (1922–1933)* (Zurich: Theologischer Verlag, 1972), 23, 154.

125. Graf, " 'Die antihistorische Revolution,' " 394.

126. In this regard, see the comments of Franks and Morgan in Rosenzweig's *Philosophical and Theological Writings*, 88–89.

127. Rosenzweig's discussion of the commonalities between Judaism and Christianity comes in his *Das neue Denken*, translated in Glatzer, *Franz Rosenzweig: His Life and Thought*, 203.

128. See the helpful discussion of Hermann's influence on Barth in Ogletree, *Christian Faith and History*, 182–83.

129. Randi Lynn Rashkover, "Franz Rosenzweig, Karl Barth and the Theology of Election," Ph.D. diss., University of Virginia, 2000, 38. See Rosenzweig's comments on human submission in his letter to Rudolf Ehrenberg from November 18, 1917, in Alan Udoff and Barbara E. Galli, eds. *Franz Rosenzweig's "The New Thinking"* (Syracuse, 1999), 59.

130. Heidegger's 1925 lecture "Wilhelm Diltheys Forschungsarbeit und der Kampf um eine historische Weltanschauung" is quoted in Bambach, *Dilthey, Heidegger, and the Crisis of Historicism*, 242.

131. Bambach, *Dilthey, Heidegger, and the Crisis of Historicism*, 220.

132. I have relied here on the version of the *Urzelle* in Udoff and Galli, *Franz Rosenzweig's "The New Thinking,"* 45. For an important analysis of the *Urzelle*, with particular attention to its philosophical roots, see Mòses, *System and Revelation*, 36ff.

133. Udoff and Galli, *Franz Rosenzweig's "The New Thinking*, 57, 62–63.

134. See the discussion in Mòses, *System and Revelation*, 39–42, as well as in Mendes-Flohr's introduction and Bernhard Casper's, "Responsibility Rescued," in *The Philosophy of Franz Rosenzweig*, 8, 102–103.

135. Rosenzweig's unpublished lecture of December 1919, "Das Wesen des Judentums," is printed in *Der Mensch und sein Werk: Zweistromland*, 526.

136. I have discussed Täubler's commitment to placing Jewish history into the wider framework of world history in "The Fall and Rise of Jewish Historicism," *HUCA* 63 (1992), 117ff., as well as in "Eugen Täubler: The Personification of 'Judaism as Tragic Existence,' " *Leo Baeck Institute Year Book* 39 (1994), 131–50.

137. See his notes for the lecture "Jüdische Geschichte im Rahmen der Weltgeschichte," in *Der Mensch und sein Werk: Zweistomland*, 539, 542–43.

138. Indeed, *ruah* was the "spiritual connection . . . that binds individuals into a spiritual community." "Geist und Epochen der jüdischen Geschichte," reprinted in *Der Mensch und sein Werk: Zweistromland*, 527. For a detailed (though somewhat elliptical) analysis of a portion of this essay, see Manfred H. Vogel, *Rosenzweig on Profane/Secular History* (Atlanta, 1996).

139. "Geist und Epochen der jüdischen Geschichte," 530 (my emphasis). Rosenzweig notes shortly thereafter that "one can speak scientifically of the spirit of history only when one seeks to become clear about the division of the body—that is, the epochs"; 529.

140. Ibid., 530–31.

141. Ibid., 533.

142. See Rosenzweig's letter of May 27, 1922, in Glatzer, *Franz Rosenzweig: His Life and Thought*, 115.

143. Ismar Schorsch argues that Graetz commenced his history with the fourth volume to "defend talmudic literature as a great national achievement of untold importance to the subsequent survival of the Jews." Schorsch, introduction to Graetz, *The Structure of Jewish History*, 48.

144. "Geist und Epochen der jüdischen Geschichte," 533.

145. Ibid., 537, 538. It is important to note that Karl Barth, Rosenzweig's theological contemporary, described Christianity in somewhat parallel terms, as a religious faith that refused to succumb to the temporal. See Ogletree's discussion in *Christian Faith and History*, 92–96.

146. For instance, at the point of the book's conception in August 1918, Rosenzweig boasted that "it's going to be quite fantastic, entirely unpublishable, equally scandalous to 'Christians, Jews, and heathens.' " Later, after the *Star*'s publication, Rosenzweig recognized that the book's deepest resonances were felt among Jews. As he noted in early 1925: "And I really believe that this is a Jewish book; not merely one that treats of 'Jewish matters,' for then the books of Protestant Old Testament scholars would be Jewish books, but a book to which the old Jewish words have come for the expression of whatever it has to say, and especially of what is new in it." Glatzer, *Franz Rosenzweig: His Life and Thought*, 81, 145.

147. The opening sentence of the *Star* is: "All cognition of the All originates *in death*, in the fear of death." (my emphasis). Meanwhile, the concluding words of the book are "INTO LIFE." See Rosenzweig, *The Star of Redemption*, 3, 424.

148. Rosenzweig regarded Judaism and Christianity as the two living embodiments of the Divine spirit. By contrast, he adopted an unrelentingly hostile attitude toward Islam, accusing it (among other sins) of affinities to both Idealism and historicism. Robert Gibbs argues that his treatment of Islam "reflects an embarrassing prejudice." See Gibbs, *Correlations in Rosenzweig and Levinas*, 113. Shlomo Pines, meanwhile, traces the influence of Hegel and the Orientalist Ignaz Goldziher on Rosenzweig's views of Islam in his essay, "Der Islam im 'Stern der Erlösung: Eine Untersuchung zu Tendenzen und Quellen Franz Rosenzweigs," in *Hebräische Beiträge zur Wissenschaft des Judentums, Deutsch angezeigt 3–5* (1987–89), 138–48, cited in Udoff and Galli, *Franz Rosenzweig's "The New Thinking"*, 186–87.

149. See Rosenzweig, *The Star of Redemption*, 340, 345, 337, 370, 337.

150. Ibid., 8–17, 97–99.

151. Ibid., 101.

152. Ibid., 102, 108.

153. Ibid., 331, 328, 332.

154. Ibid., 300.

CHAPTER FOUR
ANTI-HISTORICISM AND THE THEOLOGICAL-POLITICAL PREDICAMENT IN WEIMAR GERMANY: THE CASE OF LEO STRAUSS

1. See Troeltsch's essay, "Die Krisis des Historismus," *Die neue Rundschau* 32:1 (1922), 573. See also Karl Heussi's 1932 book of the same title, which was similarly motivated by friction between historical study and theological concern. Heussi, *Die Krisis des Historismus* (Tübingen, 1932)

2. Troeltsch, "Die Krisis des Historismus," 583.

3. Troeltsch, "Historical and Dogmatic Method in Theology," in *Religion in History*, 12.

4. Ernst Troeltsch, *Der Historismus und seine Probleme* (Tübingen, 1922). See the comments of H. S. Hughes, *Consciousness and Society*, 239.

5. Troeltsch provides a blueprint for this work of salvation in "Die Krisis des Historismus," 588–90.

6. A source of inspiration and agitation for this generation was Franz Overbeck, who set historicism and Christianity in stark opposition. In a typical formulation, Overbeck wrote: "The whole thought of locating the eternal duration of Christianity in history is an especially eloquent characteristic of the hypocritical countenance of modern Christianity—a sign that its theologians in truth are not its advocates but its gravediggers." Overbeck, *Christentum und Kultur* (Basel, 1919), 20, quoted in Thomas W. Ogletree, *Christian Faith and History*, 84. This statement recalls the renowned epitaph attributed to Moritz Steinschneider, the erudite Jewish bibliographer, regarding *Wissenschaft des Judentums*: namely, that it practitioners were merely intent on giving Judaism a decent burial.

7. Aschheim concurs with George Steiner's argument that both left and right in Weimar shared a deep sense of rupture, as well as a canon of "master texts." See his "German Jews beyond *Bildung* and Liberalism: The Radical Jewish Revival in the Weimar Republic," *Culture and Catastrophe: German and Jewish Confrontations with National Socialism and Other Crises* (New York, 1996), 34–35. See also Steiner's essay, "Heidegger, Again," *Salmagundi* 82–83 (Spring–Summer 1989), 31–55.

8. See Löwy, *Redemption and Utopia: Jewish Libertarian Thought in Central Europe: A Study in Elective Affinity* (Stanford, 1988), 18, and Gershom Scholem, *On Jews and Judaism in Crisis* (New York, 1976), 285.

9. See Rabinbach's essay, which is in part a gloss on Löwy, "Between Apocalypse and Enlightenment: Benjamin, Bloch, and Modern German-Jewish Messianism," in idem, *In the Shadow of Catastrophe: German Intellectuals between Apocalypse and Enlightenment* (Berkeley, 1997), 29.

10. Gustav Steinbömer, "Betrachtungen über den Konservativismus," *Deutsches Volkstum* (January 1932), 26, quoted in Kurt Sontheimer, *Antidemokratisches Denken in der Weimarer Republik: Die politischen Ideen des deutschen Nationalismus zwischen 1918 und 1933* (Munich, 1968), 119.

11. In his exhaustive study, Armin Mohler traces the provenance of the term to the Berlin newspaper, *Die Volksstimme* of May 24, 1848. See the updated third edition of Mohler's 1949 dissertation, *Die Konservative Revolution in Deutschland, 1918–1932: Ein Handbuch* (Darmstadt, 1989), 9.

12. The author Hugo von Hofmannsthal pointed to unity and holism as the two defining criteria of the "Conservative Revolution" in a speech from 1927. See Mohler, *Die Konservative Revolution in Deutschland*, 10.

13. On this last point, see Alan Mittleman's brief remarks on the conservatism of Hirschian Orthodoxy on which Breuer was nurtured. Alan L. Mittleman, *The Politics of Torah: The Jewish Political Tradition and the Foundation of Agudat Israel* (Albany, 1996), 18.

14. Sontheimer, *Antidemokratisches Denken in der Weimarer Republik*, 54ff.

15. See Schmitt, *Politische Theologie: Vier Kapitel zu Lehre von der Souveränität*, 2nd edition (Berlin, 1934), 49. Of particular interest is Raphael Gross's comprehensive new study of Schmitt's attitude toward Jews and the Jewish question

in *Carl Schmitt und die Juden: Eine deutsche Rechtslehre* (Frankfurt am Main, 2000), 188. See also George Schwab's introduction to his translation of Carl Schmitt, *Political Theology: Four Chapters on the Concept of Sovereignty* (Cambridge, Mass., 1985), xv.

16. See Schmitt's discussion of the "counterrevolutionary idea of the State" in the fourth chapter of *Political Theology*, 53–66.

17. For another important recent study of Schmitt, see Gopal Balakrishnan, *The Enemy: An Intellectual Portrait of Carl Schmitt* (London, 2000), 43.

18. Schmitt, *Political Theology*, 2.

19. Strauss's reference to the "theologico-political" crisis of Weimar comes in the extraordinary introduction to the English edition of *Die Religionskritik Spinozas als Grundlage seiner Bibelwissenschaft* (Berlin, 1930), translated by E. M. Sinclair as *Spinoza's Critique of Religion* (New York, 1965), 1.

20. Benedict de Spinoza, *A Theological-Political Treatise*, translated by R.H.M. Elwes (New York, 1951), 5. For elaboration on the "theologico-political" predicament of Spinoza, as well as other early modern and modern thinkers, see Steven B. Smith's *Spinoza, Liberalism, and the Question of Jewish Identity*, especially chapter 1.

21. Spinoza, *A Theologico-Political Treatise*, 6.

22. Ibid., 245.

23. Smith, *Spinoza, Liberalism, and the Question of Jewish Identity*, xiii, and Spinoza, *A Theologico-Political Treatise*, 259.

24. The writ of excommunication issued against Spinoza on July 27, 1656, by the *Mahamad* (council) of the Spanish-Portuguese Jewish community in Amsterdam refers, without further elaboration, to "the horrible heresies, which he [Spinoza] practised and taught, and of the monstrous actions which he performed." This text is included in Mendes-Flohr and Reinharz, *The Jew in the Modern World*, 50. I. S. Révah has pointed to the existence of an intriguing intellectual circle led by Dr. Juan de Prado of which Spinoza was a member and in which he may have begun to develop his heterodox views on authorship of the Bible. See Révah, *Spinoza et le Dr. Juan de Prado* (Paris, 1959).

25. Spinoza, *A Theologico-Political Treatise*, 124.

26. Ibid., 100 (my emphasis).

27. Ibid., 124.

28. Ibid., 101.

29. Lessing's remarks came in a letter to J. G. Michaelis from October 16, 1754, quoted in Alexander Altmann, *Moses Mendelssohn: A Biographical Study* (Philadelphia, 1973), 34.

30. See ibid., 604.

31. See, for instance, Isaiah Berlin's discussion of Hamann in *Three Critics of the Enlightenment: Vico, Hamann, Herder*, edited by Henry Hardy (Princeton, 2000), 347.

32. Perhaps the most renowned case of novelistic attention is Berthold Auerbach's *Spinoza: Ein Denkerleben* (Mannheim: Vassermann & Mathy, 1854). See Jonathan Skolnik's important analysis in "Writing Jewish History between Gutzkow and Goethe: Auerbach's Spinoza and the Birth of Modern Jewish Historical Fiction," *Prooftexts* 19 (May 1999), 101–26.

33. Any assertion of equivalence must take into account the fact that some of the leading twentieth-century critics were proud Jews, whereas the earlier Counter-Enlightenment thinkers often gave voice to anti-Jewish expressions.

34. See Article 114 of the Constitution of the German Republic from August 11, 1919, included in Anton Kaes, Martin Jay, and Edward Dimendberg, eds. *The Weimar Republic Sourcebook* (Berkeley, 1994), 49. For a selection of critical voices from left and right, see ibid., 309–54.

35. Benjamin, "Theses on the Philosophy of History," in idem, *Illuminations*, edited by Hannah Arendt (New York, 1969), 255, 263.

36. Benjamin, "Theses on the Philosophy of History," 257–58.

37. As in the cases of Cohen and Rosenzweig, Benjamin's resistance to historicism and its moral deficits did not preclude a constructive—in this case, essential ethical—function for historical recollection (*Eingedenken*). Such recollection disrupted the continuous flow of historical progress and allowed for reclamation of the anonymous victims of the past. Significantly, recollection was also, for Benjamin, a quintessentially Jewish act. For the scriptural mandate to Jews was *not* to investigate the future, but to remember the past (*zakhor*). Benjamin, "Theses on the Philosophy of History," 264. Earlier, in his notes for a general plan for his massive *Passagen-Werk* (perhaps from 1934–35), Benjamin writes that "[t]he historian is the herald who summons the departed to this banquet of spirits." See Benjamin, *The Arcades Project*, translated by Howard Eiland and Kevin McLaughlin (Cambridge, Mass., 1999), 912. The ethical function of the historian that surfaces here and in the last of Benjamin's "These on the Philosophy of History" stands in contrast to the dispassionate modern historian depicted in the final chapter of Yosef Yerushalmi's *Zakhor*. By contrast, Edith Wyschogrod rearticulates the Benjaminian impulse to demand ethical responsibility of the historian in *An Ethics of Remembering: History, Heterology, and the Nameless Others* (Chicago, 1998).

38. See Benjamin's notes at the end of *Das Passagen-Werk* (vol. 5 of his *Gesammelte Schriften*), edited by Rolf Tiedemann (Frankfurt, 1982), 1236, and quoted in John McCole, *Walter Benjamin and the Antinomies of Tradition* (Ithaca, 1993), 295.

39. Although Scholem had commenced informal study of Jewish mysticism during the war, prompted in part by his reading of Franz Josef Molitor, he devoted his university years after the war to an intensified study of the Kabbalah, culminating in his dissertation on *Sefer ha-bahir*. See David Biale, *Gershom Scholem, Kabbalah and Counter-History* (Cambridge, Mass., 1982), 29–34.

40. See Stéphane Mosès' discussion of the affinities between the two in "Walter Benjamin and Franz Rosenzweig," *The Philosophical Forum* 15: 1–2 (Fall/Winter 1983/84), 203. This essay, along with the article cited in the following note, provides an excellent introduction to Benjamin's notion of the redemptive possibilities of history.

41. Stéphane Mosès, "The Theological-Political Model of History in the Thought of Walter Benjamin," *History and Memory* 1 (1989), 14.

42. See the "Translators' Forward" to Walter Benjamin, *The Arcades Project*, ix.

43. In particular, a host of recent scholars has focused on Strauss not only as a political theorist, but as an innovative and important Jewish thinker who came

of intellectual age in the Weimar period. John G. Gunnell has suggested that this new scholarly impulse reflects a desire to understand "Strauss before Straussianism." His essay appears under that title in a collection edited by Kenneth L. Deutsch and Walter Nicgorski. *Leo Strauss: Political Philosopher and Jewish Thinker* (Lanham, Md., 1994), 107–28 (with a number of germane essays by Steven B. Smith and Hillel Fradkin). Among the other important contributors to this new interest are Kenneth Hart Green, *Jew and Philosopher: The Return to Maimonides in the Jewish Thought of Leo Strauss* (Albany, 1993) and his edited volume, Leo Strauss, *Jewish Philosophy and the Crisis of Modernity: Essays and Lectures in Modern Jewish Thought* (Albany, 1997); Heinrich Meier in a host of writings and editions dealing with Strauss, including a comprehensive *Gesammelte Schriften* (of which two volumes have appeared); Michael Morgan in his *Dilemmas in Modern Jewish Thought* (Bloomington, Ind., 1992), 40–67; Alan Udoff, ed. *Leo Strauss's Thought: Toward a Critical Engagement* (Boulder, Colo., 1991); Jonathan Cohen, *Tevunah u-temurah: panim be-heker ha-filosofyah ha-Yehudit ve-toldoteha* (Jerusalem, 1997), 229–94; and Ehud Luz's introduction to the Hebrew edition of Strauss's writings, *Yerushalayim ve-Atuna: Mivhar ketavim,* (Jerusalem: Mossad Bialik and Leo Baeck Institute, 2001). In his recently completed dissertation, Eugene Sheppard has provided the most overarching historical treatment of the young Strauss. See his introductory remarks on the state of Strauss scholarship in "Leo Strauss and the Politics of Exile," Ph.D. diss., UCLA, 2001, 1–6.

44. The term "hermeneutics of suspicion," as is well known, comes from the work of the French philosopher Paul Ricoeur. Its anachronistic use seems warranted in the case of Strauss, for whom esoteric writing by philosophers was a mechanism not only of conveying profound truths, but also of self-preservation in the face of a hostile ruler or censor.

45. See Strauss's essay, "Natural Right and the Historical Approach," based on his 1953 book *Natural Right and History,* in idem, *An Introduction to Political Philosophy: Ten Essays,* edited by Hilail Gildin (Detroit, 1989), 108.

46. Strauss, *An Introduction to Political Philosophy,* 99, 108.

47. *Spinoza's Critique of Religion,* 3. Strauss thereby inverts Spinoza, who had famously accused Jewish ritual, and particularly circumcision, of eviscerating Jews to the point that a vibrant political life of their own was unimaginable.

48. *Spinoza's Critique of Religion,* 30.

49. To clarify the point, Jewish assimilationists, of course, believed in the possibility, even necessity, of remaining in the diaspora. But they no longer regarded diaspora life as Exile; on the contrary, it represented fulfillment. See Strauss's Preface to *Spinoza's Critique of Religion,* 30, where he defines intellectual probity as a "new kind of fortitude which forbids itself every flight from the horror of life into comforting delusion."

50. Much of what we know about Strauss's childhood and early adulthood comes from a number of brief autobiographical sources, including his Preface to *Spinoza's Critique of Religion* (1962), a lecture/conversation at Chicago on "Why We Remain Jews" (1962), and a joint text with his friend Jacob Klein, "A Giving of Accounts" (1970). The latter two appear in *Jewish Philosophy and the Crisis of Modernity,* 311–56, 457–66. Unrestricted access to the Strauss papers (including

correspondence) may yield a richer picture, although Strauss's disinterest in auto-biographical reflection in general may mean that there are few traces to follow. In addition to Sheppard's treatment, see the useful introduction to Michael Zank's edition of Strauss's writings in English, *Leo Strauss: The Early Writings (1921–1932)* (Albany: SUNY Press, 2002), 3ff.

51. See Zank, *Leo Strauss: The Early Writings*, 6.

52. We should not overstate the case, because Strauss admitted that his house-hold, for all its observance, imparted "very little Jewish knowledge." Quoted in Zank, *Leo Strauss: The Early Writings*, 3.

53. *Spinoza's Critique of Religion*, 15.

54. Sheppard, "Leo Strauss and the Politics of Exile," 7.

55. See "A Giving of Accounts: Jacob Klein and Leo Strauss," in *Jewish Philosophy and the Crisis of Modernity*, 459. For a discussion of the "passive resistance" of rural Jews against the fast pace of modernization, see Steven Lowenstein, "Pace of Modernization of German Jewry in the Nineteenth Century," *Leo Baeck Institute Year Book* 21 (1976), 41–56.

56. "A Giving of Accounts," 460.

57. At the end of his 1959 essay "What Is Political Philosophy?" Strauss issued this judgment of Nietzsche's role in the later rise of Nazism: "He used much of his unsurpassable and inexhaustible power of passionate and fascinating speech for making his readers loathe, not only socialism and communism, but conservatism, nationalism, and democracy as well. . . . He thus prepared a regime which, as long as it lasted, made discredited democracy look again like the golden age." See the reprinted version of this essay in Strauss, *"What Is Political Philosophy?" An Introduction to Political Philosophy*, 57. See also Laurence Lampert, *Leo Strauss and Nietzsche* (Chicago, 1996), 5–10.

58. See Ehud Luz's discussion of Strauss's affinity with Nietzsche's anti-historicism in the introduction to Strauss, *Yerushalayim ve-Atuna: Mivhar ketavim*, 37.

59. Strauss apprehended this "radical historicism [as] condemning to oblivion the notion of eternity"—an impulse that comported with his own notion of a noble atheism. Strauss, "What Is Political Philosophy?" 57. For a discussion of this historicist hermeneutic in Strauss, see John G. Gunnell, "The Myth of Tradition," *American Political Science Review* 72 (March 1978), 126. Nathan Tarcov offers a competing view, though his description of Strauss's position is not inconsistent with Gunnell's argument. Thus, Tarcov defines Strauss's stance in these terms: "One must read even a great text in its context but one must first try to understand what its author understood its context to be." Nathan Tarcov, "Philosophy and History: Tradition and Interpretation in the Work of Leo Strauss," *Polity* 16 (1983), 12.

60. See the "Correspondence of Karl Löwith and Leo Strauss," translated by G. E. Tucker in the *Independent Journal of Philosophy/Unabhängige Zeitschrift für Philosophie* 5/6 (1988), 183, quoted in Lampert, *Leo Strauss and Nietzsche*, 5.

61. Steven E. Aschheim, *The Nietzsche Legacy in Germany, 1890–1990* (Berkeley, 1992), 129.

62. Leo Strauss, *Das Erkenntnisproblem in der philosophischen Lehre Fr. H. Jacobis*, reprinted in *idem, Gesammelte Schriften*, edited and introduced by Heinrich Meier (Stuttgart and Weimar, 1997), 235–98. Cf. the four-volume work of

Ernst Cassirer, *Das Erkenntnisproblem in der Philosophie und Wissenschaft der neueren Zeit* (Berlin, 1906–57). I am again indebted here to Sheppard's discussion, in which he argues that Strauss's dissertation "voiced a clear rejection of the secular liberal alliance and defiantly presented Jacobi's criticisms of Enlightenment rationalism as a compelling model of intellectual independence and moral substance." Sheppard, "Leo Strauss and the Politics of Exile," 30. See also Zank's discussion in *Leo Strauss: The Early Writings*, 6–7.

63. See "The Problem of Knowledge in the Philosophical Doctrine of Friedrich Heinrich Jacobi" in *Leo Strauss: The Early Writings*, 57.

64. Strauss, "A Giving of Accounts," 460.

65. The years 1921–22 marked an important and repercussive convergence of these three figures. In 1921 Rosenzweig published his *Star*; in the following year, Barth published the second edition of his *Römerbrief*. In the same year, Strauss also encountered Heidegger, and the meeting was a fateful one. Strauss began to attend Heidegger's lectures at Freiburg. Without understanding much of what Heidegger said, Strauss "sensed that he dealt with something of utmost importance to man as man." Strauss, "A Giving of Accounts," 461.

66. Strauss, "A Giving of Accounts," 461.

67. See Strauss's preface to his *Hobbes Politische Wissenschaft* (Neuwied am Rhein and Berlin, 1965), translated in idem, *Jewish Philosophy and the Crisis of Modernity*, 453.

68. See Jonathan Cohen, *Tevunah u-temurah*, 266.

69. Strauss, *Philosophie und Gesetz* (Berlin, 1935), translated by Eve Adler as *Philosophy and Law: Contributions to the Understanding of Maimonides and His Predecessors* (Albany, 1995). There Strauss notes that the principal difference between the modern Enlightenment and "medieval religious Enlightenment" was the esoteric tendencies of the latter. *Philosophy and Law*, 102. See also Cohen, *Tevunah u-temurah*, 267–76.

70. See Strauss's essay, "Biblische Geschichte und Wissenschaft," originally published in the *Jüdische Rundschau* 30 (10 November 1925), 744–45, and reprinted in Heinrich Meier's edition of Strauss, *Gesammelte Schriften*, 2: 359. Luz also notes Strauss's affinity for Barth in this period in his introduction to Strauss, *Yerushalayim ve-Atuna*, 2.

71. Karl Barth, "Not und Verheissung der christlichen Verkündigung," *Zwischen den Zeiten* 1 (1923), 3.

72. Gogarten, "Die Entscheidung," *Zwischen den Zeiten* 1 (1923), 41. See also the essay by Karl Barth's brother, Heinrich, "Christliche und idealistische Deutung der Geschichte," *Zwischen den Zeiten* 3 (1925), 154–82.

73. Emphasis added. Strauss made this point while acknowledging Barth's central role in the "resurgence of theology" after the First World War. See "A Giving of Accounts," 460.

74. Strauss's review of *Das Heilige* was published in *Der Jude* 7:4 (April 1923), and republished in idem, *Gesammelte Schriften*, 2: 308–309.

75. Strauss, "Zur Auseinadersetzung mit der europäischen Wissenschaft," *Der Jude* 8:10 (October 1924), and reprinted in Strauss, *Gesammelte Schriften*, 2: 343. It is important to add that in the same essay, Strauss also defended Cohen against his own teacher Ernst Cassirer, whose theory of religious myth ignored

the ethical dimension in Cohen's thought. Ibid., 348–49. See also Sheppard, "Leo Strauss and the Politics of Exile," 32.

76. "Zur Auseinadersetzung mit der europäischen Wissenschaft," 346.

77. "Biblische Geschichte und Wissenschaft," *Jüdische Rundschau* 30 (10 November 1945), reprinted in Strauss, *Gesammelte Schriften*, 2: 357, 359, 360.

78. It is helpful to recall in this context another essay by Strauss on Dubnow's work, "Soziologische Geschichtsschreibung" from 1924. Here Strauss takes Dubnow to task for not living up to the exalted standard of objectivity that he had set for himself. In the course of his criticism, we see clear evidence of Strauss's conservative disposition. To wit, Strauss suggests that Dubnow's preference for progressive regimes undermines his objectivity. By contrast, Strauss evinces empathy for Paul de Lagarde, whom he calls a "truly genuine man." See "Soziologische Geschictsschreibung," *Der Jude* 8:3 (March), reprinted in Strauss, *Gesammelte Schriften*, 2:334, 336. See also Strauss's longer essay, "Paul de Lagarde," *Der Jude* 8:1 (January), reprinted in *Gesammelte Schriften*, 2: 323–31, as well as Sheppard's discussion in "Leo Strauss and the Politics of Exile," 59–61.

79. Strauss, "Cohens Analyse der Bibel-Wissenschaft Spinozas," *Der Jude* 8:5–6 (May–June 1924), 295–314. Cf. Cohen's earlier essay, "Spinoza über Staat und Religion, Judentum und Christentum," *Jahrbuch für jüdische Geschichte und Literatur* 18 (1915), 56–150. See also Leora Batnizky's germane comments in "On the Truth of History or the History of Truth: Rethinking Rosenzweig via Strauss," *Jewish Studies Quarterly* 7 (2000), 244.

80. See "Cohen's Analysis of Spinoza's Bible Science" in *Leo Strauss: The Early Years*, 143.

81. On Strauss's opposition to this "fallacy," see Nathan Tarcov's discussion in "Philosophy and History: Tradition and Interpretation in the Work of Leo Strauss," 12.

82. Strauss, "Cohen's Analysis of Spinoza's Bible Science" in *Leo Strauss: The Early Years*, 152. Steven Smith adds that Spinoza's target was "the spiritual and political domination of Dutch Calvinists, who saw themselves as the heirs of the ancient Hebrew theocracy." Smith, *Spinoza, Liberalism, and the Question of Jewish Identity*, 18. In challenging Cohen's biographical emphasis, Strauss might also have been taking exception to the work of Carl Gebhardt, who published his *Die Schriften des Uriel da Costa* in 1922. This work focused new attention on the crypto-Jewish context in which seventeenth-century skepticism and iconoclasm à la Spinoza germinated.

83. A key feature of the Akademie's labor was its interest in collaborative projects of a grand scale, beginning with Täubler's dream of a *Biblioteca Judaica* that would include critical editions of the most important Jewish texts produced up to the eighteenth century. See my "The Fall and Rise of Jewish Historicism," *HUCA* 63 (1992), 123.

84. Ibid., 135.

85. In 1929, Strauss wrote a short piece on the Akademie in the wake of Franz Rosenzweig's death. There he noted that Rosenzweig was far less concerned with *Wissenschaft* on its own terms than with it as a tool to revitalize Judaism. See

Strauss, "Franz Rosenzweig and the Academy for the Science of Judaism" in *Leo Strauss: The Early Years*, 212–13.

86. Strauss reported on the preliminary results of his study of Spinoza's Bible criticism and its heirs in the Akademie journal. See his "Zur Bibelwissenschaft Spinozas und seiner Vorläufer," *Korrepondenzblatt des Vereins zur Gründung und Erhaltung einer Akademie für die Wissenschaft des Judentums* 7 (1926).

87. It is a variation of that theme—namely, the putative superiority of modern philosophical inquiry over its medieval precursors—that prompted Strauss's polemic against his Akademie colleague and employer, Julius Guttmann in *Philosophie und Gesetz* (Berlin, 1935).

88. Strauss, *Spinoza's Critique of Religion*, 251.

89. Ibid., 37.

90. Ibid., 259.

91. Ibid., 258.

92. See the Preface to *Spinoza's Critique of Religion*, 28 (emphasis added).

93. Strauss, "Der Zionismus bei Nordau," *Der Jude* 7: 10–11 (October/November 1923), reprinted in *Gesammelte Schriften*, 2: 318. An English translation can be found in Arthur A. Cohen, ed. *The Jew: Essays from Martin Buber's Journal*, Der Jude, 124.

94. Arendt's point was that modern anti-Semitism arose to assure that even those Jews who had long ago abandoned Jewish religious practice would continue to be stigmatized. At the same time, Arendt perceptively noted the transformation of Jews from a religious group into a group "whose members shared certain psychological attributes and reactions, the sum total of which was supposed to constitute 'Jewishness.' " Arendt, *The Origins of Totalitarianism*, revised paperback edition (San Diego, 1979), 66, 87.

95. Franz Rosenzweig used the term in a diary entry of April 3, 1922. See *Briefe und Tagebücher*, 2: 770. A brief but helpful *Begriffsgeschichte*, including reference to Rosenzweig's usage, appears in Jonathan Skolnik, "Dissimilation and the Historical Novel: Hermann Sinsheimer's *Maria Nunnez*," *Leo Baeck Institute Year Book* 43 (1998), 229–30. See Volkov, "The Dynamics of Dissimilation: *Ostjuden* and Germans," 195–211.

96. Strauss, "Der Zionismus bei Nordau," *Gesammelte Schriften* 2:317, 319, 321.

97. Ibid., 2:318. For a fuller discussion of Strauss's valorization of *Galut*, see Sheppard, "Leo Strauss and the Politics of Exile," 78–121.

98. See Strauss's introductory essay to Maimonides, *The Guide of the Perplexed*, translated by Shlomo Pines (Chicago, 1963).

99. For a discussion of Eck's understanding of "ecclesia militans," see Wilbirgis Klaiber, *Ecclesia militans: Studien zu den Festtagspredigten des Johannes Eck* (Münster, 1982), 44–45.

100. Strauss, "Ecclesia militans," *Jüdische Rundschau* 30 (8 May 1923), and reprinted in Strauss, *Gesammelte Schriften*, 2: 355, 353.

101. In writing of Zionist plans in Palestine, Breuer asserted that "Orthodox Jews, loyal to the Torah, cannot but feel a burning blush of shame and indignation rise at this public desecration of the Name of the God of Israel!" See Breuer, *Das*

*jüdische Nationalheim* (Frankfurt, 1925). I have consulted the English version, *The Jewish National Home* (Frankfurt, 1926), 79.

102. Strauss, "Ecclesia militans," 352.

CHAPTER FIVE
ISAAC BREUER AND THE JEWISH PATH TO *METAGESCHICHTE*

1. See Jacob Levinger's observations in his excellent introduction to Breuer's life and thought in Isaac Breuer, *Concepts of Judaism* (Jerusalem, 1974), 23. Pinchas Pelli laments the fact that Breuer's thought "has not received the place it deserves in the study of modern Jewish thought." See his essay, "Yitzhak Breuer: 'Torah 'im derekh erets,' " in the valuable collection of Hebrew essays devoted to Breuer edited by Rivka Horwitz, *Isaac Breuer: 'Iyunim be-mishnato* (Ramat-Gan, 1988). A similar theme was sounded much earlier by Baruch Kurzweil, one of the most incisive students of Breuer, in "Yitzhak Breuer," originally published in *Ha-arets* on December 17, 1943 and in a eulogy, "Le-zikhro shel Yitzhak Breuer z"l," also published in *Ha-arets* on November 1, 1946. Both essays are reprinted in Kurzweil, *Le-nokhah ha-mevukhah ha-ruhanit shel dorenu: pirke hagut u-vikoret*, edited by Moshe Scwarcz (Ramat-Gan, 1976), 117–22, 122–30. To date, the most comprehensive treatment of Isaac Breuer's thought is Matthias Morgenstern, *Von Frankfurt nach Jerusalem: Isaac Breuer und die Geschichte des "Austrittsstreits" in der deutsch-jüdischen Orthodoxie* (Tübingen, 1995). See also Alan L. Mittleman, *Between Kant and Kabbalah: An Introduction to Isaac Breuer's Philosophy of Judaism* (Albany, 1990), as well as his related study of the origins of Agudat Yisrael, *The Politics of Torah: The Jewish Political Tradition and the Founding of Agudat Yisrael* (Albany, 1996). Meanwhile, Josef R. Lawitschka's 1996 dissertation focuses on Breuer's notion of *Metageschichte*, a theme that will also figure prominently in our discussion. See Lawitschka, "Metageschichte: Jüdische Geschichtskonzeptionen im frühen 20. Jahrhundert: Franz Rosenzweig, Isaac Breuer und das Echo," Ph.D. diss., Berlin, 1996.

2. Breuer did attempt to provide a systematic introduction to his Jewish thought in two Hebrew volumes: *Moriah: yesodot ha-hinukh ha-le'umi ha-torati* (Jerusalem, 1944) in which he traces, in characteristic fashion, the unique historical people of the Jewish people; and the posthumously published *Nahli'el: yesodot ha-hinukh le-mitsvot ha-Torah* (Jerusalem, 1951) in which he clarifies key components of Judaism.

3. Morgenstern, *Von Frankfurt nach Jerusalem*, 208.

4. In his comprehensive study of Frankfurt as a financial center, Carl-Ludwig Holtfrerich points out that Frankfurt's Jews were disproportionately large donors to the city's leading cultural and educational institutions. See Holtfrerich, *Frankfurt As a Financial Centre: From Medieval Trade Fair to European Banking Center* (Munich, 1999), 167–68. I thank Gerald Feldman for this reference.

5. Among the leading patrons of Frankfurt's Orthodox community was Amschel Mayer Rothschild, son of the founder of the renowned banking firm. On Rothschild and the affluence of Frankfurt's Orthodox, see Mordechai Breuer, *Modernity within Tradition: The Social History of Orthodox Jewry in Imperial Germany*, translated by Elizabeth Petuchowski (New York, 1992), 220.

6. See Martin Jay, *The Dialectical Imagination: A History of the Frankfurt School and the Institute of Social Research, 1923–1950* (Boston, 1973).

7. Breuer mentions his fleeting thought of becoming a professor of history in the Hebrew version of his memoirs, *Darki* (Jerusalem, 1988), 51.

8. Rivka Horwitz notes the affinity between the two moderns and the medieval Ha-Levi, particularly with regard to their shared "theological approach to history." See Horwitz, "Galut ve-ge'ulah be-mishnato shel Yitzhak Breuer," *Eshel Beer Sheva* 3 (1986), 286. Meanwhile, another prominent Jewish intellectual, Leo Baeck, whose anti-historicist tendencies emerged in his response to Adolf Harnack (*Das Wesen des Judentums*), also preferred Ha-Levi's passion to Maimonides' rationalism. See Albert H. Friedlander, *Leo Baeck: Teacher of Theresienstadt* (New York, 1968), 101.

9. Among the most notable of them was the Hungarian-born Israeli historian, Jacob Katz, who came to Frankfurt to study at the Breuer yeshivah in 1928. Katz relates his experiences in "Yeshivat Frankfurt u-vet Breuer be-ene talmid yotse Hungaryah," in R. Horwitz, ed. *Isaac Breuer: 'Iyunim be-mishnato*, 39–50. See also the recollections in Katz's memoir, *With My Own Eyes: The Autobiography of an Historian*, translated by Ann Brenner and Zipora Brody (Hanover, N.H., 1995).

10. I. Breuer, *Darki*, 27. For an interesting comparison between German and Hungarian Orthodoxies, particularly the separatist currents within them, see Jacob Katz, *Ha-kera' she-lo nit'ahah : perishat ha-ortodoksim mi-kelal ha-kehilot be-Hungaryah uve-Germanyah* (Jerusalem, 1995), especially 277.

11. The formulation derives from the saying in *Pirke Avot* 2:2: "An excellent thing is the study of the Torah combined with the ways of the world."

12. See Hirsch's essay, "Religion Allied to Progress," in his collected English writings, *Judaism Eternal*, 238. For an excellent treatment of Hirschian philosophy, see Mordechai Breuer, *Modernity within Tradition: The Social History of Orthodox Jewry in Imperial Germany*, 69ff.

13. See chapter 1, note 115 where Simon Schwab's forceful iteration of this view is mentioned. In response, Jacob Katz offered a spirited defense of the principle of *Torah 'im derekh erets* in 1935 and was joined two years later by Jechiel Jakob Weinberg, the distinguished rabbinic figure in Berlin, in an essay published, like Katz's, in the Breuer community journal. See Weinberg's "Rabbiner Samson Raphael Hirsch zum Problem und Weltkultur," *Nachalat Z'wi* 7 (1937), cited in Jacob J. Schacter, "Facing the Truths of History," *Torah U-Madda* 8 (1998–99), 268.

14. See Rabbi Dr. Joseph Breuer, "Torah im Derech Eretz—a hora'at ha-sha'ah?" *Mitteilungen* 26 (August/September 1965), 1–2, quoted in Schacter, "Facing the Truths of History," 216–17.

15. Isaac Breuer, *Darki*, 13. Eliyahu Meir Klugman, in his hagiographic biography of S. R. Hirsch, notes that for Hirsch, "contact with institutionalized heresy, not with the heretic, was the issue." Consistent with this distinction, it seems that the IRG itself permitted nonobservant Jews to be members, but not to attain positions of leadership. Eliyahu Meir Klugman, *Rabbi Samson Raphael Hirsch* (Brooklyn, 1996), 183ff.

16. *Darki*, 64.

17. Ibid., 8.

18. Isaac Breuer, *Elijahu* (Frankfurt, 1924), 137, cited in Morgenstern, *Von Frankfurt nach Jerusalem*, 253.

19. Breuer, *Darki*, 73, 78. For an insightful discussion of the Bund, see Mordechai Breuer, *Modernity within Tradition*, 372–76.

20. Breuer, *Darki*, 52.

21. Ibid., 32, 39.

22. Ibid., 32–33.

23. Judah Ha-Levi, *The Kuzari (Kitab al Khazari: An Argument for the Faith of Israel*, introduction by Henry Slonimsky (New York: 1964), 107.

24. It was the early neo-Kantian Otto Liebmann whose work led Breuer to Kant. See Breuer, *Darki*, 41–42.

25. Breuer notes that he was more drawn to the Baden school of neo-Kantians, especially because of their treatment of "values." See *Darki*, 42, 44.

26. On this point, see the highly germane article of David Ellenson, "German Orthodoxy, Jewish Law, and the Uses of Kant," in his collection *Between Tradition and Culture: The Dialectics of Modern Jewish Religion and Identity* (Atlanta, 1994), 16.

27. See Zvi Kurzweil, *The Modern Impulse of Traditional Judaism* (Hoboken: Ktav, 1975), 36.

28. Ibid., 42.

29. Ibid., 43, 45.

30. See Breuer's essay *Lehre, Gesetz und Nation* (Frankfurt, 1910), or the Hebrew version, "Torah, hok ve-umah," in idem, *Tsiyune derekh* (Jerusalem, 1982), 11.

31. Breuer discusses this rationale for studying law in *Darki*, 53ff.

32. Breuer, "Die rechtsphilosophischen Grundlagen des jüdischen und des modernen Rechts," *Jahrbuch der Jüdisch-Literarischen Gesellschaft* 8 (1910/11), 35–64. I have consulted the English version, "The Philosophical Foundations of Jewish and of Modern Law," in Levinger's volume, *Concepts of Judaism*, 63.

33. Breuer, "The Philosophical Foundations of Jewish and of Modern Law," 74ff.

34. One of the first Hebrew studies of the Reform movement bore this link in its title. See Shimon Bernfeld, *Toldot ha-reformatsiyon ha-datit be-Yisra'el* (Warsaw, 1900).

35. See Breuer's essay, "Rabbiner Hirsch als Wegweiser in die jüdische Geschichte," *Nachalat Z'wi* 4 (1933/34), 165–85, or in the Hebrew version, "Rabbi S. R. Hirsch ke-moreh-derekh la-historyah ha-yisre'elit," in idem, *Tsiyune derekh*, 133–35. It is particularly noteworthy that Breuer criticized the "old rabbis" who "held on with all the force of their love not only to the Word of God, but also with tragic stiff-neckedness that emanated from despair over the old reality." Ibid., 135, 134, 139.

36. In his essay on Hirsch written just as Hitler assumed power in 1934, Breuer speaks of his grandfather in the following terms: "Although he was caught between the past and future, he was favored by God to see the past, represented by 'vayehi,' as continually unfolding, and the future, as embodied in 've-hayah,' as existing in reality. Thereby, he was to show to the people of Israel the path to the past, which is also the path to the future." Ibid., 132.

37. Hirsch's commentary to Deut. 4:5, quoted in Klugman, *Rabbi Samson Raphael Hirsch*, 276. See also the sixth and seventh letters of Hirsch's *Igrot Tzafon: Neunzehn Briefe über Judentum von Ben Usiel* (Altona, 1836), translated as *The Nineteen Letters* (New York, 1942).

38. Breuer, "Rabbi S. R. Hirsch ke-moreh-derekh la-historyah ha-yisre'elit," 132.

39. Breuer uses the fictional protagonist Alfred Roden to outline this stance in the novel *Der Neue Kusari: Ein Weg zum Judentum* (Frankfurt, 1934), 436. On Breuer's deviation from Hirsch over the interrelated matters of messianism and Erets Yisrael, see Eliezer Schweid, " 'Medinat ha-Torah' be-mishnato shel Yitzhak Breuer," in Horwitz, ed. *Isaac Breuer: 'Iyunim be-mishnato*, 127ff.

40. "Torah, hok ve-umah," 10.

41. "Torah, hok ve-umah," 15, 19. This point is made with even blunter force by a later, but equally intriguing and idiosyncratic Orthodox thinker, Yeshayahu Leibowitz. On the imperative of absolute submission to Halakhic obligation, a theme he repeated with great frequency, see Leibowitz's commentary to the weekly Torah portion of "Korach" in idem, *He'arot le-farshiyot ha-shavu'a* (Jerusalem: Akademon, 1988), 96–98.

42. "Torah, hok ve-umah," 36

43. Breuer, *Darki*, 34.

44. Breuer, "Epilog zum Tode Dr. Herzls," *Der Israelit* 45:17 (1904), translated in Breuer, *Concepts of Judaism*, 302, 304.

45. Ibid., 307.

46. Asher D. Biemann has explored the nuances and ambivalences of Breuer's posture toward Zionism in "Isaac Breuer: Zionist against His Will," *Modern Judaism* 20: 2 (May 2000), 129–46.

47. Breuer, *Darki*, 35, 37.

48. Breuer recalls that "[t]he concept of 'religion' was foreign in our yeshivah." *Darki*, 36. Alan Mittleman notes that this perspective was typical of German Orthodox who "retained more of a sense of peoplehood, of metahistorical, collective existence, than their Reform brethren." Mittleman, *The Politics of Torah: The Jewish Political Tradition and the Founding of Agudat Israel* (Albany, 1996), 115.

49. Mittleman notes Isaac Breuer's claim that the twentieth century was "the century of organizations" as a preface to his discussion of the political sensibility of the founders of Agudat Israel. Mittleman, *The Politics of Torah*, 93ff., 130.

50. Breuer, *Die Idee des Agudismus* (Frankfurt, 1921), cited in Breuer, *Concepts of Judaism*, 8. For an elaboration of his differences with Rosenheim, see Breuer, *Darki*, 87, as well as Morgenstern, *Von Frankfurt nach Jerusalem*, 219–21.

51. See Levinger's introduction to Breuer, *Concepts of Judaism*, 5.

52. Breuer, *Darki*, 85.

53. One thinks of this phenomenon primarily in the context of medieval (e.g., Hebrew Crusade chronicles) and early modern (e.g., post-Expulsion chronicles) Jewish historical writing , as Yerushalmi has discussed in *Zakhor*, chapters 2–3. However, it can also be seen more recently in the genre of historical writing labeled "Orthodox" or "Haredi." A good example is Chaim Dov Rabinowits, *Toldot Yisra'el: nos'im, berurim, u-vikuhim* (Jerusalem: Aharon Rand, 1994), which was originally published in 1979/80. Even as he adopts a modern narrative style (albeit accompanied by a more traditional dialogue cum commentary), Rabinowits often makes recourse to divine causality to explain seminal events in Jewish history

(e.g., the modern resettlement of the land of Israel). See Rabinowits, *Toldot Yisra'el*, 298–300.

54. Breuer, *Darki*, 87.

55. See Breuer's essay from May 1917, "Neuorientierung," originally published in the *Jüdische Monatshefte* 4 (1917), and republished in idem, *Programm oder Testament: Vier jüdisch-politische Aufsätze* (Frankfurt: J. Kauffmann, 1929), 5–39.

56. Breuer, *Judenproblem* (Halle, n.d.), 5. No printed date is listed on the first edition of this volume, thereby leading to some confusion. Whereas Breuer remembers the date of publication as 1917, Jacob Levinger believes that this was the year of composition, and 1918 the year of publication. See Levinger's discussion in Breuer, *Concepts of Judaism*, 317–18, n. 13.

57. Emphasis added. Breuer, *Judenproblem*, 77.

58. Ibid., 35.

59. I have discussed this attempt by Ben-Zion Dinaburg (Dinur), Shmuel Klein, and others—culminating in the collaborative *Sefer Ha-Yishuv*—in *Reinventing the Jewish Past: European Jewish Intellectuals and the Zionist Return to History* (New York: Oxford, 1995), 90–93.

60. While Alan Mittleman is correct in noting that Breuer affirmed the "historical revelation at Sinai," the unique "historicity" of the Jewish people was a function not only of this originary act, but perhaps even more of its ongoing survival within, against, and beyond the "visible history " of the nations. See Mittleman, *Between Kant and Kabbalah*, 195, n. 28.

61. *Judenproblem*, 38.

62. Morgenstern, *Von Frankfurt nach Jerusalem*, 231. Eliezer Schweid is intrigued, in this regard, by the parallels between Breuer and Herzl in ideological and organizational matters, especially in their respective views of Agudism and Zionism as the bearer of Jewish national consciousness. See Schweid, " 'Medinat ha-Torah' be-mishnato shel Breuer," 139ff.

63. See Rosenzweig's letter of March 28, 1924, to Breuer in *Briefe und Tagebücher*, II: 951. See also Rivka Horwitz, "Galut ve-ge'ulah be-mishnato shel Yitzhak Breuer," *Eshel Beer-Sheva* 3 (1986), 284.

64. "Unendlich hoch ueber allem, was namentlich von sogenannter nationalistischen Seite (Buber) in den letzten Jarhen geschrieben worden ist, stehen Ihre Ausfuehrungen ueber das Judentum." Breuer's letter is printed in Horwitz, "Galut ve-ge'ulah be-mishnato shel Yitzhak Breuer," 283.

65. Isaac Breuer, *Messiasspuren* (Frankfurt, 1918), 18.

66. This phrase recalls the contemporary historiographical term *Alltagsgeschichte*. The moral dilemmas attending an *Alltagsgeschichte* of Nazi Germany are addressed in the colloquium involving Martin Broszat and others, *Alltagsgeschichte der NS-Zeit: Neue Perspektive oder Trivialisierung?* (Munich, 1984). Since that time, Saul Friedländer has attempted to write an *Alltagsgeschichte* that embraces the experience of victims, as well as perpetrators and bystanders. See his magisterial *Nazi Germany and the Jews* (New York, 1997). For a more general discussion of the use of *Alltagsgeschichte*, see the volume edited by one of its leading practitioners, Alf Lüdtke, *The History of Everyday Life: Reconstructing Historical Experiences and Ways of Life*, translated by William Templer (Princeton, 1995).

67. Breuer, *Messiasspuren*, 35.

68. Ibid., 28, 79, 44, 63.

69. Ibid., 89. It in this context that Breuer dismissed Reform Judaism on the grounds that the "Enlightenment is its mother."

70. Ibid., 90, 124.

71. Ibid., 93, 100, 108. For a comprehensive inventory of the place of the *yetser ha-ra* in rabbinic thought, see the classic account of E. E. Urbach, *HaZaL: Pirke 'emunot ve-de'ot* (Jerusalem, 1982), 415ff.

72. Mittleman, *Between Kant and Kabbalah*, 57–58.

73. Isaiah Tishby notes in his study on the doctrine of evil in Lurianic Kabbalah that one of the most important ways to redeem the sparks was to "descend into the fragmented shells (*kelipot*) and to extract from them the sparks." According to the Lurianic *Sha'ar ha-kavanot*, this descent was to occur when one was praying the *shemoneh 'esreh*: "And when we are in the midst of the *shemoneh 'esreh* prayer, we are standing in the world of *atsilut* (the divine realm). . . . We throw ourselves from on high, from the world of *atsilut*, and descend to the depths of the world of *'asiyah* (the material world), like a man who throws himself from a roof to the ground." *Sha'ar ha-kavanot*, 51, 7:1, quoted in Tishby, *Torat ha-ra' veha-kelipah be-kabalat ha-AR"I* (Jerusalem: Schocken, 1942), 128ff.

74. In its most radical form—namely, the false messianic movement of Sabbatai Sevi in the last third of the seventeenth century—it was the task of the Messiah figure "to accomplish what not even the most righteous souls in the past have been able to do": namely, to descend into the realm of evil and retrieve the shattered fragments, in large part through the performance of deviant acts that exhaust the evil contained in them. See Gershom Scholem's discussion of this Sabbatian innovation in his well-known article from 1937, "Redemption through Sin," reprinted in his *The Messianic Idea in Judaism* (New York, 1971), 94.

75. Again, this is not to say that Breuer regarded the Diaspora with scorn. On the contrary, we recall that he repeatedly expressed admiration for *Golus*, believing à la Rosenzweig that it served as a bridge between past and future. For a discussion of both Rosenzweig and Breuer in this regard, see Horwitz, "Galut vege'ulah be-mishnato shel Yitzhak Breuer," 291.

76. Breuer, *Die Idee des Agudismus* (Frankfurt, 1921), 22, cited in Levinger's introduction to *Concepts of Judaism*, 8.

77. Breuer's distinctive stance is reflected in the fact that many of his Agudah colleagues regarded him as too "Palestinocentric," whereas Zionists regarded him as a deeply antagonistic polemicist, as demonstrated in his fiercely anti-Zionist pamphlet, *Das jüdische Nationalheim* (1925) as well as his novels *Falk Nefts Heimkehr* (1923) and *Die Neue Kusari* (1934). Gershom Scholem, for instances, writes in mocking terms of Breuer as "a magician-legalist." See Scholem, "The Politics of Mysticism: Isaac Breuer's *Neue Kusari*," published in idem, *The Messianic Idea in Judaism*, 328.

78. See Jacob J. Schacter, "Facing the Truths of History," *Tora U-Madda Journal* 8 (1998–99), 201–73.

79. Matthias Morgenstern notes that this episode was deemed a "catastrophe" by the Breuer family, and led Isaac to redouble his interest in Palestine. Morgenstern, *Von Frankfurt nach Jerusalem*, 224.

80. M. Breuer, *Modernity within Tradition*, 355.

81. Ibid., 380.

82. Isaac Breuer, *Darki*, 65.

83. Morgenstern, *Von Frankfurt nach Jerusalem*, 282, 286.

84. Levinger, introduction to *Concepts of Judaism*, 14. Michael Brenner concurs, noting that Breuer's targets were those "who fulfill the religious commandments but are not interested in the spiritual meaning behind them." Brenner, *The Renaissance of Jewish Culture in Weimar Germany*, 147.

85. Morgenstern, *Von Frankfurt nach Jerusalem*, 270.

86. Breuer, *Falk Nefts Heimkehr* (Frankfurt, 1923), 184, quoted in Morgenstern, *Von Frankfurt nach Jerusalem*, 270.

87. See Martin Jay's helpful synopsis in "The Frankfurt School in Exile," in idem, *Permanent Exiles: Essays on the Intellectual Migration from Germany to America* (New York, 1986), 30–31. See also Wolfgang Schievelbusch's discussion of the Institut in the context of Frankfurt intellectual life in the 1920s, *Intellektuellendämmerung: Zur Lage der Frankfurter Intelligenz in den zwanziger Jahren* (Frankfurt, 1982), 18–19.

88. This is a central theme in Breuer's seminal early article, "Lehre, Gesetz und *Nation*," where he describes "individualism [as] the bitterest enemy of traditional Judaism." See "Torah, hok ve-umah," 15, as well as Breuer's ode to heteronomy in *Darki*, 49. For a recent discussion of this motif, see Mittleman, *Between Kant and Kabbalah*, 33–34.

89. Urbach, *HaZaL*, 464, 582. As Levinger notes, Breuer himself equates the term at various points in *Der Neue Kusari* with Erets Yisrael, the Divine Kingdom, the Oral Law, and "My Lord." Levinger, *Concepts of Judaism*, 18.

90. See Breuer's discussion in his first major Hebrew book, *Moriah: yesodot ha-hinukh ha-le'umi ha-torati* (Jerusalem, 1982) revised edition 1944, 195–97.

91. Breuer, *Der Neue Kusari: Ein Weg zum Judentum* (Frankfurt, 1934), 343. Breuer also addressed the theme in the same period in a pair of articles that appeared in *Nachalat Z'wi* 5 (1934/35), 12–22, 159–68. See also Morgenstern's treatment of Breuer's notion of Kenesset Yisrael in *Von Frankfurt nach Jerusalem*, 252–53.

92. For a detailed analysis of this communitarian impulse, see Michael Brenner, *The Renaissance of Jewish Culture in Weimar Germany*, 11–65. See also the introduction to Michael Brenner and Derek J. Penslar, eds. *In Search of Jewish Community: Jewish Identities in Germany and Austria, 1918–1933* (Bloomington, Ind., 1998), ix–xii.

93. Martin Buber, "Die Losung," *Der Jude* 1:1 (1916), 1–2, quoted in the introduction to Brenner and Penslar, *In Search of Jewish Community*, xiii. Earlier, in his lectures to the Bar-Kochba circle in Prague from 1909 to 1911, Buber spoke of the Jews as a "community of blood." Buber, "Judaism and the Jews," in idem, *On Judaism*, edited by Nahum N. Glatzer (New York, 1972), 13–15. Glatzer was mindful of the fact that Buber's use of this terminology "sound[s] woefully out of place" after the Holocaust. Nonetheless, he insisted that Buber meant to convey nothing more sinister than a sense of "rootedness in one's origin, heritage, and history." Ibid., 239–40.

94. Brenner, *The Renaissance of Jewish Culture in Weimar Germany*, 49–51. Jacob Borut offers an interesting corrective to the assertion that a Jewish subcul-

ture, or series of subcultures, existed in the Weimar period. Although his distinction between a "subculture" and a *Teilkultur* is not always persuasive, he makes excellent use of local records to demonstrate that Jewish communal, ideological, and institutional allegiance was more porous than some have argued. See Borut, " 'Verjudung des Judentums': Was There a Zionist Subculture in Weimar Germany," in Brenner and Penslar, *In Search of Jewish Community*, 92–114.

95. This formulation comes from the opening clause of Breuer's "Proposed Statute for the Organisation of a Jewish Community in Palestine" appended to his pamphlet, *The Jewish National Home*, 95.

96. Morgenstern, *Von Frankfurt nach Jerusalem*, 282.

97. Breuer, *Judenproblem*, 89.

98. Writing in 1944, Breuer argued that "[t]he leaders of Agudat Yisrael did not hear the clarion call, did not understand the new era, and simply left the question of the connection between the people of the Torah and the land of the Torah as one of the 'other questions' but never as *the* question"—as he clearly thought it should be. *Moriah*, 215.

99. Baruch Kurzweil, a discerning literary critic and admirer of Breuer, claimed that Breuer's novels failed in their attempt to "free the poet in his soul." Kurzweil, "Yitzhak Breuer," *Le-nokhah ha-mevukhah*, 118.

100. Franz Kafka, *Dearest Father: Stories and Other Writings*, trans. E. Kaiser and E. Wilkins (New York, 1954), 171, cited in Mendes-Flohr/Reinharz, *The Jew in the Modern World*, 219.

101. Breuer, *Der Neue Kusari*, 448.

102. Kurzweil, "Le-zikhro shel Yitzhak Breuer z"l," *Le-nokhah ha-mevukhah*, 128–29.

103. "Few people know to judge this personality and his work adequately." Kurzweil, "Yitzhak Breuer," *Le-nokhah ha-mevukhah*, 117, 118.

104. Ibid., 117. It is important to note that Breuer's intellectual and ideological isolation was tempered by the fact that he moved to Palestine with his wife and children.

105. See Moshe Scwarcz's insightful discussion of the affinities between Kurzweil and Breuer—and of both with Rosenzweig—in his introduction to *Le-nokhah ha-mevukhah ha-ruhanit shel dorenu*, 34. I have addressed Kurzweil's antihistoricism in "The Scholem-Kurzweil Debate and Modern Jewish Historiography," *Modern Judaism* 6 (October 1986), 261–86. On the links among Kurzweil, Breuer, and Rosenzweig, see also Rivka Horwitz, "Galut ve-ge'ulah be-mishnato shel Yitzhak Breuer," 282.


CHAPTER SIX
FROM CONCLUSION TO OPENING: A WORD ON INFLUENCE, GERMAN JEWS, AND THE CULTURAL HISTORY OF IDEAS

1. For all his sharp-witted attacks, including on aspects of Orthodoxy itself, Kurzweil was born, raised, and remained (at Bar-Ilan University) in an Orthodox environment. In light of this, I have chosen to describe Kurzweil as an Orthodox thinker. His traditionalist sensibility provided urgency and a sense of purpose to his penetrating critique of the project of modernity, which he took to be "a rupture

in the continuum of Divine history." See the reverential essay by Kurzweil's student Moshe Scwarcz, "Baruch Kurzweil: ha-ish u-mif'alo," in the memorial volume, *Sefer Baruch Kurzweil*, edited by M. Z. Kaddari, A. Saltman, and M. Scwarcz (Ramat-Gan, 1975), 39.

2. Kurzweil, " 'Al ha-to'elet ve-'al ha-nezek shel mada'e ha-Yahadut," in idem, *Be-ma'avak 'al 'erkhe ha-Yahadut* (Tel Aviv, 1969), 209. I draw here on my *The Problem of History in German-Jewish Thought: Observations on a Neglected Tradition (Cohen, Rosenzweig, and Breuer)*, The Samuel Braun Lecture in the History of the Jews of Prussia, Bar-Ilan University (Ramat-Gan, 2001).

3. Leibowitz offered this observation at a symposium devoted to "The Religious Significance of History." See Leibowitz, *Emunah, historyah, ve-'arakhim* (Jerusalem, 1982), 145.

4. See Leibowitz's commentary to the weekly portion "Devarim" in his *He'arot le-farshiyot ha-shavu'a* (Jerusalem, 1988), 112.

5. Gershom Scholem, "Toward an Understanding of the Messianic Idea in Judaism," in idem, *The Messianic Idea in Judaism* (New York, 1971), 35.

6. Josef Solowiejczyk, *Das reine Denken und die Seinskonstitutierung bei Hermann Cohen* (Berlin, 1932).

7. See Abraham R. Besdin's adaptation of Rabbi Soloveitchik's lectures in *Man of Faith in the Modern World: Reflections of the Rav*, vol. 2 (Hoboken, N.J., 1989), 70.

8. Ibid., 71. Moreover, Soloveitchik's reference to Zionism as a case in which historicist principles have been applied in error distinguishes him from thinkers such as Breuer, Leibowitz, and Kurzweil, who believed that Zionism could *only* be understood in mundane—even profane—terms.

9. For an interesting modern Orthodox attempt to salvage utility for history, see Shubert Spero, *Holocaust and Return to Zion*. In line with Hermann Cohen, Spero relies on Kant's understanding of history as "a meaningful process leading toward the development of freedom; toward the growing perfection of individual and social morality." On these terms, Spero embarks on his project of reclamation, a task to which he enlists other Orthodox thinkers like Rabbi Avraham Isaac Ha-Cohen Kook. Spero, *Holocaust and Return to Zion*, 233. The obvious source of comparison to modern Orthodox attitudes is traditionalist or *haredi* Orthodoxy for whom the acquisition of secular knowledge is neither a virtue nor a necessity. The study of history in these circles has often been regarded as, for Maimonides, a "waste of time." And yet, traditionalist Orthodoxy has begun to discover the importance of writing Jewish history from its own perspective. For example, the publication of works of Jewish history and rabbinic biography by the Art Scroll imprint reflects the simultaneous processes of internalizing and resisting modern historicist norms.

10. See, for instance, Jean-François Lyotard, *The Differend: Phrases in Dispute*, trans. Georges Van Den Abbeele (Minneapolis: University of Minnesota, 1988), 57–58.

11. Lévinas asks: "What importance is there to the contest that philology and history wage for the apparent date and origin of sacred texts, if these texts are rich with intrinsic value?" See Lévinas's essay "Judaïsme et temps present," originally published in *L'Arche* in 1960, and republished in his collection of essays, *Difficile*

*Liberté* (1963; rpt. Paris: Albin Michel, 1995), 273. Elsewhere in that volume, Lévinas notes that the enterprise of *Wissenschaft des Judentums* was well equipped to identify multiple influences on past events, but it did so at the cost of losing the "spiritual significance" of Judaism. See "Judaïsme," 44. In this context, it is essential to mention Zygmunt Baumann's view of the Holocaust as the culmination of the destructive trail of modernity. See Baumann, *Modernity and the Holocaust* (Ithaca, N.Y.: Cornell, 1989).

12. Yosef H. Yerushalmi, *Zakhor*, 98.

13. See William H. Sewell, Jr., "The Concept(s) of Culture," in Victoria E. Bonnell and Lynn Hunt, eds. *Beyond the Cultural Turn: New Direction in the Study of Society and Culture* (Berkeley: University of California, 1999), 43. Or as Lynn Hunt asks rhetorically, "can a history of culture work if it is shorn of all theoretical assumptions about culture's relationship to the social world—if, indeed, its agenda is conceived as the undermining of all assumptions about the relationship between culture and the social world?" See Hunt's introduction to *The New Cultural History* (Berkeley: University of California, 1989), 10.

14. William Sewell offers a textured understanding of culture "as a dialectic of system and practice, as a dimension of social life autonomous from other such dimensions both in its logic and in its spatial configuration, and as a system of symbols possessing a real but thin coherence that is continually put at risk in practice and therefore subject to transformation." Sewell, "The Concept(s) of Culture," 52.

15. And thus, our understanding of culture is distinct from that view which maintains, as Stefan Collini has observed, that "most forms of cultural activity are essentially a disguise for the fact that Somebody is Trying to Screw Somebody Else." Quoted in Adam Kuper, *Culture: The Anthropologists' Account* (Cambridge, Mass.: Harvard, 1999), 230. Kuper offers a detailed analytic survey of different notions of culture, though he finds the term both too multivalent and imprecise for his tastes. Ibid., 247.

16. Amos Funkenstein offers an important analysis of this "fallacy" in "The Dialectics of Assimilation," *Jewish Social Studies* 1 (1995), 10.

17. See Pierre Bourdieu, "Intellectual Field and Creative Project," *Social Science Information* 8 (1969), 89–119. Bourdieu understands intellectuals in an "intellectual field" as standing in "complementary or oppositional relationships to each other." This relational approach serves as a counterweight to the long-dominant influence-based model of historical explanation. At the same time, it shifts the analytic focus from the diachronic to the synchronic plane.

18. See Graetz, *Geschichte der Juden* (Leipzig, 1900; 1870), 11: 140–41. This attitude must be juxtaposed to Graetz's far more positive view of Moses Mendelssohn's debt to German Enlightenment philosophy. That "native" influence was far more palatable to Graetz than either French or Eastern European Jewish influences on German Jews. I thank John Efron for reminding me of this important point.

19. Cf. Ze'ev Jawitz, *Sefer Toldot Yisrael metukan 'al-pi ha-mekorot ha-rishonim* (1895; rpt. Berlin: Itzkowsky, 1925) and Chaim Dov Rabinowits, *Toldot Yisrael: nos'im, berurim, u-vikuhim mi-Nehemyah ve-'ad 'atah* (1979/1980; rpt. Jerusalem, 1995/96).

20. Ben-Zion Dinur (Dinaburg), *Yisrael ba-golah*, revised edition (Tel Aviv: Mosad Bialik, 1958), 1: xxiv.

21. See Gershom G. Scholem, *Jewish Gnosticism, Merkabah Mysticism, and Talmudic Tradition* (New York: Jewish Theological Seminary, 1960), 34.

22. Although Baer spent the better part of his career as a scholar of Spanish Jewry, he tended to favor the insular pietism of Ashkenazic Jewry over Sephardic cultural openness. I have discussed this tendency in Baer's scholarship in *Reinventing the Jewish Past*, 118–26.

23. See Yitzhak Fritz Baer, *A History of the Jews in Christian Spain* (Philadelphia: Jewish Publication Society, 1961–66), 1: 240, 2: 144, 224.

24. As Scholem argued: "It takes two to have a dialogue, who listen to each other, who are prepared to perceive the other as what he is and represents and to respond to him. Nothing can be more misleading than to apply such a concept to the discussions between Germans and Jews during the last 200 years." Scholem, "Against the Myth of the German-Jewish Dialogue," in idem, *On Jews and Judaism in Crisis: Selected Essays*, ed. Werner J. Dannhauser (New York: Schocken, 1976), 61–62.

25. See Baer, "Ha-megamah ha-datit-hevratit shel 'Sefer Hasidim,'" *Zion* 3 (1938), 1, as well as my discussion of the tension between his immanentist and contextualist instincts in *Reinventing the Jewish Past*, 124.

26. With respect to ancient mysticism, he admitted that "Jewish esoteric tradition absorbed Hellenistic elements." But he hastened to add that "[s]uch elements entered Jewish tradition before Christianity developed, or at any rate before Christian Gnosticism as a distinctive force came into being." Peter Schäfer has observed that Scholem "wavers between positing plainly external 'gnostic' sources and 'vestiges of an ancient *Jewish* gnosis.'" Thus, the choice is between Jewish absorption of an outside influence or Jewish primacy in gnosticism; neither allows for a complex process of exchange, adaptation, and translation. See Schäfer, *Mirror of His Beauty: Feminine Images of God from the Bible to the Early Kabbala* (Princeton, 2002), 219.

27. Rawidowicz's lecture of February 20, 1949, "Tzvay voz zaynen ayns," appeared in *Tsukunft* 54 (May–June 1940), 287. See also an English version, "Two That Are One," in Rawidowicz, *State of Israel, Diaspora, and Jewish Continuity: Essays on the "Ever-Dying People,"* edited by Benjamin C. I. Ravid (1986; rpt. Hanover, N.H., 1998), 155–56.

28. Although a full-scale study (and appreciation) of Rawidowicz remains a desideratum, Benjamin Ravid lays an excellent foundation in his introduction to *State of Israel, Diaspora, and Jewish Continuity*, 13–52.

29. Gerson Cohen, *The Blessing of Assimilation in Jewish History*, Commencement Address, Hebrew Teachers College (Brookline, Mass., 1966). I have used the edition of this essay reprinted in a collection of Cohen's essays, *Jewish History and Jewish Destiny* (New York: Jewish Theological Seminary), 1977, 145–56.

30. Cohen, "The Blessing of Assimilation," 151. In staking out this position, Cohen acknowledged a debt to Ahad Ha-'am, the early twentieth-century Zionist and Hebrew author. Seventy years before Cohen, Ahad Ha-'am had identified two forms of cultural imitation: a negative "imitation to the point of self-denial," and a positive "imitation of competition." The latter form was healthy in that it al-

lowed Jews to import the best features of the surrounding culture into their own. Ahad Ha'am discusses the competing notions of "competitive assimilation" and "self-denying assimilation" in his 1893 essay, "Hikui ve-hitbolelut," reprinted in idem, 'Al parashat ha-derakhim: kovets ma'amarim (1895; rpt. Berlin: Jüdischer Verlag, 1930), 1: 169–77. Cf. Cohen, "The Blessing of Assimilation," 155.

31. Amos Funkenstein, "The Dialectics of Assimilation," Jewish Social Studies 1 (1995), 4, 8–9, 10–11.

32. Ricoeur, History and Truth, translated by Charles A. Kelbley (Evanston, Ill.: Northwestern, 1965), 283.

33. See, inter alia, K. A. Appiah, In My Father's House: Africa in the Philosophy of the Culture (London, 1992); Homi K. Bhabha, The Location of Culture (London, 1994); Stuart Hall, "Cultural Identity and Diaspora," in Patrick Williams and Laura Chrisman, eds. Colonial Discourse and Post-Colonial Theory (New York, 1994), esp. 402; and Edward Said, Culture and Imperialism (New York: Knopf, 1993).

34. For a particularly cogent (and anti-exceptionalist) account of this possibility, see Michael Galchinsky, "Scattered Seeds: A Dialogue of Diasporas," in David Biale, Michael Galchinsky, and Susannah Heschel, eds. Insider/Outsider: American Jews and Multiculturalism (Berkeley: University of California, 1998), 185–211. Meanwhile, Susannah Heschel, in an interesting postcolonial move, argues that the liberal Jewish scholar Abraham Geiger "reverses the power relations of the viewer and the viewed" in his treatment of the history of early Christianity. See her Abraham Geiger and the Jewish Jesus (Chicago: University of Chicago, 1998), 22. Relying on a similar set of theoretical sources, I have also discussed the process by which "a dispersed people (i.e., the Jews) struggles to define itself vis-à-vis a host society" in Reinventing the Jewish Past, 15. See my elaboration of this point in Kalonymos 4 (2001), 23–27.

35. It is entirely fortuitous—and a matter of great good fortune—that this chapter came across my desk just as I completed a draft of this book. I am most grateful to Professor Schäfer for calling my attention to his chapter and sending me a copy in galleys. See Peter Schäfer, "How Much 'Origins,' Or: The Anxiety of Influence," in Mirror of His Beauty: Feminine Images of God from the Bible to the Early Kabbala (Princeton, 2002), 230. Even more recently, David Biale has advanced a similar critique of the influence-based model of explication in the introduction to his edited volume, Cultures of the Jews: A New History (New York: Schocken, 2002), xix.

36. Barclay, in particular, attempts to produce sharper terminological distinctions by distinguishing the category of assimilation from acculturation and accommodation; each of these three terms signals a different degree and kind of immersion in Hellenistic culture. See his important methodological comments in John M. G. Barclay, Jews in the Mediterranean Diaspora: From Alexander to Trajan (Berkeley, 1996), 82–102.

37. See Lee I. Levine, Judaism and Hellenism: Conflict or Confluence? (Seattle, 1998), Erich S. Gruen, Heritage and Hellenism: The Reinvention of Jewish Tradition (Berkeley, 1998), Shaye J. D. Cohen, The Beginnings of Jewishness: Boundaries, Varieties, Uncertainties (Berkeley, 1999), and Barclay, Jews in the Mediterranean Diaspora. In his fine historiographical survey, Levine divides scholars of

Jewish Hellenism into two groups: "those who advocated a significant degree of outside influence" and "those who minimized such influence on Jewish society." Levine goes on to undertake a comprehensive review of scholarly discussion over the past half century of Hellenism and ancient Judaism. A good number of the scholars mentioned (e.g., Saul Lieberman, E. R. Goodenough, Martin Hengel) point to Hellenistic influence on Judaism, and thereby reject the model of Jewish insularity. The innovation of more recent scholarship is to suggest that interaction and adaptation may be a more refined historical measure than influence. Meanwhile, Martha Himmelfarb suggests that one of the great twentieth-century scholars of Hellenistic Judaism, Elias Bickerman, already grasped nearly seventy years ago the nuanced nature of interaction between Greek and Jewish cultures in antiquity. See Himmelfarb's treatment in "Elias Bickerman on Judaism and Hellenism," in David N. Myers and David B. Ruderman, eds., *The Jewish Past Revisited: Reflections on Modern Jewish Historians* (New Haven, 1998), 199–211. For another important adumbration, see Uriel Rappaport's distinction between two kinds of "Hellenization" in "The Hellenization of the Hasmoneans," in Menachem Mor, ed. Studies in Jewish *Civilization 2: Jewish Assimilation, Acculturation, and Accommodation* (Lanham, Maryland, 1992), 1–12.

38. Daniel Boyarin, *Dying for God: Martyrdom and the Making of Christianity and Judaism* (Stanford, 1999), 9–10. Boyarin acknowledges the proximity of his view to that of the Israeli scholar Galit Hasan-Rokem, who, in the context of Jewish-Christian relations in late antiquity, "prefers to look at the interaction between cultures in terms of dialogue rather than 'influence.' " See Hasan-Rokem, "Narratives in Dialogue: A Folk Literary Perspective on Interreligious Contacts in the Holy Land in Rabbinic Literature of Late Antiquity," in Guy Stroumsa and Arieh Kofsky, *Sharing the Sacred: Religious Contacts and Conflicts in the Holy Land* (Jerusalem, 1998), quoted in Boyarin, *Dying for God*, 10.

39. Yisrael Yuval, for instance, advocates a "dialogic approach" that holds that "Jewish existence in Christian Europe is one that features absorption, accommodation, and internalization of the values, body language, and rituals of the surrounding environment." See his *Shene goyim be-vitnekh: Yehudim ve-Notsrim—dimuyim hadadiyim* (Tel Aviv: Am Oved, 2000), 36. But Yuval also argues that the dialogic process operates in the opposite direction—for instance, when he claims that Jewish acts of martyrdom during the Crusades, including sacrifice of children, may have fueled the imagination of the Christians who invented the notorious blood libel in the twelfth century. See his chapter, "Ha-nekamah veha-kelalah," based on his 1993 *Zion* article, in *Shene goyim be-vitnekh*, especially 108–35. And yet, it is important to note that Yuval does not surrender the use or utility of the term "influence" in his work. Amnon Raz-Krakotzkin has observed this in his review of *Shene goyim be-vitnekh*, where he notes: "The concept (of influence) raises many basic questions, but is particularly problematic in the analysis of relations described here. The concept of influence assumes two well-defined and distinct identities, each of which influences the other; meanwhile, the case before us suggests a more complex and dialectical framework, a polemical framework, out of which are created differences." See Raz-Krakotzkin's review, "Ha-Yahadut ke-pulmus neged ha-Natsrut," *Ha-arets*, February 28, 2001.

40. Jeremy Cohen, " 'Gezerot TaTNaV'—ha-me'ora'ot veha-'alilot," *Zion 59* (1994), 205, quoted in Yuval, *Shene goyim be-vitnekh*, 44.

41. Stow, in *Theater of Acculturation: The Roman Ghetto in the Sixteenth Century* (Seattle: University of Washington, 2001), 69. Indeed, Stow argues that Jewish acculturation into Gentile society did not lead to the disappearance of Jews. Rather, it led to a process of "adopting individual practices and then domesticating them by subtle modification"—indeed, of "converting the external into something Jewish." Stow, *Theaters of Acculturation*, 93.

42. Taking aim against Cecil Roth's portrait in *The Jews in the Renaissance* (1959), Bonfil eschews a romanticized view of Jewish-Christian relations in early modern Europe. To the extent that Jews looked, dressed, and ate like non-Jewish Italians, it was the natural outgrowth of the often strained "encounter between the Self and the Other," as Jews struggled to preserve a measure of group distinctiveness in hostile circumstances. See Bonfil's trenchant account in *Jewish Life in Renaissance Italy*, translated by Anthony Oldcorn (Berkeley: University of California, 1994), 115. As against Bonfil, David Ruderman adopts a neo-Rothian stance that understands Jewish acculturation as robust, and not begrudging. On this view, the historian's task is "to situate the Jew within the matrix of Western civilization . . . [and] underscore their common humanity with others." Ruderman, "Cecil Roth, Historian of Italian Jewry: A Reassessment" in David N. Myers and David B. Ruderman, *The Jewish Past Revisited: Reflections on Modern Jewish Historians* (New Haven: Yale, 1998), 140.

43. See George L. Mosse, *German Jews beyond Judaism* (Bloomington, Ind., 1985).

44. Although our focus here is on intellectual and cultural historians, there has been a spate of interesting and important work by social historians recently on the nature of Jewish interaction with non-Jews in Germany. For instance, Jacob Borut seeks to modify David Sorkin's well-known thesis by arguing that Jewish communal life in Germany constituted not a discrete "subculture," but a less hermetically sealed *Teilkultur* (semi-culture) in which distinct Jewish concerns and broader cultural norms frequently intersected. Jacob Borut, "*Vereine für Jüdische Geschichte und Literatur* at the End of the Nineteenth Century," *Leo Baeck Institute Year Book* 41 (1996), 112–13. Borut elaborates on the idea of a *Teilkultur* in his book "*Ruah hadashah be-kerev ahenu be-Ashkenaz*": *Ha-mifneh be-darka shel Yahadut Germanyah be-sof ha-me'ah ha 19* (Jerusalem: Magnes, 1999), 13–21. Meanwhile, Till van Rahden utilizes the term "situational ethnicity" to describe both the textured sense of groupness of Jews and Christians and their close proximity to one another in the city of Breslau. The tightly bound and yet overlapping ethnic worlds of Jews and Christians require, according to van Rahden, a new kind of multicultural history that veers from the long regnant "paradigm of national homogeneity" in German historiography. Till van Rahden, *Juden und andere Breslauer: Die Beziehungen zwischen Juden, Protestanten und Katholiken in einer deutschen Grossstadt von 1860 bis 1925* (Göttingen: Vandenhoeck & Ruprect, 2000), 14–19.

45. Volkov, "Reflections on German-Jewish Historiography," *Leo Baeck Institute Year Book* 41 (1996), 309. In addition to Volkov, the following authors have recently treated the complex process of German-Jewish identity formation with

subtlety and sophistication: Steven E. Aschheim, *Culture and Catastrophe: German and Jewish Confrontations with National Socialism and Other Crises* (New York: NYU Press, 1996); Marion Kaplan's somewhat earlier work, *The Making of the Jewish Middle Class: Women, Family, and Identity in Imperial Germany* (New York, 1991); Paul Mendes-Flohr, *German Jews: A Dual Identity* (New Haven, 1999); Anson Rabinbach, *In the Shadow of Catastrophe: German Intellectuals between Apocalypse and Enlightenment* (Berkeley, 1997). Special mention should also be made of two articles, separated by seventeen years, that recognize the constantly evolving and interactive nature of German-Jewish identity: Gary B. Cohen, "Jews in German Society: Prague, 1860–1914," in David Bronsen, *Jews and Germans from 1860–1933: The Problematic Symbiosis* (Heidelberg, 1979, 306–337; and Samuel Moyn, "German Jewry and the Questions of Identity, Historiography and Theory," *Leo Baeck Institute Year Book* 41 (1996), 291–308.

46. Volkov, "Jüdische Assimilation und Eigenart in Kaiserreich," in idem, *Jüdisches Leben und Antisemitismus im 19. und 20. Jahrhundert: Zehn Essays* (Munich: Beck, 1990), 132. See also the important essays, including "Die Erfindung einer Tradition," in Volkov's latest collection, *Das jüdische Projekt der Moderne* (Munich: Beck, 2001).

47. Gordon, "Under One Tradewind: Philosophical Expressionism from Rosenzweig to Heidegger," viii.

48. See Gans's second presidential address to the Verein für Cultur und Wissenschaft der Juden from April 28, 1822, translated in Paul Mendes-Flohr and Jehuda Reinharz, eds. *The Jew in the Modern World* (New York, 1995), 217. I have discussed this river metaphor, as well as Franz Rosenzweig's notion of *Zweistromland*, in " 'The Blessing of Assimilation' Reconsidered: An Inquiry into Jewish Cultural Studies," in David N. Myers and William V. Rowe, *From Ghetto to Emancipation: Historical and Contemporary Reconsiderations of the Jewish Community* (Scranton, Penn., 1997), 17–20.

49. See Graf's essay, "Was heisst: 'Religion modernisieren'?" in Michael Brenner and David N. Myers, *Jüdische Geschichtsschreibung heute: Themen, Positionen, Kontroversen* (Munich, 2002), 133. Till van Rahden takes an important step in this direction in his *Juden und andere Breslauer*.

50. For an attempt to reclaim a cultural history of German Jewry from within this dark cloud, see Michael André Bernstein, *Foregone Conclusions: Against Apocalyptic History* (Berkeley, 1994).

51. I am struck by the coexistence of competing currents in contemporary literary theory. On one hand, Jacques Derrida's well-known postmodern epigraph— "il n'y a pas de hors-texte"—seems to suggest a preference for the linguistic-grammatical act of writing over biographical or historical considerations. On the other hand, we notice a group of scholars operating under the banner of the New Historicism who apply their own microhistorical techniques to literary texts. See Derrida, *De la Grammatalogie* (Paris, 1967), 227. Meanwhile, H. Aram Vesser notes that the method of New Historicism is to "seize upon an event or anecdote . . . and re-read it in such a way as to reveal through the analysis of tiny particulars the behavioral codes, logic, and motive forces controlling a whole society." See Vesser's introduction to the collection of essays he edited, *The New Historicism* (New York: Routledge, 1989).

52. Myers, *The Problem of History in German-Jewish Thought*, 33.

# BIBLIOGRAPHY

Adelman, D. 1997. "H. Steinhal und Hermann Cohen." *Hermann Cohen's Philosophy of Judaism*. S. Moses and H. Wiedebach. Hildesheim. Georg Olms.

Altmann, A. 1956. "Theology in Twentieth-Century German Jewry." *Leo Baeck Instutute Year Book 1*.

——. 1973. *Moses Mendelssohn: A Biographical Study*. University: University of Alabama Press.

Anckaert, L., and B. Casper, eds. 1990. *Franz Rosenzweig: A Primary and Secondary Bibliography*. Leuven: Bibliotheek van de Faculteit der Godgeleerdheid van de K. U. Leuven.

Appiah, K. A. 1992. *In My Father's House: Africa in the Philosophy of the Culture*. London and New York: Oxford University Press.

Arendt, H. 1979. *The Origins of Totalitarianism*. San Diego: Harcourt Brace Jovanovich.

Aschheim, S. E. 1992. *The Nietzsche Legacy in Germany, 1890–1900*. Berkeley: University of California Press.

——. 1996. *Culture and Catastrophe: German and Jewish Confrontations with National Socialism and Other Crises*. New York: New York University Press.

Auerbach, B. 1882. *Spinoza: A Novel*. Leipzig: Bernhard Tauchnitz.

Baer, Y. 1961–66. *A History of the Jews in Christian Spain*. Philadelphia: Jewish Publication Society of America.

Balakrishnan, G. 2000. *The Enemy: An Intellectual Portrait of Carl Schmitt*. London and New York: Verso.

Bambach, C. R. 1995. *Heidegger, Dilthey, and the Crisis of Historicism*. Ithaca: Cornell University Press.

Baron, S. 1964. *History and Jewish Historians: Essays and Addresses*. Philadelphia: Jewish Publication Society.

Barth, H. (1925). "Christliche und idealistische Deutung der Geschichte." *Zwischen den Zeiten* 3: 154–82.

——. 1932. *Kirchliche Dogmatik*. Munich: Siebenstern Taschenbuch Verlag.

——. 1933. *The Epistle to the Romans*. London and New York: Oxford University Press.

——. 1952. *Die Protestantische Theologie im 19. Jahrhundert*. Zurich: Evangelischer Verlag.

——. 1959. *Protestant Thought: From Rousseau to Ritschl*. New York: Harper & Row, Publishers.

Batnizky, L. 2000. *Idolatry and Representation: The Philosophy of Franz Rosenzweig Reconsidered*. Princeton: Princeton University Press.

——. 2000. "On the Truth of History or on the History of Truth: Rethinking Rosenzweig via Strauss." *Jewish Studies Quarterly* 7, 223–51.

Bauman, Z. 1989. *Modernity and the Holocaust*. Ithaca: Cornell University Press.

Beck, L. W., ed. 1963. *Kant on History*. Indianapolis: Bobbs-Merrill.

Belke, I. 1971. *Moritz Lazarus und Heymann Steinhal: Die Begründer der Völkerpsychologie in ihren Briefe, vol. 1*. Tübingen: J.C.B. Mohr.

Ben-Ari, N. 1997. *Roman 'im he-'avar: ha-roman ha-histori ha-Yehudi-ha-Germani min ha-me'ah ha-19 vi-yetsiratah shel sifrut le'umit.* Tel-Aviv: Devir: Mekhon Le'o Bek.

Benjamin, W. 1969. "Theses on the Philosophy of History." *Illuminations.* H. Arendt. New York: Harcourt, Brace & World.

———. 1982. *Gesammelte Schriften.* Frankfurt: Suhrkamp.

———. 1999. *The Arcades Project.* Cambridge, Mass.: Belknap Press of Harvard University Press.

Berghahn, K. L., ed. 1996. *The German-Jewish Dialogue Reconsidered: A Symposium in Honor of George L. Mosse.* New York: Peter Lang.

Berlin, I. 2000. *Three Critics of the Enlightenment: Vico, Hamann, Herder.* Princeton: Princeton University Press.

Bernfeld, S. 1900. *Toldot ha-reformatsiyon ha-datit be-Yisra'el.* Warsaw: Ahiasaf.

Bernstein, M. A. 1994. *Foregone Conclusions: Against Apocalyptic History.* Berkeley: University of California Press.

Besdin, A. R. 1989. *Man of Faith in the Modern World: Reflections of the Rav.* Vol. 2. Hoboken, N.J.: Ktav Publishing House.

Bhabha, H. K. 1994. *The Location of Culture.* London and New York: Routledge.

Biale, D. 1982. *Gershom Scholem, Kabbalah and Counter-History.* Cambridge, Mass.: Harvard University Press.

Biale, D., M. Galchinsky and S. Heschel eds. 1998. *Insider/Outsider: American Jews and Multiculturalism.* Berkeley: University of California Press.

Biemann, A. D. May 2000. "Isaac Breuer: Zionist against His Will." *Modern Judaism* 20(2): 129–46.

Blanke, H. W. 1991. *Historiographiegeschichte als Historik.* Stuttgart: Bad Cannstatt.

Bloom, H. 1973. *The Anxiety of Influence: A Theory of Poetry.* New York: Oxford University Press.

Boehlich, W., ed. 1965. *Der Berliner Antisemitismusstreit.* Frankfurt am Main: Insel-Verlag.

Bonfil, R. 1988. "How Golden Was the Age of the Renaissance in Jewish Historiography?" *History and Theory* 27, 78–102.

———. 1994. *Jewish Life in Renaissance Italy.* Berkeley: University of California Press.

———. Spring 1997. "Jewish Attitudes toward History and Historical Writing in Pre-Modern Times." *Jewish History* 11, 7–40.

Borut, J. 1996, 89. "*Vereine für Geschichte und Literatur* at the End of the Nineteenth Century." *Leo Baeck Instutute Year Book* 41.

———. 1999. "*Ruah hadashah be-kerev ahenu be-Ashkenaz*": Ha-mifneh be-darka shel Yahadut Germanyah be-sof ha-me'ah ha 19. Jerusalem: Magnes.

Bourdieu, P. 1969. "Intellectual Field and Creative Project." *Social Science Information* 8: 89–119.

Bowersock, G. W. 1990. *Hellenism in Late Antiquity.* Ann Arbor: University of Michigan Press.

Boyarin, D. 1990. *Dying for God: Martyrdom and the Making of Christianity and Judaism.* Stanford: Stanford University Press.

Brann, M., ed. 1904. *Geschichte des Jüdisch-theologischen Seminars (Fraenck-el'sche Stiftung) in Breslau*. Festschrift zum fünfzigjährigen Jubilaum der Anstalt. Breslau: Druck von T. Schatzky.

Brenner, M. 1996. *The Renaissance of Jewish Culture in Weimar Germany*. New Haven: Yale University Press.

Brenner, M., and D. J. Penslar, eds. 1998. *In Search of Jewish Community: Jewish Identities in Germany and Austria, 1918–1933*. Bloomington: Indiana University Press.

Breuer, I. 1904. "Epilog zum Tode Dr Herzls." *Der Israelit* 45(17).

———. 1910/11. "Die rechstphilosophischen Grundlagen des jüdischen und des modernen Rechts." *Jahrbuch der Jüdisch-Literarischen Gesellschaft* 8: 35–64.

———. 1918. *Judenproblem*. Halle (Saale): Otto Hendel Verlag.

———. 1918. *Messiasspuren*. Frankfurt am Main: Verlag Rudolf Leonhard Hammon.

———. 1921. *Die Idee des Agudismus*. Frankfurt: L. Sänger.

———. 1923. *Falk Nefts Heimkehr*. Frankfurt: J. Kauffmann.

———. 1925. *Das jüdische Nationalheim*. Frankfurt: J. Kauffmann.

———. 1926. *The Jewish National Home*. Frankfurt am Main: J. Kaufmann.

———. 1929. *Programm oder Testament*. Frankfurt am Main: J. Kauffmann.

———. 1933/34. "Rabbiner Hirsch als Wegweiser in die jüdische Geschichte." *Nachalat Z'wi* 4: 165–85.

———. 1934. *Der Neue Kusari: Ein Weg zum Judentum*. Frankfurt: Verlag der Rabbiner-Hirsch-Gesellschaft.

———. 1944. *Moriah: Yesodot ha-hinukh ha-le'umi ha-torati*. Jerusalem: Mosad Ha-Rav Kuk.

———. 1951. *Nahali'el: Yesodot ha-hinukh le-mitsvot ha-Torah*. Jerusalem: Mosad Ha-Rav Kuk.

———. 1955/56. *Tsiyune derekh*. Tel-Aviv: Hevrat 'am 'olam.

———. 1974. *Concepts of Judaism*. Jerusalem: Israel Universities Press.

———. 1988. *Darki*. Jerusalem: Mosad Yitshak Broyer.

Breuer, M. 1992. *Modernity within Tradition: The Social History of Orthodox Jewry in Imperial Germany*. New York: Columbia University Press.

Brown, C. 1985. *Jesus in European Protestant Thought, 1778–1860*. Durham, N.C.: Labyrinth Press.

Buber, M. 1972. *On Judaism*. New York: Schocken Books.

Busch, E. 1976. *Karl Barth: His Life from Letters and Autobiographical Texts*. Philadelphia: Fortress Press.

Butterfield, H. 1955. *Man on His Past: The Study of the History of Historical Scholarship*. Cambridge, Eng.: Cambridge University Press.

Casper, B. 1967. *Das dialogische Denken*. Freiburg: Wien Herder.

Cassirer, E. 1906–1907. *Das Erkenntnisproblem in der Philosophie und Wissenschaft der neueren Zeit*. Berlin: Verlag Cassirer.

———. 1951. *The Philosophy of the Enlightenment*. Princeton: Princeton University Press.

Cohen, A. A., ed. 1980. *The Jew: Essays from Martin Buber's Journal, "Der Jude"*. University: University of Alabama Press.

Cohen, G. 1997. "The Blessing of Assimilation in Jewish History." *Jewish History and Jewish Destiny*. idem. New York: Jewish Theological Seminary of America, 145–156.

Cohen, G. B. 1979. "Jews in German Society: Prague, 1860–1914." *Jews and Germans from 1860–1933: The Problematic Symbiosis*. D. Bronsen. Heidelberg, Winter: 306–37.

Cohen, H. 1904. "Die Errichtung von Lehrstühlen für Ethik und Religions-Philosophie an den jüdisch-theologischen Lehranstalten." *Monatsschrift für Geschichte und Wissenschaft des Judentums* 48: 2–21.

———. 1910. *Kants Begründung der Ethik*. Berlin: Bruno Cassirer.

———. 1915. "Spinoza über Staat und Religion, Judentum und Christentum." *Jahrbuch für jüdische Geschichte und Literatur* 18: 56–150.

———. 1918. *Kants Theologie der Erfahrung*. Berlin: Ferd. Dümmler.

———. 1924. *Jüdischen Schriften, vol. 1*. Berlin: C. A. Schwetschke.

———. 1924. *Jüdischen Schriften, vol. 2*. Berlin: C. A. Schwetschke.

———. 1927. *Kleine Philosophische Schriften*. Berlin: Akademie Verlag.

———. 1928. *Schriften zur Philosophie und Zeitgeschichte, vols. 1–2*. Berlin: Akademie-Verlag.

———. 1928. "Zur Kontroverse zwischen Trendenlungen und Kuno Fischer." *Schriften zur Philosophie und Zeitgeschichte*, vol 1. Berlin: Akademie Verlag.

———. 1971. "Affinities between the Philosophy of Kant and Judaism." *Reason and Hope: Selections from the Jewish Writings of Hermann Cohen*. New York: Norton.

Cohen, J. 1997. *Tevunah ve-temurah: panim be-heker ha-filosofyah ha-Yehudit ve-toldoteha*. Jerusalem: Mosad Bialik.

Cohen, R. A. 1994. *Elevations: The Height of the Good in Rosenzweig and Levinas*. Chicago: University of Chicago Press.

———. 1998. *Jewish Icons: Art and Society in Modern Europe*. Berkeley: University of California Press.

Cohen, S.J.D. 1999. *The Beginnings of Jewishness: Boundaries, Varieties, Uncertainties*. Berkeley: University of California Press.

Derrida, J. 1967. *De la Grammatalogie*. Paris: Éditions de Minuit.

———. 1991. "Interpretation at War: Kant, the Jew, the German." *New Literary History* 22.

Deutsch, K. L., and W. Nicgorski, eds. 1994. *Leo Strauss: Political Philosopher and Jewish Thinker*. Landam, Md.: Rowman & Littlefield.

Dietrich, W. S. 1986. *Cohen and Troeltsch: Ethical Monotheistic Religion and Theory of Culture*. Atlanta: Scholars Press.

Dilthey, W. 1988. *Introduction to the Human Sciences: An Attempt to Lay a Foundation for the Study of Society and History*. Detroit: Wayne State University Press.

Dinur, B.-Z. 1958. *Yisrael ba-golah*. Tel-Aviv: Mosad Bialik.

Drescher, H.-G. 1992. *Ernst Troeltsch: His Life and Work*. London: SCM.

Dussort, H. 1963. *L'école de Marbourg*. Paris: Presses universitaires de France.

Ehrenfreund, J. 2000. *Mémoire juive et nationalité allemande: Les juif berlinois à la Belle Époque*. Paris, Presses universitaires de France.

Ehrenberg, H. 1943. *Autobiography of a German Pastor.* London, Northumberland.

Elbogen, I. 1966. *A Century of Jewish Life.* Philadelphia: Jewish Publication Society of America.

Ellenson, D. 1994. *Between Tradition and Culture: The Dialectics of Modern Jewish Religion and Identity.* Atlanta: Scholars Press.

Endelman, T. M. 1990. *Radical Assimilation in English Jewish History, 1656–1945.* Bloomington: Indiana University Press.

Engel-Janosi, F. 1944. *The Growth of German Historicism.* Baltimore: Johns Hopkins University Press.

Faivre, A. 1996. "Des histoires en théologie: conflit de méthodes ou de croyance?" *L'Historien et la foi.* J. Delumeau: Paris, Fayard.

Feiner, S. 1995. *Haskalah ve-historyah: Toldoteha shel hakarat-'avar yehudit modernit.* Jerusalem: Merkaz Zalman Shazar le-toldot Yisra'el.

Fink, C. 1989. *Marc Bloch: A Life in History.* Cambridge and New York: Cambridge University Press.

Finkelstein, I., and N. A. Silberman 2001. *The Bible Unearthed: Archaeology's New Vision of Ancient Israel and the Origin of Its Sacred Texts.* New York: Free Press.

Fiorato, P. 1993. *Geschichtliche Ewigkeit: Ursprung und Zeitlichkeit in der Philosophie Hermann Cohens.* Königshausen: n.a.

Frank, D., and O. Leaman. 1997. *History of Jewish Philosophy.* London: Routledge.

Frankel, Z. 1851/52. "Einleitendes." *Monatsschrift für Geschichte und Wissenschaft des Judentums* 1: 5.

Friedländer, S. 1997. *Nazi Germany and the Jews.* New York: HarperCollins.

Friedman, M. 1983. *Martin Buber's Life and Work.* New York: E. P. Dutton, Inc.

Fülling, E. 1956. *Geschichte als Offenbarung: Studien zur Frage Historismus und Glaube von Herder bis Troeltsch.* Berlin, Verlag Alfred Töpelmann.

Funkenstein, A. 1986. *Theology and the Scientific Revolution.* Princeton: Princeton University Press.

———. 1993. *Perceptions of Jewish History.* Berkeley: University of California Press.

———. 1995. "The Dialectics of Assimilation." *Jewish Social Studies* 1: 1–14.

Gans, E. 1822. "Vorlesungen über die Geschichte der Juden im Norden von Europa und in den slavischen Ländern." *Zeitschrift für die Wissenschaft des Judentums* 1: 95–113.

Gardner, P., ed. 1959. *Theories of History: Readings from Classical and Contemporary Sources.* New York: Free Press.

Gay, P. 1972. *The Berlin-Jewish Spirit: A Dogma in Search of Some Doubts (15th Leo Baeck Memorial Lecture).* New York: n.a.

Geiger, L., ed. 1875–1878. *Abraham Geigers Nachgelassene Schriften.* Berlin: Louis Gerschel Verlagsbuchhandlung.

———. 1936. "Zunz: Mein erster Unterricht in Wolfenbütel." *Jahrbuch für jüdische Geschichte und Literatur* 30: 131–40.

Gibbs, R. 1992. *Correlations in Rosenzweig and Levinas.* Princeton: Princeton University Press.

Glatzer, N. N., ed. 1953. *Franz Rosenzweig: His Life and Thought*. New York: Farrar, Straus and Young.

Glatzer, N. N.. 1958. *Leopold and Adelheid Zunz: An Account in Letters, 1815–1885*. London: East and West Library.

Gnilsen, H. 1972. *Ecclesia Militans Saliburgensis: Kulturkampf in Salzburg 1848–1914*. Vienna: Geyer.

Gogarten, F. 1923. "Die Entscheidung." *Zwischen den Zeiten* 1.

Goldberg, S.-A. 2000. *La Clepsydre: Essai sur la pluralité des temps dans le judaïsme*. Paris: Albin Michel.

Goldin, J., ed. 1955. *The Fathers according to Rabbi Nathan*. New Haven: Yale University Press.

Gordon, P. E. 1997. "Under One Tradewind: Philosophical Expressionism from Rosenzweig to Heidegger." Ph.D. diss. University of California, Berkeley.

Graetz, H. 1875. *Geschichte der Juden*. Leipzig: O. Leiner.

———. 1927. *History of the Jews*. Philadelphia: Jewish Publication Society of America.

———. 1975. *The Structure of Jewish History, and Other Essays*. Philadelphia: Jewish Publication Society.

Graf, F. W. 1984. "Kulturprotestantismus. Zur Begriffsgeschichte einer theologie-politischen Chiffre." *Archiv für Begriffsgeschichte* 28: 214–86.

Grafton, A. 1993. *Joseph Scaliger: A Study in the History of Scholarship II: Historical Chronology*. Oxford: Oxford University Press.

Green, K. H. 1993. *Jew and Philosopher: The Return of Moses Maimonides in the Jewish Thought of Leo Strauss*. Albany: State University of New York Press.

———, ed. 1997. *Leo Strauss: Jewish Philosopher and the Crisis of Modernity: Essays and Lectures in Modern Jewish Thought*. Albany: State University of New York Press.

Gross, R. 2000. *Carl Schmitt und die Juden: Eine deutsche Rechtslehre*. Frankfurt am Main: Suhrkamp.

Gruen, E. S. 1998. *Heritage and Hellenism: The Reinvention of Jewish Tradition*. Berkeley: University of California Press.

Guha, R. 1988. *An Indian Historiography of India: A Nineteenth-Century Agenda and Its Implication*. Calcutta: Published for Centre for Studies in Social Sciences, Calcutta by K.P. Bagchi & Co.

Gunnell, J. G. March 1978. "The Myth of Tradition." *American Political Science Review* 72, 122–34.

Ha'am, A. 1930. "Hikui ve-hitbolelut." *'Al parashat ha-derakhim: kovets ma' amarim*. Berlin, Jüdischer Verlag, 1: 169–77.

Hackeschmidt, J. 1995. "Die hebräischen Propheten und die Ethik Kants: Hermann Cohen in kultur- und sozialhistorischer Perpektive." *Aschkenas* 1, 121–29.

———. 1997. *Von Kurt Blumenfeld zu Norbert Elias: Die Erfindung einer jüdischen Nation*. Hamburg: Europaeische Verlag.

Ha-Levi, J. 1964. *The Kuzari (Kitab al Khazari: An Argument for the Faith of Israel)*. New York: Schocken Books.

Hall, S. 1994. "Cultural Identity and Diaspora." *Colonial Discourse and Post-Colonial Theory.* P. Williams and L. Chrisman. New York: Columbia University Press, 392–403.

Hallo, R. 1983. *Schriften zur Kunstgeschichte in Kassel: Sammlungen, Denkmäler, Judaica.* Kassel: Gesamthochschulbibliothek.

Hammer-Schenk, H. 1981. *Synagogen in Deutschland: Geschichte einer Baugattung in 19. and 20. Jahrhundert (1780–1933).* Hamburg: H. Christians.

Harris, J. M. 1995. *How do we know this?: Midrash and the Fragmentation of Modern Judaism.* Albany: State University of New York Press.

Harvey, V. 1966. *The Historian and the Believer: A Confrontation between the Modern Historian's Principles of Judgment and the Christian's Will-to-Believe.* New York: Macmillan.

Heimpel, H. 1957. "Geschichte und Geschichtswissenschaft." *Vierteljahrshefte für Zeitgeschichte 59.*

Herder, J. G. 1959. "Ideas toward a Philosophy of the History of Man." *Theories of History.* P. Gardiner. New York: Free Press.

Herrmann, W. 1906. *The Communion of the Christian with God.* New York: G. P. Putnam's Sons.

Heschel, S. 1998. *Abraham Geiger and the Jewish Jesus.* Chicago: University of Chicago Press.

Heussi, K. 1932. *Die Krisis des Historismus.* Tübingen: Mohr.

Himmelfarb, M. 1998. "Elias Bickerman on Judaism and Hellenism." *The Jewish Past Revisited: Reflections on Modern Jewish Historians.* D. N. Myers and D. B. Ruderman. New Haven: Yale University Press.

Hirsch, S. R. 1836. *Igrot Tzafon: Neunzehn Briefe über Judentum von Ben Usiel.* Altona; n.a.

———. 1854. "Der Jude und seine Zeit." *Jeschurun* 1: 14–25.

———. 1942. *The Nineteen Letters.* New York: Bloch.

———. 1956. *Judaism Eternal.* London: Soncino Press.

———. 1992. *The Collected Writings.* New York: P. Feldheim.

Holtfrerich, C.-L. 1999. *Frankfurt As a Financial Centre: From Medieval Trade Fair to European Banking Center.* Munich: Beck.

Horch, H. O. 1985. *Auf der Suche nach der jüdischen Erzählliteratur: Die Literaturkritik der "Allgemeinen Zeitung des Judentums" (1837–1922).* Frankfurt and New York: Verlag Peter Lang.

Horwitz, R. 1969. "Tesifat ha-Yahadut be-mahshevet Franz Rosenzweig." *Proceedings of the American Academy for Jewish Research 37.*

———. 1986. "Galut ve-ge'ulah be-mishnato shel Yitzhak Breuer." *Eshel Beer Sheva* 3: 281–301.

———. 1988. "Voices of Opposition to the First World War among Jewish Thinkers." *Leo Baeck Institute Year Book* 32: 233–59.

———. 1988. *Isaac Breuer: 'Iyunim be-misnato.* Ramat-Gan: Bar-Ilan University.

Howard, T. A. 2000. *Religion and the Rise of Historicism: W.M.L. de Wette, Jacob Burckhardt, and the Theological Origins of Nineteenth-Century Historical Consciousness.* Cambridge and New York: Cambridge University Press.

Hübinger, G. 1994. *Kulturprotestantismus und Politik: Zum Verhältnis von Liberalismus und Protestantismus im wilhelminischen Deutschland*. Tübingen: J.C.B. Mohr.

Hughes, H. S. 1977. *Consciousness and Society: The Reorientation of European Social Thought, 1890–1930*. New York: Vintage Books.

Hunt, L., ed. 1989. *The New Cultural History*. Berkeley: University of California Press.

Iggers, G. 1983. *The German Conception of History: The National Tradition of Historical Thought from Herder to the Present*. Middleton, Conn.: Wesleyan University Press.

———. 1995. "Historicism: The History and Meaning of the Term." *Journal of the History of Ideas* 56: 129–52.

Jay, M. 1973. *The Dialectical Imagination: A History of the Frankfurt School and the Institute of Social Research, 1923–1950*. Boston: Little, Brown.

———. 1986. *Permanent Exiles: Essays on the Intellectual Migration from Germany to America*. New York: Columbia University Press.

Jospe, R., ed. 1997. *Paradigms in Jewish Philosophy*. Cranbury, N.J.: Associated University Presses.

Kaes, A., M. Jay, et al., eds. 1994. *The Weimar Republic Sourcebook*. Berkeley: University of California Press.

Kafka, F. 1954. *Dearest Father: Stories and Other Writings*. New York: Schocken Books.

Kähler, M. 1892. *Der sogenannte historische Jesus und der geschichtliche biblische Christus*. Leipzig: A. Deichert.

———. 1964. *The So-Called Historical Jesus and the Historic Biblical Christ*. Philadelphia: Fortress Press.

Kant, I. 1965. *Critique of Pure Reason*. New York: St. Martin's Press.

Katz, J. 1972. *Emancipation and Assimilation: Studies in Modern Jewish History*. Westmead, England: Gregg.

———. 1980. *From Prejudice to Destruction: Anti-Semitism, 1700–1933*. Cambridge, Mass.: Harvard University Press.

———. 1993. *Tradition and Crisis*. New York: New York University Press.

———. 1995. *Ha-kera' she-lo nit'ahah: Perishat ha-ortodoksim mi-kelal ha-kehilot be-Hungaryah uve-Germanyah*. Jerusalem: Merkaz Zalman Shazar le-toldot Yisra'el.

———. 1995. *With My Own Eyes: The Autobiography of an Historian*. Hanover, N.H., University Press of New England for Brandeis University Press.

Katz, S. 1992. *Historicism, the Holocaust, and Zionism*. New York: New York University Press.

Kellermann, B. 1917. *Der ethische Monotheismus der Propheten und seine soziologische Würdigung*. Berlin: Schwetschke.

Kelley, D. R. 1988. *Faces of History: Historical Inquiry from Herodotus to Herder*. New Haven: Yale University Press.

Kierkegaard, S. 1944. *Concluding Unscientific Postscript*. Princeton: Princeton University Press.

Klaiber, W. 1982. *Ecclesia militans: Studien zu den Festtagspredigten des Johannes Eck*. Münster: Aschendorff.

Kluback, W. 1986. "Friendship without Communication: Wilhelm Herrmann and Hermann Cohen." *Leo Baeck Instutute Year Book* 31: 317–38.

Klugman, E. M. 1996. *Rabbi Samson Raphael Hirsch*. Brooklyn: n.a.

Köhler, W. 1941. *Ernst Troeltsch*. Tübingen: J.C.B. Mohr.

Krieger, L. 1989. *Time's Reasons: Philosophies of History Old and New*. Chicago: University of Chicago Press.

Kuper, A. 1999. *Culture: The Anthropologists' Account*. Cambridge, Mass.: Harvard University Press.

Kurzweil, B. 1969. *Be-ma'avak 'al 'erkhe ha-Yahadut*. Tel-Aviv.

———. 1976. *Le-nokhah ha mevukhah ha-ruhanit shel dorenu: Pirke hagut u-vikoret*. Ramat-Gan: Bar-Ilan University.

Lampert, L. 1996. *Leo Strauss and Nietzsche*. Chicago: University of Chicago Press.

Lamprecht, K. 1909. *Moderne Geschichtswissenschaft: Funf Vorträge*. Berlin: Weidmann.

Lange, P. 1972. *Konkrete Theologie? Karl Barth und Friedrich Gogarten "Zwischen den Zeiten" (1922–1933)*. Zurich: Theologischer Verlag.

Lawitschka, J. R. 1996. "Metageschichte: Jüdische Geschictskonzeptionen im frühen 20. Jahrhundert: Franz Rosenzweig, Isaac Breuer und das Echo." Ph.D. diss. Free University, Berlin.

Lazarus, M., and H. Steinhal. 1860. *Zeitschrift für Völkerpsychologie und Sprachwissenschaft* 1.

Leder, R.S.J. 2000. "Torah Truths." *Los Angeles Jewish Journal*.

Lee, D. E., and R. N. Beck. 1954. "The Meaning of 'Historicism.' " *American Historical Review* 59: 568–77.

Lehman, J. H. 1975. "Maimonides, Mendelssohn and the Measfim: Philosophy and the Biographical Imagination in the Early *Haskalah*." *Leo Baeck Instutute Year Book* 20: 87–105.

Leibowitz, Y. 1982. *Emunah, historyah, ve-'arakhim : ma'amarim ve-hartsa'ot*. Jerusalem: Akademon, Bet ha-hotsa'ah shel Histadrut ha-studentim shel ha-Universitah ha-'ivrit bi-Yerushalayim.

———. 1988. *He'arot le-farshiyot ha-shavu'a*. Jerusalem: Akademon.

Lévinas, E. 1965. *Difficile Liberté*. Paris: Albin Michel.

Levine, L. I. 1998. *Judaism and Hellenism: Conflict or Confluence?* Seattle: University of Washington Press.

Levine, P. 1995. *Nietzsche and the Modern Crisis of the Humanities*. Albany: State University of New York Press.

Levy, R. S. 1975. *The Downfall of the Anti-Semitic Political Parties in Imperial Germany*. New Haven: Yale University Press.

Liebeschütz, H. 1967. *Das Judentum im deutschen Geschichtsbild von Hegel bis Max Weber*. Tübingen: Mohr.

———. 1968. "Hans Cohen and his Historical Background." *Leo Baeck Instutute Year Book* 13.

Lowenstein, S. 1976. "Pace of Modernization of German Jewry in the Nineteenth Century." *Leo Baeck Instutute Year Book* 21: 41–56.

Löwy, M. 1988. *Redemption and Utopia: Jewish Libertarian Thought in Central Europe: A Study in Elective Affinity*. Stanford, Stanford University Press.

Lüdtke, A. 1995. *The History of Everyday Life: Reconstructing Historical Experiences and Ways of Life*. Princeton: Princeton University Press.

Luzzatto, S. D. 1894. *Igrot ShaDaL*. E. Graeber. Cracow: 1867.

Lyotard, J.-F. 1988. *The Differend: Phrases in Dispute*. Minneapolis: University of Minnesota Press.

Maimonides, M. 1965. *The Guide of the Perplexed, vol. 2*. Chicago: University of Chicago Press.

Maranz, F. 1993. "Did the Exodus Really Happen?" *The Jerusalem Report*. Jerusalem, April 8, 1993: 16–20.

McCole, J. 1993. *Walter Benjamin and the Antinomies of Tradition*. Ithaca: Cornell University Press.

Meinecke, F. 1959. *Die Entstehung des Historismus*. Munich and Berlin: R. Oldenbourg Verlag.

———. 1972. *Historicism: The Rise of a New Historical Outlook*. London: Routledge and K. Paul.

Meinecke, S. 1991. "A Life of Contradiction: The Philosopher Franz Rosenzweig and His Relationship to History and Politics." *Leo Baeck Instutute Year Book* 36: 461–89.

Meir, E. 1994. *Kokhav mi-Ya'akov: Hayav ve-yetsirato shel Franz Rosenzweig*. Jerusalem: Magnes Press.

Melber, J. 1968. *Hermann Cohen's Philosophy of Judaism*. New York: Jonathan David Publishers.

Mendelssohn, G. B., ed. (1843–45). *Moses Mendelssohns Gesammelte Schriften*. Leipzig: F. A. Brockhaus.

Mendelssohn, M. 1983. *Jerusalem, or on Religious Power and Judaism*. Hanover, N.H.: University Press of New England.

Mendes-Flohr, P. R., ed. 1988. *The Philosophy of Franz Rosenzweig: Proceedings of the Fourth Jerusalem Encounter*. Hanover, N. H.: Published for Brandeis University Press by University Press of New England.

Mendes-Flohr, P. R. 1991. "The Study of the Jewish Intellectual: A Methodological Prolegomenon." *Divided Passions: Jewish Intellectuals and the Experience of Modernity*. idem. Detroit: Wayne State University Press, 23–53.

Mendes-Flohr, P. R. 1999. *German Jews: A Dual Identity*. New Haven: Yale University Press.

Mendes-Flohr, P. R., and J. Reinharz, eds. 1980. *The Jew in the Modern World*. New York: Oxford University Press.

Menger, C. 1884. *Der Irrthümer des Historismus in der deutschen Nationalökonomie*. Vienna: A. Hölder.

Metz, K. H. 1984. " 'Der Methodenstreit in der deutschen Geschichtswissenschaft (1891–99)': Bemerkungen zum sozialen Kontext wissenschaftlicher Auseinandersetzungen." *Storia della Storiografia* 6: 3–20.

Meyer, M. A. 1966. "Great Debate on Antisemitism: Jewish Reactions to New Hostility in Germany, 1789–1881." *Leo Baeck Institute Year Book* 11: 137–70.

———. 1967. *The Origins of the Modern Jew: Jewish Identity and European Culture in German, 1749–1885*. Detroit: Wayne State University Press.

———. 1971. "Jewish Religious Reform and Wissenschaft des Judentums: The Positions of Zunz, Geiger and Frankel." *Leo Baeck Instutute Year Book* 16: 19–41.

———. 1988. "The Emergence of Modern Jewish Historiography: Motives and Motifs." *History and Theory* 27: 160–75.

Michael, R. 1961. "Cohen contra Graetz." *Bulletin des Leo Baeck Instituts* 4: 301–22.

———. 1993. *Ha-ketivah ha-historit ha-Yehudit mi-ha-renasans 'ad ha-'et ha-hadashah*. Jerusalem: Mosad Byalik.

Mittleman, A. L. 1990. *Between Kant and Kabbalah: An Introduction to Isaac Breuer's Philosophy of Judaism*. Albany: State University of New York Press.

———. 1996. *The Politics of Torah: The Jewish Political Tradition and the Founding of Agudat Yisrael*. Albany: State University of New York Press.

Mohler, A. 1989. *Die Konservative Revolution in Deutschland, 1918–1932: Ein Handbuch*. Darmstad: Wissenschaftliche Buchgesellschaft.

Morgan, M. L. 1992. *Dilemmas in Modern Jewish Thought*. Bloomington: Indiana University Press.

Morgenstern, M. 1995. *Von Frankfurt nach Jerusalem: Isaac Breuer und die Geschichte des "Austrittsstreits" in der deutsch-jüdischen Orthodoxie*. Tübingen: Mohr.

Mosès, S. 1990. "Franz Rosenzweig mul ha-Tsiyunot." *Ha-Tsiyonut u-mitnagdeha ba-'am ha-Yehudi*. H. Avni and G. Shimoni. Jerusalem: ha-Sifriyah ha-Tsiyonit, 321–25.

———. 1992. *System and Revelation: The Philosophy of Franz Rosenzweig*. Detroit: Wayne State University Press.

Mosse, G. L. 1985. *German Jews beyond Judaism*. Bloomington: Indiana University Press.

———. 1985. *Toward the Final Solution: A History of European Racism*. Madison: University of Wisconsin Press.

Moyn, S. 1996. "German Jewry and the Questions of Identity, Historiography and Theory." *Leo Baeck Institute Year Book* 41: 291–308.

Myers, D. N. October 1986. "The Scholem-Kurzweil Debate and Modern Jewish Historiography." *Modern Judaism* 6: 261–86.

———. 1992. "The Fall and Rise of Jewish Historicism: The Evolution of the Akademie für die Wissenschaft des Judentums." *Hebrew Union College Annual* 63: 107–44.

———. 1994. "Eugen Täubler: The Personification of 'Judaism As Tragic Existence.' " *Leo Baeck Instutute Year Book* 39: 131–50.

———. 1995. *Reinventing the Jewish Past: European Jewish Intellectuals and the Zionist Return to History*. New York: Oxford University Press.

Myers, D. N. 1998. " 'The Blessing of Assimilation' Reconsidered: An Inquiry into Jewish Cultural Studies." *From Ghetto to Emancipation: Historical and Contemporary Reconsiderations of the Jewish Community*. D. N. Myers and W. V. Rowe. Scranton: University of Scranton Press.

———. 2001. "Hermann Cohen and the Quest for Protestant Judaism." *Leo Baeck Instutute Year Book* 42: 195–214.

Myers, D. N. 2001. *The Problem of History in German-Jewish Thought: Observations on a Neglected Tradition (Cohen, Rosenzweig, and Breuer). The Samuel Braun Lecture in the History of the Jews of Prussia*. Bar-Ilan University. Ramat-Gan.

Neher, A. 1986. *Jewish Thought and the Scientific Revolution of the Sixteenth Century: David Gans and His Times*. Oxford: Oxford University Press.

Niethammer, L. 1992. *Posthistoire: Has History Come to an End?* London and New York: Verso.

Nietzsche, F. W. 1980. *On the Advantage and Disadvantage of History for Life*. Indianapolis: Hackett Publishing Company.

Nipperdey, T. 1983. *Deutsche Geschichte, 1800–1866*. Munich: C. H. Beck.

Nirenberg, D. 1996. *Communities of Violence: Persecution of Minorities in the Middle Ages*. Princeton: Princeton University Press.

Nowak, K. 1987. "Die 'antihistoristische Revolution': Symptome und Folgen der Krise historischer Weltorientierung nach dem Weltkrieg in Deutschland." *Troeltsch-Studien: Umstrittene Moderne, vol. 4*. H. Renz and F. W. Graf. Gütersloh: Gütersloher Verlagshaus Gerd Mohn.

Ogletree, T. W. 1965. *Christian Faith and History: A Critical Comparison of Ernst Troeltsch and Karl Barth*. New York: Abingdon Press.

Otto, R. 1958. *The Idea of the Holy*. London and New York: Oxford University Press.

Overbeck, F. 1919. *Christentum und Kultur*. Basel: Benno Schwabe.

Pasternak, B. 1949. *Safe Conduct*. New York: New Directions.

Pines, S. 1987–89. "Der Islam im Stern der Erlösung: Eine Untersuchung zu Tendenzen und Quellen Franz Rosenzweigs." *Hebräische Beiträge zur Wissenschaft des Judentums, deutsch angezeigt* 3–5: 138–48.

Pocock, J.G.H. 1999. *Barbarism and Religion (Narratives of Civil Government, vol. 2)*. Cambridge: Cambridge University Press.

Poma, A. 1997. *The Critical Philosophy of Hermann Cohen*. Albany: State University of New York Press.

Popper, K. 1957. *The Poverty of Historicism*. London: Routledge and K. Paul.

Rabinbach, A. 1997. *In the Shadow of Catastrophe: German Intellectuals between Apocalypse and Enlightenment*. Berkeley: University of California Press.

Rabinowits, C. D. 1995/6. *Toldot Yisrael: nos'im, berurim, u-vikuhim mi-Nehemyah ve-'ad 'atah*. Jerusalem: n.a.

Rand, C. G. 1965. "Two Meanings of Historicism in the Writings of Dilthey, Troeltsch and Meinecke." *Journal of the History of Ideas* 25: 503–18.

Rashkover, R. L. 2000. "Franz Rosenzweig, Karl Barth and the Theology of Election." Ph.D. diss. University of Virginia.

Rawidowicz, S. May–June 1940. "Tzvay voz zaynen ayns." *Tsukunft* 54.

———. 1998. "Two That Are One." *State of Israel, Diaspora, and Jewish Continuity: Essays on the "Ever-Dying People"*. B.C.I. Ravid. Hanover, N.H.: Published by University Press of New England for Brandeis University Press.

Raz-Krokotzkin, Amnon. 1996. "Yitsuga ha-le'umi shel ha-galut: Ha-historyografiyah ha-tsiyonit ve-yehude yeme ha-benayim." Ph.D. diss. Tel Aviv University.

———. 1998. " 'Le-lo hesbonot aherim': she'elat ha-Natsrut etsel Scholem ve-Baer." *Mada'e ha-Yahadut* 38: 73–96.

Reill, P. H. 1975. *The German Enlightenment and the Rise of Historicism.* Berkeley: University of California Press.

Renz, H., and F. W. Graf, eds. 1987. *Unstrittene Moderne: Die Zukunft der Neuzweit im Urteil der Epoche Ernst Troeltsch.* Troeltsch Studien Band 4. Gütersloh: Gütersloher Verlagshaus Gerd Mohn.

Révah, I. S. 1959. *Spinoza et le Dr. Juan de Prado.* Paris: Mouton.

Rickert, H. 1924. *Die Probleme der Geschichtsphilosophie.* Heidelberg: C. Winter.

Ricoeur, P. 1965. *History and Truth.* Evanston, Ill., Northwestern University Press.

Ringer, F. 1997. *Max Weber's Methodology: The Unification of the Cultural and Social Sciences.* Cambridge, Mass.: Harvard University Press.

Rohls, J., and G. Wenz, eds. 1988. *Vernunft des Glaubens: Wissenschaftliche Theologie und kirchliche Lehre.* Göttingen, Vandenhoeck & Ruprecht.

Rosenbloom, N. H. 1976. *Tradition in an Age of Reform: The Religious Philosophy of Samson Raphael Hirsch.* Philadelphia: Jewish Publication Society of America.

Rosenstock-Huessy, E., ed. 1969. *Judaism Despite Christianity: The Letters on Christianity and Judaism.* University: University of Alabama Press.

Rosenthal, E.I.J. 1975. "Hermann Cohen and Heinrich Graetz." *The Salo Wittmayer Baron Jubilee Volume.* Jerusalem: American Academy for Jewish Research, 725–43.

Rosenzweig, F. 1924. *Hermann Cohens Jüdische Schriften.* Berlin: C. A. Schwetschke.

———. 1937. *Kleinere Schriften.* Berlin: Schocken.

———. 1955. *On Jewish Learning.* New York: Schocken Books.

———. 1971. *The Star of Redemption.* New York: Holt, Rinehart and Winston.

———. 1984. *Der Mensch und seine Zeit: Zweistromland.* Dordrecht: n.a.

———. 1987. *Mivhar igrot ve-kit'e yoman.* Jerusalem: Mosad Bialik.

———. 2000. *Philosophical and Theological Writings.* Indianapolis: Hackett Publishers.

Rosenzweig, R., and E. Rosenzweig-Scheinmann, eds. 1979. *Der Mensch und sein Werk: Briefe und Tagebücher.* The Hague: Martinus Nijhoff.

Rotenstreich, N. 1972. *Tradition and Reality: The Impact of History on Modern Jewish Thought.* New York: Random House.

Rothacker, E. 1960. "Das Wort 'Historismus.' " *Zeitschrift für deutsche Wortforschung* 16.

Rubanowice, R. J. 1982. *Crisis in Consciousness: The Thought of Ernst Troeltsch.* Tallahassee: University Presses of Florida.

Rubaschoff, S. 1919. "Erstlinge der Entjudung: Drei Reden von Eduard Gans in 'Kulturverein.' " *Der jüdische Wille* 2.

Rubenstein, E. 1999. *An Episode of Jewish Romanticism: Franz Rosenzweig's The Star of Redemption.* Albany: State University of New York Press.

Rudavsky, T. M. 2000. *Time Matters: Time, Creation, and Cosmology in Medieval Jewish Philosophy.* Albany: State University of New York Press.

Rupp, G. 1977. *Culture-Protestantism: German Liberal Theology at the Turn of the Twentieth Century.* Missoula, Mont.: Scholars Press for the American Academy of Religion.

Safranski, R. 1998. *Martin Heidegger: Between Good and Evil.* Cambridge, Mass.: Harvard University Press.

Said, E. 1993. *Culture and Imperialism.* New York: Knopf.

Saltzman, J. D. 1981. *Paul Natorp's Philosophy of Religion within the Marburg Neo-Kantian Tradition.* New York: Georg Olms.

Schacter, J. J. 1998–99. "Facing the Truths of History." *Tora U-Madda Journal* 8: 202.

Schechter, S., ed. 1887. *Avot de-Rabbi Natan.* Vienna: n.a.

Schievelbusch, W. 1982. *Intellektuellendämmerung.* Frankfurt am Main: Die Hessen-Bibliothek im Insel Verlag.

Schmied-Kowarzik, W., ed. 1988. *Der Philosoph Franz Rosenzweig: Die Herausforderung jüdischen Lernens.* Freiburg: K. Alber.

Schmitt, C. 1934. *Politische Theologie: Vier Kapitel zu Lehre von der Souveränität.* Berlin: Duncker & Humblot.

———. 1985. *Political Theology: Four Chapters on the Concept of Sovereignty.* Cambridge: Massachusetts Institute of Technology Press.

Schnädelbach, H. 1983. *Philosophie in Deutschland 1831–1933.* Frankfurt am Main: Suhrkamp Verlag.

Scholem, G. 1960. *Jewish Gnosticism, Merkabah Mysticism, and Talmudic Tradition.* New York: Jewish Theological Seminary Press.

———. 1971. *The Messianic Idea in Judaism.* New York: Schocken Books.

———. 1976. *On Jews and Judaism in Crisis.* New York: Schocken Books.

———. 1979. "Mi-tokh hirhurim 'al Hokhmat Yisra'el," *Hokhmat Yisra'el: Hebetim historiyim u-filosofiyim.* P. Mendes-Flohr. Jerusalem: Merkaz Shazar, 153–68.

———. 1981. *Walter Benjamin: The Story of a Friendship.* Philadelphia: Jewish Publication Society of America.

Schorsch, I. 1994. *From Text to Context.* Hanover, N.H.: University Press of New England.

Schorske, C. 1998. *Thinking with History: Explorations in the Passage to Modernism.* Princeton: Princeton University Press.

Schwab, S. 1988. *Selected Writings: A Collection of Addresses and Essays on Hashkafah, Jewish History and Contemporary Issues.* Lakewood, N.J.: C.I.S. Publications.

Schwab, S. 1934. *Heimkehr ins Judentum.* Frankfurt: n.a.

Schwarzschild, S. S. 1955. "Two Modern Jewish Philosophies of History: Nachman Krochmal and Hermann Cohen." D.H.L. thesis. Cincinnati, Ohio, Hebrew Union College.

Schweitzer, A. 1968. *The Quest of the Historical Jesus.* J. M. Robinson. New York, Collier Books/Macmillan.

Scwarcz, M. 1975. "Baruch Kurzweil: ha-ish u-mif'alo." *Sefer Baruch Kurzweil.* M. Z. Kaddari, A. Saltman, and M. Scwarcz. Ramat-Gan: Schocken, 37–46.

Sheppard, E. 2001. "Leo Strauss und the Politics of Exile." Los Angeles, Ph.D. diss. University of California, Los Angeles.

Sieferle, R. P. 1995. *Die Konservative Revolution*. Frankfurt am Main: Fischer Taschenbuch.

Simon-Nahum, P. 1991. *La cité investie: la "science du judaïsme" français et la République*. Paris: Editions du Cerf.

Skolnik, J. 1998. "Dissimilation and the Historical Novel: Hermann Sinsheimer's *Maria Nunnez*." *Leo Baeck Institute Year Book* 43: 225–37.

———. 1999. "Writing Jewish History between Gutzkow and Goethe: Auerbach's Spinoza and the Birth of Modern Jewish Historical Fiction." *Prooftexts* 19: 101–26.

Smith, S. B. 1977. *Spinoza, Liberalism, and the Question of Jewish Identity*. New Haven: Yale Univeristy Press.

Sockness, B. W. 1998. *Against False Apologetics: Wilhelm Herrmann and Ernst Troeltsch in Conflict*. Tübingen: Mohr Siebeck.

Solowiejczyk, J. 1932. "Das reine Denken und die Seinskonstitutierung bei Hermann Cohen." Ph.D. diss. Friedrich-Wilhelms-Universitat, Berlin.

Sontheimer, K. 1968. *Antidemokratisches Denken in der Weimarer Republik: Die politischen Ideen des deutschen Nationalismus zwischen 1918 und 1933*. Munich: Nympherburger Verlagshandlung.

Sorkin, D. 1987. *The Transformation of German Jewry, 1780–1840*. New York: Oxford University Press.

———. 1996. *Moses Mendelssohn and the Religious Enlightenment*. Berkeley: University of California Press.

Spinoza, B. 1951. *A Theologico-Political Treatise*. New York: Dover.

Stauss, B. and B., ed. (1939). *Hermann Cohen: Briefe*. Berlin: Schocken.

Stein, S., and R. Loewe, eds. 1979. *Studies in Jewish Religious and Intellectual History Presented to Alexander Altmann on the Occasion of His Seventieth Birthday*. University: University of Alabama Press.

Steiner, G. Spring–Summer 1989. "Heidegger, Today." *Salmagundi* 82–83.

Stern, F., ed. 1958. *Varieties of History*. New York: Meridian Books.

Stieg, M. F. 1986. *The Origin and Development of Scholarly Historical Periodicals*. University: University of Alabama Press.

Stow, K. 2001. *Theater of Acculturation: The Roman Ghetto in the Sixteenth Century*. Seattle: University of Washington Press.

Strauss, D. 1972. *The Life of Jesus Critically Examined*. Philadelphia: Fortress Press.

Strauss, L. 1930. *Die Religionskritik Spinozas als Grundlage seiner Bibelwissenschaft*. Berlin: Akademie-verlag.

———. 1935. *Philosophie und Gesetz*. Berlin: Schocken.

———. 1952. *Persecution and the Art of Writing*. Glencoe, Ill., Free Press.

———. 1965. *Hobbes Politische Wissenschaft*. Neuwied am Rhein and Berlin: Luchterhand.

———. 1965. *Spinoza's Critique of Religion*. New York: Schocken Books.

———. 1989. "Natural Right and the Historical Approach." *An Introduction to Political Philosophy: Ten Essays*. H. Gildin. Detroit: Wayne State University Press.

———. 1995. *Philosophy and Law: Contributions to the Understanding of Maimonides and His Predecessors*. Albany: State University of New York Press.

Strauss, L. 1997. *Gesammelte Schriften.* Heinrich Meier, ed. Vol. 2. Stuttgart and Weimar: J. B. Metzler.

Tal, U. January 1964. "Liberal Protestantism and the Jews in the Second Reich." *Jewish Social Studies* 26.

———. 1975. *Christians and Jews in Germany: Religion, Politics, and Ideology in the Second Reich, 1870–1914.* Ithaca: Cornell University Press.

———. 1976. "Theologische Debatte um das 'Wesen' des Judentums." *Juden in Wilhelminischen Deutschland, 1890–1914.* W. E. Mosse. Tübingen: Mohr Siebeck, 599–632.

Tarcov, N. 1983. "Philosophy and History: Tradition and Interpretation in the Work of Leo Strauss." *Polity* 16: 5–29.

Tishby, I. 1942. *Torat ha-ra' veha-kelipah be-kabalat ha-AR"I.* Jerusalem: Schocken.

Troeltsch, E. 1916/17. "Die Ethos der hebräischen Propheten." *Logos* 6: 1–28.

———. 1922. *Der Historismus und seine Probleme.* Tübingen: n.a.

———. 1922. "Die Krisis des Historismus." *Die neue Rundschau* 33: 572–90.

———. 1991. *Religion in History.* Minneapolis: Fortress Press.

Tucker, G. E., trans. 1988. "Correspondence of Karl Löwith and Leo Strauss." *Independant Journal of Philosophy/Unabhängige Zeitschrift für Philosophie* 5/6.

Udoff, A., ed. 1991. *Leo Strauss's Thought: Toward a Critical Engagement.* Boulder, Colo.: L. Rienner Publishers.

Udoff, A., and B. E. Galli, eds. 1999. *Franz Rosenzweig's "The New Thinking".* Syracuse: Syracuse University Press.

Urbach, E. E. 1982. *HaZaL: Pirke 'emunot ve-de'ot.* Jerusalem: Hotsa'at Sefarim 'al-shem Y. L. Magnes, ha-Universitah ha-'Ivrit.

van Rahden, T. 2000. *Juden und andere Breslauer: Die Beziehungen zwischen Juden, Protestanten und Katholiken in einer deutschen Grossstadt von 1860 bis 1925.* Göttingen: Vandenhoeck & Ruprect.

Vesser, H. A., ed. 1989. *The New Historicism.* New York: Routledge.

Vielmetti, N. 1970. "Die Gründgeschichte des Collegio Rabbinico in Padua." *Kairos* 12: 1–30.

Vogel, M. H. 1996. *Rosenzweig on Profane/Secular History.* Atlanta: Scholars Press.

Volkov, S. 1985. "The Dynamics of Dissimilation: *Ostjuden* and German Jews." *The Jewish Response to German Culture from the Enlightenment to the Second World War.* J. Reinharz and W. Schatzberg. Hanover, N.H.: Published for Clark University by University Press of New England, 195–211.

———. 1990. "Jüdische Assimilation und Eigenart in Kaiserreich." *Jüdisches Leben und Antisemitismus im 19. und 20. Jahurhundert. Zehn Essays.* idem. Munich: Beck, 131–45.

———. 1996. "Reflections on German-Jewish Historiography: A Dead End or a New Beginning." *Leo Baeck Institute Year Book* (41): 309–20.

———. 2001. "Die Erfindung einer Tradition." *Das jüdische Projekt der Moderne.* idem. Munich: Beck, 118–37.

von Bruch, R. 1988. *Deutsche Geschichtswissenschaft um 1900.* Stuttgart: Franz Steiner.

Wallach, L. 1959. *Liberty and Letter: The Thoughts of Leopold Zunz*. London: East and West Library.

Weinberg, J. 2001. *The Light of the Eyes*. New Haven: Yale University Press.

Weiss-Rosmarin, T. 1936. *Religion of Reason: Hermann Cohen's System of Religious Philosophy*. New York: Bloch.

Welch, C. 1985. *Protestant Thought in the Nineteenth Century, Vol. 1, 1799–1870*. New Haven, Conn.: Yale University Press.

———. 1985. *Protestant Thought in the Nineteenth Century, Vol. 2, 1870–1914*. New Haven, Conn.: Yale University Press.

Wiener, M. 1974. *Ha-dat ha-Yehudit bi-tekufat ha-emantsipatsyah*. Jerusalem: n.a.

Wiese, C. 1999. *Wissenschaft des Judentums und protestantische Theologie im wilhelminischen Deutschland: Ein Schrei ins Leere?* Tübingen: Mohr Siebeck.

Wieseltier, L. 1981. "*Etwas über die jüdische Historik*: Leopold Zunz and the Inception of Modern Jewish Historiography." *History and Theory* 20: 135–49.

Wilde, O. 1988. *The Picture of Dorian Gray: Authoritative Texts, Backgrounds, Reviews and Reactions, Criticism*. New York: W.W. Norton.

Willey, T. E. 1978. *Back to Kant: The Revival of Kantianism: German Social and Historical Thought, 1860–1914*. Detroit: Wayne State.

Wittkau, A. 1992. *Historismus: Zur Geschichte des Begriffs und des Problems*. Göttingen: Vanderhoeck and Ruprecht.

Wolf, I. 1822. "Über den Begriff einer Wissenschaft des Judentums." *Zeitschrift für die Wissenschaft des Judentums* 1: 1–24.

Wolin, R. 1994. *Walter Benjamin: An Aesthetic of Redemption*. Berkeley: University of California Press.

Wyschograd, E. 1998. *An Ethics of Remembering: History, Heterology, and the Nameless Others*. Chicago: University of Chicago Press.

Yerushalmi, Y. H. 1989. *Zakhor*: Jewish History and Jewish Memory. New York: Schocken Books.

Yovel, Y. 1980. *Kant and the Philosophy of History*. Princeton: Princeton University Press.

Yuval, I. J. 2000. *Shene goyim be-vitnekh: Yehudim ve-Notsrim: dimuyim hadadiyim*. Tel-Aviv: 'Am 'oved.

Zunz, L. 1845. *Zur Geschichte und Literatur*. Berlin: Veit und Comp.

# INDEX